PENGUIN BOOKS

The BUST Guide to the New Girl Order

Marcelle Karp and Debbie Stoller are the editors, and, together with art director Laurie Henzel, the founders and publishers of *BUST* magazine.

Marcelle Karp, a.k.a. Betty Boob, is an award-winning television producer (Lifetime, Fox, HBO) and director. In her spare seconds she writes for *Spin, Details,* and *Jane* about the zeitgeist of all things girl.

Debbie Stoller, a.k.a. Celina Hex, has written about feminism and girl culture for *George, Ms., The Village Voice,* and *New York Newsday,* among others, and also pens a column about women and pop culture, "The XX Files," for *Shift Magazine* (www.shift.com). She holds a Ph.D. in the Psychology of Women from Yale University.

You can check out their award-winning web site at www.bust.com.

THE

BUST

GUIDE

TO THE

new girl order

edited by
marcelle karp
& debbie stoller

PENGUIN BOOKS
Published by the Penguin Group
Penguin Putnam Inc., 375 Hudson Street, New York, New York 10014, U.S.A.
Penguin Books Ltd, 27 Wrights Lane, London W8 5TZ, England
Penguin Books Australia Ltd, Ringwood, Victoria, Australia
Penguin Books Canada Ltd, 10 Alcorn Avenue, Toronto, Ontario, Canada M4V 3B2
Penguin Books (N.Z.) Ltd, 182–190 Wairau Road, Auckland 10, New Zealand

Penguin Books Ltd, Registered Offices: Harmondsworth, Middlesex, England

First published in Penguin Books 1999

7   9   10   8   6

Illustration credits for page one: 1. Clockwise from top left corner—Sylvia O'Reagan
from *The Best of American Girlie Magazines*, Taschen Publishers.   2. Advertisement from
Eyeful Magazine.   3. Detail of illustration by Ley, *Latin Senoritas Magazine*, February
1966.   4. Detail of photo of Mabel Santley, c. 1875.   5. Rama—Tahe, c. 1928, both from
The Pin-Up: A Modest History.   6. Advertisement from *True Secrets Magazine*, September
1963.   7. Advertisement from *True Story*, n.d.   8. From *The Best of American Girlie
Magazines*, Taschen Publishers.   9. From *The Pin-Up: A Modest History*.   10. Advertisement
from *True Secrets Magazine*, September 1963.   11. Rosita Davis from *The Best of American
Girlie Magazines*, Taschen Publishers.

LIBRARY OF CONGRESS CATALOGING IN PUBLICATION DATA
Stoller, Debbie.
The bust guide to the new girl order / Debbie Stoller and Marcelle Karp.
p.   cm.
Includes bibliographical references.
ISBN 0 14 02.7774 9
1. Teenage girls—United States—Psychology.   2. Teenage girls—
United States—Attitudes.   3. Body image in adolescence—United
States.   4. Self-esteem in adolescence—United States.
I. Karp, Marcelle.   II. Title.
HQ798.S82   1999
305.235—dc21   98–31893

Printed in the United States of America
Set in Melior
Designed by Carole Goodman
Art Direction by Laurie Henzel

ACKNOWLEDGMENTS

Debbie and Marcelle would like to thank: Lydia Wills, for helping us get our act together and take it on the road, and without whom this book would never have happened; Courtney Hodell, our first editor at Penguin, for functioning not only as editor but also as a therapist who coaxed us through our numerous fears about writing; Laurie Walsh, our new editor at Penguin, for always giving us an extension when we needed it, for being on our side, and adding much coolness and brilliance to the manuscript; all the people who have helped us along the way, but especially the contributors, those who took the time to write, illustrate, shoot, etc. (for *free!*) and be a part of *BUST,* because without y'all, *BUST* would be a bunch of pages with just Debbie and Marcelle's meanderings; and last but not least, Laurie Henzel, for being an understanding and soothing influence on us both, for playing a much-needed smart and level-headed Kate to our often flighty Farrah and Jaclyn, and for being the only third of the *BUST* triumverate who has taste: without your vision and drive, we would still be somewhere in the photocopy ghetto.

Debbie would like to thank: Best friends Jodi and Fran, who were not just supportive in real life, but were also the imaginary, encouraging eyes that looked over my shoulder when I was too afraid to write another word; Wednesday, for her endless patience and reassurance; little-sister Meg, for reading the manuscript and giving me input on my chapters, and soul-sister, Kim, just for being so Drew-like; Michael, for giving me good loving, being my one-man cheerleading squad, and, especially, for giving me the sweet, nurturing support without which I would have imploded long before the completion of this manuscript. And, of course, my dad, for having so much faith in me, and my mom, for being the first, and most wonderful, woman in my life.

Marcelle gives props to her family of friends: I would like to give a shout out to those who have been more than a support network to me over the years; you've been surrogate siblings, tear-wipers, partners-in-crime. Thank you for lasting, for not running away, and for being such a vital part of my real and not-so-real life. Starting with the girls: Anne-So, Cathie, Denise, Farai, Janet, Jax, Kelly, Lizz, Maria, Melissa, Mikki, Ronit, Sia, Tiggy's Mom, Wendy Bott, and Wendy Shanker; the boys—Dean, Jack, Jake, Jerry, Fabien, Kendryck, Matt, Matthew, Olive. Thanks to the advisory committee for your pearls: Arthur, Christina, Peggy, Penn, and Girls Against Boys. And to my mom and dad, well, there are no words to express how much you mean to me. To paraphrase Sandra Bernhard, without you, I wouldn't be.

CONTENTS

There's
been a lot of talk lately of
defining our generation, this generation
of late twenties, early thirties, non baby-boomer
slackers. They call us Generation X. They talk about our
difficulty committing to jobs, difficulty taking on responsibilities, difficulty becoming adults. But there has been very little talk about Generation XX, we women slackers, the girls having a
difficult time becoming women, and the adult fears that are particular to
being female: having children, fear of becoming "spinsters," dealing with
men who can't "commit," being way more than two boys away from being virgins,
aging and our body image, to name a few. There are a ton of women's magazines
out there, but they all seem to tell us that being an adult woman is a major bummer. They tell us to exercise, just say no, decorate your apartment, get a facial,
diet diet diet, how to deal with the married man, how to deal with the single man,
cooking, how to keep your man, how to avoid sexual harassment at the office, how to
avoid date rape, etc. Only *Sassy* magazine, devoted to the newly found freedom and sexuality of the teenage girl, seems to understand that being a girl can be really fun.
That being independent is a cool thing, that girls make great friends, that boys are
only part of the story, that the way you look doesn't matter all that much and that
beauty comes in many shapes and colors, that you buy clothes because it's fun to buy
things you like, fun to listen to music that floats your boat, excellent super fun
to say yes to cute boys, yes to wild car rides, and yes to life. Those of us
older girls who get off on reading *Sassy* do it as a sort of guilty pleasure:
sure, it makes us feel good, but it also makes us feel like losers because
the only magazine we can relate to is meant for teenagers! One by one we
think to ourselves: why didn't I grow up to be the type of woman who
relates to *Mademoiselle* or *Essence*? What kind of weirdo am I? And
mostly, we get to feeling really lonely, and really afraid.
We are the women who were raised on feminism, who pitied
our mothers for being choicelessly house bound, and
looked down on those girls we went to high
school with who got married to
the   first   guy

they

fucked, had kids, and worked

in shoe stores. We wanted to have

choices, to have careers, to not be tied down, to

hold onto our freedom, and to become sexually "experi-

enced." And we were sure that neither our gender nor our race

would stop us. But somewhere, somewhere in our girl-brains the

idea had been planted—when we were young, when we watched "The Brady

Bunch," when we were forced to take "homemaking" while the boys took

"shop"—that we would, of course, be married to successful men and be ready

to have families by the time we were, well, at least definitely by the time we

were thirty!!   Instead we find ourselves nearing or past thirty, still in dat-

ing hell, still trying to figure out our sexual identities, still sleeping too

late, forgetting to do the fucking laundry and wearing dirty underwear, not know-

ing how to cook, worrying about the electricity being turned off again, being in debt

to our creditors, not having any savings, and hearing the TICK TICK TICK of our god-

damned biological clocks. When we were in our early twenties we thought that that bi-

ological clock and "juggling career and family" stuff was yuppie bullshit for women

who wore beige stockings or relaxed their hair. We knew better. We would figure it

all out, in our own radical bohemian thrift-store ways. Surely it would happen to us

in its own time. Surely we'd figure out what we wanted to be when we grew up. Surely.

And yet it hasn't. We haven't figured it out. And now here we are. But look around

you—there are a lot of us here. Lots and lots of us. It's not just me, it's not

just you, there are a whole heap of us late twenties early thirties groovy girl-

women. And we need to hear each other. We need to help each other. We need

to laugh at each other. We need to speak to each other. So speak.

We wanna read you. We wanna recognize ourselves and laugh. We wanna

have fun. We wanna get mad. We wanna BUST! love,

your editors the left one &

the right one

The Birth of BUST

Remember, if you will, a time before the Spice Girls, before Buffy the Vampire Slayer and Xena the Warrior Princess, before Angela and Rayanne and Jordan Catalano. A time when Courtney Love was only pretty on the inside, when Liz Phair's audience was just a small tape-recorder in her bedroom, and Janeanne Garafolo was still performing standup comedy in rinky-dink clubs. A time when "You go, girl" was only a drag queen's mantra, and "girl power" had yet to become a marketer's wet dream.

The year was 1992—the year after punk broke. It was then that a couple of overeducated, underpaid, late-twenty-something cubicle slaves, working side-by-side at a Giant Media Conglomerate, began bonding over a shared love of *Sassy* magazine and obscure records by The Fall. Graduates of the Punk Rock school of thought, we had stomped our way through the eighties in lipstick and combat boots and thrift store dresses, members of a growing army of new-wave feminists who were inspired by women like Patti Smith, Excene Cervenka, Barbara Kruger, Cindy Sherman, bell hooks, Debbie Harry, Chrissie Hynde, Kim Gordon, Pam Grier, Susie Bright, Cynthia Heimel, Salt-N-Pepa, and of course, Madonna.

But now, in our late twenties, it seemed that our comrades-in-arms had disappeared. In the media, women our age were being represented as either corporate clones or jazzercising jigglebunnies. And except for an outspoken group of younger women who were calling themselves "Riot Grrls," it looked like our generation of feminists was getting swept under the rug. Out of sight, out of mind. The more we talked to each other about this sorry state of affairs, the clearer it became that we needed to do something. Not only did we want to let the younger girls know that we older girls had never given up on feminism, but we also wanted to create a place where girls of all ages could let their voices be heard, in all their fierce, funny, feminist glory. Thus, the idea for *BUST* was born.

The name came to us in a flash. *BUST* was at once sexy and aggressive, a joke that would be instantly recognizable by the girls we wanted to reach—it was a mystery wrapped up inside an enigma. This was not going to be *Ms.* magazine for juniors, but rather *Sassy* for grown-ups. But, twenty-something slackers that we were, we dropped the idea almost as soon as we had it.

It wasn't until a year later that we picked it up again. With *BUST,* we wanted to start a magazine for women like ourselves—women who couldn't relate to the body sculpting tips of *Cosmo* or the eyebrow tweezing directions of *Glamour.* Women who wore ripped sweaters instead of the angora ensembles that were being modeled in *Vogue.* A magazine for broads who weren't afraid of any f-words—from feminism to fucking to fashion—where we could work out the kinks of our ideology while trying to figure everything else out—like how to deal with the apparent epidemic of boy disease, the general lack of creative career opportunities, and how to live without being economically dependent on every paycheck. Wouldn't it be nice, we thought, if we could feel pleasure and pride in reading a women's magazine rather than shame and alienation?

Yeah, it would be nice. But how could we start? Neither one of us had an MBA degree or knew anything about publishing. So we decided that we would just do what we could on our own, with a publishing budget of zero. We knew that whatever we lacked in financial resources, we could make up for in talent: we had an abundance of smart-ass, outspoken friends, and we asked them to write for us. We suggested that they write under pseudonyms in order to encourage 100 percent honesty (and to keep ourselves from having to get unlisted phone numbers). As a way to inspire our writers—since we would not be able to motivate them with the promise of money—we decided to create theme-related issues that would allow them to focus on a single topic and beat it until it cried uncle! We were also lucky enough to have friends who were designers, and we asked them to use their new-fangled computers (this was 1993, remember?) to lay out the pages for us. Lastly, we agreed to post a call for submissions in each issue so that we could publish stories from *BUST*-y girls from every corner of the country. Now all we needed was to distribute our so-called magazine around the world.

Unfortunately, we had no idea how to do that. We were vaguely aware that there was a world of 'zines out there, a community of do-it-yourself publishers. So we trotted on down to the local 'zine store, See/Hear, asked a lot of questions, and picked up the bible of all 'zines, *Factsheet Five.* It turns out that they produced a "Zine Publisher's Resource Guide," a manual that listed tons and tons of places for us to sell our zine. We got a post office box, we got a bank account, we got e-mail. Everything was falling into place and we were on our way.

"A Day in a Life" was the first issue of *BUST.* It was only 29 (count 'em!) pages long, and we made five hundred copies, Xeroxing and stapling till our wrists ached. Shortly after we had gotten it out there into the world, we started getting fan mail from readers, submissions for our next issue, and more orders (we ended up making another five hundred copies). It was then that we began to realize that we were onto something big. Inspired by that first issue's success, we pooled our money together so that we could actually print the next issue all professional-like, and asked a groovy designer, Laurie Henzel, who we knew from our Big Media Conglomerate days, to join us as a third partner in crime. With an art director to guide us, *BUST* finally began to develop into a magazine whose look was as brazen as its voice. The two thousand copies we printed of the "Fun" issue, our second, quickly sold. With the number of submissions that were arriving in our Post Office box each day, the fan letters we were receiving from all over the world, and the positive reviews we were beginning to get in other 'zines, those what-am-I-gonna-do-when-I-grow-up feelings that had plagued us throughout our twenties were beginning to evaporate. We didn't just know what we wanted to do, we knew what we *had* to do: we must, we must, we must increase our *BUST.*

Five years down the line, *BUST* has developed from an AA cup to a C cup, and we continue to grow. We've increased our distribution from 1,000 to 32,000 copies, a small step for magazines, but a giant leap for zinekind. We take whatever money we make—from subscribers, sales, advertising—and invest it into the next issue, growing *BUST* step-by-step from a handmade rag into a full-on glossy mag with color. Our lives have changed dramatically, but still not enough to give up our day jobs. *BUST* continues, to this day, to be a labor of love. Much like crime, *BUST* doesn't pay, but the fact that each issue is the collaborative, and voluntary efforts of at least fifty writers, designers, illustrators, photographers, editors, and proofreaders, lets us know that being a part of *BUST* is rewarding in its own way.

In *BUST,* we've captured the voice of a brave new girl: one that is raw and real, straightforward and sarcastic, smart and silly, and liberally sprinkled with references to our own Girl Culture—that shared set of female experiences that includes Barbies and blowjobs, sexism and shoplifting, *Vogue* and vaginas. It was obvious to us that it was time to take this voice to a broader audience, to collect the best of *BUST* and put it into a book. And so here you have it: *The BUST Guide to the New Girl Order.* Of course, today we have *Jane* and *Honey* and *Nylon,* we have Daria and Sabrina and Felicity, we have Ally and Bridget and Veronica, we have Ani and PJ and Missy, we have Claire and Parker and Christina. Can we just say we saw this coming? So wake up and smell the lipgloss, ladies: The New Girl Order has arrived.

— Marcelle Karp and Debbie Stoller

THE

GUIDE

TO THE

new girl order

Leslie Day

1

Our Womanly Ways

I'VE GOT TWO WORDS FOR YOU: TITS AND TWAT. WE GIRLS ARE
obsessed with them, and boys, well, (straight) boys just gotta have 'em. These two terrific T's are the most sexified parts of our bodies, the most fetishized, the very hot
spots of our pleasure zones, and we pamper, powder, and play with them to our
heart's content. However, our bodies are more than these twin peaks; it's not just
stacked and snatch, it's also our hips and our dimples and our toes and, well, our
weight. We poke and prod our bodies with a psychological microscopic lens that ranges
from the schizophrenic to the esoteric. But as we try to grow into and learn to accept our
own bodies in a world that is full of mixed messages, it's possible for an unabashedly
feminist sense of fun, pride, and pleasure to emerge. Ah, the joys of our womanly ways.

Boys seem to have it so easy: Simone de Beauvoir argues in *The Second Sex*
that "at the moment of puberty, boys also feel their bodies as an embarrassment, but

being proud of their manhood from an early age, they proudly project toward manhood the moment of their development; with pride they show one another the hair growing on their legs, a manly attribute." There is little mystery to the body by boy, a sporty number that is often competitive and occasionally crude: grow a few inches, pop boners, maybe suffer through an embarrassing voice change, and voilà, what a man, what a man, what a man. Proud. Posturing. Pumped.

But where boys are driven by their need to achieve, girls are propelled through puberty by something else, something less celebratory, more painful. As Peggy Orenstein tells us in *Schoolgirls: Young Women, Self-Esteem and the Confidence Gap,* "For a girl, the passage into adolescence is not just marked by menarche or a few new curves. It is marked by a scathingly critical attitude toward her body and a blossoming sense of personal inadequacy." The pretty poison formula begins coursing through our veins while we are still little girls—be good, eat right, look pretty, and then you'll marry Prince Charming! We're thrust into a pool of other girls who are cuter, skinnier, more of something we are suddenly aware of not being ourselves. "A girl's identity and her sense of worth is suddenly wrapped up in her bra size, something she has no control over," Judy Mann says in *The Difference.* This is an argument that did little to help the ever hopefuls: those girls taunted by the Itty Bitty Titty Committee, who mimicked Judy Blume's Margaret by desperately chanting, "I must, I must, I must increase my bust," and who sometimes ended up falling just a little flat.

It really doesn't seem fair that so much of a girl's self-worth depends on the boob patrol. A boy isn't judged and scrutinized on a daily basis by his penis size—his package is tucked in his pants. Instead of compare-and-contrast cock contests, boys brag; a girl's breasts, however, are always on display, front and center, and are therefore vulnerable to evaluation. As soon as boobs bud, they become an unconcealable barometer of worthiness. Self-conscious, a girl looks inward, more embarrassed by her new body than excited and proud, not fully realizing yet that her coming-of-age should be a point of celebration, exultation, discovery. The bigger, the better, the tighter the sweater.

But then, we grow up and realize: "TITS!!! I got them! They may be an A or a triple Z, but I got 'em." Suddenly, boobs once hidden by baggy shirts now get put on display by baby T's. And we *BUST* girls, we love our breasts. We love the strength we

2

derive from them, the sense of femininity they endow us with, their ability to seduce and attract. Sure, there is the occasional insecurity of not passing the pencil test, or not being a desired cup size, or of falling a little too low, but for the most part, our breasts do wonders for us—we can share them if we like, show them off, or remain selfish. Breasts empower us.

Let's face it, our culture is obsessed with breasts. And nowadays, if a girl wants 'em bigger (or smaller), she can make it happen easily. In Marilyn Yalom's *History of the Breast,* an unnamed female psychologist calls implants a "status symbol" and maintains that a "woman can buy the perfect body the same way she can buy anything else." If she can afford the operation, that is. (If she can't, there's always the Wonderbra.) Or the legal fees. Implant manufacturers such as Dow Chemical, Bristol Meyers, Baxter, and 3M were taken to court for failing to warn recipients of the risks involved with implants. But while awareness grows as to the dangers of breast augmentations, boob jobs are still popping up everywhere.

Have men driven women to prettify, boobify, skinnify themselves? Some feminists think so. In *Backlash* Susan Faludi states that the medical profession, as well as the male-dominated media and fashion industry, are guilty of conspiracy against women. And Susan Brownmiller, in her book *Femininity,* opines that "enlarging one's breast to suit male fantasies" furthers the exploitation of women. Plastic surgery offers some women the opportunity to indulge men, to appease men, to continue to give men more of what they want: big-breasted bombshells that they cannot, do not, will not need to take seriously. In objectifying women and compartmentalizing them ("she's got big ta-tas"), the patriarchy can keep on keeping on. But only if the girls let them.

Of course, there are feminists who are pro-enhancement. Feminist scholar Jan Breslauer wrote an article about her implants for *Playboy,* "Stacked Like Me," in which she proclaimed, "This boob job is empowering." She goes on to argue that although "I know the party line on breast augmentation that women who have surgery are the oppressed victims of a patriarchal culture . . . feminism is about having control over life and one's body." Many famous women, including Courtney Love, Jane Fonda, Cher, and Nina Hartley, agree that a woman's choice to mold her body does not make her a victim. If bigger boobs are what she wants, it's her right to choose both as a feminist and as an individual. Is it a demolition job or home improvement?

It's strange that in our sexual lives, we are so breast obsessed, when sex really happens "down there." "The worst thing about being female is the hiddenness of your own body. You spend your whole adolescence arched over backward in the bathroom mirror trying to look up your own cunt. And what do you see? The frizzy halo of pubic hair, the purple labia, the pink alarm button of the clitoris—but never enough! The most important part is invisible. An unexplored canyon, an underground cave and all sorts of hidden dangers lurking within," says Erica Jong in *Fear of Flying.* In the '70s, *Our Bodies, Ourselves* encouraged women to take a mirror and get *in* there and see what makes us so sugary and spicy, to not feel scared or embarrassed or even shameful. You would think we'd be curious from childhood games of "doctor," but in fact, while we're fascinated with what's "down there," the actual sexual discovery doesn't occur until we start to actually rub and press and get off. We don't learn about our power from the Human Sexuality 101 classes, we learn by doing, on our own or with another. Touching our vaginas isn't oh-so-'70s, it's oh-so-now.

Plenty of women in the '90s are all for checking out their doll parts. *Sex for One*'s Betty Dodson and performer/goddess Annie Sprinkle have done vagina tours, if you will, for audiences in order to educate, enlighten, and entertain. Betty holds masturbation workshops for women, and Annie has been known to sit spread-eagled with a clamp between her legs and her cervix on display. Annie feels very strongly about pussy because, she says, "It's fun. . . . The cervix is so beautiful that I really want to share that with people. . . . I think it's important to demystify women's bodies. It wasn't until recently that anyone was allowed to look at pussy. . . . a lot of women have never even seen their own, and . . . in a way I wanna say 'fuck you guys, you wanna see pussy? I'll show you pussy.'" The power of pussy is a force to be tapped into, especially if you get really good at your Kegels. As Julie Covello points out, boys touch themselves several times a day, at the very least—every time they go to the bathroom. What a gift! So why shouldn't we be having the same fun with our Sacred Yonis!

During an interview in a Lifetime special, Roseanne Barr-Pentland-Arnold-Thomas (nowadays known simply as Roseanne) half-jokingly said that one time she had considered running for President: her slogan would have been "Put New Blood in the White House Every 28 Days." Thank the Goddess above that our bodies constantly remind us how special femaleness is—leaks, spills, cycles, and all. Having your period is a fact of life. From the moment we see those first little spots of blood on our cotton undies, we join ranks with our moms and girlfriends. This is OUR time of the month, a natural state of our girlie experience and nothing to be ashamed about. Women in the '90s are lucky (ha!) enough to have access to tons of information about sanitary napkins, tampons, and other women's hygiene products thanks to a multibillion-dollar health and beauty industry, mainstream women's magazines, and savvy media. And yet, we still have lingering doubts and conflicting feelings about our smells, our vaginas, and our periods. Is it because we have been conditioned by a society to feel embarrassed about our supposed "sewers"?

Historically, many patriarchal societies treated a menstruating creature differently. For example, Jews sent their married women to the mikvah for a monthly ritual cleansing (a practice that is still very much a part of today's traditional Orthodox and Conservative Judaism). According to Dr. Helen Fisher in *The Anatomy of Love,* primitive cultures secluded their women in "menstrual huts." In *For Her Own Good,* Barbara Ehrenreich and Deirdre English point out that in the 1800s "medicine had 'discovered' that female functions were inherently pathological." Public health officials, in their war against germs, subjected menstruating women to "new hygienic standards" because they were considered dirty, unclean, and unsanitary by the mostly male public health officials. Please. The patriarchy of yore would definitely have incarcerated Donita Sparks of the band L7 had they seen her at the Reading Festival in England in the early '90s. There Sparks, in response to the mud-throwing audience, reached between her legs, pulled out her tampon, and threw it at the crowd! You go, girl!

Susie Orbach declared that "fat is a feminist issue." And for our gal Roseanne, "fat" is an F-word not to be feared, but flaunted. What we see with Roseanne is what we get—a body that is not an object of shame. "Well I'm fat. I thought I'd point that out." Finally, a voice that defies the you-must-look-like-this messages of the not-so-subtle pop media. Oh, let us count the ways we love Roseanne. In her sitcom, her stand-up routines, and her personal life, she is loquacious, loud, and lewd. Roseanne is not another Weight Watchers spokesperson, another large-girl-gone-slim "success sorry." In fact, for most of her sitcom years, Roseanne's show opened with a camera panning around the dinner table, while Roseanne and her family/cast members

5

laughed and ate, reaching over each other as families do during a meal. Chowing down on television, how normal! In Roseanne's world, food is never an enemy; it's an integral part of it. Whereas fitness guru Susan Powter and her ilk espouse the virtues of slimdom under the guise of good health, Roseanne glorifies the reality of the Real Live Girl. The way these fitness freaks confront their bodies as their nemesis, always needing to be tamed, taut, and thinner, makes girls feels worse; we need more Roseannes and Camryn Manheims, women who accept their size with poppy fresh pleasure rather than fall victim to it with self-imposed torture.

Somehow, the body whole can turn into a psychological battleground. We spend a lot of time figuring out ways to lose weight, strategically planning our exercise schedules and checking out the competition—the other girls' merchandise. Call it catty, call it unsisterly, but we're guilty of it. Measuring ourselves against the girl next door is already destructive, but nothing does a more damaging mind-fuck than our fascination with models and the reed-thin bodies that make them (models) millions of dollars. If we dare go over a desired weight, we'll starve, or worse, purge until our faces are riddled with burst capillaries. We diet, we gobble laxatives, we wear girdles. In coveting the "ideals" of model figures, we condemn our bodies ourselves to eating disorders, continually punishing ourselves for not being "thin enough."

The Body Shop took little baby steps toward embracing the real body by girl in one of their advertising campaigns: "There are three billion women who don't look like supermodels and only eight who do." This copy accompanied a photo of a paint-by-numbers, Barbie-like head tacked onto a naked Rubenesque doll figure. This kind of Body Shop model doesn't leave the bitter aftertaste of inadequacy that this year's version of Kate Moss does. It's clear that the Body Shop ideology is on our side, condemning lookism (the disease of judging the body) and encouraging *being yourself.* Finally, it's okay for us to look like us! Will this pioneer campaign influence others and encourage women to covet real bodies? Only time will tell. But the Body Shop is starting something the *BUST* girl is hungry for: Reality.

We *BUST* girls are not immune to feeling insecure about our bodies, but we're smart enough to know that we don't need to be victimized by it. Instead of admiring superfreaks, it's important to remember that there are plenty of famous women with bodies that don't quit being real, who don't make you feel alienated and weird, that are crazy, sexy, cool. Rock chicks Kim Gordon, Cibo Matto, Bjork, Queen Latifah,

Missy Misdemeanor Elliot, Salt-N-Pepa are divine—they prance and pose and wink and growl without looking like they've been liposuctioned and airbrushed into toothpickville. Models, to me, are the real freaks of nature: too tall, too thin, too pretty to be perfect in any sense of the word. It's the real girl I aspire to be, the one who is sexy and having fun, the one whose snarliness doesn't feel objectifying or demeaning, but does feel like positively raw girl power and that feels right. I'm just a girl and more.

Don't forget, as Marcia Ann Gillespie reminds us, "Women's bodies have long been considered little more than malleable clay to be reshaped to meet whatever the standard of the day, no matter the risk, discomfort, or pain." The fact is, reinforced ideals which result in our internalized negative body images have always been wreaking havoc on us chicks. It's time to say FUCK YOU to that shit. It's time to say "Mirror, Mirror on the wall, I don't care that I'm not six feet tall!" Whether you are a truly toned athlete (or even someone like Sporty Spice, who is by no means an athlete but is finally giving girls everywhere a cue that being a tomboy and/or a jock is cool!) or whether, like me, you are a 100 percent soft couch potato, you don't need to torture yourself about your body. Your scale doesn't need to be your enemy, you don't need to throw out the tape measure, you don't have to give yourself Special K tests. All these parts of ours—our tits and hips and lips—are power tools. And it's time that we, the grande dames of the New Girl Order, defy the backlash with a proverbial middle finger and bust through the Reviving-data of Ophelia's low self-esteem, stop shoving our fingers down our throats, turn our back on skeletal standards, enjoy being the girl with the most cake and ask: Can I have some more?

— *Marcelle Karp*

✕

Thanks for the Mammaries: The Rise and Fall of My Boobs

by Ophelia Lipps

I'm single again, and rapidly beginning to lose touch with my body. As soon as I stop having sex regularly, I begin to live from the head up, considering my body with only the most critical and insecure of thoughts. I forget what a powerful instrument of desire and sensation it can and has been; that my body has become a map of the most beloved areas of past lovers: this one adored the back of my neck, and that one was seduced by my lower lip, and the other was ignited to animalistic passions by the taste of my sex.

But of all my various body parts, my breasts have the most interesting story to tell. And it is one which, surprisingly, keeps changing.

I was a very late bloomer. When the other girls at school started to develop figures and I remained flat as a board, I started to get desperate. One day I was walking home from school, heavily worrying about my dilemma. How is any boy ever going to find a skinny, flat-chested girl sexy? I wondered. I was terribly insecure about my shortcoming, and was certain that I would never develop breasts. But suddenly it came to me. I remember the exact instant, the exact place I was in my daily walk home. We had been reading *The Great Gatsby* at school, and I had seen pictures of the flat-chested flapper women of the '20s, with their sinuous serpentine sexuality. That would be it. I would be serpentinely sensuous. Maybe the boys could get turned on by imagining my slinky, dark-skinned body curling and slithering around their legs, chests, necks. That would certainly make up for my lack of breasts.

Still, I continued to stand naked in front of the mirror every day, tensing my pectoral muscles to convince myself that there were, indeed, two shallow mounds beginning to form on my chest. I didn't pad my bra but I did take to frequently wearing my cream-colored, French-sleeved Huk-a-Poo shirt, which gave the appearance that I had at least some semblance of boobage. But at twelve, and then at thirteen, I remained a rail-thin Flatsy-doll. So I continued to arm myself against the hordes of cruel eighth graders with the secret belief that I was intensely desirable to those boys out there who were searching for a rail-thin olive-skinned beauty.

In ninth grade I finally got them. But by then I had so thoroughly accepted my membership in the Itty Bitty Titty Committee that I wasn't even the first to notice them. It happened during homeroom, when I was kidding around/flirting with the two boys who sat in front of me. Somehow the subject of boobs came up. "Well, I know I'm totally flat," I said, feeling the confidence of my serpent-scenario. "No you aren't," the boys said casually. But then, one of them looked at me with extremely serious dark eyes and said, in a softer voice, "Believe me, you're not."

That was the day I officially got breasts, the day they were noticed.

I didn't really appreciate them, however, until I was fifteen and I got invited to a party with some of the high school bad boys. "Everyone knows they can get a girl to second base by the fourth date," a friend told me. I was shocked. Not those boys. I didn't believe it. I hadn't even been French-kissed yet.

So there I was, at the party, when all of us decided to go out to the woods and smoke cigarettes. Then, suddenly, as if it had been planned, each boy chose a girl and together they'd disappear into the trees. I was nervously sitting on a rock figuring I wouldn't get picked when the young, pale, dark-haired boy, the baddest of the bad boys, the one I had a secret crush on, came up to me and took me by the hand. I stood up, silently. He pressed his lips against my lips, then his tongue was in my mouth. I liked it. He was serpentinely sensuous, long and lean. He rolled his tongue around my mouth, he rocked his hips against my hips. When everyone went back into the basement, the two of us found a place under the Ping-Pong table. The lights went out. Quickly his hand was under my shirt, then inside my bra. In that moment, my breasts had no size. They were only sensation and heat. That hand grabbing and squeezing my breast felt like it had reached right into my rib cage and was holding my heart. My stomach tightened. I felt light-headed, and I loved it.

That was the day that I realized that breasts were not just for the boys, but for me, too.

At seventeen I lost my virginity to my first real boyfriend. Our lovemaking was focused on my learning to fuck and give blow jobs. In the summer after high school he came to stay with me at a relative's house and wanted to have sex. I felt too embarrassed to do it under the roof of my aunt's house, and refused him. But one

9
—

night after everyone had gone to sleep, we started to make out. Since I wouldn't have sex with him, we remained in a state of extended foreplay. That night he sucked, licked, and nibbled at my breasts for so long that I almost came. It was, in fact, the only time I ever even got turned on with him.

College was a blur of beer and blackouts, during which sex took place in a sort of sleepwalk. I wandered through those years in a bulimic haze, gaining weight, getting bloated, completely out of touch with my body, my size, my sexuality.

But in graduate school all of the unhappiness of college melted away and I became thin again, without even trying. I felt sexy again, and I felt serpentine. In the meantime my breasts had fully developed to a size D cup, and, with visions of Edie Sedgwick dancing in my head, I took to wearing boob-flattening bras in order to achieve my desired look of gamine leanness. I had no idea the kind of power I was hiding away by doing so.

I learned all about that power when I met him.

He was an art student whom I'd had my eye on for months. He had shoulder-length blond hair, was tall and thin, and had the most beautiful face. I was finally introduced to him at a party by a roommate who also had a crush on him. She was gorgeous, with wild white-blond hair, full lips, and very pale skin. We all got drunk at the party, and, somehow, the two of us got him to come home with us. We seduced him. I figured he was into her and that the only way I'd get to sleep with him at all was if I slept with both of them, so I did.

He slept the whole night through with one hand holding my breast. The next morning she got up to go somewhere, and he woke up and grabbed me, held me, rolled me over, fucked me, buried his head between my breasts. Then we talked. He admitted to having had a crush on me for a while. He told me how he'd watched me dancing at the party the night before; how he'd studied my body, my moving outlines on the dance floor, and how it had turned him on. "But," he said, "your breasts are much bigger than I thought. It was a surprise when you took off your shirt last night." He rolled me onto my back and grabbed them, one in each hand, and kissed them, teased them, worshiped them.

That was the day I realized I had, not just breasts, but big breasts.

The boy and I fell in love, and I spent the next four years with him sleeping beside me, my back curled into his stomach, his arm over my shoulder and his hand cupping my breast. I loved his hair and he loved my breasts. I threw away my boob-flattening bras and bought the kind with underwires, he grew his hair longer and longer. I nestled my head into his hair at night, he nestled his between my breasts. My breasts were a constant source of pleasure to him. He fucked me between them, licked and bit and kissed them till I came—he even made drawings of them! I began to wear clothing to flaunt them more and more, and started to experience them as a symbol of power, the power I had over him, the power of my sensuality, the power of boobs. We'd watch Madonna on MTV and I'd identify with her boob-centrism.

When it ended, I was devastated. I obliterated my sadness with tequila, and went out every night, trying to find a replacement for him, using the only weapon I thought I had. I'd wear this particular black ta-ra-ra-bustier that held my boobs front and center, so that people would notice them before they noticed me. That was my armor, and my boobs were my power. I got drunk wearing my bustier and I picked up a lot of men that way. And because I presented my boobs so prominently they got a lot of attention on those many one-night stands. But it did nothing to still my sorrow.

I've since given up my desperate drinking and have had a number of romances. Some of my lovers have been turned on by my breasts, some of them have neglected them. I was starting to get very self-conscious about the effect of gravity on my breasts, thinking they would only disappoint any future lover, but was encouraged by my most recent boyfriend, who was used to going out with women my age and knew exactly where to find my boobs when I'm lying on my back (they no longer stand at attention and tend to disappear when I am in that position).

I love being a woman and I love having breasts. I love the attention they can get and the way they can turn on a lover. I love that they have a direct line to the rest of me, that someone kissing my nipples can make me wet between the legs. And I love that they have a function—that I will one day be able to nourish another being from them, hold a baby born of my body against myself to feed it. And there will begin a whole new chapter in the history of my breasts, one that has yet to be written.

11

A Fine Spine

by Nancy E. Young

(Note: Scoliosis is lateral curvature of the spine. It is often detected at puberty and is more common in girls, for reasons unknown.)

I was escorted to the waiting room—in a thin white cotton gown and robe. The only things of my own were my kneesocks. I dreamed of bolting the building, although I didn't know where I would go once outside.

My name was called. I went into a room full of obtrusive technology. A southern-twanged technician patterned my body into specific stances. Something akin to a cafeteria tray was given to me to hold in front of my reproductive organs—for protection.

The technician would leave me alone. She wore all kinds of protective garb as she stood behind a screen. In addition to the tray, I was given this calming advice:

"Hold your breath."

Buzz . . .

"Don't shoot, don't shoot." My dry tongue tried to push out the syllables as he pointed and aimed at me.

"Okay, you can breathe now."

I sat on a padded exam table covered with crunchy crumply tissue paper. After developing the X rays, the technician would check their clarity and measure the degree of the curves. Bending and straining to look into her work area, I asked for a progress report. Her response was crisp silence or a memorized rejoinder to wait for the doctor's explanation.

That was the visit when I had crossed the fine line—my curves had worsened. The doctor's monotone monologue with my mother was a declaration that I must wear the Milwaukee Brace.

Jones's fish market was a white overlookable store, a few blocks away from City Hall. Only a reluctant connoisseur of catfish, I found myself willing our Oldsmobile to stop there. Instead, Mom turned into the lot on the left, gravel leading up to "Al's and Joe's Body Parts." (Multisyllable words like *prosthetics* are prohibited in the South.)

Slowly, I stepped out of the car and into the Parts office. I announced myself to the redheaded receptionist, who checked my name off in between bites of peanuts. My mother sat in an institutional orange plastic chair, completing the four-page questionnaire about insurance and me.

During my third attempt to read *Fish and Game*'s latest article on bigmouth bass, my name was called. Mom followed me back like a newly trained dog on a leash, willing to please but not sure where to go. She was posted outside my changing room as I listened to the receptionist's instructions to undress. She casually pointed to the back of the door.

"Now, put on these two here bodysuits. Take off everything else, including your jewelry. They'll call for you shortly."

"Excuse me, you want me to put both of them on?"

"Yes ma'am, I sure do. You'll understand why later."

Reluctantly, I stacked my clothes on top of a nearby filing cabinet. The two thin white bodysuits had short sleeves and no crotch. After many pulls downward, they fit a bit below my butt. No bra, no panties, no socks, no robe, no jewelry, only Mom.

Her voice at the door willed me out and down the stubby hall to an open workroom on the right. There, Al and Joe were anxious to greet us with breath smelling of fish. I quickly noticed Al's yells directed to Joe, who had hearing aids bulking out of each ear.

Mom seemed to be the only whole-bodied person around.

Pointing to an encyclopedia drawing tacked on the yellowing wall, Al traced the development of the Milwaukee Brace. Invented and improved by Dr. Walter P. Blount in 1945, the success rate for avoiding surgery by preventing further curvature was 80. Al explained how girls fitted continued with horseback riding, biking, and even gymnastics, as I tried to look defiant and swallowed lots.

Al handed Mom their business card, which as an afterthought listed the

13

credential of Orthotist in the bottom right-hand corner. Seating her in a rusted folding chair, they led me to the spot of honor in the middle of the room. *Arkansas Gazette* comics covered the floor where I stood and there were three metal bars holding up something white, which I at first mistook for a noose. Joe yelled this was a harness, to keep my body aligned and erect.

He placed the straps under my chin and fastened them at the back of my neck. Al joked that I would be mummified, but quickly shut up under the glaring expletive of my mother's stare.

Arms out like a T, shoulders straight but not up, I felt the plaster-wet bandage Velcro to my shape. The bandages were passed from man's hand to man's hand, each winding them halfway around my 29-inch chest. Joe at my front needing guidance, Al yelled directions from my back through my right ear. As they continued their conversation, I felt like an unwilling stand-in for a farce. Tightening through the waist, I avoided my mother's eyes as the men wrapped below my belly button. I was conscious of my dark pubic hair, and the bandages at least offered me a curtain from eyes and hands.

Although I needed to scratch my nose, Al warned me not to sneeze or move. Like swallowing a laugh during church, I was temporarily distracted by my effort to resist.

"Hey old man, watch out!" yelled Al as Joe almost dropped the bandage. "It's hard for him to concentrate on a purty young gal," stage-whispered Al. "Mainly we do feets and leg parts."

"Do her feet?" yelled Joe as he began another layer around my chest.

"Heck no, coot. Keep on wrappin'."

As their oxygen-wasting conversation continued, I wanted to disintegrate. Another twenty minutes and the wrapping was over.

I was mandated to stand still, like there was another option, while the fast-drying plaster hardened the bandages. As its grip on me tightened, I felt pulled down by the weight. Like conversations at airports before departing for a long trip, the words Mom and I exchanged were mainly to fill the crevice of each minute, which we felt.

Hearing Al's and Joe's yells almost drowned out the final tick of the timer; their return was welcome. Al revved and ran a sawlike machine down my left side as

14

Joe held on to the mold. Within seconds, the mold was apart from my skin, but the relief passed quickly.

With goose-pimple erect skin, I raced down the hallway to reclaim my clothes and take off the remaining bodysuit that the plaster had not absorbed. I folded the suit and placed it on a four-year-old copy of *Vogue* with Twiggy on the cover.

Two weeks later, Gertie and I were new to each other. I never called her my "Milwaukee Brace" or "It"—somehow the personification made her easier to take.

All of a sudden, I became a teenager who could not dress myself. This was especially awkward in a shut-up-about-sexuality home like mine. The problem of getting dressed, as well as what to wear, belonged to me and, by default, Mom. Because of the leather padding, which covered from above my belly button to the bottom of my hips, I needed some fabric sandwiched in between Gertie and me. After buying a package of boy's Fruit of the Loom T-shirts, I refused to wear a complete one, which I feared would add to an asexual appearance. We cut the sleeves and collar off of each one, and I was left with rounds of soft cotton cloth.

Once in a bra, panties, and T-shirt dreg, I had to put her on front first. She opened up in the back, with two long metal columns appendaged with three buckles. The front was one long breast-splitting piece of metal and all was hooked up to a collar, which fenced about three inches around the circumference of my neck. There was a chin piece attached at an uncomfortable height, to force me to strain my neck higher. Gertie was awkward and heavy, and my body had to shrug her into the right place. Mom would first screw the ¾-inch bolt into the collar while I held up handfuls of my long curly hair. Next, she tightened a belt which pulled the two-piece leather girdle as snug as I could take it. Tighter was better. Threading the left side piece through the bars and to the front, I was then able to attach it in two places.

Being just on the precipice of fleshing out enough for clothes from the junior department, I now had to select them carefully. Any idea of "hiding" Gertie was ridiculous, since she peeked out of any opening given to her. I looked for baggy pants and tops; I quickly learned that the needles of the buckles poked holes and gnawed at my clothes. The leather girdle also stressed by its constant rubbing. Still, even with the protection of the T-shirt, Gertie dug deep red marks (about two inches wide and three long) above each hipbone. These tattoos were signs of a proper fit, and they stayed with me for several years.

15

Me and My Cunt

by Janine Guzzo

It's a normal day in upstate New York. Not only is it raining and muggy and hot, but it's also my day off, which means I get to do anything I want. So I'm hanging out in my living room, sweating, and I decide to check out my pussy. Not for genital warts or anything, but just because I share the opinion of many other women that we don't check out our own cunts enough. In fact, if I took the amount of time I spend critically examining the fat on my ass or the stretch marks on my tits and compare it to the time I spend ignoring most other parts of my body, I would have to come to the conclusion that I am kinda fucked up.

So there I am with a mirror, naked on the living-room floor, looking at my cunt, which I think is pretty neat-looking although my unliberated boyfriend thinks all snatch looks like roast beef sandwiches. Well, that's why he's unliberated. Anyway, I'm alternating squeezing my labia together so that they pop out like a purple wet butterfly, with stretching them out, and I mean stretching them. All stretched like that, the colors are perfectly visible. The parts closer to my body are really red, deep scarlet. And then they darken gradually to bluish purple and then to almost black. Now I know that this deep color is because I am Sicilian, but suddenly this evil critical voice perks up and says, "Well, how come none of the chicks in porno movies have black labia?" So I'm like, well maybe there are no Sicilians in the industry, which I know can't be true. And I also know that I'm not suffering from some weird labia disease, but there I am. Got my labia and mirror positioned as before, still looking in the mirror, yet I am no longer with myself. Thoughts turn to just why is it that in the all pornos I've seen, which is a moderate amount, only women with cute symmetrical powder-pink pussies are featured? Do I possess an ugly vagina? Like I need to think about this shit on my day off, when I'm uncomfortably hot and only half awake.

The BUST *Guide to the New Girl Order*

I come back to where I was, the living-room floor, checking myself out, and I'm kind of pissed that this should even be a consideration. What exactly is an ugly vagina but one that doesn't work? And mine works just fine. So I begin masturbating, still watching myself in the mirror, watching my belly and my thighs and my face and my boobs and my cunt, and I have an awesome orgasm, and then I do it again, and have another. And then I feel immediately weird that I just watched myself beat off. What would my shrink say, if I had one? Oh fuck it. It's my day, it's my body, and I can get off any way I want. I've got a big ass, stretch marks on my tits, an asymmetrical pussy, bluish-black labia, but you know, I think I'm beginning to like this body. Well shit, it's only taken twenty-four years.

✄

Sex, Lies, and Tampax

by Isadora Bimba

"Is it in yet?"

"No."

"Try a different angle. Is it in yet?"

"No! I can't find the right hole, let alone try a different angle!"

"Is it in yet?"

"I'm not sure. It's halfway in. This really hurts, you know!"

"Maybe it's in the wrong place."

I looked down at the tampon. "Tampax Slender Regular." I knew that this bright piece of pure white cotton was about to change my life forever.

I crouched there in the bathroom still staring at "it" and then fixated on the dried-up mud that had collected in the corner. My vagina was wide open, taking a rare whiff of fresh air, as the conversations I'd had about this piece of crumpled cotton were stirring in my mind.

I guess if I had been a born-and-bred American this day would not have been so important, but having come from a more archaic culture, things such as tampons were taboo unless a girl was married.

After enduring summer camp in Idaho for one year using nothing but pads, I was determined to break all tradition and find a more comfortable method of blood control. It's not that I preferred tampons to pads—I had never tried them—but somehow I knew there was something more comfortable to use, especially when riding a horse or a bike. There must be something less bulky—something that doesn't go up your ass and pull on your hair. Something that doesn't leak all over your clothes at unexpected moments.

I was always stigmatized as the voluptuous, ethnic one in my early teens. I guess what came with that is more blood, more hair, bigger hips, a larger ass, and definitely the most torturous ways of dealing with those features. (I haven't even mentioned the mind-over-matter exercise that I partake in every month when I get my bikini-line waxed.)

On that day I was twelve years old and away from home, and I thought, "Goddamn it, I'm going to learn how to put one of these up my cunt 'cause I'm not going through the same thing I did last year at Summer Camp Olympics." It was bad enough being excused from swimming at school because I was "indisposed," and having to watch my classmates swim while I sat and sulked from the galleria. But at least at school there were other people like me who couldn't use tampons and therefore got "indisposed." At camp, that vocabulary didn't exist.

"What do you mean you've never used a tampon?"

"You lose your virginity when you use a tampon."

"Oh come on! You break your hymen, yeah, but you don't lose your virginity."

"Well, isn't it the same thing?"

"No, it's not. Besides, you don't always break your hymen. My friend told me that in some cases it just expands and the tampon doesn't break it."

"Well, if it's not broken then how the hell does the blood come down? And if it just expands then how does the tampon go all the way in?"

"Look, it doesn't matter anyway. If you want to learn how to wear one I can help you."

I was shown a tampon and instructed to read that little booklet that lies on top of every box. That secret little book was going to free me from my closed-minded culture.

I was advised to put some Vaseline around the cotton to ease the passage into the vagina. After an embarrassing episode in which I was the first ever camper to buy a box of tampons at the snack store, and a good three days of trying to find the right hole—I gave up, and pretended to have succeeded in my quest, thereby swallowing my pride and any embarrassment involved in having bought the damn things.

But now I really had no excuse not to participate in the water activities. I prayed for rain but I also picked the activity where I didn't have to use a bathing suit—the crawfish race.

I moved along the shallow water catching those little black creepers from turned-over rocks. I moved so fast and caught so many that I won the race. To my amazement, that won my team the entire event, and the prize was to throw the winning team into the water. Before I could run, one of the cowboys lifted me up and dunked me into the river.

My head burst through the water. Oh God—I could feel the cotton bulge between my legs, expanding as the natural spring's water penetrated the cotton, enabling it to bleed. I didn't know whether I should get out or stay in until everybody was gone. Either way, I was humiliated and disgusted.

I finally rushed out of the water while everybody was preoccupied with splashing contests, and ran to the bathrooms. I stood in the shower crying, trying to figure out how to save myself from all the confusion. Why did I have to be so different? Why, after having asked my mother if I could use tampons, had she said no? Why, after having prodded her further and telling her I would go to the doctor to get a professional answer on the matter, had she said no? Why, after having gone to the doctor, unnecessarily spread my legs, and heard that there is only one way of losing one's virginity, and that it's not by using a tampon, had she still said no?

"What's the big deal anyway?" I wondered. "It's my virginity. And if God gets pissed off, then I'll just have to find out when I die. Besides, nobody makes a big deal about my brother's virginity and he's definitely lost it. My mother boasts about his sexual activity as though it were something to be proud of. Aren't God's rules equal for everybody?"

My cheeks burned as I thought, "Fuck it! It's my cunt and I'm going to do with it as I please!" Overcome with rage, I realized that all I had been taught about virginity was a lie. God wasn't going to punish me. God would never scorn what is essential about birth—or maybe he would, since the Virgin Mary conceived without having lost it. But hey, I wasn't the Virgin Mary, and besides, I planned to have a lot of fun in my life.

I took a tampon from my cubby-hole and locked myself in the stall. In one movement I angled my hand parallel to my stomach, found the hole, and shoved. I felt the harshness of the cotton as it clung to my vaginal wall but I shoved harder until I could feel that bone that was so beautifully illustrated in that secret little booklet, and then I pushed on the second cardboard, releasing the tampon into its natural area.

I stood up from my crouch, collected myself, and went back out into the campgrounds. I looked over at the wild landscape and realized that for the first time in my life, I had taken things into my own hands, literally. And if I had just lost my virginity, I couldn't have found a better person to have lost it to.

A Visit to the Museum of Menstruation

by Nancy E. Young

Our nation's capital: home to many manly monuments, including the Lincoln Memorial, the White House, and now, the Museum of Menstruation. All right, the Museum of Menstruation (affectionately known as MUM) is really in a suburb of

Washington, but this shrine to the blood of every woman is challenging the phallus quo of sight-seeing in D.C.

MUM was founded by a man, Harry Finley, which makes its existence even more curious. It currently resides in the downstairs of his home. The town is one of those Anywhere USA type of 'burbs. There is no sign in front of his house advertising the existence of MUM. A quick walk through the back door and one enters a '70s flashback: a wood-paneled den with thick carpeting and that most sacred piece of furniture, the beanbag chair—purple, no less. All available space is consumed by a continually rotating set of exhibits reflecting different aspects of menstruation.

Harry is the founder, curator, and heart and soul of MUM. He is friendly, knowledgeable, and easier to talk to about menstruation than your mom. Sure, women share solace with each other during "that time of month" for which we have countless nicknames (why can't we just say it?!?!?), but have you ever thought about the larger implications of your blood? Harry has. Who is this man who has the balls to go where no man—or woman—has gone before?

Harry was an army brat, the son of a colonel, and he lived all over the USA and Far East as a kid. His family tree includes a grandfather who invented the Miss America pageant(!). Among his straight jobs have been working as a math teacher, cartoonist, watercolorist, and graphic designer. Harry has worked for the feds for over twenty years. His black half-Burmese cat, Mack C. Padd, and new cat, Minnie Padd, maintain a round-the-clock vigil at the museum. Read on for a *BUST* conversation with MUM founder Harry Finley.

Harry, whenever I tell people about your museum, the first thing they say is "a museum of what?!" So after repeating the name, I get to gauge their reactions. Could you share with us the type of reactions you've had—especially what have been the most positive and the most negative?

The most positive have been from very liberal (and intelligent) women and groups such as Planned Parenthood, midwives who have visited me, etc. There have been many people who have encouraged me, including from Finland, Australia, and England. Criticism has come from as many sources. I got a letter from Cheyenne, Wyoming, saying that I should be burned at the stake and "May God close your

Harry and visitor of MUM
photo: Nancy Young

horable [*sic*] museum." Someone wrote *The Washington Post* that because of people like me the next century would be our last as a "superior nation." And my family is pretty upset.

Why are you, a man, fascinated with this subject in the first place?
Here's why I did it:

1. I'm very curious about many things and got interested when I started collecting magazine layouts, ads, and illustrations when I was hired as the art director of a small magazine in Frankfurt. I had never done magazine layout before, and I needed samples of what other people had done to study. Among them were menstrual hygiene ads from many different countries. It struck me that different countries approached this semi-taboo subject very differently, and I started to get intrigued by the marketing problems involved, and the history of it.

*The **BUST** Guide to the New Girl Order*

2. I like women and this is a seldom-discussed aspect of women.

3. The museum combines my interest in design and the feeling that I am doing something worthwhile.

4. It's not often that someone gets the chance to do something no one else has done, and I've got that chance.

5. It livens up my pretty dull life. This is actually the most important point.

Do you think the museum would be the focus of so much attention if you weren't a man?
Probably not. A woman writer for *Self* magazine said the fact that I'm a man also lends more importance to the subject, because of the generally higher level of respect given to men—sad, but possibly true. A woman doing this kind of thing might be regarded as just another far-left feminist with some kind of anti-male ax to grind.

How many visitors have you had since you opened?
About 350 to 400. Since I'm gone eleven hours a day at a full-time job, people can visit only on the weekends by appointment (with rare exceptions).

Have the visitors been mostly women or men?
About 95 percent women. I think men come mostly as bodyguards.

Do you allow children in your museum?
Sure, but only with adults. There have been maybe five or six kids under eighteen.

Have you had visitors from other countries?
People from Norway, England, Australia, Germany, and Canada have visited.

How much time do you spend on the museum weekly?
I spend anywhere from ten to forty hours. I always have projects hanging over my head. Right now, it's completing the next newsletter, preparing the next exhibit, a

display of the first commercial tampons ever made, and making a computerized inventory of the museum contents—about four thousand items—for an Italian medical publisher who wants to publish a bilingual catalog of the museum. I show visitors around on weekends, answer mail, and fulfill requests for information. It's a tough second job I've made for myself and I force myself to take time to do nothing every weekend—I would go nuts otherwise!

What is the weirdest thing you've learned about menstruation?
That I know more than most women about it. It's truly silly, people's attitude about menstruation.

For our male readers out there, what do you see as the role of men in menstruation?
More understanding, I suppose, and less nervousness. Up till fifteen years ago menstruation was never a topic of discussion between me and my girlfriends—but then I was never interested anyway.

At what age do you think females and males should be taught about menstruation?
Earlier than puberty, so there won't be so much shock.

Okay, Harry, here's a very important question to us women. Do you believe in PMS?
Yes.

What are some of the common myths about menstration? Do they differ by gender—that is, are there some myths that men have that women don't, or vice versa?
Many myths are disappearing, like the one about not bathing or washing your hair during a period. It probably started during the last century, when women were regarded as fragile creatures with all kinds of problems not shared by men. Men in general have as little to do with menstruation as possible—almost all associations are bad.

I'm curious about how menstruation has infiltrated other aspects of our culture. Do you know of any songs that make reference to menstruation?
There are, but I know zilch about popular music.

What about books or movies that are known for menstrual references?
The film *Carrie* is best known, but there are other references, usually negative.

Have you ever read Gloria Steinem's piece from *Outrageous Acts and Everyday Rebellions* about "if men could menstruate"?
Yes—it's very funny. Wouldn't it be great if women could feel a little better about menstruation?

You have a celebrity corner in the museum (display famous people in feminine hygiene product ads) which is quite fun. Can you tell our readers who is there?
Carol Lynley ('70s actress) and Susan Dey as teenagers before they were famous, and Cathy Rigby after she became famous as a gymnast (she was once America's hope in the Olympics, but flopped). Someone sent an ad of a well-known TV actress (unknown to me though), but these ads are still a bit taboo.

Could you talk a little about the cultural differences regarding menstruation around the world?
Menstruation is regarded positively in some parts, negatively in others, and seemingly neutrally in others. There is no universally bad attitude as I believed when I started this. This is what surprises—and pleases—me. The first men to really think about it must have been stunned—as I was. In a squeaky-clean society like ours, menstruation is evil, because it's blood, unpredictable, a mess, and appears in the most embarrassing spot for any woman in our society. And then she has to wear a diaper in many cases. This is part of the reason it is so interesting—it is at total odds with the ideals of our society, especially women's ideals.

What do you think of the women's liberation movement in the USA?
It's great and should continue. Women must be given equal access to opportunity, regardless if they take it or not. People in power—usually men—don't like sharing power. Few people do.

How is the role of women impacted by menstruation?
Aside from severe PMS, which is very unusual, very little. I used to think that

menstruation was a big handicap for women, but I no longer do. Our society can make it less of a handicap if we stop being so stupid about it.

Who invented the modern Kotex as we know it? What kinds of items preceded the Kotex?
The word Kotex was invented by the Kimberly-Clark Corporation about 1920 for their cheap, disposable pad made of cellulose-form wood pulp instead of the usual cotton that women had used for centuries. Kotex means C(K)Ottonlike TEXture, and it was supposed to be easier for women to say than "sanitary napkin" to a male sales clerk. But it wasn't, and Kotex didn't really begin to sell until the company told stores to put boxes of it on the counter next to a coin box, so women didn't have to say a word. Kotex was not the first disposable commercial napkin. Curads was one of its predecessors, as was Johnson & Johnson in the 1890s. Women usually made their own pads from diaper cloth and pinned them to their underwear or bought a commercial belt or special underwear. There are many strange patents in the last and present century for pads and pad-holding devices.

When did tampons appear?
Commercial tampons appeared in the early 1930s, for example Wix and Fax, o.b.-like tampons without applicators. Fax didn't even have a string—you tugged on the gauze which covered the tampon—which came before Tampax (1936).

Is there one person who is credited with inventing Kotex?
Kotex was originally invented as a bandage by the company Kimberly-Clark for American soldiers in the First World War, and probably invented by a man. However, it is only because American nurses used it in France at that time as a menstrual pad that it dawned on the company that it would make a good pad.

26

What about tampons?
Tampax, although not the first commercial tampon, was invented by a man, the Denver osteopath Dr. Earle C. Haas, who said, "I just got tired of women wearing those damned old rags, and I got to thinking about it." (Quoted from the official history of Tampax, *Small Wonder*.) He apparently knew nothing of tampons made in the past. Haas's invention was actually the tube applicator with the tampon (patented in

1933), but there was at least one other commercial tampon before Wix, which had no applicator.

Given the time they were developed, do you think women were involved in the process or just men?
It seems that it was mixture, but mostly men. Isn't it a shame that women couldn't have gotten more involved? But I have several patents of pads from this century which were either developed by women or in partnership with men.

What do you think of the past and present dangers involved in menstrual products, specifically tampons?
Dioxin and other chemical residues, especially in tampons, are dangerous. They are there because of the way the paper and cotton are made. There are products (NatraCare and others, and now Tampax cotton tampons) which avoid most or all of these chemicals. Pads are probably less dangerous because they sit outside the body rather than inside, but a woman can still absorb chemicals from the pads. Toxic shock is still a problem, but companies are very concerned about lawsuits, so they have been more cautious about instructions for use and the composition of the tampons. One solution is to use a menstrual cup like the Keeper, made in Ohio. I have read of no medical problems. You let the cup fill up after it is inserted in the vagina, pull it out, empty it, and reinsert. It is promoted as lasting ten years, and costs about $3.50 per year on that basis. But many women don't like the idea of emptying a cup, putting it back in, getting their hands bloody, etc. But it sure is cheap, ecological, and comfortable when used correctly.

So you think the cup is the most effective form of protection?
Yes, but I understand women's objections to it.

If you could have your ideal MUM, what would it look like and what would it include?
It would be a low modern building with some landscaping and an enclosed garden in the back. Inside would be a main exhibit hall showing menstrual customs from around the world, the history of the menstrual hygiene industry, art, etc. There would

be a temporary exhibit space, an auditorium for general women-related topics, a book/gift shop, and a German-style café with great pastry, great coffee, where you can stay as long as you want.

And finally, for readers who would like to see MUM in person or get your newsletter, how can they do this?
The newsletter is free. Call (301)459-4450 and leave a message, e-mail hfinley@mum.org, or write P.O. Box 2398, Landover Hills Branch, Hyattsville, MD 20784. The Web site is at http://www.mum.org. To arrange a visit on a weekend, give me a time you want to come—it'll almost always be okay in the afternoon on Saturday or Sunday. Bring friends or male bodyguards if that makes you feel more comfortable, although no one has ever failed to reappear after visiting the museum—and I think almost everyone has enjoyed it. Some people even laugh a lot!

POSTSCRIPT Harry has asked the editors to add the following notation in the book: "I am now looking for a public place for MUM and until I find it the museum is closed. It was open almost every weekend for four years, and I had to recapture the weekends for myself." Log on to the MUM Web site for updates.

Myth of the Black Butt

by Ayanna Sullivan

When I think about the sinister "Myth of the Black Butt," a bleached blank space replaces any decisive thought in my brain—I am desperately ambivalent about defining it as a myth; I actively oppose any stereotypes, including the ever-popular "black women naturally have bigger butts than white women." However, it's damned hard to actively oppose anything that often appears to be true.

*The **BUST** Guide to the New Girl Order*

There is no sound scientific evidence I've heard of that proves this general myth—although a few assholes in France conducted "research" in the late 1800s by dissecting the corpse of Sartje Baartman, a South African slave/circus act dubbed "the Hottentot Venus." They tossed her buttocks and genitalia in a jar of formaldehyde and placed them on display like a freaky biological joke.

Anyway, I do know what I see: Black women generally have more poundage on the back end than less-melanated females. That's why I brace myself when I try on jeans designed to fit the average (read: skinny White) woman. Now some Black women having "mo' junk in the trunk than a White girl" (as a '70s relic might say) would mean nothing if it weren't for the omnipotent European beauty standard reinforced in this so-called melting pot. (And I would like to point out, that because this is a so-called myth, not every Nubian Beauty has a big old butt). In a utopian ideal USA, Black women and White women, Latinas and Asians, Indigenous sistren and everybody else could sing the same song of lower-body love. We could celebrate this love with a pair of jeans that didn't slice up our rectums. We could sport bikini drawers without the mighty yeast beast growling from inadequate back fabric lodged in our back and front cracks. We could wear a size 7 in the waist and the hips! But we can't. And this European beauty standard yields more than just denim crisis. I know firsthand what it does.

Psychic damage occurs when a caramel-skinned five-year-old (like me) sees predominantly vanilla faces on her favorite shows (*Wonder Woman, The Love Boat,* and *Charlie's Angels*), in animated Disney flicks, and in her mother's *Family Circle*s. She then privately decides that she wants to look like a skinny, creamy, blond princess instead of her life-sustaining mother, aunts, and grandmother. After all, these "healthy" Black women just didn't look like all the rich stars.

At thirteen, her eyes wander past those coveted alabaster faces to their crack-pipe thin, bottomless bodies. She's starting to notice on her own now, also becoming aware of her own shape now, that boys and men stare at her bow legs and widening thighs.

And she gets a little confused about the mixed messages she's receiving. You see, when she's prancing around her mostly Black West Philadelphia neighborhood, the boys and the dirty old men appreciate her butt for all of its fullness. They cackle and sing classic odes to the Black physique like "Brick House," "Big Ole Butt," and "Bad Mamma Jamma." When she follows their probing eyes, they're not staring down "boobs" (as the White girls at the all-White girl's schools call them), they're sweating ass. This shameless lust makes her uncomfortable; instead of her mother's brainy but beautiful child, she's reduced to a BBQ rib at a pork fest. However, there don't seem to be any cultural or racial implications in their hungry commentary. The boys are straight-up nasty; the old men are straight-up dirty.

By tenth grade, when her butt and hips spread for real, so does her cultural confusion. Although she consciously acknowledges the danger of accepting the obvious Euro beauty standard—because her politically and culturally aware parents taught her right—she compares herself to the White girls anyway. She can't help it. Mass media still poison her psyche with the skinny, flat-assed ivory "ideal."

So she tries to at least compare herself to mass-media Black girls. But the Black girls on TV, in magazines, on BET, and beyond are very similar to the chicken bones she begrudgingly admires in *Mademoiselle.* Mainstream's melanated flavors of the month like Vanessa Williams, Jasmine Guy, and even Robin Givens just don't have mo' junk in the trunk like many of the girls around her way. And although the boys and men are sexually attracted to her hindquarters, they only yell "That's my wife" when a Lisa Bonet type walks by. This reverence tells her that only thin, light-skinned Lisas are marriage material. She's just a piece of ass.

Her butt is a source of sexual confusion as well. On one hand, she loves cramming each meaty cheek into a pair of fitted Calvins. She needs that lustful commentary on her "oven stuffer roaster" to feel attractive because it's 1989 and "light is right." On the other hand, the supposed "fuckability" of her butt makes her feel nasty before her time; she's had no parts of sex yet, and the idea of a man wanting her for "that ass" makes her sad. Like any melodramatic daughter of a self-professed womanist, she wants males to dig her mind, even at first glance.

Years later, her first ass tap is a debacle. Preorgasmic exclamations to "Move that big ass, girl!" shut the tryst down. She tries to take his wannabe compliment as such, but his nonromance smacks her right back to her thirteen-year-old's sexual confusion. As images of brown buttocks in glass and auction blocks fill her head, she begins to despise him. She wonders if he ever urged his lighter ex-love the same way during sex. She wonders if he likes her butt better than her mind. Then she decides he's not worth the wonder and leaves him alone. She has economic issues to take up with her butt.

Socioeconomically, she's been placed on this college-preparatory, private-school, grudgingly middle-class, "mainstream" (read: predominantly White) path where her ass is not an asset. In her mind only flat-butt, white and small-boned, light-skinned, straight-nosed, wonder-if-she's-Black, flat-assed chicks get the play in this "real world" she hears grown folks grumbling about. In fact, her butt, her bow legs, and her pigeon-toed prance all seem hopelessly unsophisticated in a world of anatomically correct Barbie dolls. Barbie will probably be her competition in any job market beyond her block, so when her mother tells her "now you have some hips," she secretly worries that what is natural to her will be an economic obstacle. And it sucks.

So coupled with the natural self-hate that arrives with female adolescence, she quietly resents her naturally plump butt. And it hurts.

I'm twenty-three now and fully functioning in the "mainstream" (read: predominantly White) job market. The dualism continues. I still sport my butt in Crown Heights, Brooklyn, where I dwell, but cover it on 34th and Fifth, where I toil. Occasionally—neurotically—I stand naked in the mirror and stomp to count the resulting butt jiggles. I grapple with the fact that I'm a 5/6 or 7 in the waist but a borderline 9/10 in the hips and ass. The dirty old men and teenage boys and Black college grads still show their appreciation of "love" when I pass them by. The mass media chicks still have minimal backside. But I realize now, as I observe the mostly White women that I work with, that many of them don't fit the beauty standard either. A couple even have gluteal endowment to rival mine. But I still contend that a White woman in a pair of tight Levi's packs a different set of cheeks than a Black woman in that same pair. After all, White girls don't have decades of the "Loose Woman" stereotype to contend with. Their buttocks have never floated in a jar of formaldehyde as a biological phenomenon.

I would love to say, "*Damn it, I love my beautiful African behind all the time!* It is part of my heritage and those who hate it, fear it." But privately I sometimes fear my natural roundness when no one's looking. Then I think about Ms. Bartman and every other Black woman who's been on this journey and I thank God. Body issues and all, I'm damned proud of who I am.

31

My Left Hand

by Ann Rex

For as long as I can remember, I have always been obsessed about my weight. I was worried about how my body looked long before I ever picked up an issue of *Cosmo,* long before I realized that models were actually people behind the cool gazes and stretched bodies, long before I realized the difference between skinny mirrors and fat mirrors. As early as the age of ten, even, I monitored my body's growth. I'd place my tiny hand on my upper thigh, my self-appointed barometer of policed weight control, making sure that the width of my thigh did not exceed the width of my outspread hand.

As I blossomed into a full-fledged voluptuous teenager, my obsession seemed to expand exponentially. In high school, I was the leader of my own little rat pack of girls; I was a Heather, an "IT" girl, and so my so-called friends adopted my every-thing—from my outfits to my mannerisms—in their efforts to be just like me, popular. I always felt like I had to live up to my "image"—a manipulated concoction of perfect body, brains, and bravado—in order to maintain my hierarchical status. To be the "IT" girl my minions had pegged me for, I had to spend a lot of time *being* her, being a troublemaker, being the girl with the most cake, being a touchy and untouchable entity. But I could never just be. And to further aggravate matters, such as my dilemma of quelling my insecurities about my body, my problems, my needs while still being a cool chick, I had no one to turn to when I felt weak, unsure, heavy.

As I got older, the self-inflicted pressure to be this girl increased. My fears manifested themselves in my ravenous appetite. I had a sweet tooth; it began at break-fast with a can of Coke and the potpourri of junk food I shoveled into my mouth just continued from there. When I was seventeen, my father warned me that my butt would balloon into a Goodyear blimp if I kept up the pace of my "diet." Concerned, I immediately cut out carbonated drinks from my daily intake.

In the summer of my eighteenth year, I discovered my left hand. I learned that I could still be this girl—the one with an effervescent personality and a perfect body—and be in control of my weight while still eating everything I wanted. So while the other little rat packers counted calories, I gloated about not getting bloated.

My left hand and I had an unusual first date, and like the first time I fucked, it hurt and I cried. I thought this was going to be easy. I thought I could eat as much as I wanted and get rid of it all and everything would be fine, I'd still be skinny. I didn't expect the tears, I didn't expect the pain, the gagging, the bile. But I was not to be daunted—the challenge of perfecting my skills had been triggered, the goal of having it all loomed on the horizon and I was only going to remain thin if my inept left hand would become a skilled crafts hand. In short, I was hooked by the southpaw.

And so, I turned into a shove-your-fist-in-your-mouth-till-your-knuckles-bleed kind of gal. My life became a constant merry-go-round of overeating (bingeing) and cheating (purging), a free ride of brownies and pasta, an eyes-closed whirlpool of gradually degenerating degrees of self-control. My left hand became my heroine; not an instrument of destruction but of reconstruction. A beacon of hope, of keeping everything under control, of having my cake and purging it if I had to. And so I lived this sort of hazy nether beat-the-scale world for quite some time. I was fueled by my acute desire to remain popular, to have the best-looking boyfriend, to be a straight-A student, to be a perfect daughter, and to keep my perfect body. And as I got older, and *Cosmo* finally did infiltrate my life, this perspective of perfection was based on everyone else's, and yet no one's. It came from an amalgam of body parts I had seen on *The Brady Bunch* (they had great hair) and in magazines and other women's bodies in my life whom I had looked up to and at, who functioned as role models, teachers, what have you, women like my mom—the kind of woman I aspired to be like, to look like too.

At the height of my first (yes, there were two!) bout with bulimia, I was bingeing and purging up to eight times a day. My left hand was adept at getting rid of food without much effort. In and out, I used to say. However, the toll the binge/purge cycle took on my body was another story. By the end of the day I would lie down, fatigue-ridden from the day's events. My eyes were often puffy from involuntary tears, complete with burst capillaries turned into raspberry speckles all around my cheeks and eyes. Not a pretty picture.

When it finally occurred to me that I had a problem I sought therapy. I knew I needed help, but finding the right kind of help proved to be even more devastating than admitting I had a problem. In the end it was actually my brother who came to my aid by basically threatening to tell my parents. And the idea of shattering their image of their perfect daughter was so terrifying to me that I stopped after months of sometimes gentle, sometimes rough brother-sister therapy/intervention. A week before I turned twenty-two, I gave my left hand an extended, overdue vacation.

For the next four years, my body healed itself. My knuckles were no longer red from the constant scraping against my teeth. The back of my throat was no longer irritated all the time, having been scratched to bits by my fingernails. I had energy, I felt great about myself. Things started to "happen." I was out of college; I met the most perfect man in the world who ended up being the most perfect boyfriend for the next few years; I pursued a career. And I had a great body, again.

Unfortunately, I relapsed. After four years, my career was going nowhere, I lost my perfect boyfriend, I didn't like my friends. I began to see lumps and bumps in my thighs, the kind I'd never seen before. In short, all my fears had come back to haunt me, except this time I knew I was fat. By then, models had names, MTV flooded the senses, AIDS prohibited uninhibited sexual behavior. By then I had the awareness I did not have at eighteen; I was painfully aware of how inadequate I had become in my old age. I read those horrible un*BUST*y magazines and I knew what "willowy" and "lithe" referred to and I knew it wasn't me.

I began to hate my body. *Hate.* I wanted to be like the thin models, except I knew I couldn't be; I was short and I was fat. I hated to see my reflection in the mirror—I felt horror every time I saw yet another piece of me expand or sag. I would not be catching anyone's eye if I remained looking this way, because after all, what else could I offer to a guy who might be fantasizing about some current hot babe/media goddess when, in fact, I was anything but?

And so it began, except this time, it was not an experiment. Every time I looked at my left hand, I knew, I fucking knew that what I was about to do was self-destructive. I knew about destroying the electrolyte balance, and I knew how the acid produced in my belly would rot my teeth. But once I relapsed I could not stop. The familiarity fit my left hand like a glove as the bingeing and purging again became a part of my everyday lifestyle.

All the old habits returned, the feasts, the treats. I began carrying a compact toothbrush, floss, and toothpaste with me at all times. The purging process had its own set of rituals. I would lock myself in the bathroom while the shower loudly ran cold water to muffle the gagging and coughing sounds, so as not to arouse the suspicions of my roommates. And then, once the purge was complete, I would draw a nice lukewarm bath, to soothe my shaking body and rid myself of the accompanying, necessary evils (bile-filled mouth, puffy eyes, racing heartbeat). Then the self-abuse would begin, the utter hatred, the abysmal shame, the unreality of it all. Depression would sweep over me.

I began to believe that therapy was the only way out. I was bulimic. I was addicted to bingeing and purging. I needed help. I was just too emotionally volatile. After almost every purge, I would swear up and down never ever to do it again. Sometimes I would succeed for a day or so, but if I was just slightly upset, the evil bug would come back, over and over again. And this cyclical behavior was not going to stop unless I sought help.

Because this second bout was not like the first time. There was something more pathetic and desperate about this round. This time everything hurt. Not just my body, but my heart and my mind were much more worn out than when I had been bulimic in my teens. The puffiness didn't dissipate as quickly as it once did, the capillaries took longer to repair themselves, and the fatigue was unshakable. I was the worst kind of addict; I lied to everyone, pretending everything was okay, perfect in fact. Three years into the second round, I got the scare of my lifetime.

I had been in the bathroom for over an hour. My knuckles, scarred from never healed scabs, were bleeding, my fingers had turned into pruny prongs, my irritated throat was punctured by my insistent relentless attempt to purge the evening's bacchanalian binge. I could feel the pop pop pop of blood vessels in my face exploding each time I leaned over. My eyes were heaving closed, every pore in my body was gasping for air, and I was panicking, because nothing was coming out. I mean, I had eaten a lot of food and not a damn morsel was coming out, no matter how many fingers I stuck into my mouth. Nothing was working and I was getting worried. The longer the food sat in my stomach the sooner it would get digested and I would get fatter soon if something didn't give.

I didn't know what to do, so I decided to stand up and get some water. However, I was so disoriented, I could barely stand. Instead I lay down on the cold tile bathroom floor for what I thought was a few minutes, but when I finally popped my eyes open, dusk had turned to dawn and panic set in.

Oh god, what had I done? Was I going to die, now? Like this? Possibly from a heart attack and then my roommate would find me, arm drenched in bile, toilet bowl full of halfhearted spew? What would my parents say? She died because she thought she was fat? Oh god oh god oh god. Suddenly I was afraid, not just roller-coaster butterflies in my stomach afraid, no this was a deeper fear. Terror had set in, a pure unadulterated unconditional cold heartless sensation that bled blackness. Ohmigod. I'm not sure how long I sat in the murkiness of my mind's revolt; I had no grasp on myself, my sense of anything. But then, as if someone, maybe me, flicked a switch, it happened: the epiphany. I suddenly did not feel clammy, but happy, this bizarre giddiness that came from this well of knowledge. It was over. I was going to be okay. Just like that.

What? Yeah. I'm not saying cold turkey works for everyone, but I just sat up and I was fine. I had been abusing my body for years, how could I be "just fine"? But, the prophetic gaze into the nadir of my soul reminded me that I could get better. I was still fat, no question, I still felt fat, but if that feeling could be dealt with, then maybe I could accept and learn to love the body that I had. My terror angel had waited to rear its ugly head, always just lurking on the horizon, just waiting for the right moment to go Boo! And when it did, I woke up.

Truth is, I still miss the perfectness of my body; I don't have it anymore. But my idea of perfection has changed; so maybe in a perfect world perfect doesn't really exist. In my world I am okay, and that kind of feeling is just about perfect. The models, well, they still haunt me, but frankly, being 5 feet 11 inches tall thinthinthin and heartachingly beautiful is not a norm, it's an anomaly. Models stand out because they are so different than the rest of us, and different is still cool.

I am different too now, new on the inside. No matter how many times a lover will oooh and ahh over my DD-size breasts, I still wonder how he will react when he sees what they really look like when the bra is off and they hang so gloriously low.

Does this mean I'll lop them off so they'll look like someone else's breasts? Nope. It just means I am still insecure about my body but at least now I don't want to punish myself for it. Now I can eat as much as I want with a group of people and not have to be embarrassed about excusing myself from the table at just the right moment. Because now when I go to the bathroom during a meal, it's because I have to pee, and that makes me feel really good.

She Ain't Heavy, She's My Lover

by Andrew

The young men at the bar were all in agreement about Sandy. "Oooooh," said one of them with a squinty, disgusted look. Another just lifted his upper lip and exclaimed, "Sandy?" as if that were enough.

I had slept with Sandy the night before. Her scent still lingered on my fingers and in my underwear. I was remembering how much fun we both had; how exciting it was when I first saw her in her bra and when she first took her shirt off. What a woman!

These three guys had all slept with her, too, yet they had all written her off as someplace to go and later, recall. In short, a war story. "Man, I'm glad I lived through that one!"

I could only remember how the two of us had sat around in the White Horse Tavern the night before, talking about literature over cheap beer and laughing. How we had poured ourselves into a cab to her place, exhilarated about what was about to happen.

And here, the following night, I was listening to the other heroes express their relief at having lived through the ordeal. Something was definitely wrong.

37

This was a time when skinny, flat-chested body types were in vogue. Fat was very out. Sandy was not a fat woman by any stretch of the imagination, but she definitely was not skinny either.

In the coming weeks something else gnawed at me. When I thought about it, a lot of the great times I had had in the sack were not with the lithe, heavily advertised as-seen-on-TV body types, but with "larger" women, with breasts and buttocks. As a matter of fact, there seemed to be a direct correlation between how crazed the sex was that I had with women and their distance form the "normal" female body I was supposed to desire. I began to realize that I was not really attracted to the publicized female form at all; I was attracted to larger, more developed female bodies. All of this hit me with a wave of disgust. I felt I was a freak. I was ashamed of myself.

It stuck me that these larger women were also ashamed. We were lovers cast aside by the popular culture. I had never made a conscious decision to be attracted to a certain body type, but here I was made to feel embarrassed by something I couldn't control. To make matters worse, I constantly had to listen to friends put down women I thought were attractive. "Man, did you see the jugs on that one?"

There was a certain discomfort that these friends seemed to feel in being attracted to a female form that was not popularized. But they distinctly *were* attracted to them; that was evident from the way they were constantly preoccupied with fuller-formed women, if only to express disgust, which was the way they were being taught to behave. For some strange reason, men were supposed to be attracted to starving women who stood in front of cameras to make money. The women in front of cameras were skinny because the nature of photography makes the human form look heavier than it is in reality. It seemed reality was taking a backseat to its own image.

This was over twenty years ago. Things have not changed that much, although it is now okay for women to work out and be healthy. And there is a new aesthetic developing among men and women that deems it acceptable for a woman to be large. Read large: not a euphemism for fat.

I still can feel slightly embarrassed in a crowd when I'm accompanied by a woman who does not fit the "norms" of show business. Why, I don't know. At the same time I have to listen to media types make statements like "the curvaceous Cindy Crawford." Cindy Crawford wears makeup well. She is not curvaceous.

And still someone always seems to be crowing about how fat some woman is while many of my male friends wear enormous potbellies that push out their shirt buttons in a silly expression of physical unawareness.

I married a big woman. I love her. It took me an awfully long time to understand who I am and what I desire. Thank God for that much.

Danny Maloney

2

Feminists Fatale: BUST-ing the Beauty Myth

Who was it that said clothes make a statement? What an understatement that was. Clothes never shut up.
  —Susan Brownmiller, "Femininity" (1984)

IT'S SATURDAY NIGHT AT MY HOUSE, AND ALL THE GIRLS ARE
here. We're all feminists, of course, but we don't all look the part. Some of us shave
our legs, some of us shave our heads; some of us wear miniskirts, some of us wear
pants; some of us keep up with the latest trends, some of us wouldn't know the latest
trend if it hit them upside the head. Still, when I bring out my beauty bucket, which
contains about fifty colors of nail polish, in every shade imaginable from blue to
bronze, all of us get to work. Passing around the little bottles from hand to hand, we
make our choices and revel in these moments of total girlified glamour. It's almost
a guilty pleasure. After all, we are the women who grew up during feminism's
bra-burning heyday, who learned about *Roe v. Wade* while we were still reading
Dick and Jane.

   We've come a long way, baby. It was in 1968 that Robin Morgan and her
group, New York Radical Women, handed out leaflets inviting women to attend a
protest of the Miss America Pageant in Atlantic City, New Jersey. Taking aim at "the
degrading mindless-boob-girlie symbol" that they felt the pageant promoted, the
organizers complained that "women in our society are forced daily to compete for
male approval, enslaved by ludicrous 'beauty' standards we ourselves are conditioned to take seriously." Among the many events that the pamphlet promised would
take place at the rally, one stands out: "There will be . . . a huge Freedom Trash Can,
into which we will throw bras, girdles, curlers, false eyelashes, wigs, and representative
issues of *Cosmopolitan, Ladies Home Journal, Family Circle,* etc.—bring any such
woman-garbage you have around the house." (Contrary to popular myth, no bra burning
actually took place at this event; in fact, not a single item of lingerie was harmed.)

   Thirty years later, it seems that we gals have rummaged through that trash
can and recycled just about everything in it. Only now we call it "reclaiming." From
lipstick lesbians to rouge-wearing riot grrls, today's vampy visionaries believe that it
is possible to make a feminist fashion statement without resorting to wearing Birken-
stocks 24-7, or hiding our figures in power suits. We've taken out our shoulder pads
and stuffed them into our bras, no longer disguising ourselves as men, but as women.
Because it's as clear to us as it is to RuPaul that fashion is a costume, that femininity
is a masquerade, and that sometimes we *like* to play dress-up. We want to shout out
to all the nonbelievers who still think that the only true feminist is a hairy, scary
feminist: "We're here, we use Nair, get used to it." Can I get a witness?

The **BUST** *Guide to the New Girl Order*

In the past few centuries, feminists have had plenty to say on the subject of fashion, most of which can be summed up by a single statement: They're against it. In 1790, women's rights vindicator Mary Wollstonecraft argued that it was women's addiction to adornment that was keeping them down. "[Women's] minds are not in a healthy state," she wrote, explaining that "[their] strength and usefulness are sacrificed to beauty." By the mid-1800s women's bodies were not in a healthy state either. To achieve the newly stylish "S-curve" silhouette, women had taken to squeezing themselves into tight-laced corsets, with little or no consideration for their internal organs. It was at this time that Elizabeth Cady Stanton began to advocate an outfit that was most likely the nineteenth-century equivalent of a muumuu and sweatpants: a midlength dress worn over puffy pantaloons. But the women who gladly donned these so-called "bloomers" quickly discovered that not everyone took kindly to the idea of women wearing the pants in the family. The bloomer brigade soon found themselves trailed by jeering mobs of men who pelted them with sticks and stones. Ultimately, the costume was abandoned, as much for the embarrassment it caused its wearers as for how ugly it looked. As Stanton would later admit, the overall appearance of the outfit was "not artistic."

A strict, if more artistic, dress code for men and women remained in effect all the way up until Robin Morgan's day, when feminists and hippies alike once again advocated a free-to-be-you-and-me, unisex style of clothing. Men grew their hair long on their heads, women grew their hair long on their legs, and anything "unnatural" was thought to be oppressive. But for those of us born into the '60s and '70s, all was not ponchos and pantsuits. On the one hand, we could appreciate the no-frills look of people like Kristy McNichol and Patti Smith, but on the other, we were thoroughly seduced by the groovy glamour of Laurie Partridge and Cher. We understood very clearly what feminists, and our mothers, meant when they said, "It doesn't matter what you look like on the outside; it's what's *inside* that counts," but we still felt tempted by those ads that promised we could "be a model, or just look like one." And oh, how could we resist the siren song of Clairol's Herbal Essence shampoo (the original one), the sexy slickness of Bonne Bell's strawberry-scented lip gloss, or the pop-art perfection of Maybelline's pink-and-green tubes of mascara? These coveted items were our all-access passes to the exciting world of teenage girlhood, a mask that let us look older than we felt, a protective coat of war paint that gave us the confidence to go out and capture that elusive boy.

Maybe we were just being duped by Madison Avenue, who, by the '70s, had taken to selling us women's lib in the form of cosmetics and antiperspirants ("strong enough for a man, but made for a woman"). But for us, fashion had little to do with feminism, and everything to do with female bonding. After all, the land of clothing and hairstyles was where we held our all-girls, no-boys-allowed pajama parties, whether we were drooling in front of the boob tube over Farrah Fawcett's perfectly feathered 'do, or just hanging out at the local Pants Place Plus. We never thought that our pursuit of style in any way held us back from our pursuit of equality. We'd grown up with none of the clothing restrictions that had so obviously (to us) kept our mothers in the oppressive chains of patriarchy: white underwear, white gloves, tight girdles, and heels. We had Earth Shoes, jeans, and a wide variety of T-shirts in our closets hanging right next to our miniskirts and go-go boots. We had what no other generation of women before us did: a choice. And we intended to keep it.

By the time the 1980s rolled around, however, a generation of lip-gloss-wearing liberationists came to understand that being fashionable *and* feminist was still considered to be a conflict of interest. Those of us old enough to attend college in those years quickly learned, in our women's studies classes, that any woman who dressed *too* sexy was a traitor to the cause—after all, what self-respecting woman would ever *choose* to wear uncomfortable, skintight, or skin-revealing clothing? Susan Brownmiller defended her decision to swear off skirts "because the nature of feminine dressing is superficial in essence," and it was agreed that dressing like a sex object meant you were asking to be treated like—well, an object. So although we stridently claimed the freedom to wear whatever we wanted, it was the unspoken understanding that no woman could expect to be taken seriously unless she dressed like a man. Enlightened women at universities everywhere began retreating to the safe neutrality of overalls and jeans, while women in the corporate world donned pin-striped pants and blazers.

But then, when Madonna crossed the borderline from the MTV screen into our collective psyches, we suddenly had a poster girl for postmodern fashion. Whether she was wearing a bra, a midriff-revealing T-shirt, or fishnet stockings, Madonna managed to transform each of these items from a scarlet letter of sexual submissiveness into a red badge of courage. She dressed like a sex object, but she acted like a sex subject—an explosive combination if ever there was one. So while the press took offense that Madonna was setting feminism back by presenting herself as a "boy toy," no one seemed to notice that her biggest fans were not straight men at all, but rather, young women. Suffocated by the high-school version of the Virgin/Whore complex (dress demurely and you're a prude; dress sexy and you're a slut), girls were happy to have at least one of these options invested with some power. And unlike previous va-va-voom girls such as Marilyn Monroe—whose shtick involved playing dumb about their own sexiness, as if they were too innocent to even know about such things—Madonna's over-the-top image was far from accidental. From Harlow to harlot, Maddona's ever-changing sexual personae were carefully chosen, and completely under her control.

So instead of throwing out the bra with the bathwater, as earlier feminists had done, Madonna suggested that the trappings of femininity could be used to make a sexual statement that was powerful, rather than passive. It was an idea that had widespread appeal, and it convinced a nation of Madonna wannabes to say good-bye to the "natural" look and hello to a new style of feminine display that involved layers of lingerie and bottles of bleach. At the same time, women like Annie Lennox and Grace Jones were putting a seductive spin on androgynous dressing. Irony had become the must-have accessory of the decade, and feminism was finally being set free of its antifashion stance. Inspired by these and other glamour gals of the '80s—Cyndi Lauper, Exene Cervenka, the Go-Gos—many of us made pilgrimages to our local Salvation Army, buying up '50s dresses that made a pointed statement about just how different we were from prefeminist housewives, and vampy '40s gowns that allowed us to camp it up in our new role as feminists fatale. We dressed like girls, we dressed like boys, we dressed like women, we dressed like men. Every item in our wardrobes was chosen to convey our unwillingness to conform to traditional ideas about gender and sexuality. Suddenly, Simon de Beauvoir's statement that "One is not born, but rather becomes, a woman" could be heard in a new way: as a slogan for postmodern feminist fashion.

It was with this same sense of irony that Courtney Love, as Madonna's heir apparent in the '90s, burst onto the scene. In her little-girl dresses and bright red lipstick, Courtney Love gave more the impression of a child playing dress-up than of an adult rock star. Her girlie-girl style, coupled with her very unladylike, out-of-control performances, helped to convey her rebellion against the stereotype of the demure, selfless female, and won her a loyal following of young women who were grasping for a model of female adulthood and sexuality that could include anger and aggression.

Courtney also helped bring the gynocentric gestalt of the Riot Grrls front and center. The baby-doll dresses that she helped to popularize, and which soon became a mainstay of mainstream fashion, were directly descended from this loosely defined movement of young women. Gathering together in latter-day consciousness-raising groups, the Riot Grrls represented a new breed of feminists who were determined to embrace, and no longer apologize for, everything that was traditionally girlie, and therefore just as traditionally marginalized—including ultrafemmey fashion. Taking their cue from the queer movement, Riot Grrls worked to reclaim sexist slurs like "slut" and "bitch" by scrawling those words in lipstick or Magic Marker across their bodies. They even resurrected the word "girl" itself, by injecting it with a fierce, double-r growl. With their legs unshaven and their hair sprinkled liberally with baby barrettes, Riot Grrls took to the streets holding hands, wearing thrift-store dresses with combat boots, and carrying Barbie lunch boxes as purses, their look sending out a cacophony of messages about femininity, feminism, and fashion.

These days, girls everywhere are sporting clothing from companies with names like Poontang, Tart, Girly, and Label Whore. Started by a growing number of young female designers, these labels reveal a tongue-in-chic sensibility that is definitively feminist. Their influence can be found on everything from T-shirts in New York City boutiques that read "Whore" and "Girls Kick Ass," to watered-down versions appearing in malls across the country that read "Brat" and "Girls Rule." One company even makes a line of underwear that has a kitten illustration over the crotch accompanied by the words "Pussy-scented." Ironic, obnoxious, and unapologetically female, these designers have added a new meaning to the words "fashion statement."

Of course, nothing's become more synonymous with Girl Power than the colorful, sparkly nail polish that is being worn by everyone from Riot Grrls to Spice Girls. Whereas for years women could only choose from shades of red, pink, or coral for their manicures, new nail polish lines by Urban Decay, with their slogans "Does pink make you puke?" and "Look like a person, not a doll," and Hard Candy, started by a girl just out of her teens, are staging a full-frontal assault on the idea that cosmetics are just about trying to be "pretty." Girls are snatching up colors like Roach Brown, Slime Green, and Puke Orange, and painting them on in an act that is almost as ornery as it is ornamental. "Yes," they seem to be saying, "we like decorating ourselves. But it's not necessarily because we're trying to please *you*."

Even mainstream companies are beginning to add a more brazen edge to their beauty products, with their own lines of nontraditional nail polish and makeup. The cosmetics firm M.A.C. paid lipstick service to the notion that makeup is politically incorrect when they used transvestites and lesbians as their product spokesmodels. Now it seems even the boys want a piece of the girlie action—Hard Candy recently introduced a new line of nail polish just for men, called Candy Man. So while we laugh at Cynthia Heimel's statement that "wearing makeup is an apology for our actual faces," we know that we're looking for more than just "facial improvement" when we step up to the makeup counter and plop down $12 for a tube of Viva Glam— we're looking for a way to grab glamour by the balls, and have some fun with the idea of femininity.

Unlike our feminist foremothers, who claimed that makeup was the opiate of the misses, we're positively prochoice when it comes to matters of feminine display. We're well aware, thank you very much, of the beauty myth that's working to keep women obscene and not heard, but we just don't think that transvestites should have all the fun. In our fuck-me dresses and don't-fuck-with-me shoes, we're ready to come out of the closet as the absolutely fabulous females we know we are. We love our lipstick, have a passion for polish, and, basically, adore this armor that we call "fashion." To us, it's fun, it's feminine, and, in the particular way we flaunt it, it's *definitely* feminist.

—*Debbie Stoller*

47

Do you know your ABC's...
ANIMAL PRINTS
BOOTS!
EYELINER
KOHL
FLIP
JEWELRY
BUST
KNEE SOX

Girl's Fashion Tips for Boys

by Girl

Long ago, before I realized I was going to be a permanent resident of the Island of Misfit Toys, I made little experimental forays into the Land of Feminine Beauty. I tried out all the colors in my sister's eye-shadow arsenal, attempted some misguided plucking, etc., trying outwardly to pass, but even then I knew it was all a farce. I knew there was a reindeer game being played and not only did I not want to learn the rules, I didn't even want to learn the language of being a Girl (my nom de 'zine has everything to do with not feeling grown-up and nothing to do with feeling feminine). I'm not a tomboy or anything, just . . . an Aquarius. The astrological profile in chilling black and white. "I don't mind combining the male and female in myself" and "I'm a little confused about my female identity . . . I don't like being gender identified." Ouch.

Okay, so maybe you don't believe in that stuff. Let's just say that I can't figure out how to surf the subject/object rules of society and I'm confused. I want to change the world instead of, Goddess forbid, learning to cope with things as they are. Because things as they are kinda suck.

Representation of self—as you would like to be seen, as you desire to be, as you desire to be desired—is insidious cultural programming for girls (and by the way, I don't think gender is destiny). I want to be looking, not looked at. However, I'm still captive to the program, damn it. It's hard to be the Subject of my own life when to walk down the street means getting hassled, turned into somebody's little power-trip Object—a daily humiliation compounded by the even greater daily humiliation that, in spite of all your beliefs and passionate commitments, you still want to be attractive, you want the attention, to be the object of desire. You can't help it. I hate it. (Of course, being valued as a piece, as chattel, means that one day you will devalue, meet

52

indifference, and the invisibility will be imposed upon you instead of chosen in this particular marketplace . . . but that's a whole 'nother story.)

I'm not into trying to switch places, to attain male-type power (I believe that female-type power is of an entirely different order and I happen to prefer it), but I think it's a healthy exercise to try. In recent pop culture, strong women have objectified men for the vicarious pleasure of other women—Courtney, Salt-N-Pepa, Ada in *The Piano*—so I thought my contribution might be a little reversal, to offer all those guys out there the chance to be a Love Thing and to encourage women to actively engorge their tumescent tissues of desire.

So men—be brave. Take chances. Try to please women—imagine yourself as the object of their desiring gaze. It's fun, and you'll be contributing to the end of Western civilization as we now know it.

Dos

- **Long underwear** Making special sneak previews from below collars, pushed-back sleeves on firm forearms, beneath torn jeans or skatepunk shorts, in full skanky glory under a T-shirt for that bad bi-level effect. Why is long underwear so great? I think I used to assign it a heavy boys-only kind of domain; now that I wear it myself it's extra sexy on men.

- **Sideburns** Pant pant, pant. I go crazy for sideburns of almost any dimension or design. This is one of those mysterious deals where I seem to have been programmed during the '70s (unbeknownst to my preteen self) to fetishize an odd secondary sex characteristic. (God, could it have been triggered by Spock? It wasn't Neil Diamond—maybe Neil Young? Perhaps these things are best left unexamined.) Anyway . . . I do have an erotic attachment to that site on the male body, the spot just before the ear where sideburns begin—it's a luscious place to plant a long, slow kiss. Now let's see, where was I?

- **Braids** Short and nappy, woven with beads, cowries, colored threads, a pair of shiny ropes falling over collarbones, one long thick plait down the back. Treat your hair like the beautiful expressive ornament it is.

- *Tattoos* In nonpublic body areas, for private viewings. For girls' eyes only.

- *Middle part* Another example of preadolescent programming. Hair parted in the middle is charmingly dorky, especially if it's a grown-out shag. Somehow I associate it with someone who doesn't have all the answers (like where to get a good haircut).

- *Bracelets* Even with a huge paramilitary geek watch, bracelets fascinate and transform and beguile. Necklaces can get icky (like fat gold medallions and puka shell chokers) and are probably too often about manly powers, like neckties, but even spiked leather cuffs seem sort of sweet and vulnerable. Or is that just me?

- *Lucky T-shirts* Perforated with ancient holes from unscrewing beer caps or the near-invisible spray of battery acid, collar torn from four thousand yanks over the head, soft as moleskin from four thousand washes, silkscreen gone with the rinse. Beyond comfortable, approaching fetish object.

- *Pierced noses* Maybe because this used to be a females-only adornment in India and I relish any gender signifier getting fucked with. Also, holes=receptivity.

- *Skirts* Few nonrock stars seem to have the impunity for this. I like to look at men's legs. That skatepunk-jammie look is kinda skirtish.

- *Patchouli* Any dark earthy essential oil. Musky smells to enhance your own glandular secretions and all those pheromones flying around.

- *Gap teeth* Not precisely fashion; a mark of beauty, a show of antivanity (well, maybe just poverty?). Flaws can be most haunting.

- *Nehru jacket* Like a suit, but liberated from all the dreariness of business, professionalism, etc., it turns you into a man capable of resistance, nonviolence, incense burning, love bead wearing, and international diplomacy, too.

- *Pirate earrings* Big, heavy, round. Pendulous. Shiny. Daring.

54

The BUST *Guide to the New Girl Order*

Don'ts

- **Turtlenecks** Despite my thing for Illya Kuryakin in his sleek black one, I'm afraid the only place left for this garment is *Sprockets*. Non-black turtleneck associations: Sears catalog, dickeys, slimy Euro-trash pseudosuavity, golf, ascots, slacks . . . stuff like that.

- **Pectorals** I prefer my men flat-chested, thank you. Concave, even.

- **Sunglasses** I don't care if you really really need them for road safety, on the sidewalks 99.9 percent of the time they are a big fat nasty affectation. (At night? So glamorous! Be a junkie—or just look like one.)

- **Wallabees** Weejuns, wing tips, white socks. No.

- **Stretch jeans** Black, size two, on hairdye rocker dudes with legs so skinny you can almost hear the wind whistling through them; legs so skinny they attach to the spine without benefit of butt. Always with needlenosed Chelsea boots.

- **Warm-ups** Or anything manufactured with the intent to be used in, required for, advertised with, or in any way referring to, exercise of any kind.

- **Cologne** A crime against olfaction! Get out of my neighborhood! (Okay, so I bought Old Spice for my father once; maybe I thought he'd turn into the Ghost of Mrs. Muir and sprout a peacoat and duffel, but then I was way too young to know any better.)

- **FL_NN_L** Can't even mention it anymore—poor, innocent, soft-napped cloth.

- **Leather** I mean leather clothes, against the skin. Unless the wearer is incandescent-incendiary enough to blow Jim Morrison, Mel Gibson '82, and Mrs. Emma Peel right out of the water. Try at home first.

55

Feminists Fatale: BUST-ing the Beauty Myth

- **Thick necks** Wider than the head? You may think it's an affliction, not fashion, but I say it's a lifestyle choice. Nothing is by accident, right?

- **L.L. Beanism** Please don't wear anything that looks too sporty, outdoorsy, rustic, waterproof, downy, snowshoey, hunty, or campy—I mean camping-y. It signals a total numbness to subtle visual stimuli, and clogs your pores.

- **Bikinis** "Ballhangers" is what sweet, freckled, nice-Catholic-girl Nancy from the dorm called them, in a mock-salacious spicy growl. BVD's and boxers are far preferable, or no underwear at all . . . even if it's only because you didn't do laundry. Ballhangers remind me of big mustaches.

- **All Black** Please! So boring, so safe. Zzzzzzz. Only Johnny Cash and Metallica are exempt from this category.

Gotta Git That Stick

by Esther Gyn

What is it about those shiny and lovely tubes of color that make me feel like the diva I was on my twelfth birthday? Lipstick is my bag. It is the only cosmetic I will happily drop $16 a pop on. Lipsticks have the color of life and I want them everywhere. Color on lips makes me feel like a million bucks . . . the feeling divas die for. I have lips of Twiggy, Soho Scarlet, Wall Street Wine, Rubine, and Evening in Paris. It is attitude in a stick, and I never want to live without it.

My love of the color and the glamour of makeup must have had something to do with my being a ballerina when I was little. I would work for months with blisters and sore legs to get the chance to take center stage. Recitals were fun but it also meant the season was over and another long year's wait to do it again. I studied really hard and then got to strut my stuff. It was heaven. But the ritual of putting on the stage makeup was the best, most interesting reward. I got to wear and spray and roll up all the things my mom did. It was like being welcomed into a special tribe. It was the grown-up world of primping and expectation, a ritual about doing your best and looking a part. The part I got to play was that of a ballerina princess queen, which was all that I wanted and more. The real beauty was that I was a good dancer. I was prepared, my costume fit (which was difficult in a glitter outfit), and then I got to show it all off. The makeup was the true icing on the cake; it was mystifying and dreamy and I loved it.

Those days ended in my early teens, and my love of arty pageantry declined into a typical teenage rebellion stage of "Everything *Vogue* thinks is great is really a media trick to get you to distort your mind and body." (I still believe this to a degree.) Lipstick was on a scale with devil worship. No colors brighter than a shadow graced my butt or face. I claimed to be au naturel. Bright (attractive) colors were a sign of stupidity and innocence, and wearing makeup was a political sellout to a culture that exploited women sexually. But in truth I was a beauty bulimic. At night I feasted on all the fashion and beauty magazines my beautiful, stylish, but short and chunky mom bought religiously, and by day I vomited the political rhetoric about the exploitation of women in magazines. It was a perfect setup.

In reality my rejection of beauty, of the culture of makeup and the ritual of primping, was a rejection of male attention. I thought boys only liked me for my outside and not for who I really was. My girlfriends were also a problem. More than once a girlfriend would like a boy and the boy would end up liking me. I did not want the boy, but just the same I was blamed for drawing him from her. This was always too painful to bear. I withdrew from any expression of healthy sexuality. Sexuality, beauty, and confidence were dangerous. Attraction and desire I deemed uncontrollable and deadly to friendships. So, at fifteen, I suppressed what sexuality I had discovered and the rest remained hidden. For the time the world was colorless and I dressed the way I felt.

I remember the day my doom and gloom started to crumble. I was shopping with my mom my freshman year in college. At once she spotted me looking over and

57

over again at a "sweater of color." Like a cat she sallied on over and leapt at the opportunity. "It's great! You look terrific! Oh, honey . . . what else do you like?" I was a dead woman. My mother beamed and I stood in front of the department store mirror smirking. Secretly, she had won. My mom is the ever-optimistic color-me-beautiful queen. Nothing is too bright, too daring, or too sacred not to wear with style. Our day ended and I walked out with two bright tangerine sweaters. The day had dawned. My mother's daughter had come around. It was the beginning of the end of my colorless, lifeless idea of beauty.

I am my mother's daughter, but it took some time to warm up to the real test: red lips. I made the first attempt in my Greek Tragedy class (how fitting). I was a first-year student, in with lots of crunchy granola graduate students. I psyched myself up, walked in with fire engine red on my lips, and went down in bloodred flames. The loud and proud attitude I fantasized my lips would give me failed miserably. I froze in front of all those pale faces and I felt instantly stupid. By the end of the class, my fire engine was smeared on my hands, pants, and socks—basically anywhere I could hide my ambition.

But I did not give up. After all, I had been a ballerina and I'd danced many tragic stories. The phoenix rose, and within six months I was a lipstick connoisseur. Folks, remember my adage: A little red lipstick will always brighten your day.

Lipstick is my way to be a queen every day. I prefer those snot shops of color—Bendel's, Barney's, Saks—where the colors are great and the variety excites my attitude. It is my big indulgence. I love to treat myself and I do it regularly. Currently I stock nine lovely reds, a sea of browns, burgundies, and corals, and even one very special tangerine flip. It is a cheap thrill that makes me feel alive, and to be alive is to be beautiful. Lipsticks are a spice in life, a spice I taste regularly. Whenever I go out I always check—keys, lipstick, money—and yes, honey, it's in that order.

58

The Joy of Slacks

by Tabitha Rasa

I wear pants all the time. I mean, I almost *always* wear pants, so much that my friends remark on it. They'll say, "You know, I've never seen you in a skirt," and other similar comments. I wear pants to work, too, and the progress I've made is that I now wear nicer pants than I used to. Now I mostly wear what you might call "slacks," and it seems to please my work higher-ups a little more than the faded black jeans did.

I've been at the same job for several years and I guess I've gotten easier to be around, although my real marker for how angry I am and for how high up I've pushed the walls around me is whether I'm wearing combat boots. I'd been trying not to wear them at all but then I sprained my ankle really badly and I had to start wearing them again and I swear it only made my anger worse. So now I wear slacks that are a little too short and along with my boots, y'know, I'm starting to look a little Amish. (Although the Amish would definitely frown on all this anger.)

Lately I've sort of *had* to wear pants, which bums me out, despite my love for them. I quit smoking and put on about ten pounds, and I can't fit into a lot of my clothes, and now it's not such a free choice, it's more that I'm wearing pants because I fit into them. My friends have spelled out for me that (contrary to what I think) I'm not fat, I've just gained some weight, and not even that much. But I've been so wigged about it, I've seriously considered starting smoking again just to lose the weight. One friend started smoking again several months ago and I can tell she's lost weight and it's just really hard not to think about using it as a diet method. Since none of my old jeans really fit anymore, I started wearing wide-leg pants—fortunately they have been enough in style lately for me to get away with it—because they were more comfortable. I feel so ashamed to admit this in such a public forum as this, because I feel like I'm discussing Depends and my bladder control problem or something. Fat and eating are pretty shameful issues in this country. And I never had much of a problem with them before I quit smoking and I was glad I didn't. So my reaction to all the shamefulness of the issue is just to get hugely pissed off.

Actually, this entire topic pisses me off. It's a hugely irritating issue in my world. Most of what's beautiful is dictated TO me. I get bombarded with that fucking waif and

59

before that, junkies, and before that, skinny girls with breast jobs, and so on, and then I'm surprised I'm so angry. Much, much of my life today is spent in the service of growth, healing, spiritual seeking, but when I consider what to wear and how to groom myself, what I see doesn't strike me as particularly natural, healthy, or normal.

Still, when I try to change my attitudes about beauty, it's such a Sisyphean task I just don't have the heart. Day after day I'm hit with more images of unhealthy role models, more hatred of the (actual) female form from Calvin Klein, more media molding away from nature and toward shaving my legs plucking my eyebrows liposuctioning my ass holding in my belly worrying about underarm odor worrying about cunt odor do I have dandruff putting on makeup waxing my underarms and "bikini line" trimming my pubic hair and so on. Guys do what? Maybe think about growing a Vandyke now and then? They certainly aren't required to be so UNNATURAL in order to have sex appeal.

So where was I? Talking about slacks. Well, the good news is that it's much cooler with boss types to wear them to work than it ever used to be. Thanks to Katharine Hepburn, among other steely babes. Plus it helps to work in not-for-profit. Today I called one of my co-workers at home, where she is spending a medical leave because her leg is fucked up. She had to get a brace and has to do some physical therapy. I expressed sympathy for her, to which she responded, "Oh, but I can wear slacks and cover it up. . . . Thank goodness we can wear slacks to work nowadays." Yep. Thank goodness.

When I was a kid I climbed trees and I raced my bike with the other kids around the dirt track down the street and I had a fort and I played football and I played Little League baseball and I pulled all the other kids' loose teeth for them and I got punched in the face and got a bloody nose and I wiped out on my bike. And I can't imagine doing any of that shit with a skirt on, nor would I have wanted to. I wanted to wear jeans like everybody else. But there's more. I also hate being "femmy." I can count on one hand the times in my life that I've worn lace. I had a hard time adjusting to having breasts (even though I wanted them so badly I sent off for that Mark Eden thing). I was always a tomboy and I'm still a tomboy and I don't want anybody to think of me as femmy!

During all this kid stuff, all the bike riding and tree climbing and dirt under my fingernails, that's when bell-bottoms hit (the first time, that is, in the '70s). They were the first fashion trend in which I consciously participated. I remember a friend told me she'd heard they were going to go out of style, and I claimed I'd never give them up. I thought they were tremendously romantic. Once when I had a crush on A. J. Lojek I remember doing this sashay-y walk back and forth in front of where he and the rest of my brother's Little League team were practicing (by this time I didn't play anymore), and I just loved how the bell-bottoms swooshed around my red All-Stars. So when they were revived recently, since I was in on them the first time, I felt legitimized. I didn't even wear full bell-bottoms this go-round; I just felt good knowing I'd been there in the '70s.

I guess what it comes down to is that I love clothes that carry power. As Celina Hex said to me, "If they wouldn't let us wear pants for so long, there must be something really powerful and important about them." Wearing pants is definitely powerful in my mind. As a kid, I wore pants in order to do everything all the other kids in my neighborhood were doing, and all the other kids in my neighborhood—ALL of them—were boys. And today, I wear pants with my beloved army boots and it makes me feel powerful and safe and strong. I can stomp around the subway listening to bands of hard women on my headphones and nobody gives me shit.

Growing Out of Layers

by Chessie Sequel

At the age of eight I was used as a guinea pig so some scissors-happy beauty-school dropout could try her hand at a Carol Brady Shag. The experiment was a failure and in an effort to correct the cut, I continued to have it chopped up for the next two years. Fashion hit me at the age of ten, after my first version of the Toni Tennille cut. I was one of the first in my school to get one, so people were actually noticing *my* hair. It is thick and wavy, so this was a high-maintenance style which required a big workout: blow-drying my locks up and under with a round brush after every washing and then Pssst'ing it into place with Breck (pink can). This held for a day, then started to curl up, so I used a clamp curling iron to reset. I was even able to achieve the second version of the Tennille (two vertical flip rolls on either side of the face) by using the roll back–hold–dry–quick release twirl-down technique taught to me by a variety of stylists—that's what they were beginning to call themselves—eager to sell round brushes and clamp curling irons and see me again "every six weeks" for maintenance.

I was hooked on clamp irons until short and sassy Dorothy Hamill rose to fame and they gave me a Wedge. Once you were plopped down in the chair, it was snip, blow, straighten, style (up and under), a few "do-it-yourself tips," and off you went. The problem with this was that after leaving the chair, I could never achieve the perfect wedge and ended up looking very dorky at the end of two weeks. I blamed it all on myself, thinking I lacked dexterity and wishing for straight hair. In retrospect, it was poor crafting on the part of the stylist. By this time I was heavily into inhaling Clairol Herbal Essence. My sister, three years older, had preferred Lemon Up when she was my age. She had a low-maintenance Laurie Partridge.

Julie Wilson

In high school things got better. Cher opened a few new doors and Gypsies became the rage. Hiding in French braids or Indian braids, or under bandannas tied Stevie Nicks–style was easy on bad hair days. Then *Charlie's Angels* hit and I got layers. I was able to achieve a semblance of the "Farrah" by bending down and brushing forward until just damp, then grabbing the crown with that same old round brush, concentrating the air, and pulling up and back. I had to buy a bent brush to achieve volume and smooth it into shape (couldn't afford hot rollers) before a light spray with Miss Breck (blue can). It all seemed to be to a higher end because the "Farrah" framed my face and in combo with all the hiding and pulling back you could actually see me. People started saying I was pretty. I wore makeup for the first time and got hooked on pulling the left side back with Goody barrettes and letting the right side hang demurely in front of my eye. After mastering this, boys took interest, and I found myself out at the local teen disco boogying to the *Saturday Night Fever* sound track.

Off to college in the big city, where some salon flamer convinced me to get my bangs spot-permed on purple rods. I wore it top-heavy during two years of junior college, one of those all-girls schools where everyone was getting pregnant. We learned the hard way not to put chemicals on your hair when your hormones are changing because it will fry and ruin your graduation. Thank god for those new bristle-edge curling irons which helped to smooth and straighten the frizz. After an emotional year and several trims my dead hair went away. I started dating a rapper who insisted I wear a red Kangol beret at all times. I switched to a construction hat on-site so I could make cash for a four-year academic institution. Upon graduation, I went corporately blunt and stayed corporately blunt except for weekends at the Hotel Amazon when I'd twist the sides up on top and don some door-knocker earrings and bright red lips (still dating the rapper).

It took Bo Derek and her ancient African hairstyle to hip me to the fact that scalps need to breathe and after miserable scalp circulation problems I found a great Japanese coiffure, dumped the rapper, and went short. It has since grown in.

She's coming out of the closet now and respectfully gets rinsed with nettles and chamomile, massaged with jojoba and almond oil, gently washed with yucca and treated with aloe. After cleansing, it drips dry without so much as a comb, forget mousse, brush, or gel. I wouldn't even finger comb if it didn't get knotty, and I want to keep my job. Now she's free and full when she wants. I never asked my hair how she felt. Had I, she probably would have said, "Leave me alone for Christ's sake." Like the rain forest, she wants to remain untouched.

The Mysterious Eroticism of Mini-Backpacks

by James Reling

The other day I was in a department store with my friend Brendan and, after circling the aisles a few times to make sure no one was watching, we ventured over to the mini-backpacks. I was in awe of the different colors and sizes and textures of mini-backpacks. Some had buttons, latches, and zippers. There were clear plastic packs that took away any sort of mystery about what was contained inside. There were tightly sealed bags with drawstrings. They all had different lengths of straps to fit the personality of the wearer, from high on the small of the back to riding low on the hips of more-developed physiques.

Brendan and I giggled as if trying on bras as I worked up the courage to try one on. It was very awkward at first and I even needed Brendan's help guiding my arm through the strap. Once on, I noticed the immediate comfort and realized the advantage of the mini-backpack. I could barely feel its presence, yet it encouraged me to stand more upright and proud, working with my spine rather than oppressing it like most larger models. Blushing somewhat at the thought of someone happening to see me in the midst of my gluttony, I walked over to the mirror and turned around for a peek. It was perfect for me. It had red and white horizontal stripes and a cute little icon of a kitten batting lazily at a balloon.

I realized that not only could I fit my little writing notebook in the pack, but my favorite pen, too. I could put in one of those cute stuffed animals my girlfriend has given me, or better yet, a real kitten or puppy with its head poking out around the drawstring. I could put in a pair of very cool sunglasses for sunny San Francisco days, and a roll of quarters for laundry. A handful of tissues for my runny nose, some guitar picks in case I decided to take up guitar, some rave flyers, a toothbrush for those wild over-nighters, some breath mints, a bus map, a mixed tape, an eyepatch, and an X-acto knife for removing pictures out of library books. The possibilities were dizzying. I was about to pass out when I was yanked back to reality by Brendan's frantic voice scream, "Let's get out of here!" I looked toward the counter, where the cashier and her friend were pointing at me and laughing. I went terribly red and realized the intimacy of trying on mini-backpacks. It was much more feminine than a bra; it was the whole essence of femininity and here I was galloping around with it on my back.

There is something about these mini-backpacks that I find extremely erotic. Just like women, the backpacks come in all shapes and sizes, colors, and degrees of durability. Watching a woman who is wearing one forces you to wonder, "What's inside?" What *could* be inside? A brush? A wallet? Why would you want to carry your wallet on your back? Isn't that just inviting people to try to steal it? No, it can't be a wallet; it has got to be something much more precious and mysterious, like the keys to life itself. Just like women hold the power of reproduction, the mini-backpack also holds some kind of enigmatic power. Mini-backpacks are even sort of like vaginas: they are pouchlike and have the capacity to hold a limited amount of items. To wear a mini-backpack is to display your vagina on your back for all to see. This isn't a vulgar display; it is a proud and colorful display that takes a certain amount of self-confidence and exhibitionism. You can identify a woman's personality from a distance by her mini-backpack, and just to clue in you men, stay away from the women with the transparent ones. I have to admit that I have had fantastic, lust-driven dreams of stealing a mini-backpack from a woman and hiding away in a dark corner to empty its contents on the floor and filter through them, trying to swallow the secrets before I am discovered. I could never do this, though; I have too much respect for the secrets of femininity.

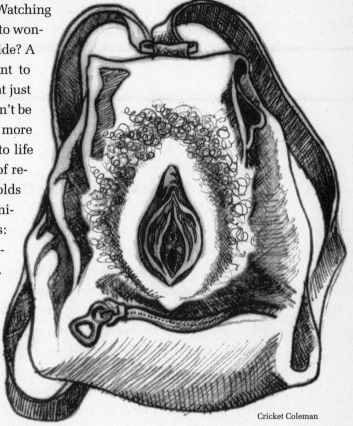

Cricket Coleman

Embarrassed by my audience at the store, I pulled off the pack, hung it back on the rack much sloppier than it had been previously, and bolted. I decided then that

I would only put on a mini-backpack in the future if it was owned by a consenting woman with whom I was very much in love and with whom I planned to spend the rest of my life. My current girlfriend is not really the type to wear a mini-backpack; she's into larger, masculine backpacks full of books and some presents for me. So I will probably never get to wear a mini-backpack again. But I will always have that one intimate moment alone with myself in the world of fashion.

✖

Vogue *vs.* Harper's Bazaar: *It's a Catfight!*

by Jayne Air

My relationship to fashion—and fashion magazines—has always been a very love-hate affair. As in, I love them and they make me hate myself. Unlike women's "service" magazines, which get me all contemptuous, magazines like *Harper's Bazaar* and *Vogue* get me all flustered and insecure and giddy, not unlike the first day of school, when I was scared I might not rate and thrilled to think that I might, that this year I might have bought the perfect button-on cover for my wooden-handled purse and be sporting the cool Bonnie Bell Lipsmacker.

In fact, with their brilliant photography and other worldly models and delicious and highly improbable clothes, *Vogue* and *Harper's Bazaar* are the ultimate bitchy high school. Reading them longingly, I'm reminded of my favorite line from *Heathers:* as Heather Two fixates on Heather One's red headband, Heather One, enjoying her undisputed stylistic superiority, snaps, "Jealous much?!"

It must be the undercurrent of high school bitchiness that made me so overjoyed to learn that the editrices of *Vogue* and *Harper's Bazaar* (Anna Wintour and Liz Tilberis, respectively) are rumored to hate each other's guts. Ever since I heard about it, I've entertained fantasies of the two of them on tippy Manolo Blahniks in a boxing ring, ready to

66

rip each other's eyes out: "Bitch! You tried to steal Steven Miesel!" "Idiot! I saw you wearing water socks at the Royalton last week!"

I hope you're not expecting to read about how fashion is evil and tries to get us to throw our backs out and spend all our money on long skirts and then switches to short ones. Or that they are lockstep and stupidly conservative and don't care a fig for innovation, except when they do things like fall all over Alexander McQueen one month and savage him the next.

Because while those things might be true, I just can't be angry at *Vogue* and *Bazaar* for being fashion magazines for the same reason I can't get mad at a horse for not being a cow. If we want Susan Faludi, we can read *Backlash*. And if we want comfort and durability, we can get ourselves an L.L. Bean catalog.

Why You Shouldn't Burn Your Fashion Magazines—The Long Explanation

Vogue and *Bazaar* are annoying—even infuriating—for all the reasons we already know, but I can't stay away from them for long. And as I cast about for why I love them so, I realize that I adore them for the simple reason that they acknowledge a universal truth: that women are more interested in other women than just about anything else. And that fashion—far from being all about enslavement to men (except maybe the ones who make it)—is an elaborate performance girls put on for other girls.

Here's an example: My friend Sally and I go to Bloomingdale's on our lunch hour because I need a bag. Sally—a girl who won't wear shorts even if it's 110 degrees and once refused to speak to a man simply because he was wearing a braided belt—holds up a brownish beige number, knockoff of that putrid Prada plaid from last season. "Demented!" she chimes. Nice shape—fun pattern—on sale.

Just as I get excited, I get insecure. Will I hate it tomorrow? Will it look good with my Product coat? What had seemed like a solution now feels like the biggest problem in Christendom.

Sally takes the situation in hand. "Pretend you don't know me." Hooking the bag over her shoulder, she strides past me purposefully, making toward lingerie. A few seconds later she returns. "Well? Did you fascinate on me?"

Laurie Henzel

"Yeah."

"Then buy it."

Duh. For one second I had forgotten what Sally and I long ago agreed must be the basis of all style decisions: getting other girls to notice you.

Where the Real Compliments Are

Let's face it—who really cares if men like your clothes? "Lookin' good!" "Wow!" or "Hey baby!" mean very little coming from the mouth of someone whose idea of attractiveness and fashionability is Jennifer Aniston. And as charming and enlightened and aesthetically forward as your boyfriend or husband is, he thinks a girl wearing Daryl K. hip huggers and Velcro New Balance sneakers looks plain weird.

You, on the other hand, know she's cool, and that there's no greater compliment than a sidelong glance from such a girl as she checks you out. And though you're not a mean person, you can't help but hope that as she looks at you she is thinking, "Why does she look so good? Where can I get those boots? Why do I look so dumb?" Not because you're a competitive little bitch, at least not exactly. But because you want a compliment to mean something. And when a woman fascinates on you, it is meaningful.

Except in those instances when it's dangerous and infuriating. "It's like she was studyin' ya'," an alarmed Bertie warns Margo in *All About Eve*. And of course she's right—Eve is sinister because she admires Margo so much, she wants to become

The **BUST** *Guide to the New Girl Order*

a better Margo than Margo herself. And she pretty much does it, stealing her clothes and her roles and almost her man. Whoa. Feminist film theorist Jackie Stacey called it an "ur-text of female fascination," and when I read that, my life was changed forever. Now I had a name for that thing that went on between women, a term other than derisive ones like "narcissism" or "jealousy" or "bitchiness" or "momentary lesbianism" or whatever else the freaked-out guy I was with at the time called it when I stared at another woman or she stared at me.

The Part Where I Finally Get to the Magazines

As near as I can figure it's female fascination that motors the engine of *Bazaar* and *Vogue,* those glossy wonderful hateful stupid despicable frothy stupid insignificant utterly important depressing empowering insulting magazines under scrutiny in this very column. So which one wins, you ask: *Vogue* or *Harper's Bazaar*?

Well, as far as I see it, *Vogue* has one insurmountable handicap: the very fact of Anna Wintour. Is it just me, or is the magazine infused with a much greater sense of anorexia of both body and spirit since her mean little reign began? It's as if Anna's on a one-woman mission to exorcise the ghost of the late, great Diana Vreeland, with all her excesses and gorgeous enthusiasms. Anna's always bashing us over the head with every form of minimalism and carefulness and dumb debutante worship in the book. What a fraidy cat she is, from her fraidy-cat sunglasses even indoors to her fraidy-cat little bob and her fraidy-cat, conventional sensibility. All of which just makes *Vogue*'s fashion forays like "techno color"—about what kids are wearing in clubs—all the less credible and all the more laughable. Wow, they even ran a fraidy-cat sidebar on what's in and out in club culture. Like, under the out column, "Predawn drug run," and under the in column, "Predawn doughnut run (ditch hardcore house for Krispy Kreme)." Who knew that the ladies who lunch were so very in touch?

On the other hand, when you pick up *HB*, you can just hear the stylists screaming, "Sweetie, darling, it's genius!!!" as they shoot the hairless pink cat next to a pink, Lucite-heeled Prada mule. I also give them big points for Cynthia True's hilarious piece on one of the most important issues in the life of a freelance writer: what to wear in front of her computer. And even more points for her solution: slinky, film-noir-esque lingerie.

Sure, it can be as dumb and out of touch as *Vogue* (especially when they run pieces on the goodies you get when you ride first-class on the Concorde) and there's less to read, but *Bazaar* has more madness and charm and over-the-top fashion insanity to it.

But however you get it, wherever you get it, don't forget to get your female fascination. Fabulous sweetie darling.

Be a Model, or Just Act Like One

by Lu Cashmere

I was flattered. My public relations maven of a pal had just called me to plead a favor. "We're producing a fashion show and some models backed out at the last minute to walk the runway for Donna Karan. Are you free? It would look great on your résumé," she added, stroking my ego. She had just asked me to live the dream of every starry-eyed sapling who ever wanted to become a model. And now, given the honor, perspiration laced my brain cells. If I did this, wouldn't I be spitting all over the Equal Rights Amendment? Would I betray my sex and then get caught up and be transformed into an insufferable narcissist? Wasn't I way too muscular in the gams? And wouldn't I be singled out as an impostor?

With all these doubts swirling around me like Kamikaze bees, I squared my shoulders, cleared my throat, and heard myself reply, "Well, if you really want me, I'll do it."

I spent the early afternoon toying with the idea of immortality. After all, didn't I, a femme fatale in my own circle, deserve to be more collectively recognized? But should this include being placed on a pedestal for a genetic achievement I could take no responsibility for? Was I ready to plunge into a genre where men revered the model as a superior breed of the female gender? Models, after all, were women men would walk on all fours for, as though they were in a category above other females. These definitions were just what Lu the Teenage Suffragette had grown to abhor, and yet with every step closer to the performance space, my faith in myself was elevating to new heights.

After all, I thought, hadn't a grueling eight-month isometric regimen rewarded me with a killer bod? And didn't my peers often refer to me as "the Greek Statue"? By the time I had arrived for rehearsal, my conscience was in fine form, and I was ready to become the contemporary counterpart to mythological yore. Fuck my degree. Fuck EOE. This was equal opportunity. If society rewarded beauty, then I was ready to work them curves.

Inside the venue where we were to exhibit our inventories, two bland-looking females bantered in white-trash trailer park jargonese. Ah, the Midwestern contingent. I felt no kinship for these, my comrades-in-arms. As I thought of my new attitude about flaunting what one has, the set director flailed her arms in resignation. British, lithe, and bald, she used cigarettes and petulance as her personal stage props. My entrance had interrupted some stage direction that was being about as well received as an anklet under panty hose. The temperamental Brit's seizure seemed to have been brought on by a spoiled brat named "Katya," whose defiant airs were, at present, scrutinizing me. "Are those curls on you for real?" she moaned as she languorously filed her talons. Standing out in high relief to her was a willowy black woman reading a psychiatry textbook. "Are you from the Esmeralda Agency, too?" she asked me. She was a Princeton student named Aquachiniqua, and what I learned from her in the next couple of hours left an indelible mark on me.

Nearly all of the seven girls who were there wanted to be models more than any other profession invented. They knew Cindy Crawford's cup size, they prayed they had the next hot look of the moment, and they incessantly hogged any mirror in sight to the point of perversion. Three of them had no idea what was going on when someone blurted "NAFTA." Some of them were workhorses, others quite the bonbon loungers, and certainly there were those who felt they were destined for stardom and therefore above any criticism or supervision. On the other hand there were girls, like

71

Aquachiniqua, who were in it for what they could get in a capricious industry while hitting the books in case they failed. And Aqua had an added agenda: she wanted to shatter some racial stereotypes and offer the couture houses some reason to turn to ethnic models.

After tedious rehearsing, and with Gloria Steinem's foray as a *Playboy* Bunny flashing before my eyes, I was beginning to realize that the arrival of kosher lipsticks to the cosmetics market could be discussed in earnest for only so long. The more time I spent with these women, the more I noticed everyone's physical flaws. And although none were perfect, these girls certainly had thick skins. Not one ounce of blood within them would betray the insecurities they had all learned to repress. And here I was, once a confident gal, reduced to an inanimate object and getting used to the idea that strangers would be entitled to offer or withhold their stamp of approval without ever knowing the contents of my "package."

Once the rehearsals were over, the gowns arrived. The girls snatched at them like piranhas. I guess that's what all those trappings on women are to men anyway, a lure to ensure allure. I stared incredulously. Somehow, I had expected the girls to act as dignified as if they were in some well-crafted Hollywood production. I imagined designers doling dresses to all the girls they envisioned wearing them. Instead, I realized I'd better move fast if I wanted to wear something I thought would suit me.

Amid this chaos stood "Katya," carrying on a love affair with the looking glass. Aquachiniqua and I rolled our eyes. Scratching my head, I climbed into an Ava Gardner number as I overheard some girls complain about the lack of dressers. Since I'd never had more than a roommate to zip me up, it was easy to go on being the populist. I styled my own hair while "Katya" pouted over her limp strands, which were freshly dyed blond. While Aqua and I applied our own makeup, "Katya" demanded personal attention. Finished first, Aqua and I were a designer's wet dream; we even began to help the others. Meanwhile, pseudo-quadriplegics like "Katya" got molly-coddled. We were ready to torch the coif of every self-deluded hussy who thought she deserved to get the red carpet treatment in life.

Out on the runway, I was a walking oxymoron. Or maybe I was just a moron. Five minutes earlier, after hours of reinforcement, I had been persuaded that my looks and abilities were superior. Now, under the spotlight, my doubts returned. The attention was so magnified. I was not prepared to be distracted by propositioning men on the sidelines, the need to stifle an itch I couldn't scratch, or the desire to illuminate my face with a smile when the script called for a pensive gaze. I wasn't prepared for all the staring and sizing up that went on. My diaphanous blouse made me feel liberated and bovine all at the same time.

Ever since that day I've found myself less able to handle the mob mentality of beauty. I used to think that whatever her strengths were, a woman should use her abilities to the greatest advantage as long as no harm came to others. Now I feel that if Anna Nicole Smith's low-IQ cleavage ruins it for the rest of us who are trying to elevate a chap's perception of an attractive woman as a thinking human being, then I will place my vote with Susan Faludi. Because I still resent men who let their dicks lead them around, even if now I know I can provide the scent for their fox hunt.

Titillation complete and festivities over, I kissed Aquachiniqua on both cheeks in parting. And, seeing "Katya" within earshot, I added, "It was a pleasure to work with someone true to her black roots."

73

3

Sex and the Thinking Girl

I. What's Fun Got to Do with It?

"Are we having fun yet?" This question was posed by the title of a recent book about women and sex, and thirty years after the "sexual revolution," it's about time someone asked. Things have certainly changed a lot from way back in the '50s, when our mothers saved themselves for marriage, never touched themselves "down there," and used vibrating massagers for, well, actual massages. "Nice girls don't" was the saying at the time, a time when just sitting with your legs uncrossed could get you branded a hussy; when *Playboy* centerfolds were average-looking girls with average-looking bodies, and the only people who went to see porn movies were those who wore raincoats.

So, *are* we having fun yet? Of course, today we no longer have to deal with an unfair sexual bias that brands men who sleep around "studs," and women who do the same "sluts." Of course, today women are just as sexually satisfied as men, and men go down on women in the same numbers as women go down on men. Of course, today women don't have any old-fashioned "hang-ups" about their bodies, they have no discomfort about bringing up the issue of birth control (or disease control) with their partners, and thirteen-year-old girls are just as comfortable masturbating, and talking about it with their friends, as boys are. And the multibillion-dollar porn industry produces as many movies intended to enhance women's solo-sex adventures as it does for men. Of course . . . NOT.

In the 1990s, the effects of the feminist movement can be clearly felt in the boardroom, but its influence in the bedroom is less apparent. Let's set aside, for the moment, the fact that women are paid only seventy-five cents to the man's dollar, and turn our attention to the equally depressing but lesser-known statistic that while 75 percent of men report having orgasms during partner sex on a regular basis, only 29 percent of women do. Ouch! There's an orgasm gap out there that hasn't budged since the days when *Donna Reed* actually believed that *Father Knows Best*. Unfortunately, there are a whole lot of women who most certainly *aren't* having fun yet. The insidious sexual double standard that keeps men hard, and women hard up, is alive and well and living in America.

II. The Way We Were

In the beginning was the pill. In the early '60s, the availability of this brand-new form of birth control suddenly gave women, who had always been told to "just say no" until marriage, the option to say "yes." It paved the way for the sexual revolution, which wasn't about transforming sex or the way people had it, but about making sure that everyone had *more* of it. Free sex, free love, everything was free, especially the women. They were free to have premarital sex with as many men as asked them. They were free to perform oral sex without having hang-ups. They were free to be traded in wife-swapping sessions. They were free to become the fantasy fuck-mates that men had always wanted but were afraid to ask for.

*The **BUST** Guide to the New Girl Order*

When, later in the same decade, the feminist movement was being reborn, one of the first things its leaders realized was that the sexual revolution hadn't revolutionized much for women at all. Sure, girls were having more sex, but it was just more of the same old *bad* sex that didn't recognize their needs—or even their anatomy. Everyone from psychoanalysts to medical doctors was still claiming that the only truly mature orgasm was achieved through vaginal intercourse alone, and any woman who demanded clitoral stimulation was misguided if not downright sick. Maybe men needed to work on their staying power a little bit, the thinking went, but a woman who didn't get off on the old in-and-out routine was simply labeled "frigid."

Tired of this kind of dick-centric reasoning, second-wave feminists believed that once men and women were equal, the world would witness the birth of a new style of sexuality—one that would bring women's needs front and center. According to their somewhat naive and Utopian vision, the sex of the future would become the cosmic coupling between two equal partners, who would slip out of their natural-fiber clothing, crawl sweetly between flannel sheets, touch and lick and kiss and—don't forget the clitoris!—bring each other to loving, heavenly, sensual, spiritual orgasmic bliss. No dominance, no submission, nothing kinky, nothing perverse—there would be no spanking and no yanking. In other words, people would stop fucking, and start making love. This is how Gloria Steinem describes it in her essay, "Erotica vs. Porn": "Imagine images of people making love; really making love. Those images may be diverse, but there is likely to be a mutual pleasure and touch and warmth, an empathy for each other's bodies and nerve endings, a shared sensuality and a spontaneous sense of two people who are there because they *want* to be."

For others, no matter what women and men did together in bed, sex between them could never really be freed from its power-play underpinnings because of the whole penis-and-vagina thing. The physical fact of one body penetrating another was enough to make some women claim that all heterosexual sex was actually a form of rape. "There is never a real privacy of the body that can coexist with intercourse: with being entered," wrote Andrea Dworkin. "The thrusting is persistent invasion." For these women, the only truly liberated sex was between two women. Certainly, lesbian sex would be free from any traces of power or violence

77

or domination. But then a lesbian named Pat Califia came forward and gave that simpleminded idea a combat-booted kick in the ass. Here was a woman, a lesbian, who was into S & M, B & D, and assorted other outrageous acts and everyday initials. It was the kick felt round the world, and it marked the beginning of the feminist sex wars.

Before Pat and her group, Samois, made their voices heard in 1979, there was the belief that feminists were pretty much of one mind when it came to sex. They had already organized against pornography (forming groups like the awkwardly named WAVPM—Women Against Violence and Pornography in the Media), and no one was challenging Robin Morgan's assertion that "pornography is the theory, and rape is the practice." It was agreed that there was no room for dominance or submission in the bedroom, and that its presence there all these years was simply evidence of women's historical subjugation. What to do, then, with lesbians who were tying each other up, spanking one another, and calling each other "sluts"? Many feminists thought this was an example of women participating in their own oppression, that the worst aspects of male-female relationships were now being re-created by women themselves. In other words, this kind of sex was politically incorrect. Many feminist bookstores refused to carry Pat's books, and a number of protests were held. These S & M lesbians, many felt, were simply not "true feminists."

But how could women's sexual pleasure *ever* be considered "incorrect"? The last thing any of us needed was to have one set of rules about what constitutes appropriate sexual behavior for women to be replaced by another. Never mind the well-publicized brouhaha that erupted over pornography within feminism's ranks: the debate there was focused on freedom of speech, rather than what turned women on. Even most "pro-porn" feminists weren't arguing that there was anything in the stuff that could help women get their rocks off, but rather that if we allowed the government to get into the business of censoring speech, it would be the speech of women and gays and minorities that would be silenced first. Women were arguing over semantics, over policies, over laws. Feminists fought against feminists in this war of the words. In the fray, our focus turned to issues of power and of politics, and turned away from what was really at stake all along: our pleasure.

78

III. Girls Just Wanna Have Sex

When Freud asked his classic question, "What do women want?" he said it as though he thought it was some kind of top secret information that we chicks had, but just didn't feel like sharing. The problem is, of course, that it is very difficult for us to know what we want. I mean, how could we? We are given so many conflicting messages about what's expected from us—what we're supposed to look like (as fragile and beautiful as Kate Moss, as pneumatic and crass as Pamela Lee, as sexually aggressive as Lil' Kim, and as sexually demure as Jewel), what we're supposed to do (have orgasms from straight intercourse), and how often we're supposed to do it (a few fucks before marriage are okay, as long as we really *love* the guy)—that it's simply impossible to find a place that we can fit into comfortably. When they say that women hit their sexual peak at age thirty-five, it's not hard to understand why. It takes us that long to figure out what the hell we want.

The message guys get is a lot clearer. "I have a dick, therefore I fuck" is what most men are encouraged to believe. A male sex-advice columnist once remarked that "guys feel they have the right to whatever it is that gets them off," and it's true. Women, on the other hand, have a very hard time thinking this way. It's still the case that if you like having sex a lot, you're a whore, and if you don't, you're frigid. If having a guy come all over your face doesn't send you into shivers of sexual ecstasy, well then, there's probably something wrong with *you*. To confuse matters even more, we are given the not-so-subtle message that sexual attractiveness and sexual satisfaction are one and the same. If we just cut all the fat from our diets, go to the gym three times a week, and wear the right lingerie, we'll be able to attain sexual nirvana. Of course, that's not how it works. The thing we women are never encouraged to do is to focus on what actually makes us feel good.

79

IV. Sexual Revolution Grrl-Style Now

In the '90s, the women of the New Girl Order are ready to go out and get what's cumming to us. Our mission is to seek out pleasure wherever we can find it. In other words, if it feels good, screw it. Vibrators in hand, we're ready to fight the good fight.

1. Exile in Guyville

One strategy we've used is to try playing by the boys' rules. Our motto has been "If you can't beat 'em, join 'em"—if it seems like we can't arrive at a balance of power between the sexes, then at least we want our fair share of it. Madonna preached that boys should be *our* toys, and we tried playing with them as much as we could. When Deborah Iyall belted out "I might like you better if we slept together," we brazenly sang along, threatening boys with the promise that we could be just as singleminded in our quest for sex as they were.

Of course, this strategy has also led to a good number of disappointments. No matter whose rules we play by, sometimes it feels like we just can't win. Erica Jong realized this way back in 1973, when, describing her ideal of the "zipless fuck," she wrote: "It is free of ulterior motives. The man is not 'taking' and the woman is not 'giving.' . . . The zipless fuck is the purest thing there is. And it is rarer than the unicorn." Liz Phair echoed that refrain when she expressed her disillusion with guys who "Fuck and Run," and Courtney Love let us know how she felt about many men: "They get what they want, and they never want it again."

Nevertheless, it's important that casual sex remain a part of a girl's repertoire. When a book like *The Rules* encourages women to use sex as a bargaining chip—as something to trade for that elusive male commitment—it suggests that, for women, sex can't be considered a reward in itself. But whether you're sleeping with a guy on the first date to prove what a sexual rebel you are, or waiting till the fifth to show what a respectable woman you are, you aren't sleeping with the guy for the only reason that should matter: because you're so hot for him that just thinking about it gives you a wettie. This is what having sex like the guys is all about: It's not about numbers, or emotional detachment. It's about desire; it's about going after what you want.

2. Whose Power Is It, Anyway?

In addition to taking long journeys into the land of the one-night stand, another strategy we've used is to question each and every assumption about women, men, sex, and power. And there are so many. Take, for example, Simone de Beauvoir's observation, in *The Second Sex,* that "in birds and mammals, [the male] forces himself upon [the female], while very often she submits indifferently or even resists him." Now, I don't mean to question Simone's extraordinary perceptive abilities, but what, exactly, does she think constitutes an "indifferent" bird? Seen from this angle, a girl can never come out ahead—even when she's giving head. A woman who gives a blow job is often said to be "servicing" a man, while he remains comfortably in control—disregarding the fact that there are few things more vulnerable than a man with his penis in someone's mouth. In deciding who's zooming who in the bedroom, men, women, and feminists alike are always bringing their own biases along for the ride. Whenever they do that, the male always seems to come out on top.

It's this matter—of who's really in control when it comes to sex—that may account for some of the confusion surrounding the subject of date rape. Under the guise of increased sensitivity to women's needs, seminars are being given on campuses nationwide that are teaching men to ask their partner's permission for each and every sexual move they make. But turning sex into a game of "Mother, may I" only reinforces the idea that a man's place is in the driver's seat when it comes to sexual encounters. Just like in the '50s, the woman's only role is to play the part of sex police. Do we still really believe what Mother always told us—that men only want one thing? Because if you flip that coin over, you'll see that the other side says that women always want *more* than just sex.

Reducing the number of date rape incidents is not just about teaching the guy to take "no" for an answer—it's also about teaching women to be more vocal about what they want, and don't want, from their partners and from themselves. On this subject, Camille Paglia wrote, "A woman who goes upstairs with a brother at a fraternity party is an idiot. Feminists call this blaming the victim. I call it common sense." While Paglia, as usual, is overly harsh, I agree that the girl should be prepared to protest loudly, and, if need be, violently, when that frat boy makes an unwanted move on her. But I also understand that this is not such an easy task for women, who have been taught from the get-go to be polite and make nice. Mary Gaitskill admitted that she was unable to do it when she was date-raped: "I let myself be drawn into sex because I could not face the idea that if I said no, things might get ugly. . . . I was unable to stand up for myself because I had never been taught how." In the end, she concludes,

"I had, in a sense, raped myself." Demanding that men obey a strict set of rules with us would mean putting the responsibility for our sexuality back into their hands. It would mean giving up the power and independence that have been so hard for us to win. As Gaitskill points out, it would, in a sense, be raping ourselves.

These days, guys are so afraid of being accused of dominating us that we have to practically beg them to act like sexual barbarians when we want them to. "I say to men, 'Okay, pretend you're a burglar and you've broken in here and you throw me down on the bed and make me suck your cock,'" feminist Lisa Palac said in a 1994 *Esquire* article trumpeting the new "Do-Me Feminism." "They're horrified," she continued. "It goes against all they've been taught: 'No, no, it would degrade you!' 'Exactly. Degrade me when I ask you to.'" Unfortunately, the past decades' sex wars have left the threat of "politically incorrect sex" hovering like a sword of Damocles over our beds, leading both men and women to second-guess their own desires, and ruining everyone's fun. It's time to get away from this idea that power and pleasure make strange bedfellows: our generation of garter-belt feminists have found ways to use power to our advantage, and in ways never before thought possible. Like Lisa Palac, we can even manage to be aggressive about our desire to be submissive.

3. You Gotta Fight for Your Right to Pornography

Our ideal of sexual freedom is less about some old-school vision of egalitarianism and more about the simple ideal of equal opportunity. We don't have a problem with pornography, unless, of course, it doesn't turn us on. With X-rated movies available for rent at every local video store and Hooters considered a family restaurant, we realize that American porn culture is here to stay. So, rather than trying to rid the world of sexual images we think are negative, as some of our sisters have done, we're far more interested in encouraging women to explore porn, to find out whether it gets them hot or merely bothered. This is not to say that we don't see most of the currently available porn as being ruthlessly sexist. "I could criticize pornography until the cows come home," writes sexual intellectual Susie Bright, "but I will not criticize the power of pictures to arouse me: to arouse passion or ideas, erections or damp panties, fears, curiosities, unarticulated yearnings, and odd realizations."

Of course, pornography itself might need to change if women are going to derive the kind of pleasure from it that men have enjoyed all these years. Never mind the old "men are more visual" argument—if that were the case, women would never have been able to master the fine art of eyebrow plucking and lip lining. No, the fact is, the current crop of available porn has very little in it to appeal to women. "Paunchy guys with overgrown mustaches who had little to offer except their big dicks weren't our idea of sexy. We wanted bad boys with angel faces who understood the meaning of seduction," explains Palac. Filmmakers like Candida Royalle are stepping in to fill that void by imagining erotic movies that are more in line with female fantasies and making them a reality. While the female market for fuck films is still far less than that of men, it's a central tenet of our version of feminism to acknowledge that it exists at all.

4. Work It, Girl

The final frontier for the feminist sex avenger is the subject of sex work. While the "bad girl" of the past was simply any girl who had sex before marriage, today we have all become the bad girls of our mother's generation. The line that traditionally divided bad girls from good girls now merely separates the sluts from the whores. In *Pretty Woman,* when Richard Gere says to Julia Roberts, "I never treated you like a prostitute," no one stops to ask what he means; in our culture it is simply assumed that prostitutes deserve to be treated badly. But as long as women are punished for being sexual—whether for fun or for profit—we are all in danger. "We have a great deal to teach each other," outspoken feminist and prostitute Carol Queen writes. "No bad girl, no sexually deviant woman, can afford, in a misogynistic and sex-negative society, to ignore lessons learned by the other ones."

So we advocate for prostitutes' rights, or explore the world of stripping as a potentially liberating experience. We've even transformed a variety of sex-work venues and re-created them in our own image. Today, one can find burlesque shows that feature women stripping for other women, and feminist-minded erotic cabarets

83

that cater to a mixed audience of men and women. And while women are still a long way from becoming regular consumers of sex work themselves, that, too, is perhaps merely a matter of time.

V. Babes in Boyland

The terrain of sexuality is one that has until recently been conquered, navigated, and mapped out by the male of the species, leaving women behind to find our way in the dark. But, as sexual freedom fighters, we've crossed enemy lines and are getting ready to release women from the shackles of the evil double standard. From fucking around to cursing like sailors to watching porn to shaking our booties at the local strip joint, we are sexual adventuresses who, unlike our foremothers, don't dare to assume that we know what "female sexuality" is all about. Call us do-me feminists, call us prosex feminists, just don't call us late for the sale at Good Vibrations. In our quest for total sexual satisfaction, we shall leave no sex toy unturned and no sexual avenue unexplored. Women are trying their hands (and other body parts) at everything from phone sex to cybersex, solo sex to group sex, heterosex to homosex. Lusty feminists of the third wave, we're more than ready to drag-race down sexual roads less traveled. Ladies, start your engines.

84

Betty & Celina Get Wired: Part I

Celina's Story

by Celina Hex

It's a spectacularly sunny spring day in New York, and even the sidewalk on Sixth Avenue is all glittery. I'm on my lunch hour and on my way to Eve's Garden, a woman-oriented sex-toys shop in mid-Manhattan. I'm going there to meet my co-editor, Betty Boob. Our mission: to solicit advertising for the upcoming Sex issue of *BUST*. Our purpose: to buy the Hitachi Magic Wand vibrator, which had been recommended to us by a very reliable source.

I'm feeling less sunny and more embarrassed by the time I reach the place— a nondescript office building on West 57th Street. Just entering the building makes me feel self-conscious: Will the lobby guy ask me where I'm going and ask me to sign some book? Does he entertain himself by trying to guess which women are on their way to the sex shop? And do I look like "the kind of woman" who is? And why why why do I feel so fucking embarrassed anyway?

He says nothing. I take the elevator up and walk down the hall to the door, which is marked with a small plaque. I quickly slip inside. Whew—safe.

Betty's not there yet so I wander around the incense-scented-yet-air-conditioned office space. Sex tapes line the shelves against one wall; feminist, lesbian, and erotic self-help books are along the other. At the far end of the store is what I've come to purchase; there are three long shelves full of dildos, ben-wah balls, and other assorted mechanical, plastic, and rubbery devices lined up like a toy army. Something about it all starts to feel pathetic and sad.

For one thing, all of the sex devices seem so unnatural. I mean, there are, like, no natural fibers or plant materials or organic substances of any kind. What they do have are lavender dildos made of creepy-crawler goop, egg-shaped vibrators of pink plastic, and large, beige and white vibrators. Not at all sexy or sensuous, these devices are marketed as "massagers" and they look it—they have the practical design and cold lines of household appliances. I feel like I am at Sears, and I am not inspired.

85

There are other erotic substances, however, that are more to my liking: a bottle of clove-scented soap strikes my fancy, and some other groovy-smelling bath stuff, which I buy. Finally Betty arrives.

We peruse the shelves of vibrators, both a little too nervous to touch them. Betty asks the woman behind the counter whether she carries the Hitachi Magic Wand. The woman nods her head knowingly. "We call it the Cadillac of vibrators," she says, and walks us back to the shelves. She points out the Magic Wand, which is, in fact, just about the size of a Cadillac. It's the length and width of my arm from elbow to wrist, and the vibrating part is the size of a small fist. She turns it on for us. Other people in the store turn their heads. The thing is loud.

I'd always thought vibrators were only about the size of a, well, you know— a hot dog. Obviously, this thing was intended for external use only. I didn't like the looks of it. I hated it. But I wasn't about to turn back now, and so I bought it.

The lady put my goodies in an unmarked pink plastic bag, and I walked back to work, slightly nervous. Would people ask what was in the bag? What if the bag ripped, right in the elevator, and everyone saw? It annoyed me that my pursuit of physical pleasure should be so embarrassing to me. I was trying to feel empowered, sex-positive, and daring. Instead I kept feeling like a shriveled-up pathetic spinster with a ridiculously oversized toy. There was clearly some kind of subconscious fear that kept telling me that maybe I *was* buying a vibrator because I couldn't get a man. I don't know what men tell themselves when they rent porn videos or go to a strip club, but I don't think they feel pathetic or embarrassed, and it's probably because the pursuit of sexual pleasure is accepted as an intrinsic part of their lives, in whatever form it takes. A girl's sexual pleasure, however, is supposed to depend entirely on a man. A woman who can please herself without a man is somehow threatening. And, maybe, even to herself.

Still, I wanted to try it out that night. I took a long candlelit bath with the clove soap to, you know, get myself in the mood, and read the pink instruction pamphlet that came with the device. Then, finally, it was time to do the deed.

I found an extension chord, and then turned off all the lights in my apartment before I even plugged in the damn thing—I was so afraid that someone across the street might be able to see through my curtains and see me. I left my CD player on loud, to drown out the noise. ("Honey, is that girl next door using her blender at

1:00 A.M.? What on earth is that noise?" "Well, she's single, isn't she? She's probably using a vibrator! Ha ha ha!")

After a few awkward moments I found a position that felt good, and just as I was easing into it—Whoops! There it is!—I had an orgasm in record time. I wasn't even really ready for it yet, it just happened. I mean, in like two minutes. Weird. And yeah, it felt good, but it somehow wasn't as satisfying as I'm used to—it was similar to the kind of laughter that comes out of you when you're tickled; it's laughter, all right, but it's not as good as when you're really laughing, hard, deep, and from your belly. Damn, I thought, this was supposed to be so great. I started to try again, but to no avail. And for the moment, I was secretly glad that I didn't like it that much; that it wasn't better than a man.

I gave it another shot the next night, and the next—and I have to say, I'm getting more used to it. But I still can't last very long—maybe I should think about baseball when I'm doing it. The amazing thing is that I don't need to be in the mood—I barely even need to come up with a fantasy for myself, which, in the past, could sometimes take so long and get so complicated that I would fall asleep before I even got off. And I like the newfound power; I can get off whenever the fuck I want to, and even when I don't want to. The capacity is there, it's in my body, it's simple, it's a reflex, and it feels good. It feels damn good, in fact, and with my vibrator my orgasms are guaranteed (or my money back?).

So I have to wonder—if men came with a vibrating attachment, if I could be that assured of coming every single time I slept with someone—would I behave more like a man? Would I suddenly want to sleep with almost any man who offered? Would it be easier to think of men as sex objects, if they, in fact, *were* sex objects? An object I could masturbate with? An object I could use to make me come? Because, the trouble is, a large percentage of men I've slept with, especially the one-night stands, don't make me come. And I know I'm not alone in this; more than one woman has confessed to me that she is able to give herself better orgasms than any man.

Now don't get me wrong: I'm not saying that sex with a vibrator is better than sex with a man; it's just that it's more reliable. Which is why, perhaps, we women look to men for more than orgasms, and is maybe why we tend to have sex with men we really like, with men we could fall in love with. And why we

87

tend to emphasize the whole interpersonal-communicating-with-another-being thing when we talk about sex. Because, after all, there has to be some reason to sleep with them, right?

Betty and Celina Get Wired: Part I

Betty's Story

by Betty Boob

Before

My best gal pal gave me a little toy called The Beaver for my thirtieth birthday. I was almost thrilled; I'd never owned a toy before, and certainly never one like The Beaver. The Beaver was a black beast, made of undulating rubber, propelled by an attached battery pack. On its shaft was a miniature replica of a beaver, whose tongue gyrated to and fro, depending on the speed. (I reckoned if it were in ultra-high-speed mode, it could probably serve as a guillotine.) To top off the mood, the head, or the phallus, of this toy had a smiley face; apparently in the country where The Beaver is manufactured, it is illegal to produce sex toys. In order to avoid getting into trouble each sex toy has to be presented as an actual toy. As for me, the sight of this pleasure-inducing character was enough to put me off and make me run screaming back to my hand: my lovely adept little hand, which I used daily, nightly, hourly to pleasure myself. And, after years of constant use, I was beginning to get a tingly feeling in my wrist, which in my hypochondriac-esque mind could mean only one thing: carpal tunnel syndrome. Imagine having to explain to people that the bandage on your wrist was because you jerked off too much. My gal pal had given me The Beaver with the best of all intentions; unfortunately, it was the wrong toy for Betty Boob. And so began my quest for the right toy.

During

One day, I was sitting in a bright kitchen with my friend, Lisa. I was lamenting about The Beaver. (It had recently been adopted by my dogs as a quim-scented chew toy.) Lisa hushed me up with three reassuring words: "Hitachi Magic Wand." Hmmm. I consulted Celina Hex. She was as much in the dark as I was about the Wand, so we decided to go pick one up. Each.

Where does one venture for a Magic Wand? If I were in San Francisco, I would go to Good Vibrations. I wasn't in San Francisco, however, although I would soon learn that Good Vibrations offers an extensive catalog featuring toys that would bring new meaning to the word "pleasure."

We agreed to meet at the same place that my best gal pal bought The Beaver.

As usual I was late; upon walking into the store, I found Celina looking a little uncomfortable (although later on I realized that perhaps it was just me projecting). I decided to brave the storm and went directly to the lady behind the counter. I rambled on and on about *BUST,* and I was doing really well until I awkwardly stuttered "So what's the deal with the Magic Wand?" I had said the "magic" words apparently, because before I knew it, I was standing before the dildo section. I almost felt at home once I saw a replica of my friend The Beaver, displayed prominently, alongside a bunch of other Beavers, in a variety of different colors.

I stood in awe as the lady from behind the counter casually went into a how-to-tell-if-a-vibrator-is-good-for-you speech. Before the eyes of three other people, including a man, she used me as her mannequin, first gently and then roughly, demonstrating on my pelvic area the pros and cons of each vibrator. And, of course, asking my own opinion. Frankly, I couldn't tell the difference from one vibrator to the next although I did nod every time she asked if I liked said model. I couldn't feel much at this point except moisture, and in fact I was a little numb at the soul spot where she kept pressing the heads of the aforementioned vibrators on me. Even after all the demonstrations, I was as clueless as I had been when I walked in. The only thing I did know before, during, and after was that Celina and I knew we were going to buy a Hitachi Magic Wand anyway.

I couldn't wait to get home and try my new toy.

So I dashed home and quickly hid the wand. After all, I had a roommate,

89

male at that. He would have heard me, or the pleasure beast, right? Oh boy, I thought, that is not going to be good. No, no, no! I'll just have to wait, I figured. Before I hid my wand, however, I carefully took it out of the box for a sneak peak at my new toy. Originally designed as a massager of sorts, it has fast become an appliance de pussy. Now ladies, let me warn you, because even though the lady from behind the counter used a Magic Wand on my clothed person, for some reason the size of the Magic Wand didn't really register. Well, I am telling you here and now: The fucker is huge. And thick, and, well, it definitely does not look like The Beaver. It's a lot smoother, cleaner, almost CLINICAL. At that point I was just hoping there would be an instruction manual.

A number of days passed and I had still not made friends with the wand. By the fifth day, I was beginning to suspect that I was avoiding it. It was on this fateful day that my roommate went out on a date. Feeling like a supreme lonely loser, I got stoned, you know, to relax, and soon succumbed to this blurry lazy-hazy state. I began to feel horny. Feeling bold and daring, I dug the wand out from the Secret Hiding Place. It took me forever to get into a comfortable position, but once I did, I turned it on, to the low cycle, and my dog perked up. I had to shoo her away. After all, I was about to have a private moment. And then I got nervous. What if I began to come, and I got electrocuted? What if the swirling head some-how got caught in my pubic hairs and ripped them out? What if a neighbor walked past my apartment door and heard me moaning, or the Magic Wand whirring? Before I knew it, I was no longer horny, just cranky. And extremely, neurotically paranoid. I thought about the scene in *Risky Business* when Tom Cruise is at-tempting to masturbate—his fantasy interrupted by his own fears of getting caught. God, I thought, I am such a wimp.

A few more days passed and I began to get pissed off. And impatient. In fact, I was masturbating manually with more passion in the last few days than I had been even before I bought the wand. I wondered if I was going to be able to set a new world record for masturbating.

Another gal pal took pity on me and sent a few porn tapes my way. Just watch this, she said, you'll be able to do it.

So the following day, I waited for my roommate to go to work. Once he left, I popped the tape of porn into the VCR. I fast-forwarded through the tapes, mentally jotting down the scenes I would want to return to. There were a lot of girl-on-girl scenes, which made me happy. I like watching femme porn: there is something so artistically sculpted about these women. Their bodies are supernatural. I don't hate these girls like I hate models, who are freaks of nature. No, the bodies of porn stars are specifically designed for aesthetically stimulating pleasure. These chicks are short, tall, white, black, bleached; they're natural, flat, siliconed beyond belief. (It's always fun trying to point out the ratio of real versus fake boobs.) Each lady is sculpted in her own special way. Oh, and they are curvy, bringing dimension to their femininity, unlike models, whose flatboard bodies leave you feeling, well, flat. These female porn stars put the male porn stars to shame. Male porn actors aren't as carefully tended to. Some of them are in shape, some aren't, some have hair, some don't, some are huge, some are average. They certainly don't have that special quality the girls have. But I digress.

It was not too long before my visual aid, my Magic Wand, and I fell into sync. Before I knew it, I was screaming out names, of bouncers, of people behind counters, of people I kind of know but not really, and they were all there, invading me, joining me, indulging with me.

After

It's been a few months since my first time. I finally got over being intimidated by a "contraption." After all, it had taken me years before I could even show myself how to manually masturbate. The leap from hand to wand wasn't really that big of a jump. And I must say, I am quite pleased with Magic Wand. Very pleased. Beyond pleased. It's my guess that by the time the motor runs out on my Cadillac I may have carpal tunnel syndrome. I still use my hand; there's no substitution for the real thing. But the Magic Wand can do things, faster usually, that sometimes I can't. Bottom line is for me, I need the pleasure. I want it. And to the end, I will get it any way I can.

Fiona Smyth

Way After

I don't know what day it is today but all I do know is this: I am heartbroken again. Again I have waited for the boy to call and yet again he has not called. And yet again I am falling apart. Not just little by little. No. All at once. All day I have had a lot to do, calls to make, work to finish. And yet again all day all I have accomplished is checking my voice mail 172 times. And he hasn't called. I am so emotionally exhausted there is only one thing I want to do: cry. So there I am, just wandering aimlessly around my apartment. What to do, what to do. And probably because I am so blinded by heartbreak, so numb within my mind, I do not notice that the Magic Wand is just lying there on the floor. Just like that. Quickly I pick it up and the dimmer in my head begins to brighten. Hey! There may be a way to clear up the Betty Boob blues.

Betty and Celina Get Wired: Part II

Celina's Commitment

by Celina Hex

Since buying my first vibrator four years ago, I have only one regret: that I didn't get one sooner. Why didn't I get one, say, when I was fifteen? Why didn't I have one during all those difficult years of college, where it could have come in so handy as a way to relax after a grueling test? Where, in fact, I could have done myself a huge favor by not going out, getting drunk, and picking up some dumb-ass frat boy in my search for sexual healing, a strategy that usually only left me, come morning, with beer breath, razor-stubble burn, and someone whose name I couldn't remember. All those nights would have been much better spent cuddling up with a cute, vibrating little pleasure device, and would have been far more sexually satisfying, as well.

When it comes to vibrators, the question should not be "Is it better than a man?" but "Is it better than your hand?" The answer to the first question is, simply,

"It's different." The answer to the second is a resounding "Yes!" Listen, masturbating is fun, but sometimes you need a little jolt of electricity, so to speak. For men, that's where girlie mags, porn movies, or a good set of binoculars comes in. They save men the work of having to come up with their own fantasies. For me, the fantasy was never the hard part—it was the manual labor that could get to me at times. My little Magic Wand takes care of all that, freeing me up to focus completely on conjuring up my elaborate, perverted, and sick little sex scenarios.

Ever since I've gotten one, I've been on a mission about vibrators. "Every girl deserves a helping hand" is my motto. In fact, I think a vibrator would make the perfect bat mitzvah or sweet sixteen gift. Just think of all the orgasms a girl might otherwise miss out on. I mean, I know plenty of women who didn't have their first orgasm until they were in their twenties, but not a single man who hadn't had one by the time he was fourteen. Why is that? I don't know. Maybe boys have the advantage because they have a penis that gets hard and screams "stroke me!" at them in the middle of the night. We girls have to learn it all ourselves, and, after a few furtive attempts, well, I think I just gave up. There was nothing to see, nothing that squirted—I'm not even sure that at that age I knew that women really *could* have orgasms. And while I knew the size of my breasts down to the last centimeter (because they, at least, were getting talked about), I had no idea what a clitoris looked like, let alone what one was. That little anatomical illustration that came inside my Tampax box diagrammed my nether parts in loving detail, to make sure I didn't shove that thing up the wrong hole, but it neglected to include the clitoris. In this culture, we don't even need to practice female castration to separate a girl from her clitoris. If nobody bothers to tell her she has one, there's a good chance she may never find it.

Oh sure, I learned about the birds and the bees as a kid. I learned about how babies are made, about the whole penis-and-vagina thing. How I had ovaries and a uterus and how that little egg would come out once a month. Later, in junior high school health class, I was taught how I could keep from contracting diseases, how to avoid getting pregnant, and how to deal with the messy monthly blood, but nothing about how to find my little pleasure bud. After puberty, it seemed, all my time would be taken up just keeping my genitals safe from unwanted mishaps. Well, I'm here to say to the girls of our nation: ASK NOT WHAT YOU CAN DO FOR YOUR CUNT, BUT ASK WHAT YOUR CUNT CAN DO FOR YOU!

Of course, one of the best things it can do for you is give you orgasms.

"I'm getting these breast implants for myself" is the standard explanation given by women who are about to undergo the surgeon's knife, but I say, if you *really* want to do something for yourself, go get yourself a vibrator. If as many women bought themselves vibrators as they do breast implants, the world would be a better place. Maybe we need to start telling women that using a vibrator helps you lose weight, or that using the vibrator helps tighten your vaginal muscles, which will increase *his* pleasure. Maybe then they will be more likely to get them.

Because I'm sick of women who don't have or use vibrators responding with a sort of disdain when the subject of them comes up. They usually kind of scrunch up their noses with disgust, a response which always suggests, "Darling, I'm so sexually satisfied I don't need a vibrator." Can you *imagine* men responding in like form to the topic of porn. "You watch porno? Yo, dude! How gross!" Yeah, right. Most women don't even seem to know what vibrators actually look like or how they are used. For one thing, few people know that vibrators come in a wide variety of shapes and sizes, from small egg-shaped things to the larger ones that are sold right in your local Radio Shack as "massagers" (which is a good place to get one without embarrassment, since the men who work there don't seem to know that that's what they're used for, either). Even fewer people know that the vibrator is mostly intended for external use. Let me say it loud and clear: A vibrator is not a dildo, although some of them can be used in that way. A vibrator is just meant to be held against your clit until you explode with pleasure. Class dismissed.

To be honest, I used to be one of those women myself. I was very uncomfortable about buying my first vibrator, and I, too, thought it meant I was some kind of dried-up old spinster or something. But ever since I finally went through with it, it has become so important to me that, like my answering machine, I can no longer imagine what life was like without it. I'm mad that we women have been scared out of getting them; that they aren't more normalized in our culture. If we can talk about feminine hygiene sprays and yeast infection treatments on TV, why can't Hitachi run ads featuring a dancing little Magic Wand that promises to give "pure feminine satisfaction"? Can't Victoria's Secret have Dennis Miller or some supermodel let us in on what Victoria's Secret *really* was—that she had a supercharged vibrating love machine that never let her down?

Until then, I've got my work cut out for me. Taking my cue from the riot grrls' chant—Grrls Need Guitars!—I've come up with my own rallying cry: Vixens need Vibrators! Say amen, somebody.

Betty & Celina Get Wired: Part II

Betty's Breakup

by Betty Boob

When Celina and I decided to document our vibrator experience in *BUST*, I was quite apprehensive about the Hitachi Magic Wand and its wonders. I was a dedicated *au naturel* gal but once I got down with the Wand, I was hooked. Talk about a hoo-ha! Girl, this is a hoo-ha that vibrates through your whole body, leaving you tingling for minutes on end, face flushed with after-sex glow, with no muss, no fuss, no stinky fingers. My hoo-ha's were quite intense, and in the beginning, came as quickly as I liked, depending on how much control I could exert over my horny self. I suppose it's always like that in a given honeymoon period—you just can't get enough.

Forsaking my hand, ignoring the lapping tongues of ardent lovers, I became obsessed with the Wand, constantly strategizing about when I would return to the round bulbous head of my poontang machine as I went to work, did the laundry, or spent the rare night at my lover's. If I ever had a problem before with punctuality, now it was epidemic; I was always late, in meeting friends, attending concerts or doctor's appointments. I was purely in pursuit of my constant state of pleasure. The Wand became my priority.

I couldn't bear to be apart from my Wand. I traveled with it, to Los Angeles, Paris, and London (well, naturally I got one of those European adapter gizmos). Once I was stopped by a Vancouver customs officer. The man savagely pulled my precious Wand out of my bag and asked me what it was. Obviously, I was not going to lie, so I said, "Well, that's my vibrator!" He turned a beet red and ushered me very quickly

96

onto the plane. The beginning of the end of another vibrator was also my fault: I had mangled, bent, and twisted the cord so much from repositioning the Wand during our special moments that the protective sheath started to suffer from the wear and tear and simply cracked: eventually the zing I got wasn't only because of my whirring dervish. I figured I should go get a brand-new model pronto. Another Wand got accidentally chewed to bits by my dog one night, which freaked me out because it meant I would have to wait until noon the next day before Eve's Garden was open in order to get a new one. Oh, the horror!

As I began using my Wand more, like up to 3 or 712 times a day, my clitoris became a little moody. Sometimes it took a little longer for my hoo-ha to come. If I held it in the same position for too long, my vagina would get a little sweaty. Once, I smelled something akin to a motor burning, which would distract me to no end. I brought the Wand back to the store where I purchased it to ask the salesperson to inspect the motor. The motor was fine. It was me who was having the problem.

My problem was overusage. A typical day went like this: once when I awoke, once after breakfast, a couple of times over the course of the afternoon, and quite a few times once the sun set. Even my dog knew the Wand came before her walk did. And the constant pressure of the Wand was something I (okay, my clitoris) was getting accustomed to.

I noticed that my Wand usage affected my sex life with real live people too. At a point in time where my relationship with the Wand had gone from a novelty to a necessity, I met a boy that I fell for, hard, the kind of hard where he was sharing my bed every night of the week. He was a fun fuck and exhibited carnal skills (pussy friendly, maintaining erection, and always always always coming inside me—unless we indulged in other activities) that are important to me. The only thing that did not occur were hoo-ha's. As much as I was aroused by him, and the things he did to my body, I never ever had a hoo-ha unless I participated manually. I didn't mind so much at first, because I had the Wand to come in for cleanup after he left in the morning. And oh, how I looked forward to my Wand time. It wasn't until I noticed how sore my vagina was becoming that I realized that all the fucking and the increasingly long sessions with the Wand were beginning to take their toll on my pleasure zone.

After a few years of consistent Magic Wand usage, it was taking me up to 45

97

minutes to locate my special place with the Wand. On occasion, my arm would go numb from enduring the long time of holding the vibrating mechanism in the same position, literally vibrating against my forearm. I became paranoid that I was getting carpal tunnel syndrome in my elbow. I just was not enjoying my masturbatory moments with the fervor I once had. I started to worry and wonder: Was it him? Was it me? What was happening with my hoo-ha's and the Magic Wand?

Quite honestly I have never been the most orgasmic woman in the world—it takes a lot of foreplay to get me going, although I usually, with a little help from my end, come through. I thought about my sex life pre-Wand: it was busy, that's for sure, with plenty of clitoral orgasms. And post-Wand? Well, I realized, the hoo-ha's were not as aplenty; I always knew that if I wasn't achieving orgasm with the person, I'd get some with the Wand.

Could it have been that my clitoris had developed a certain liking to the whirring of the Wand and its constant throbbing pressure that never let up? Did I in fact develop a tolerance? Maybe. There was no way I could attain that kind of pressure from the mushiness of a tongue, unless I kept my lover's whole jaw in place for an extended amount of time, using it as one would use a bucking bronco!

Whoa.

I guess that's when I started to think about breaking up with my boyfriend. I mean, I could not possibly leave my Wand. How could I? It was such a part of my pleasure, my thoughts, my lifestyle. But then again, there was this really super-fantastic boyfriend. And maybe I was selling him short—I knew he had the hoo-ha potential in him, he just needed a chance. But on the other hand, I loved the Wand. And even though it did not have the potency it once did, I could not resist the power of the Wand; it had a certain magic over me.

The Wand had power over me. It was then that I had my sad epiphany. I couldn't possibly allow an inanimate object to dictate my life. I needed to break free. It was obvious that in my case, I could not handle having a real-life lover and the Magic Wand as a lover. I had to make a choice: it had to be one or the other.

And that's why I ended up breaking up with the Hitachi Magic Wand, pathetically staring at the bottom of an empty garbage can after breakfast on that fateful day.

Of course, now it is a year and a half later and I am without lover and without Wand. I miss the now ex-boyfriend a lot because I was, in fact, nuts about him, but I suspect I miss the Wand even more. I go through phases—when I am in between lovers or when I am sleeping with a lover who is boring, which lately has been de rigueur—when I consider reconciling with the Wand. I wander into Eve's Garden and stare longingly at the display thinking, Okay, just this once I'll just buy the Wand and use it once and then maybe give it to someone as a hand-me-down. Surely I must know some girls who wouldn't mind a hand-me-down, I tell myself before I realize I sound like a loser addict, like that stupid dumb junkie boyfriend who says, "Just this once," but you know it means "Here I go." So I don't buy anything, except maybe a porn tape, and it's back to Ms. Hand. Which, you know, ain't so bad.

More Than a Blow Job: It's a Career

by Dixie LaRue

My friend and I made up a game once to pass the time. It's a little intellectual and moral exercise we call "The White Room." Say you're in a small white cubicle with no windows and only a mattress on the floor. Being realistic, how much money would it take to give a blow job to (insert repulsive celebrity)? The ground rules were (1) you don't have to talk to them, nor they to you (that lowered Donald Trump's price considerably); (2) always remember you can give the money to charity; and (3) there is an interesting anecdote factor that shouldn't be discounted. (Imagine telling friends and family about the time you had Henry Kissinger's member in your mouth!) Needless to say, this game can provide hours of brainteasers and is a good icebreaker at any party.

99

I suck cocks. I am a woman who likes to put penises in her mouth, and then suck said penises for all they're worth.

Why is it that the term "cocksucker" is considered so vile as to be hurled as the most slanderous insult imaginable to only the most cretinous of jerks? I say, let's take back the word and appropriately apply the label to those of us who wear it as a proud badge of honor.

I was an adolescent girl somewhere in the middle of the junior high social food chain—something with a spine but not cuddly enough to make it as a plush toy. Okay-looking, but not even junior varsity cheerleader material in the blond and pastel world of South Florida aesthetics. Though slim with a good figure, my nose was a bit too bulbous and my hair a bit too curly for anyone to mistake me for Charlie's or anyone's angel. I didn't mind not having a boyfriend really. I had no interest in being on the receiving end of some high-fivin' quarterback—vaginally or conversationally. I was saving myself (vaginally and spiritually) for my first true love.

But everyone wants to be wanted, especially insecure and bored teenage girls. I quickly found my niche—and my calling—in the wonderful world of blow jobs. Blow jobs were a small planet in our teenage deb sexual universe, something to be dimly aware of out past Neptune and far from the solar brilliance of IT. In our eighth-grade baseball lexicon, cocksucking was called "fourth base," beyond the pale of the deflowering home run. Fellatio was an exotic ritual performed by French courtesans or the hopelessly skanky.

Imagine the impression one could make on a fourteen-year-old boy when you pulled fellatio out of your bag of tricks. Because of misplaced delicacy, Southern Baptist conditioning, or insipid squeamishness, I found myself nearly alone in my field. I was Tiger un-Beat-able. It wasn't long before I developed a sense of craftsmanship, a pride in my craft not unlike an artisan blowing glass in Old Williamsburg. I wasn't blowing glass, but my work too required delicacy and precision. The only things transparent though were my newfound friends.

Fellatio well suited my needs and my madcap slut persona. Like a prostitute, I never kissed my Styx- and Journey-lovin' paramours. That would have been too intimate, and frankly, too gross. Cocksucking entailed little face-to-face contact, almost no pain or small talk, no fear of disease, and bestowed upon me a certain

100

status as a "hot babe." (If only in my own eyes, which is, after all, where it counts.) I often referred to myself as the "lathe of heaven."

Naturally, in college the field was more crowded. A virgin in tramp's clothing, I honed my craft to include a special, shall we say melodramatically hearty rendition of the swallow. Deglutition is still no-woman's-land for many a young maid. You'd think the legions of bulimic sophomores would welcome the upchuck support (not to mention the much-needed protein), but most still drew the line. (Girls: The gag reflex is your friend. It brings up saliva and is handy for replenishing moisture for the duration.)

As adult sexual politics became more apparent, so too did my predilection for cock-suckage. It was one of the few times a girl could feel as though she were making an impression. Usually my friends and I just felt, well, used. Sucking cock, you felt important. No longer acted upon, above or below the waist, now you were the actor, the doer instead of the "do-ee," or worse, the "done-to." For once, you had the upper hand. Fellatio put you in the driver's seat.

Which brings me to my cocksucking pet peeves. As a proud practitioner, I do not like "backseat drivers." Of course, some well-intentioned directions, some laudatory guidance is appreciated. But barking out speeds and constantly demanding an ever-changing increment of pressure is downright obnoxious. I especially resented having my head steered. As an artiste, I don't like being some saliva-producing middleman between a guy's dick and his hand. Gentle hints tempered with praise are not only more encouraging, they're only polite. My other peeve is, shall we say, an absence of obdurance. If I've got your penis in my mouth, goddamn it, it better get hard. I've got feelings too you know, and your little internal struggles with your God or some goofy whore/Madonna complex could really screw up my game.

Another little-talked-about dilemma is the whole neck-cramp issue. Usually I could go on forever if not for the crimp in my neck. I get around that now by propping up some pillows for my head to rest on, but I can see where that could take away some of the romance.

Boys: I'm told another peeve is your steadfast ejaculation even when you've been nicely asked not to. While I've always held that if you've got the business end of a penis in your face, into your life a little rain must fall. Boys: it would behoove you to show a little consideration. And girls, be a good sport. (One friend of mine was so pissed at this betrayal she got up and spit it in his face.) And whatever you do, girls, don't think of tadpoles. Remember, this is the very stuff of Life; a little pickles and bleach never hurt anyone.

The heady mix of pleasure and power makes fellatio my number one sex act. Really. Straddling your sweetie's thigh and devouring his penis is fabulous. I've always felt that sex—when done correctly—always comes out even. (Though not necessarily simultaneous.) Cocksucking is not at all unselfish. It's not at all degrading. It's not, as Germaine Greer once said, like being attacked by a giant snail. When it comes down to it, you don't make love to a body part. You make love to a whole human being.

Some of them just happen to have a hard, pulsating, veiny protuberance down your throat.

Footnote: All-time highest price for "The White Room" was "not enough money in the Universe" for Martin Balsam.

How to Be as Horny as a Guy

by Lady J.

WARNING: Horniness may lead to sex. Be prepared, and follow safer-sex guidelines.

Don't be fooled. Horniness is not just hormonal. Learn why guys are walking woodies and use their secrets to enjoy more and better sex!

1. Skip one expendable girlie activity per day. Instead, use that time to masturbate. Get good at it. Buy books on technique. Become a sexual dynamo. Next thing you know, you'll be looking for someone to show off your talents to. (Good girlie activities to skip: removing unwanted hair, popping zits then covering them with makeup, folding T-shirts, cleaning boyfriend's kitchen.)

2. Every time you go to the bathroom, touch your clitoris. Well hey—they touch their penises! Tell me that doesn't change their attitude just a little. And while you're at it, keep some sexy reading material by the throne—you may end up touching yourself more than once.

3. In your mind, replace all advertising images made to titillate men with images made to titillate you. Every ad that you see that has a sexy woman in it, imagine the ad with a man instead. Picture a Guess Jeans Boy spilling his popcorn all over a movie theater floor. Instead of Calvin Klein's Obsession model Kate Moss, place Ewan MacGregor or Will Smith sprawled nude, facedown on the sofa. Imagine the "St. Pauli Guy" or the "Maidenform Man." It doesn't take much to visualize a world full of tempting torsos and inviting smiles.

4. Ogle men. Check out dude's bods. Assertively seek out sexy butts, chests, legs, packages, etc., as you go through the day. When you find something appealing, look at it closely, memorize its shape and detail. Save these images in your brain in a "smile file." Whenever you feel like it, refer to this file and relive these golden observances. Create new and different fantasy lovers out of parts you have on file or just drive yourself wild with them alone or with a friend!

5. Drink booze and smoke pot.

6. Wear comfortable clothes. How can you be "in the mood" when you're hobbling down the street in heels with your underwear riding up your butt? (Exception: bondage clothes.)

7. Eliminate the fear of pregnancy and STDs. Keep condoms with you at all times (at work, in your gym locker, car, or lunch box). Remember: "Desire turns to doubt when you're caught without!" If necessary, eliminate intercourse entirely. There are plenty of other cool things for the two of you to do. Grind his butt cheeks! He can screw your armpit!

8. Get together with your girlfriends and talk about sex and men. Work yourselves up and then go out hunting. Feel empowered and in control, then move in on your victim.

9. Have orgasms every time you have sex. Before him, with him, next to him, alone in the bathroom, wherever. You deserve it! Girls that say yes to sex are girls that get off.

10. Watch porn. Sure it's gross and sexist, but it makes you think about sex and that makes you horny. If you can't stomach a video store, tapes can be ordered from porn magazines. TIP: Gay porn has the hottest guys!

Lesson Number One

by Scarlett Fever

He pushes me inside a yellow cab and stuffs himself in beside me. I hear the first gunshots exploding like Chinese firecrackers in February as the door slams closed.

"Drive," he says to the cabbie. "Relax, babe. It's over." He drops a bloated pink hairless hand onto my thigh.

"Consulate Hotel. West 49th Street," he says speaking to the driver, and looking at me, the question in his eyes.

I don't say anything. *How bad can it be? He's not mean. I need a car. I need his money to get it.*

"I need three n' a quarter, 'Lloyd.'"

"Okay, three hundred and twenty-five dollars it is then." He smiles at me, rubbing his pink hand up and down my thigh vigorously, anticipating. I catch Abu Ben Taxi Driver looking at us in the rearview mirror. Listening in. Deciding what I am. What "Lloyd" is. The vodka from my last drink rises back up my throat and tastes awful.

Next week I can drive into the city in the car I bought with the money from my first trick.

The hotel room: the lights are out, the blinds open. The room is lit only by a full moon and the streetlights below. "Lloyd" lies naked on the bed, a great white beached whale. His skin is iridescent in the moonlight, broken only by an archipelago of eczema that dots his massive body, the source of the medicinal aura that floats around him at all times. I stand at the bathroom door, my clothes at my feet, and try to imagine the feel of his skin, the texture of the rash. I leave my body. My heart and soul float across the room, settling sadly into the wing chair in the corner. A voyeuristic sadistic pleasure keeps me watching as the scene unfolds. I watch myself, in awe of what I'm capable of.

I see myself in the moonlight, breasts full and plump, ass round and creamy, hips rolling seductively as I walk over to the bed. My face a blank mask of concentration and focus as I look down at him. Thinking about what? The car? The money? The task at hand?

"Lloyd" lies on the bed, legs spread wide, stomach rising up above everything, a 350-plus-pound island of flesh lit blue-white by garish streetlights, waiting for me.

He reaches out entwining his chubby fingers in my dark curly pubic hair and shoves his thumb inside of me (an audible gasp bubbles out of my mouth, escaping into the night). His thumb probes deeper, twirling around.

"Suck my cock," his voice no longer whiny, no longer begging. He pulls his thumb out of me, pushes me toward the end of the bed, and shiny with my juice he sticks it in his mouth and suckles.

Proportion takes on a profound meaning when a man's cock is surrounded by so many pounds of flesh. Finding it alone is a labor worthy of Hercules. Tucked inside the many folds of his massive thighs, deep inside the crevices below his bellies, I watch myself root through his flesh like a pig after truffles. Holding a belly up with my elbow, a thigh away with my hand. Finding my prey, my pound of flesh, short and

105

Pamela Hobbs

hard, no bigger than his thumb or a pale breakfast sausage, I bend and take him into my mouth. Covering it with my own saliva, stroking him slowly, making him harder, squeezing and pulling, rubbing my breasts while he cranes over his belly to watch, squeezing my nipples, getting us both ready. He lies there, unable to move, a giant turtle on his back, a great sea mammal washed ashore and abandoned, at my mercy. My juices are flowing. I touch myself, separate the damp hairs, the outer labia, the inner labia, open myself up and rise up, rise up, Venus rising from the foam. I close my eyes and mount him as best I can.

"Suck this." I knock his hand away from his mouth and stick my fingers, my whole hand, slick with my own juices, in his mouth.

I ride him, leaning forward as he grabs my tits, pulling painfully at my nipples. I grip his round arms and ride him, forgetting about his rash, his size, his lack of size. I ride and pump and thrust and grind. I moan and curse and Oh baby, and yes, yes, yes as he comes inside me, I ride some more, pulling on my own nipples now, rubbing my clit up against the overflow from his big firm belly, bringing myself to climax. I stroke his immense round gut as I feel him shrinking, I contract inside and try to hold him there a bit longer. Shrinking. Shrinking. He slips out.

And I think about where I will go in the cute blue Pinto I will buy with his money.

The money, the real reason I'm here, I tell myself. Yet, even today, when I describe it, my juices flow and the tingles grow in the secret place deep inside me. His flesh repulses me, the act of selling myself does not. Having someone desire me so much that he will pay me, pay what I ask, opens me up inside.

To be in charge.

To be in control.

To be paid.

He's coming out of the bathroom, already having washed my scent off and stuffed himself back into his oversized brown polyester slacks when I realize no money's changed hands yet. No crisp bills waiting quietly on the nightstand like in the movies.

"'Lloyd,' uh, are you leaving?" My clothes are on the bathroom floor. He stands at the doorway to the bathroom, a wall of flesh between me and my clothes. The fluorescent bathroom light creates a gargantuan silhouette, his huge polyester behind the only thing reflected in the mirror.

"Yeah. Look, I gotta go see what kind of damage was done in the club tonight. You can keep the room, babe. I paid them for the whole night." He struggles into the brown-and-gray plaid sport coat, pats me on the head, checking his pockets as he does so, and heads toward the door.

"I don't wanna stay here all night. We *talked* about the money, 'Lloyd.' What about the money?" I don't want to let him escape. I grab up my clothes, and pull them on without washing him off of me. Liquid Lloyd runs down my leg.

"Look, I don't have the money with me."

"What do you mean, you don't have the money? You paid for the cab, the room . . . ?"

I came here to get paid, to turn a trick.

"That's about all I had on me. I have just enough to get home from here. Everything else is in the safe at the club. Do you need cab fare or are you okay?"

Cab fare, you mammoth pig? I need three hundred and twenty-five dollars. I need your head on a platter. I need my fucking money.

"Okay? Okay? I'm not okay. What about my money? You said you'd pay me three"—*It's not a trick if I don't get paid. If I don't get paid it's just a nightmare—*"hundred and—"

"Hey," he interrupts, his inflated Macy's Thanksgiving Day parade balloon hand on my naked shoulder, "do you think I'm trying to cheat you?" *Yes, that's exactly what I think.* "What did you want me to do, tell the guys on the stairs to wait, don't shoot up the place till I get money outta the safe to give to my girl?"

"But I thought you had money with you. . . ."

STUPID, STUPID, STUPID. STUPID BITCH.

"No, doll." He speaks softly, like you do a child. "You stop by the club tomorrow night and we'll straighten everything out. Okay?"

I'm such a stupid bitch.

I nod silently and sit there, even quieter, watching in the mirror as he kisses me good-bye. Silent as I watch the door close after his fat shit-brown polyester ass. Silently I sit as my heart and soul walk over and rejoin me, a little thinner now, a little paler. Silent as I finish dressing and head down to the subway and back home. I can panhandle whatever I need for the Long Island Rail Road.

Or maybe it wasn't like that at all. Maybe I was too scared or too stupid to ask for the money afterward. Maybe there was just a chubby girl having sex with a huge fat man, expecting him to keep his word. Maybe it wasn't sensual at all. Maybe it was a dirty little room in a cheap hotel with no full moon, only the streetlights and the eczema.

Stupid bitch.

Lesson number one: Get the money up front.

One Sick Puppy

by Lust

Dogs give great head. But I digress.

When I was twelve and living in the 'burbs, we had a small stub-nosed dog named Toby. He was irresistibly cute, a puppy pinup with as many neuroses and vices, namely an unquenchable thirst for attention and sex. He humped everything in the house: a little stuffed bunny, my dirty underpants, the loops in grandma's quilt. He repulsed me.

For one thing, dog penises are wet little aliens living inside man's best friend. They are not of this world. Either they look like a drippy corn dog or a melting creamsicle. Neither is attractive with a panting, hyper, buggy-eyed dog on the other end. To make matters worse, Toby was unscrupulous: any soft, smelly thing would do. I caught myself staring at him with a grimace on my face. Watching and grimacing and mesmerized.

At twelve, my orgasms came at mysterious times. I didn't understand what caused the body-cramping rush between my legs and made my month when it happened. I didn't connect sex and the little "o," and I never connected sex and Toby. He was masturbating, but I didn't know that yet. All I knew was that our dog was a barking hormone, and that he was getting the coveted rush every time I saw him hump something.

He knew I was weak, and he wore me down. (Thank God he wasn't feeding me pickup lines around the house.) Whenever I was sitting on the floor, he would make a heroic dive between my legs. Of course, I would shove him away in disgust and snidely congratulate my mom on her fine choice of a lecherous dog. But between you, me, and the cat post, despite his alien organ and his species, Toby sent a tingle up my spine every time.

One night, after my parents had gone to sleep, I was sitting on the floor making a bead necklace. My legs were spread to form a V with the strings and beads scattered in between. I was wearing only a T-shirt and underpants. Toby ran in to investigate, sniffing at my beads and trying to steal some string. It occurs to me that this was a ploy to make me laugh so he could make his next move. (You see this in bars every night: a couple of Long Island iced teas, a lot of laughs, the tie gets loosened, the leg goes up on her stool, a few witty whispers and bang! He's in.) It worked. I laughed as he licked my knee. But slowly and deliberately, he moved toward my panties like a bloodhound, and out of amused curiosity, I didn't fight it. He poked around and drew deep breaths as he licked the outside of my underpants. The tingle started. With the courage of late night and a heady sensation surprising my body, I pulled the panties aside. I spread my legs. He hesitated, sensing a setup, and proceeded cautiously, then with relish. If a dog can sense a human's fear, he may also have an innate smell for our arousal, because Toby buried his soft face and tongue into me with confidence, tasting my approval. He licked between my lips and gently burrowed deeper as I inched toward him and grew wet. The hotter I was, the deeper he went. When I quickly stood up to take off my underpants and make a full commitment, he was literally smacking his lips. All disgust forgotten, I fell back down and spread my legs, frozen with an o-shaped smile on my face as he enthusiastically went to work.

Fast-forward fourteen years. I live in New York City. I'm sitting with a TV-producer friend in a dark, smoky East Village bar slurping free drinks and winks from the bartender, who occasionally gives us a dollar for the jukebox. Sex and relationships, our favorite victims, were being torn apart as usual. Good head came up—no pun intended—and I slid into a drunken revelation of the best head I'd ever gotten. You know the punch line—my tireless Casanova was a foot-high dog. She screamed. Her

best head was also a dog, although taller than mine; she always got the better-looking guys. Was this some disease of the suburbs spread by Wonder bread and Milk Bones? I started to wonder if maybe all my middle-class friends harbored secret dog fantasies. The bar seemed to grow smokier, the music muddled, and the crowd closer as we leaned into the lush details of our conversation.

I decided no secret this fun, and perhaps this common, should be kept from my boyfriend. He might be disgusted, but he might pick up some pointers. Reasons why dogs give better head than men: (1) they don't care when you took your last shower; (2) they would put the Energizer Bunny out of business; and (3) they don't

Sex and the Thinking Girl

have razor stubble. One of the only drawbacks is that I don't want to be penetrated by a dog and Toby never penetrated me—but I do want to be penetrated by something. After listening to my story slack-jawed and short of breath, I don't think my boyfriend liked the fact that I cooed about Toby's technique, but he knew that the ace would always be in his hand (or mine) and he offered the best of both worlds: dog porn.

In making our selection, there were two requirements: lots of booze and an expert in the field. Destination: Times Square. The first porn shop we visited was your basic all-purpose mall of movies, with bright casino lights and neatly organized sections. "Oh, no no no, we have no animals. You see little shop there—see?" He pointed. "They have animals." With great care, he gave me detailed directions to rival the instructions my father had given me to find the SAT testing site across town. It boiled down to two streets and a murky sign. We found it. With a shit-eating grin on my face, I told the man behind the counter, "Give me dog head." With the weary look of experience, he pulled "The Russian Master Dog" and popped it in for a free preview. "Lot of dog head. I tink dis is de best." He watched, nodded approvingly, and put it in a brown bag. $39.95. The video had been dubbed from a European copy and covered its horrendous production with thunderous dog panting and scrambled instructions from the director. Although there were brief head scenes, it was mostly the dog getting head and forced penetration, enjoyed by neither the dog nor his fat human costar. Alas, The Russian Master Dog is no Toby, just a porn dog, doing it for the money. Well, maybe I'm not as perverse as I thought, but it was fun to remember my long-lost Toby and my innocent orgasm.

And that's the moral to my story: the big O doesn't have morals. If it feels good downstairs and no one gets hurt, girlfriend, fuck morals.

Fear of a Black Cat

by Hapa Wahine

One of the most valuable pieces of straight-girl-gets-boy advice I ever got was from my grandmother, God rest her soul. She said that to keep a man happy, all a woman had to do was sit on his face. Well, she prefaced it by detailing all the shopping for lingerie, bathing, and primping she'd have to do beforehand, but that stuff wasn't critical and it certainly is *not* what I remember most profoundly. "Sit on his face," she said. I will remember those words for the rest of my sexually active life.

It has only recently occurred to me, though, that the oral sex I give with pleasure is by no stretch of the imagination returned in kind and hasn't been for, well, years now. You may be asking, as I know I have, "What the hell is that about?"

The only answer I came up with is that perhaps it's because I'm not white and the men that I date are. While none of these men ever have any qualms about dating me, seducing me, getting me off, or having sex with me, a biracial woman, it would seem that going down on me is out of the question. Their mouths never seem to quite make it to my nether regions, and, if they do, it's never for more than a peck here and there. (A little advice to you boys: If you're too scared to do it, then don't even bother hinting at it. I don't need you exacerbating my case of "blue clit," and if you do, I may have to kill you.)

Sex can be an intimate act, but oral sex is intimate in a very profound and real way. You may be able to fool yourself and "play off" having sex with someone, but there's no denyin' it once you've got your face in a woman's crotch, your tongue inside her, your nose pressed against her clit, your mouth lapping up her juices (not that I can *picture* it, or anything . . .). Based on that assumption, I would venture to guess that the reason for the reluctance to perform the undeniable deed is ultimately a matter of fear; or more precisely, gross misconceptions about my anatomy.

First, there are the predominantly white media, which continue to perpetuate an ideal which is neither realistic nor helpful to me in my er . . . cause. I had access to mass-media pussy at a very young age and noticed that, according to the "men's maga-

113

zines," all pussy was created equal: all vaginas were presented as neatly trimmed, cute little pussies; all of them were generally of the same size, shape, symmetry, and perfect shade of pink. No one pussy was in any way different or more outstanding than the other, and they certainly were not so different or so outstanding as to belong to a woman of color. It's been a while since I've perused the pages of any of those mags, but I'd be willing to guess that things haven't changed much in the past twenty years. It's no wonder, then, that the men who grow up consuming those white girl, cookie-cutter pussy pictures would carry those same images with them into adulthood—and into my bedroom.

We've all heard the same tired old "big strappin' buck" stereotypes about Black men and of the "teeny-weeny pee-pee" stereotype about Asian men, but what of the false notions about Black and Asian women? Some of the ones I've heard are doozies, from Asian women having horizontal vaginal openings to Black women having an unusual amount of sweat glands so as to produce an inordinate amount of stench. And I'm expected to *live* in the face of all this? No wonder nobody's giving me head—my pussy is sideways and sweats profusely!

Aside from these ridiculous notions and the media's predilection for cute boxes, there is the matter of my own inhibitions to deal with—after all, I cannot get what I do not explicitly ask for. But, let's make sure we're all clear here: I'm afraid to ask for head, not because I don't take great pride in the beauty of my body, but because I think the potential head-giver is afraid and unwilling. My fears about his fears—the possibility of rejection—tend to keep me from openly asking for this particular pleasure. It's easier to complain about not getting it than it is to conquer the wrongness of it. Yes, my construct may be flawed, but it's difficult to challenge one's own paradigms in the throes of passion.

I would gladly concede to any men who would argue (or, better still, demonstrate) that I'm just dead wrong in my analysis here. Until then, I'll have to be the adult and open up the dialogue with my lovers. I can just hear the conversation now: "Not all women are the same . . . not all pussies are the same . . . some are light, some are dark . . . whatever the case, every one looks, smells, and tastes different . . . any questions?"

Since I'm now asking for what I want, I'll start by saying this—not just for my own cunnilingus-deprived self, but for my grandmother as well: Eat me! Trust me—we'll all be glad you did.

114

My Friends Don't Touch My Boobs

by Training Bra

"Can't we just be friends who have sex?"

How many times have you heard that before? Well I'm here to tell you that friends don't have sex. Friends are just that—friends. I guess it all depends on how you classify friendship. I always thought it was about people you have this connection with, and can trust and tell secrets to. That definition can also describe a boyfriend or a girlfriend, but there's one important element missing—passion. I'm talking about that sexual tension, that spark, that desire, that throw-up feeling in your stomach when you see them. Now correct me if I'm wrong, but isn't that what makes you like someone as more than a friend? If you are wondering why I didn't use the word "chemistry," it's because I do have a certain chemistry with my friends—that's what makes our friendships special. Now, sexual chemistry, the kind that says, "If I don't lick a line down to your navel right now, I'll explode," that's another story.

Maybe it's just me, but I have friends who, if we were both naked in front of each other, still wouldn't get turned on in the least. Then there are those people who, when I only picture them naked, make me forget my name. To me, these are the people I like as more than friends.

Regardless of how you distinguish your platonic friends from your not-so-platonic friends, once you start having sex on a very regular basis, something more than "do you wanna share my cookie" is going on. How can you be sleeping with someone for a long time and not get those feelings of friends/lovers all mixed up? I can't lie next to you night after night and consider you just a friend. Casual sex might be it for some, but not for this girlie. I don't care if my friends kiss people right in front of me, they can do whatever they want. But how can I be with you in the morning, and then watch you try to pick up someone later that night?

This is where the grrrl part comes in. I don't want this to make me bitter, but

115

I have to be for right now. I just don't get the whole male species. It's that fucking boy disease, I tell you. How do they have the nerve to say, "I still want to have sex, but I don't want you around as my girlfriend"? How annoying is that? Don't say you care for me and then degrade me like that. Go ahead and be my friend—be my best friend, if you want. But remember, my friends don't touch my boobs.

Boy-dello

by Ann Magnuson

Y2K is here and prostitution is finally legal. I'm one of the first customers at one of the first bordellos that cater exclusively to women. That is to say, a whorehouse where the whores are men and the women are the johns. It's not like those tacky old male cathouses from the past. None of those red lamps, flocked wallpaper, or fake Tiffany lamps. No, this place looks like a luxury retirement community in Palm Springs—sunny, bright, with lots of floor-to-ceiling windows that provide us with breathtaking vistas of the desert's big sky country with its emerald green golf courses and blooming cacti.

Inside, the pristine decor boasts a tasteful color scheme in pale pinks and greens while rays of bright sunlight stream biblically in through the sunroofs. The air-conditioning keeps us and the hundreds of flowering plants that fill every nook and cranny perfectly cool.

All of us are, for the most part, middle-aged; our ages range from late thirties to well into the seventies. I even think I see an octogenarian or two. At any rate, we are all very well preserved, well coifed, well groomed, freshly perfumed, and smiling.

So many smiles. The ones in the wheelchairs are the happiest. My, but it's the cheeriest, sunniest group I've ever seen, and we're all giggling as we ride the elevator to the upper level, commenting on the rosy aroma of potpourri that fills the air.

The men are in the auditorium. We can see them through the giant picture window. Their backs are to us but it doesn't matter. We can tell that they are the handsomest, sexiest men alive.

They are all young and could each earn top dollar as international male supermodels. Many have long, flowing hair. Some sport goatess. Other are clean-shaven with the latest marine-style jarhead cut. It goes without saying that they are all extremely virile and oh so cute. I want to hold and cradle each and every nude one of 'em in my arms.

They sit in plush chairs in rows facing a giant reproduction of Titian's *Bacchanal*. Each of the hunky males reads from books. The classics: Dostoevsky, Plato, Ayn Rand. One is even working his way through the entire encyclopedia. He's my favorite. I love the way his nose is buried in Volume P-Q.

The men read because they want to. At least, that's what we're told. But we know it's mostly because the management insists that each male possess the virtues of the world's greatest lovers, and since romance and poetry are an essential part of a complete erotic experience, we ladies appreciate getting our money's worth.

Besides, there's nothing worse than a dumb lay.

Waste: A Short Story

by Lisa Glatt

Skipper and I are having problems. He's dissatisfied. It's all there in Skipper's face, in his flushed, unshaven face, all the problems we are having, all his dissatisfaction. He bites his lower lip and ruffles his eyes together and doesn't even look like Skipper. We've been together for six good years with great sex two to four times a week and decent conversations, and all of a sudden over coffee and bran muffins last Sunday morning, his face changes shape; he's hard to recognize. Really. And he looks at me and blurts out that he's never been happy with me, that I've never made him completely happy. He says that I've never fully satisfied him, sexually, that is. I tell him that he's the best sex I've ever had, and besides that, there's love here. Right, I tell him, right? And Skipper looks over my head, out the window, maybe at the oak outside the window, and says nothing.

Later that same Sunday, Skipper returns from grocery shopping, and I'm standing in the kitchen pouring wine into glasses, wearing his favorite black teddy. I help him unpack the groceries and feel silly putting away milk and onions and cheese in such an outfit. Skipper sets the toilet paper on the table. I hand him the razors and soap. It's fine, he says, you look great. But his face looks weird, like he doesn't mean it.

We sit on the couch, drinking. Skipper doesn't look any more familiar and I don't feel any less silly. This was a bad idea, I say, and remind him of what he said earlier.

What can I do? What do you want me to do? I say, and as soon as the words leave my lips I regret them.

You could pee on me, Skipper says, if you loved me, you would pee on me.

Skipper thinks all our problems stem from the fact that I refuse (have always refused) to pee on him. If you did this one thing for me one time, Skipper says, you'd see that it's okay, you'd see me love it, and that would make it okay for you, better than okay. Skipper says that he's never loved anyone as much as he loves me and that he's never asked anyone else for urine. And that's why, Skipper says, he's never been peed on. It doesn't occur to Skipper that the other women he slept with, but didn't quite love, might not have peed on him either; I am the only woman in the world selfish enough to refuse him.

Debra would have peed on me, Skipper says, nostalgically.

Then why didn't you ask Debra? Why don't you call Debra right now?

Because I didn't love Debra the way I love you, he explains. I didn't trust her the same way.

Maybe you should have, I tell him.

Pee isn't such a big fucking thing to ask for, Skipper says. And he puts his wine down and walks to the den.

A couple days later I'm eating lunch at Sam's Seafood with my best friend, Claire. Claire has just finished telling me about her new lover, Lilly. Lilly, Claire says, is the most gifted woman in the world. Good, good, I say absently, and I must look upset—maybe my face, too, is changing shape under all this pressure—because now Claire won't let up. What's wrong with the two of you? she keeps saying. And I surprise myself when I blurt out, Skipper wants me to pee on him, he's always wanted me to pee on him. I tell Claire that Skipper's blowing this pee thing out of proportion, that he's blaming my refusal for his every unhappiness. Claire is trying not to laugh. She raises the napkin to her mouth and pretends to wipe something away. And the laugh is there, there in her napkin.

Is this funny? I say. Claire, what the hell's so funny? Skipper's face is all skewed up into a stranger's face, he wants my urine, and you're laughing.

I'm sorry. I'm really sorry, Claire says.

I tell Claire that I can't pee on Skipper, that I can't imagine my life without him, but I can't imagine peeing on him either. If I peed on him, I say, I wouldn't be able to look at myself, talk to my mother on the phone, or pee the same way again.

Claire puts the napkin in her lap. She leans in. Maybe there's something else wrong with the two of you, maybe Skipper's using this pee thing as an excuse to leave you, maybe it's symptomatic, she says.

He really wants the pee. He's wanted it from the beginning. You just don't know, I tell her.

The waiter pops out of nowhere and sets two bowls of creamy soup in front of us. He smiles oddly at me, like he knows, like he stood somewhere listening. Can I get you anything else? he says. Perhaps some water? I think I see a smirk. We're fine, I tell him. Did he hear us? Do you think he heard us? I ask Claire. Who? The waiter, did he hear what we were saying? Don't worry about it. It doesn't matter. But if he heard— Claire interrupts me then and says, You can't worry about what people think. You just can't worry. She picks up her spoon. I read about a man once who would only have sex with his wife if she barked like a dog. Imagine, barking like a dog—for your husband, she says. This is different, I say. Maybe, she says.

The first year Skipper and I were together, I thought he would grow out of this urine thing. I thought it was more a fantasy than something he really wanted. The

119

night he brought it up, we were in bed, my head on his stomach. I was looking at the wall, noticing the cracked, yellowish paint. If this room's going to be our room, I said, we should paint it. What do you think of one red wall? Red walls drive people insane, he said. It's been proven. What about a rose color then—a pale, pale red? Maybe, he said. And moments later, with his hand in my hair, he asked, What do you think about urine? Urine? Urine.

We were at that stage in our relationship where I wanted so badly to be loved by him, and said things, not necessarily reflecting my own feelings, but things meant to please, to entice, and to mystify him.

I've never thought much about it. What about it?

Do you think it's ugly?

Not really ugly. Necessary, I said. Urine is necessary.

Do you think it's sexual?

I'm not sure. It might be sexual.

And later, watching him sleep, watching his tough jaw, his barely open lips, I remember thinking, this man wants my urine. And I was oddly flattered—that he would want even my waste. I thought him not a freak, but an enigma. An enigma, however, I would refuse and refuse and refuse. An enigma I am still refusing.

Had he insisted that night, I might have crouched and let go, might have balanced my eager hips above his stomach or crotch and given him that. But he did not.

After lunch, Claire and I stand outside Sam's.

Is this about control? Claire says. Is this about remaining pretty?

You don't understand, I say. It's something Skipper wants that I don't want just as badly.

It'll be okay, Claire says, holding my shoulder.

He's growing a beard, I say.

I thought you hated beards, she says.

I suppose it could be worse. Skipper could ask me to kill someone. Or he could ask me to tie him up and stick pins in his feet. Or he could ask me to bark before sex, bark like a dog. Demeaning, that's what barking like a dog is. And I suppose peeing on him isn't half as ugly as him wanting to pee on me. You don't want to pee on me, do you? I asked him a year ago. And he said, I just want to be peed on. Still, I'm not about to pee on anyone, not even Skipper.

Skipper says I won't pee on him because I'm worried about society, what the world thinks, what the world would think if I peed on him. He says people are miserable, that they shoot each other on freeways, torture each other in dark rooms, judge each other for all bad reasons, and all he's asking for is a little pee. He says people think and worry too much about what others are doing in bed, and the reason, he says, is because they're so dissatisfied with their own sex lives and worse, he says, they hate their bodies and their bodies' functions.

Peeing, Skipper says, is a glorious function, and you're too fucked-up worrying about the world to enjoy it.

It's just not sexual to me, I say. It's waste, I remind him.

You've been poisoned, he says.

When I was in college I dated a bartender named William. William was six feet tall with brown, curly hair, and older—nearly thirty. His hands were smooth and tan—the fingers long and elegant. I sat at his bar one night and watched him poor drinks; I was excited by those fingers.

I was twenty and all my friends had boyfriends. I wanted a boyfriend. I wanted more than anything for William to be my boyfriend.

On a Friday night I went to William's apartment to watch movies. He'd promised me a musical and what I got was a lengthy porno film. Near the end of the film, a naked woman lay on wet grass, in the middle of a meadow maybe, and a man in an orange cape, carrying dynamite, approached her. The woman had yellow hair that fell across her cheeks. Hair like straw. And the man stood above the woman, looking down at her, at her naked body, at her straw hair. He said one word. Open, he said. He stuck the dynamite inside the woman and began to whistle. He lit the dynamite. The dynamite sizzled and crackled and the man continued whistling. I sat on the couch next to William in my short, black dress, watching him watch the woman, watching him watch the dynamite, listening with him to the sizzling and crackling. When the woman blew up, the caption read: The Big Bang. And William laughed and laughed, a big, deep laugh from the bottom of his guts. I hated him then. I felt the hate on my face. It was hot and scarlet; I thought he could see it. I tried hard to wipe the hate off my face, hoping William would like me. Would touch me. Would be my boyfriend. He started grabbing at me, at my neck and hair, at my skirt. And I was dry inside, all dry, no matter what William did with those elegant fingers. And I remember thinking: We are ugly and deserve each other; we deserve this. And I helped him with my zipper.

When I tell Skipper about William, Skipper shakes his head. This urine thing is not about violence, he says. I don't think sticking dynamite inside a woman is sexy. Don't confuse me with that bartender. There are lines I don't want to cross, I say. I am not that bartender. I know, Skipper. I don't want to hurt you or make you ugly.

The man in the movie whistled, I say, I think it was The Star-Spangled Banner.

On Friday night Skipper and I have dinner at Claire's. With Claire and Lilly. We eat bread, salad, and pasta. White sauce. Claire is glowing, there is a red ring all around her. I look at Lilly and wonder if she knows Skipper wants me to pee on him.

I watch Claire watch Lilly.

I watch Lilly watch Claire.

Skipper leans toward me. Part of love is objectification, he whispers emphatically.

I drink glass after glass of wine. Every glass is a preparation. I'm ready for a fourth. I follow Claire to the kitchen. I ask her to open another bottle. She's wonderful, I say, you've never looked rosier. Do you like Skipper's beard?

I think it looks good, she says. But you hate it, don't you?

I'm going to pee on him tonight, I tell her.

Are you sure? Is that okay for you? If not . . .

Tonight, I interrupt her, is pee night.

Is that enough?

Pee night, I repeat.

Why are you drinking so much?

Preparation. The peeing person must prepare, I say, and I laugh, all the way back to the table, I laugh.

On the way home, in the car, I am not laughing. I am looking out the window at the road, at the black trees. Skipper has one hand on the wheel and one hand on my thigh.

What if I wouldn't fuck you, what if I loved you, lived with you, did everything sexually for you, but wouldn't fuck you? Would you stay with me, would you be satisfied? he asks.

Yes, I say.

But would you miss it, the fucking part? Would you want me to fuck you?

It depends.

Would you try to talk me into fucking you?

Yes, I tell him.

We are in bed. The pillows are fat against the headboard. The sheets are white. Crisp. Skipper is naked. I wear a blue silk gown. I am kissing his neck and ears. He is touching my hair, moaning softly.

What do you think about urine? I ask him.

I lay him down on his back. I drink the glass of water I've brought into the bedroom. I drink it down, simply, easily. I set the empty water glass on the nightstand. Skipper is breathing hard now, astonished. I am crawling on top of Skipper, enjoying this. I start to lift off my gown.

No, he says, leave it on.

I pull the gown up, gather it at my waist. I crouch above his stomach, near his crotch, and let go.

As the hot urine falls from my body onto his body, down the sides of his body, on the white sheets, I am overcome with anger. I try to stop peeing, I try for the sake of us to stop, to stop this peeing, but I cannot.

And moments later, Skipper is on me, moving inside of me. The gown is wet and tight and tangled about my waist. I am looking at the empty water glass. Skipper is looking at my cheek, kissing my face—grateful. I feel his beard, his red and brown beard, his new beard. The room is pungent. My gown is pungent. Thank you, Skipper says, thank you. And as I move with him, loving him, I am leaving him. I will leave him. It's as sure as anything.

Fiona Smyth

4

Men Are from Uranus

*"Remember the man shortage? Those were the days. I was watch-
ing the Promise Keepers on TV and boy, do we have an excess!"*
—Barbara Ehrenreich, October 16, 1997

THE NOVEMBER/DECEMBER 1997 ISSUE OF MS. ASKED, DO MEN
Get It? Have all men really and truly integrated feminism into their own lives? The
conclusion: No. At least, not many. If every single "man" got it, you would not hear
about men struggling with issues of their own masculinity in the face of feminism,
Hillary would be Presidentrix, and Lord knows, those pied pipers of anti-chickdom,
Robert Bly and Warren Farrell, wouldn't have successful writing careers. With all the
talk of men's movements—the so-called earnest attempts of the Million Man Marches
to "atone," the Promise Keepers reclamation of their "rightful" role as the Head of

Household—you have to wonder, *What is going on here?* Men are still excluding women, men are still pushing women around, men are still being . . . goddamned men. Is this as good as it gets?

Anti-girl perpetrators need to and must be held accountable for their actions because in order for men to get it, they need to know what the "it" factor is. Writer Allan Johnson believes that men are oblivious of the insidiousness of the patriarchy, that the enlightened ones need to help the unenlightened ones, to inform them about the evils of "male privilege and the male-dominated, male-centered, male-identified system that underlies and enforces it." But I don't think that we can leave "it" in the hands of men; "it" still feels like women's work. If we leave it to the boys to wake up and do something about us, we'll be waiting a long, long time in our stained aprons and chipped blue nail polish. Let's face it, between role models as diverse as Charles Barkley, Bill Clinton, and RuPaul, men are bombarded with so many conflicting messages about how to behave, perhaps *getting* the she-thing is too much of a challenge.

To paraphrase Simone de Beauvoir: First we must ask, What is a man? Man is the appendage boy, the "X" Factor, and the father spirit; he is the Buddhafied Beastie Boy and the American Gigolo; he is O. J. Simpson and Jeffrey Dahmer; he is LL Cool J and Will Smith; he is Kurt Cobain and James Dean, he is Slick Willie and Rambling Roger. He is Sugar Daddy, Papa Bear, Candy Man. He is a feminist and he is a misogynist, Zeus and Beelzebub, philanderer and monogamist, saint and sinner, anima and animus. He is a walking erection, a big spender, a lover, a husband, a partner, a child—he is all of this and more, a heady package of myth and reality, of good and bad that makes this luscious fuckable gender what they are.

Confusion abounds. Even in TV land. Here's a telling exchange from *Roseanne:*

"Oh Dan, you're such a . . . a man," exclaims Roseanne.

D.J. asked, "Dad, why did Mom call you a man?"

"Because she's mad at me," Dan replies.

"I thought it was good to be a man," D.J. says.

"Oh no, son," says Dan. "Not since the late '60s."

" 'Manhood' needs to be redefined in a way that allows women equality and men pride. Our culture desperately needs new ways to teach boys to be men," Mary

Pipher writes in *Reviving Ophelia.* She also urges people to find a "model of manhood that is caring and bold, adventurous and gentle. They need ways to be men that don't involve violence, misogyny, and the objectification of women. Via the media and advertising, we are teaching our sons all the wrong lessons." And how. Just listen to anything by Guns N' Roses, or for that matter, any album with a naked lady on the cover. There's dark, handsome, pseudo-sensitive Trent Reznor earnestly confessing, "I want to fuck you like an animal," and the aggro-naughty lads of Prodigy merrily chanting, "Smack My Bitch Up." Witness other pop-cultural icons who are the generation next of antigirl: the nerdy boss and the conniving smirker of *In the Company of Men,* Beavis and Butt-head, and any contestant on MTV's *Singled Out* (another parade of thick-necked, scary behemoths sporting six-pack abdomens and baggy Bermuda shorts, who just scream, "I'm a date rape poster boy so don't take back any nights!"). Or comedian Martin Lawrence, as evidenced by his opening monologue on *Saturday Night Live:*

> "I gotta say something: Some of you are not washing you ass properly. Now, I don't know what it is that a woman got to do to keep up the hygiene on the body. I know I'm watching douche commercials on television. And I'm wondering if some of you are reading the instructions. I don't think so. 'Cause I'm getting with some of you ladies, smelling odors, going, 'Wait a minute! Girl, smell this, this is you.' . . . Put a Tic Tac in you ass!"

This is out-and-out horrible and it was broadcast on national television (granted, NBC had lil' Martin on tape delay, and never reran the original monologue in repeats). But for each of us who saw this and went OH MY FUCKING GOD, there may have been others that thought, *Gee, maybe Martin is onto something. Maybe his hatred of women, veiled in comedy, is really something to listen to. Maybe women do need to be spoken to in a way that gets a certain point across. Now where are those Tic Tacs?*

Oy. We could start our own girlie version of *Network's* battle cry, "I'm mad as hell and I'm not gonna take it anymore."

Robert Bly, the *Iron Jerk* himself, seems to think that the second sex possess magical, mystical, albeit ultimately evil powers. Bly refers to women as a "force field" which depletes the male species of its Samson-like emotional and physical strength. According to Simon Reynolds and Joy Press in *The Sex Revolts,* Bly has this theory in which "a generation of young men—soft males—have grown up confused and unhappy because women have sapped their energy and need a resurrection of male initiation rites to induct them completely into the instinctive male world." This is exactly the Neanderthalesque mentality we must eradicate from the dialogues and behavior of men.

As Ann Roiphe says, "Misogyny and the cruelty of a system that deprives women of worldly opportunity are real and worthy adversaries." See, women are ready to take these adversaries on. According to Catharine MacKinnon, approximately 85 percent of working American women will be or have been sexually harassed. In 1986, Mechelle Vinson sued her employer for alledgedly forcing her to have sex with him in order to keep her job. This case, argued in the Supreme Court, established that sexual harassment was illegal. In 1992, Anita Hill spoke out about the behavior of her former boss, Clarence Thomas, and in doing so raised public awareness about the pervasiveness of sexual harassment. These women, Goddess bless, fought back. Because if men are allowed to get away with treating women in ways that are abusive and disrespectful, we are sending all the wrong signals to boys, especially in the cases that get the media blitzkreig riled up. As a result, we get stuck with a generation of boys that cannot socialize or work with girls. And if boys can't learn how to play with girls, how will they grow up to be men that can work with women?

Unfortunately, there are plenty more examples of boys who cannot just hang with the homegirls. Swinging the pendulum all the way over to the criminally disturbed portion of the male population we find Ted Bundy, Robert Chambers, Alex Kelly, O. J., and all the other wolves strutting around in pleasant-looking sheep's clothing. Take for instance the shocking case of the brutish jocks who allegedly raped a mentally impaired girl in Glen Ridge, New Jersey. In his nonfiction account of this incident, *Our Guys,* Bernard Lefkowitz shows how these high school nimrods—the shining glory of their puny worlds simply because they were athletes—were sheltered by a community-sponsored belief that "they were put on earth to stomp anyone who was weaker than them. Girls were an easier target because they weren't as strong as them and they had been taught not to complain about how they were treated. Girls were their toys." To men of this kind, girls are disposable objects, conveniently subhuman. We're breakable, rapeable, killable. When men like these commit crimes of violence against others, punishment becomes a valuable consequence of these actions as some of *Our Guys* were (jail time, probation), and best-selling books written about them remind us that these men exist, that antigirl behavior is not a thing of the past but a threat for our futures.

Antigirl behavior can also include crimes of the heart. The quintessential bad boys, experts at the old love 'em and leave 'em philosophy, are perhaps every smart girl's Achilles' heel. According to *Bad Boys*, by Carol Leiberman and Lisa Collier Cool, many women fall into the trap of "glamorizing male characters who are dishonest, daring, defiant, or even dangerous to women." We decide that "good boys are dull . . . bad boys have the power to excite, to make things happen." A conflict of feminist doctrine, but a verification of our humanity; we are capable of making mistakes. This is why Elizabeth Shue's prostitute sticks by Nicholas Cage's loser alcoholic in *Leaving Las Vegas,* why the Shangri-Las dream about the Leader of the Pack, and why I still love the video-store boy. Although lust and sexual desire are to be cherished and relished, doing so at the risk of our emotional well-being doesn't make such men worthy of us. Being too forgiving can be dangerous. Holding men accountable for their actions may result in tire tracks in your driveway, but it guarantees that you won't get fucked over by yet another bad-for-you boy.

Men confuse sensitivity with feminism. The sensitive man is not necessarily a feminist. He is more likely someone in touch with his feelings, his yin and yang, his ability to say "ouch" when he falls down. But does that mean he understands the issues of equality between the sexes? Not automatically. If a man really wants to get down with the feminist cause, then he needs to believe in it and his actions need to validate his beliefs. He has to put his money where his mouth is; otherwise he is simply yet another guy who is still confused about how to behave, how to feel, how to communicate, and how to treat his fellow humans, with an eye on your boobs instead of an interest in your mind. And you get a recipe for disaster, girl wise.

> Some women may not need men to open mayonnaise
> jars, to bring in money, to pump gas or change tires, to carry out
> the garbage, but many of us need them, father by father, mate by

mate, as partners in the home. That is not politics. It is bottom line reality, the kind that hits you at two in the morning when in the darkness the corridors of your own home seem unfamiliar and shadows threaten. —Anne Roiphe, *Fruitful*

But all is not lost—there are some amazing progirl guys out there, boys who are smarter, better, *BUST*ier than the average Joe. Take, for example, the guys from bands like Fugazi, Girls Against Boys, and the Jon Spencer Blues Explosion. These indie rock poster boys seem more enlightened because, as Ann Powers argues, their world has been "influenced by feminism." Then there is the *BUST*iest boy ever, Sonic Youth's Thurston Moore, a classic example of a man who espouses progirl values both in his songs and in real life (you'll see when you read our interview with him in this chapter). Soooo, maybe there is hope for mankind. Think about it. We have the potential to be pairing up with the boys actually raised on feminism. Sons of women who were daughters of the revolution. Women who were sexually liberated, their feminist consciousness and their miniskirts raised. And as these daughters of '50s conservatism began to discuss their new ideas, their '70s feminist legacy was passed on to our '90s boys, who had front-row seats to their mother's ch-ch-changes. As their moms divorced and dated jerks/mensches, or stayed with their fathers and had affairs/lived happily ever after, these boys watched and took notes. Mama said treat women "right." Make friends with girls. Get with feminism. These enlightened boys are crush-worthy and, more importantly, us-worthy. It could be that you know a *BUST* boy already. Maybe he is your brother or your best male friend, the first man you fall for or the first man who loves you. Maybe he's your daddy.

For me, watching my father muddle through his adulthood taught me a lot about men and feminism. His mother, a concentration camp survivor, smuggled her three sons out of Nazi Europe to Israel via a POW stint on Cyprus, where she raised them on her own. My father understood from a very young age that women are capable of doing anything. He called Grandma a feminist. And when he married, he encouraged my mother to do her "thing." By day, he was a New York City taxi driver; by night, he was a mentor, a disciplinarian, and a fixer-upper. He tried to teach me how to cook, he explained why Gloria Steinem and Betty Friedan were important women, and he turned me onto eight-tracks (Patti Smith and Bruce Springsteen). My father did not encourage me to stop my education after high school and find a husband like all the other Jewish girls in my class were planning on doing. He insisted I graduate college and pursue a career of my own—he recognized the importance of a woman's financial independence. He wanted me to have the chance to raise my own family but without compromising my ambition. My father was not a perfect person or a great husband; I was always aware of his quirks and faults but overall, he was a good man and an amazing papa. My father empowered my feminism.

When I think of my ideal guy (because there is no such thing as a perfect man), I think of what my father taught me: When boys are bad, they need to be punished and I don't mean punishment dominatrix style, but rather taken to task for wrongdoing. If a man hits you, report him. If a man is emotionally abusive to you, leave him. If a man lies to you, deal with him. If a man behaves in vile sexified Peter Pan ways that reek of Boy Disease (a term coined by one of the original *Sassy* gals, Christina Kelly), the "come here, go away" thing, the old "loved for ten minutes, shunned for a lifetime" way, call him on it. Because if girls still continue to feel hurt, angry, confused, bitter, and betrayed about the way they're being treated, then boys will still be getting away with their proverbial IT. And that has to end. As we struggle with the everyday disappointment of Boy Disease and celebrate the thrill of Girl-Boy Love, it's our duty to challenge boys to be better human beings, to engage them in an intimacy that extends beyond the physical, into the personal, and the political. Mary Pipher points out that "there is something eerie about teaching our daughters how to fight off rapists and kidnappers. We need classes that teach men not to rape and hurt women. We need workshops that teach men what some of them don't learn: how to be gentle and loving." This isn't brain surgery, this isn't Lacanian philosophy, this is not a battle of the sexes resurrected from the '70s; it's simply an urgent call to action for all of us to condemn unacceptable antigirl behavior. It's your basic honesty-respect-consideration equation, elements of a Girlie Principle that is second nature to the second sex but not yet a priority for the other sex. Boys need to get "it," and get it quick. Because in this new girl order there is only one kind of boy we want, and he is a *BUST* boy.

— *Marcelle Karp*

Fear of a Boy Planet

by Celina Hex

This morning I must have seen at least forty or fifty men. I mean, I know I must have passed them while I was in the park walking my dog, on the way to the subway, in the croissant shop, on the street, in the elevator. But I'm not really sure. Because, even though they must have been there, I didn't really see them. I do remember this one older man on the subway. I remember him because the train was very crowded. We were straphanging beside each other when a seat became available in front of us. I felt like sitting, but he was about seventy years old and tired-looking, and I thought I'd let him sit down. He didn't, though. That seat stayed empty for a whole stop until some girl, younger than I, sat down. I remember the man because I felt a little angry at him—why the hell didn't he sit down, anyway? I just don't understand them.

I definitely remember seeing women today, though. There was the stressed-out-looking one trying to squeeze her way onto the S train, the younger one who didn't even try and resigned herself to waiting for the next train, the girl with the great curly hair who was walking on the street in front of me, the woman I always see at the croissant shop who has pencil-thin plucked eyebrows and who always looks stoned, there were the three F.I.T. students with their book bags and homemade clothes, there was the girl carrying the book that looked interesting (but I don't remember what it was anymore). I always feel an immediate connection with women, an identification, a secret shared feeling that we are from the same planet, and in our momentary eye contact there is a recognition that suggests that we understand we are part of the same underclass, the same underground army.

But the boys and men I saw today all passed before my eyes as part of a large blur, a grayish-bluish blur of tallness and movement and largeness and stubble, a blur of black shoes and pants and jackets and short dark hair punctuated only occasion-

132

ally by a pair of glasses or a hat. The men seem to be interchangeable, like extras in the movie that is my life—the same guy who played the guy on the subway platform later reappears as the guy driving the cab or the guy crossing the street beside me on the way home.

I do remember, however, one guy I saw today. He was a tall boy with a blond ponytail who was coming out of a grocery store. I saw him immediately, I saw him in slow motion, pan to close-up of his face, I saw that his Technicolor blue eyes were looking at mine and for a second I could almost smell the scent of his hair and I wondered where he was going and it seemed that to smile at him or follow him could possibly change the entire direction of my life, but I kept walking and I didn't turn back to see if he was turning to look at me still. I kept walking and I figured he was probably on his way to visit his girlfriend, anyway.

In my life men seem to be perpetually relegated to the status of "them" in the cosmic "them" and "us." It's as though my senses, through evolution, have been finely tuned to only seeing a few out of the masses of them, the same way my cat automatically, almost despite himself, chases after objects that are of a particular shape and speed. There are only a few who break through the hazy field of "them," and to me those few are like a drug, like incense, they seem to be more than mortal, they are pure and enormous and powerful and, most seductive of all, they don't seem to need women. Those are the few (the brave, the proud) who do not belong to either the world of "them" or of "us."

I'm thirty years old and I've been doing this mating dance for almost half of my life and you'd think that men would start to make more sense to me, that they'd begin to seem less like aliens, but instead, the opposite has happened. I am more confused by them now than I ever have been. They walk among us, but they are not like us. It's little wonder that with this kind of attitude it's hard for me to get dates.

But I don't know what else to do. When I was younger, boys held out the promise of so much love and fulfillment and excitement and adventure, but then my heart got broken, and it got broken again, and after I cried and felt like a zombie for a week or a month or a year I got optimistic again and got all into some guy and then got my heart broken again. And now I have this thirst for a boyfriend, for a man in my bed, for a man to overwhelm me, overcome me, or just come over. But I know it means that the crying is going to have to come again and the fear and the stifling

133

feeling of losing myself and of feeling like a fool for loving the alien. I'm thirty and I'm just exhausted by it. I don't think humans were ever meant to be kept in a holding pattern of adolescent angst for this long—and after a while something happens to us, something changes, something just gives up.

And like a riot grrl or a girl who got her favorite toy taken away I want to put on combat boots and have a screaming, thrashing temper tantrum about all of this disappointment and all of this anger and sadness. I want to lash out against something, but there is nothing to really hit against, my fury is muffled by a soft, cushiony "acceptance," an attempt to grow older gracefully, without malice or hatred, because there are so many of them I'm angry with that just to start thinking of it makes me exhausted. But mostly my fury is tempered by my fear, which seems to have made a more comfortable and permanent place for itself inside of me over the years.

I'm pissed off because this was all supposed to be so much fun. Being single and frolicking on the beach and drinking Sunkist or having quick dark sex and walking home at dawn with your hair smelling of a stranger's semen, not having to worry about being "tied down" by a husband or a kid, free to pursue our "careers," an ultimate fulfillment, boys would be there, romance would be there, it was all a given. After all, single people have more freedom and more sex and more romance, right?

Well, maybe boys do. All I know is that my girlfriends and I gather together on an regular basis to mourn or laugh over the latest romantic fiasco or lack of one, while we get older, our biological clocks ticking, worrying about how we're ever going to get the boy thing right in time to have a baby. And we're getting more pessimistic by the day. Suddenly we see our futures as a mysterious black hole, because we may not end up being part of a family portrait like we'd always expected, and may instead be hanging out and dating and eating Doritos and worrying about our rent until we're ninety.

134

But if that's how it's gonna be, then I want to start planning for it now. Because I don't want to live out the rest of my life trying to stifle a tantrum. And I want help in the planning—because there are a lot of us who are trying to figure this out. The loneliest thing about this is feeling like I'm the only one to be going through it, that all the rest of us *did* end up with the lives we were raised to believe we'd have, that there's something wrong with me for not being there. But I know that many of us who did get married got divorced a few years later, and that some of us who are having babies now no longer feel they can easily fit themselves into a family portrait either. It's clear that the lives we thought we'd have aren't even a possibility anymore. We are the strong, independent, smart, thinking, laughing females who like to be called "women" but think of ourselves as girls, living in apartments that we call our "rooms," loving and losing and beginning to give up our girlhood idea that we'll ever really feel like "grown-ups," that we'll always consider ourselves "girl-friends" even if we become wives, that we may even feel like children even if we ever become mothers, and that we'll always need to have our friends around to go out and play with.

Girlfriend, Listen Up

by Cassandra O'Keefe

Girlfriend, listen up: When a man says, "I'm no good at relationships. I have been alone for so long, perhaps I was meant to always be alone!" or "You'll probably come to hate me, deep down I'm a real asshole," take him at his word and run like the wind! Yes, it may be a cry for help from the depths of a lonely soul, and it never fails to awaken the nurturing I-have-enough-love-for-both-of-us nature, but SO WHAT?! Don't be a fool, you've fallen into this pit before, we all have. What woman can resist the "I walk alone. No woman can defrost the iceberg that once was my heart" bit? Well, maybe Camille Paglia, but who the hell looks to her for guidance? Nope, when your heart starts aching listening to the woes of an unloved boy, cry if you must, hold his hand, whisper that you love him. (A little-known secret: this is a prime situation for the most fabulous sex.) You want to show him that he can be loved, he wants to show you that he is capable of receiving love. So dive right on in, but then . . . GET THE HELL OUT! RUN AWAY! SAVE YOURSELF!

Your instinct will be to save this wretched creature, your own survival won't enter into your usually trustworthy intellect. Come on! You want to save something? Think big. Save the whales, save the rain forest, there's plenty of work out there for a compassionate heart. Why waste it?

Look, I love men. I really do. Nothing makes me more weak than a beautiful boy. That's my problem. I want to be in love, but sheesh, I don't want to work that hard at it. I'm not blaming them—the '80s brought forth the sensitive male. Suddenly it was okay for them to share their innermost thoughts, their deepest pain, their (yeeccchhh!) feelings. I have as many male friends as female, and both always ask the same question; "If women are looking for a nice guy, sensitive, caring, loving, etc., then why do they always go for the jerks?" I'll tell you why—because the man who will forget your birthday, storm out when you cry, and basically treat you like dirt is letting you know, straight up, that he is a pig. No mystery, no surprises, no "You have given me a great gift. You have taught me how to love. This is a gift that I finally feel confident to share . . . with someone else. Happy birthday." I have a suspicion that this whole "I had a bad childhood, I am not worthy of love" routine is really an insurance policy against relationships. When the going gets tough, he can check out with his integrity intact simply by stating, "I was completely honest with you from day one. I said you would hate me, and you do. I said I was an asshole, and I am. I gave you fair warning, and you fell in love with me anyway, stupid. This is all your fault. Happy birthday."

Still not convinced? Still whining about how much he needs you? Yes, they are vulnerable and misunderstood, all they need is a little tenderness. The same could be said for mass murderers. How would you like to be a guest on the next *Oprah* entitled "Women Who Love Serial Killers"? Imagine yourself squirming in your seat while a caller from Tuscaloosa, Alabama, berates you for not seeing through your man's charade of not being good enough for you. Or how about "Women Who Fall for Forest Animals" on the next (insert the name of the most debasing talk show you can think of here)? You'd die of embarrassment when your mom called in weeping about how it was all her fault for taking you to see *Bambi* when you were four years old. It's not completely inconceivable. Deer are cute, they look fragile, and terrified of life. But I wouldn't get involved with one, for crying out loud.

My point is you just can't win, but that's no reason not to play. When you connect with the unloved—and you will, we are drawn to them like moths to head-lights—take it for all it's worth. Listen to their songs of woe, cry your eyes out over their crummy childhoods, take it all in like a good book or fascinating film. They are sincere in their sadness, and their hunger for love creates the kind of kissing that sends your knees on a coffee break. Did I mention that the sex goes beyond swell? Trust me, it kills ya. It is romance in all its bittersweet glory, and that you should not deny yourself. But when you find yourself falling hopelessly in love . . . GET LOST! RUN!! Start looking for the swine of your dreams. They're not hard to spot. Go to a sports bar, drop your purse, and as you bend to retrieve it, if you hear, "Hey honey, while you're down there, heh, heh, heh," this is your mating call. No, he probably won't remember your birthday, but he won't be whining about his needs while you're out saving baby seals either.

The Curse of the Mama's Boy

by Betty Boob

I was in my girliehood prime when I first became acquainted with the dreaded Oedipus complex. My grandmother's blatant dislike for my mother coupled with Grandma's viselike emotional grip on my dad made for many, many problems for everyone in our immediate family. Grandma frequently denounced my mother, which resulted in subsequent acts of verbal abuse from Dad to Mom. I knew something sinister and suffocating was happening, something inherently unhealthy between the three of them, which affected the rest of us. My mother's only ally was my aunt Rivka (she was married to my father's brother Moish), whom Grandma didn't like either. However, my aunt Rivka didn't take Grandma's nonsense: early in their marriage, Uncle Moish had made his decision to stand by his wife; my father never did.

I did not want to end up in a situation like this when I grew up and fell in love.

Fast-forward to the Great Love of my life, "D." When we began living together, "D." had been estranged from his mother, *Mother,* for ages. A year into our relationship, while "D." was on a business trip to where *Mother* lived, they kissed and made up. That didn't bother me. I thought it was unhealthy not to have a connection to one's parents. But something began to gnaw at me, an emerging familiar pattern I noticed in their correspondence and frequent long-distance phone calls: *Mother*'s similar Grandma-like hold on "D." When *Mother* decided she wanted to come to meet the woman who was "stealing her 'D.'" (yes, she did say that), my guard was obviously up. And not because she was planning on staying in our one-bedroom apartment for three weeks over Christmas, but because I could see that *Mother*'s presence had turned into something sinister and suffocating; when later she denounced me, he believed her. *Just like my father.*

Three months after she returned home, not easily, mind you, I left him.

It was then that he realized he had believed in the wrong woman. By the time I declared I was no longer in love with him, he was prepared to renounce all ties to his mother, which, had he done that before, at the time while she was calling me names, would have meant something. But this was now, and now I was feeling hurt and betrayed. By now I had passed a threshold of pain. By now, my girliehood ghosts were screaming at me, "I told you so, didn't I?"

It still hurts even now to think about it all.

Now that I'm a little more relationship weary (wary), I still think you can't *really* tell you are going to have problems with his mom when you first begin going out. People are always so polite at first; it's not until you put a hand suggestively on his knee in her presence that a potential problem may arise for her and then maybe for you. She may make a suggestive derogatory comment in passing to him about you, or she may open her arms and invite you to call her Mom too. It can always go either way. His response, his reverence, his respect for his mom may cloud his perception of you no matter which way she goes. And since I know that not even a pair of Calvin's could come between a boy and his mom, concerns about the kind of woman my boyfriend's mother is come up, as do questions like *Who raised this guy?*, *Does she know how to let go?* and *How much work am I gonna have to do?*

So here are some of my own guidelines:

- The depth of Mommy love is potentially unfathomable, so make your diagnosis prudently and as objectively as you can. If it is at unhealthy proportions he could:

  a. be Norman Bates incarnate;

  b. hate his mother and therefore treat you like a moldy doormat;

  c. love his mother so obsessively, he consistently screams "Mommy" when inside you (ewwww);

  d. oh, just draw your own nightmarish conclusion and break up with him ASAP.

- When hooking up with the man who has lost his mother or is an orphan, beware of the Fantasy Mother Who Could Do No Wrong button.

- What if you're at his mom's place and there he is sitting on his butt as Mama caters to his every beck and call? It's rather disillusioning, actually. You may develop a horrible lack of respect for him thereafter and may need to dump him.

- Ah, and those out-of-town moms! Sometimes those absentee moms have Real Meaningful Input in their sons' lives. But sometimes they forget that their baby boy has grown up. And the son? Well, if he forgets that you exist and doesn't make time for you when Mama visits, then honeygirl, light up a cigarette and fill up your social calendar with a new Mr. Right Now. This boy doesn't deserve you. If he is the stand-up guy you have fallen for, he'll make it clear that there are two very special women who exist in his world. Now this is a boy who knows where he'll be resting his head to sleep—next to *yours*.

- A strong boy will know to put you first, *always*. A normal boy will be conflicted. And a boy who is a wimp will always be held emotionally hostage. Stay away from door number three.

My Dream Mom is the one who knows the difference between motherly love and romantic love. This mom, who did such a good job at raising him, lends

139

herself to the best kind of mother-you relationship—one with the understanding that you can both love her son without wanting to (still) control him. You may not ever be best friends, you may get annoyed at their little in-jokes, but if she gets the controlling thing, you have a pretty good chance at a healthy, happy relationship with her.

I don't really have THE solution to the Mommy Problem, other than being aware that boys' feelings about their moms are complicated. Feeling jealous as their knowing looks cut a hole in your heart or fretting about her approval can be stressful but it's important to remember that in order to make your relationship with him work, there has to be room for her too in your lives. And while *you* know that it's *You First Always* (repeat the mantra, girls, and be proud), moms don't. After all, Mom *did* come first.

The last thing you ever want is to feel resentful toward his mom. Because when you're not looking, the words "mama's boy" will slip out of your lips, which will result in flaccid-penis action, and really, no one wants that.

Both Sides, Now

by Talin Shahinian

Men: alien species, genetic mutations, animal, vegetable, mineral? The more I think about it, the less I seem to know. It's like a vast research project that I'll never finish. My brain teems with all the conflicting data: my father, my older brother, crush-worthy friends of the family, the born-again Christian pastor I grew up hearing every Sunday, my supposed first boyfriend—the nasty, moody son of a Baptist minister—art fags, college buddies, men I hung out with in the goth/punk/new wave clubs

I inhabited in the late '80s, the men I know in similar scenes now, and all my male friends, foes, loves, and acquaintances, past and present.

I was talking about men with a gay male friend of mine recently (he said he was having just as much trouble figuring them out as I, and he's a man, which made me feel a bit better) who said he thought people are most attracted to the gender they have the hardest time understanding and getting along with. Then he said, "But how does that explain bisexuals?" and we both had to laugh, because I am well known as one who "colors outside the lines." His hypothesis made sense to me, though. I seem to have much unfinished business with men, and a need to figure them out, which may explain why I find myself more interested in men than women recently. My nature is terribly inquisitive; I just have to know and understand everything, and men perplex me far more than women. My friend also told me an amusing quote he heard from a friend of a friend. This woman said, "Men are like Rubik's cubes, boring and frustrating, but you fuck with them anyway." We laughed. Most of the time I don't find them boring, sometimes very frustrating, but I fuck with them because I enjoy it.

Sartre said that when we make assumptions about a whole group of people, when we say we know them, understand them, it is at that moment we stop truly perceiving them. There was a time in my life when I let that happen. For a time I ceased to perceive men. Well, I was sick of men, I had endured enough damage and heartbreak at their hands, so when I fell in love with a woman, I used it as my ticket out of testosterone-land.

I swam to the isle of Sappho and set up camp. As for men, I fell back on facile conclusions and false divisions. I had checked out of boy-town. It was easier. I took a class in feminist theory taught by a philosophy grad student who was a radical lesbian separatist. Though I was against separatism, and she and I argued points a lot, I did find myself influenced by the class and her. We read Mary Daly, Andrea Dworkin, and Catharine MacKinnon. I became antiporn, and against S/M, though I was strangely fascinated by both. (The fascination with intelligent and interesting smut has lingered, by the way, long after my Daly and Dworkin books have become coated in thick layers of dust.)

My female lover and the lesbian, gay, and supposedly bisexual alliance on campus wanted me to be a lesbian, because it made them more comfortable. Being bi-sexual was a misunderstood and controversial identity. I was under massive pressure to conform to the "alternate" standards of the queer community, and to make my insecure lover happy. I finally gave in and dubbed myself a lesbian. I rationalized to myself, that after all, these were my friends, I loved my girlfriend, and if we stayed together I wouldn't ever be dating men again anyway. Part of me believed this, and another part of me thought I was full of shit (especially when I caught myself day-dreaming in class, imagining certain male professors sans vital articles of clothing). All the paradigms had suddenly shifted, transforming men into the grand taboo, which multiplied their attractiveness immediately. Straight white men were the enemy, so no wonder I dreamed about them at night. Ever the rebellious iconoclast, I balked at the thought that one gender was verboten, even in my fantasies. So I regularly gave my girlfriend heartburn by digging men who had nice chests in the movies we'd watch on our VCR.

Strangely enough, even though I had some contact with some straight white men, I bought into their demonization quite a bit. I either viewed them as evil incar-nate or I assumed total superiority in a fit of lesbian feminist chauvinism. Of course women were superior to men, of course lesbians were superior to everybody. I look back on my attitudes with incredulous horror; could I have ever engaged in such simplistic thought? Unfortunately, yes.

I now strive to view people as individuals, regardless of gender. Everyone is a mixed bag. Some men are evil and so are some women. People of both genders can be assholes and do rotten stuff. Believe me, I learned the hard way that being with a woman does not ensure a kinder, gentler relationship, or some kind of sisterly parting if you break up. When my girlfriend and I broke up, I had the opportunity to learn more about female evil than I ever wanted to know.

142

When I saw how truly heinous women could be, I realized I had nothing to lose in giving men another try. They couldn't be any worse, could they? So I emerged from my Sapphic enclave and embarked on a rigorous research project. My subject: the other half of the species. Like a mad scientist, I'd get these rare flashes of brilliance, and feel so clever as I unearthed some likely hypothesis to explain them. It was at these moments that I became convinced I had them pegged: I knew what made them tick, I knew all the buttons to push, I knew how to turn them on and off, manipulate their interest, control them with the deftness of a seasoned dominatrix. I felt so smug and self-satisfied as I'd flex my bitch-goddess muscles. I was just starting to sing "I know what boys like" at just about the moment I fell on my ass, knocked off my femme top pedestal by some maddeningly unpredictable behavior on the part of some man. Damn! Then I'd have to start all over again, feeling like some pathetic little slave girl who'd crawl on my hands and knees to worship at the secret shrine of black leather jackets, black jeans, combat boots, and sweat.

Their remoteness and ability to keep emotional distance confounds and fascinates me. I covet the cool, the edge, the detachment, and the icy silence that some men seem to possess, while I feel like an open book, some kind of transparency, with my heart on my sleeve. Which brings me to the subject of "Mr. Alternative" and "Mr. Sensitive"—often interchangeable types, or two components of the same man. These identities are largely created out of male vanity. These men want to believe that they are more enlightened and evolved than other men. They are often worse, because they have all these lofty ideals, which they'll almost always undoubtedly betray. Furthermore, their self-delusion is often so complete, that for a while you might actually believe that they are "different," and by the time you figure out you're dealing with a big ole wanker, you've been royally fucked over. Not only will you have a broken heart, but you'll have wasted valuable time listening to his endless self-congratulatory speeches about how fucking enlightened he is. Because behind every "Mr. Alternative" and "Mr. Sensitive" I've found men who still buy into the virgin/ whore complex, or some other ludicrous myth about women, or who start foaming at the mouth when they find out I'm bisexual, or are just too fucking cool for words 'cause they're like "alterna-dudes," bohemian slackers, or some other equally gag-worthy thing.

The person who really saved my life during the postbreakup period with "The Beast" (what a friend had dubbed my ex-girlfriend) was a longtime friend who just happened to be male. I'd known him so long and we had been through so much together that I didn't even think of him in gendered terms that much anymore; to me he was simply Jonathan. As time went on, though, we'd be talking on the phone, and I'd realize that I was hearing his voice, but had no idea what he was saying. Instead I was listening and imagining him taking off my dress. We became a couple. And during the last four years of our tempestuous relationship, he has taught me plenty about

143

men. For instance, when I told him I was writing this article, he said: "I better not be in the sucky boyfriend category; at least say something nice about me." I assured him that I would, so, for the record: Jonathan is a great lover, has really nice thick, dark, curly hair, is highly intelligent, creative, supportive, cute, and thoughtful (and he's gonna owe me for the next coupla months or so . . .).

Anyway, I'll be continuing my, ahem, experiments. I'll probably never totally understand men, but I plan to have some fun gathering my research.

Watching Him Fuck Her

by Girlbomb

I knew the minute it started. We were at that bar, the No-Tell Motel, and he did his trick with the coin. He can flip a coin through his fingers, over the tops of his knuckles, smooth. I suppose I once found this novel. They were sitting just too close on the sofa, trading hot shoulder, and I was smoldering deeper into my vinyl stool, getting sticky and drunk. It was Friday night. Fuck Night. 2:30 A.M. I saw him slide the quarter slyly from his pocket. "Plato was a fascist," he told her, shooting his cuffs. "He thought he could dictate reality." I watched the coin flash and turn, admired his technique. She looked lamblike up at him, nodded yes. And so she was his for the having.

"Katz wants to have sex with you," I told her. We're candid like that. "What, are you kidding?" Her tinny, cordless voice pitched a little high at the end. So she already knew. "No way. You think?" Of course she knew. Claudia's a seasoned professional. You don't have to tickle her palm for her to get the point. That's why we hang out. We're both women in the know. "Don't do it," I warned her. "For your own good." "Ucch, I would never," she said. Like I don't know. Like I don't know her, like

144

she's not practically my evil twin. Like her motives are a mystery to me. I've been there, I know. Women. You always want to think you're the one who's different. But then, you're just the one who's next.

I met Katz through this chick Irma I used to work with. Irma was cute, and she had her own little thing going on, but she was vapid, and Katz was bored of her. He likes to flirt, he gives great banter, and he says a lot of witty offhand things—insults usually, but so you laugh, so you like it, if you can keep up. What he mostly does is, he pays a lot of attention. He tilts his head while you talk. He nicknames you, casually. He says precise, perceptive things to you about art and philosophy. You start to peruse him while in the bath. I ran into him in the street, on Broadway, alone. He looked me up and down and smiled as we parlayed. "So how's Irma?" I asked him. He rolled his eyes. "Who even knows." We smirked at Irma. "You should call me sometime," I told him. "We'll do a movie." "I'll do that," he said. "I think I will." The rest was automatic.

"Is Katz coming out tonight?" she wanted to know. "I don't know," I said slowly. Things must be thickening, I thought. Claudia's usually more discreet. "Did he call you?" "Why would he call me?" she squealed. She's got to get that voice thing under control. "He doesn't even have my number."

Katz and I were over, but he was still around, in that indistinct, uncommitted ex-boyfriend way of his. Or not really ex-boyfriend, Claudia reminds me, as we never officially went out. "Really, you guys were just seeing each other," she said. "For, like, three months, Claudia." "It was almost a year ago, though, wasn't it." Her fake offhand-musing voice. Casual. "I mean, aren't you guys just friends?" Like she doesn't know. Certain men are just taboo. "Well you know, as far as I'm concerned," she told me, "he's my dead dickless brother." And I thought, yah, whatever.

"It isn't you," he had said. "Apparently it isn't," I said right back. "Apparently, it isn't me." He dumped me in a restaurant, which I hate, because you can't make any kind of scene, and if you even cry the waitress knows and smirks all about it. "Why are you making this such a big deal?" Katz had resorted to whining. I was smoking up a small storm. He showed me his empty palms, nothing to give or to hide. "I just think we shouldn't put pressures on us if we're going to stay friends." The bile shifted in my gut and I put down my fork. "It will be hard for us to stay friends," I told him, "once I dismember you with a saw." But what are you going to do? You can't argue your way out of dumped. And there were already other girls. "Look," he said, final. "I'm just not looking for that kind of relationship." What a tired, tired line. He wasn't even trying. "Oh, blow yourself," I told him, got up, and walked out.

We were at the bar, getting woozy and snide. Katz hadn't shown up, and I could feel the dead wait for him between us, heavy like a lead purse. "I'm bored," said Claudia, making overlapping wet rings with her glass on the bar. "It's slow tonight," I said. She kept peeping over my head at the door, a spastic periscope. "Ucch," she told me, withering back down. "I don't feel like competing with any of these women for any of these men." I surveyed again the women in the crowd and instantly, exhaustedly, hated them all. I don't know if I ever noticed before how much I am capable of hating women. Especially when I drink. Especially women who look like me. This one chick by the back wall had my same shoes. I hated her. I knew why she was wearing those shoes, she was wearing those shoes to be stylish and cute and get fucked by a man. Contemptible. Like I don't know. Girl, please. I've spent 20 full minutes applying the no-makeup look. "Ucch." Claudia leaned in over me, hissing. "What does she, shellac her hair?" We tend to hate the same women, that's why we're friends.

He insists that I broke up with him. "Not that we were ever officially going out, or anything." I say it before he can. Katz's story is, I was sick of him not acting the way I wanted him to—which is true—so I dumped him in a restaurant—which is a psychotic revision of history. "I still thought we should see each other," he tells me, which means: He though he should still be able to come by my house and have sex with me, or call me up late when he was feeling neurotic, yet simultaneously remain free to nakedly scope other women, even while sitting across the table from me at brunch, without me pitching a fit. A likely story. The long, drawn-out, likely story of my life. Months later, I still wanted to take him home from bars. Except I knew he wouldn't go. "You know, I ran into Claudia on the street the other day," he mentioned, you know, incidentally. "Really." "Yeah." Dot dot dot. "How is she?" "You tell me," I said calmly. "You saw her." "Yeah. Hmmm." I was quiet, waiting, eyes closed over the phone. A year later, and he was still number one on my autodial. "So, you think you guys will be at No-Tell tonight?" "Who even knows," I told him, tired. There's just no telling, with men.

"Life is so existential," said Claudia. She was in high shine. Katz leaned over her, his arm against the wall. They both had the smirk on, I noticed. It seems I noticed everything very much that night. I was in a hyperaware state of drunk, stuck to my seat, struck dumb with déjà vu and blinding strobe. "We're going to go get coffee at Veselka," she came over to tell me. He was putting on his coat. I could invite myself, but why. I already knew. Claudia and I are the same kind, we want the same things. But there's only so many of them, and there's so many of us. You do what you have to. "Is that okay?" she asked me. I watched Katz light a cigarette and face the back wall, waiting for Claudia, waiting for me. "Hello," said Claudia. "All right?" And I just kept watching, and I didn't say anything, because Katz had just spotted the look-alike girl in the shoes. And for one bright lucid moment I knew, if we all just stood there long enough, he could skip right over Claudia, and spare us. "We're going," she said. Oh what the hell, I thought. Why not let her suffer him. I was there once, soon enough she'd be here. I saw the coin turning in Katz's hand. He would fuck her, and fuck her over. I knew how it was. I felt him watching us, women. Let him have her then. "Don't do anything I wouldn't do," I told her, and kissed the whole thing good-bye. Like I didn't already know.

Manthing

by Tammy Whynot

You come home early in this white-hot July day with a migraine. You were wearing your bright yellow hand-painted shamaness dress, but it failed to cheer or cure you. Now you're lying on your bed, merciless sun pouring in and the fan whirring and oscillating, catching the light with each left turn and throwing it back in your eye—not a happy thing for a migraine sufferer.

You're hoping that, having OD'd on painkillers, you'll be in some sort of acceptable shape for dinner this evening. You guess it's a date. It's with a guy. If only you could just drift off for even half an hour, you'd be all set. Unfortunately, this is a new apartment and the new and obnoxious sounds won't permit a healing catnap. There's the five-year-old who lives upstairs who never walks, but runs and jumps his way around the apartment, and then there's the landlord and his family downstairs and they're all running in and out of the screen door, which, from your current location and perspective, sounds like a small explosion every time it slams behind one of them.

The phone rings and you know it's a manthing. It's your "date" calling to finalize plans. Where's that fucking phone? Everything's out of place from the move and the desktop phone is plugged in awkwardly to a wall-mount jack. You try to raise your voice a few octaves so that you won't sound too pathetically ill and confirm sushi at seven. He's so glad that you like sushi since it's his absolute fave and he just seems to go on and on about it. You find a polite way out of the conversation and mention the migraine so that you'll perhaps have a safety valve later if need be.

Exhaustion from pain finally puts you out for a short while, and upon awakening you look and feel like you've been dragged through a knothole, but your throbbing brain is taking a time-out. You apply approximately six inches of makeup to mask the dullness your complexion has taken on from all the discomfort and drugs. You find the effect to be rather corpselike but it'll have to do since this is as good as it gets tonight.

Manthing arrives and is somewhat accusatory and punitive about your situation, rather than sympathetic like a good and interested "date" should be. He drops some subtle criticism of your use of painkillers, stating for you that you feel worse having taken them than you would had you recovered from the migraine without such manipulation. At this point, you don't need to ask to know that he has never experienced a migraine. Of course, nothing matters at all at this point since your malaise has apparently ruined his evening and his attitude has ruined yours.

At the restaurant, he tries to impress the living hell out of you with his incredible sushi knowledge. He's from a landlocked state in the Southwest, where, you're certain, sushi is a real traditional dish. He harasses the Italian-American waiter by ordering the various fillets by their Japanese names and getting them wrong. He special

148

orders a "yummy roll," telling the waiter to see if the chef knows what it is, and sends him off with "That's all for now but there will be continuous ordering of food."

When the harried waiter returns to ask how the yummy roll is made, manthing feigns an insulted rage. "What! Isn't your sushi chef any good? Isn't he Japanese?" You sink in your chair. Your headache is coming back with a vengeance as you listen to manthing stumble over his list of ingredients. He doesn't even seem to know what the fuck is in it, and makes up some sort of version of a California roll, which isn't even traditionally Japanese. You have a fleeting thought that this might be a good time to call him a stupid bastard to his face, but you don't have the energy. Also, as you do not have the energy to go on listening to his endless and uninteresting monologue, which he, no doubt, is mistaking for scintillating conversation, you excuse yourself to go to the bathroom. On the way you make eye contact with our waiter and put on your best save-me-from-this-nightmare-hell-date face.

Now would be a good time to rinse your face with cold water, but that would mess up your funeral good looks. So you sit down on the oriental-style chair under pink track lights and rest your head against the wall. Eyes closed, you take in and release the deepest breaths you can muster before returning to the scene of the crime, which this date has become.

During dinner your position in your chair gets lower and lower. Manthing's pseudoholistic psychobabble puts you in mind of other men whose method of charming their way into your pants was through pretentiously "alternative" channels. Your favorite example was the manthing in college who practically begged you to sleep with him and, when you wouldn't, told you that you weren't a "spiritual seeker of Truth." You told him you were unimpressed with his couching his erections in terms of the East. Then there was the manthing in his second year of recovery who, despite his Twelve Step rantings, obviously missed his drugs a real whole lot. He seduced you; then, no doubt feeling super "empowered," left as quickly as possible. There was the actor, the wanderer, the would-be rock star, the feminist, etc., etc. Mostly these affairs had nothing to do with you, and they certainly had nothing to do with either party's higher life goals. The fact is, regardless of the content of the dialogue, the dynamic is always the same: low self-esteem manthing needs to exert control, finds a vulnerable woman fully socialized to be a second-class citizen (you), takes a

149

nosedive toward the Achilles' heel and attempts possession of the entire organism. And he's probably not even good at cunnilingus.

You're brought back to the present as manthing hails the waiter and orders another $30 worth of food. Great, another half hour of this shit. This date was over in the car on the way to the restaurant and there's still no end in sight. You wish you were more conniving and could use his need to spend a lot of money to your advantage. Better to let it pass so as not to have him think you're encouraging him in any way. At this point manthing's punitive side reemerges and it's as though he's trying to pull you by the hair out of your ailing state. Mr. groovy manthing is all pissed off because, chances are, with you so miserable he'll never get laid tonight. You guess that this is at least a little more interesting than when he was talking about using zinc oxide last summer so that his appendectomy scar wouldn't keloid. You choose not to take the obvious cue to ask him why that would be exposed to sunlight.

Finally, with a doggy bag full o' raw fish, he's ready to go, but not without a little mocking laughter at the amount of the bill, as if to say it was nothing compared to what he's used to. In front of your house, you go for that safety valve so as not to have to suffer through any kind of prolonged good-bye. He acknowledges that you need to go to sleep immediately. The only thing you feel you need to do immediately is get the hell out of that car before he tries to kiss you, as this will induce vomiting. You repress a smile as you think of his reaction to having his precious yummy roll re-gurgitated into his lap.

You don't return his calls, knowing he'll be headed back to the desert in a couple of weeks. He was just passin' through and soon it'll be time to hit the road. This familiar scenario has always been the foundation of considerable pain for you. For the first time you can't wait for a manthing to walk out of your life. And the best part is, you never let him in.

Dont's for Boys

by Betty Boob, Miss Mara, John-Boy, Jimmie C-A-Go-Go

Here's the deal. We LOVE men. We do. Really. It's just that sometimes, we just don't get it. Does the term BOY DISEASE mean anything to you? It should. Here is a rather thorough set of guidelines to follow in order to avoid this horrible virus in the Valley of the Dolls.

In the Beginning . . .

Before we even get to the "relationship" stage, everyone goes through that awkward should-we-or-shouldn't-we phase. You know, do I like him/her, should I ask him/her out, do I consider him/her a friend or what. The key to this stage is honesty. If you remain honest about your feelings, no one gets hurt. Remember, honesty is the best policy.

- If you like me, ask me out. We're not in high school anymore. If I liked you, I'd ask you out.

- If we go on a first date, and it doesn't go well, don't bother with "I'll call you." Leave, gracefully.

- If we fuck on the first date, it doesn't mean I am waiting for an engagement ring to appear on the second date.

- Sex out of the gate is tough stuff all the way around. That's a fact. Maybe it was a mistake, maybe it was bliss, maybe it was the booze, but whatever it was, let's not ignore it. Maybe we'll just be friends, or maybe we'll never see each other again, but at least we'll know.

- Don't use being drunk as an excuse for "accidentally" kissing me. If you kiss me, drunk or not, you have a BIG KISS to deal with.

151

Men Are from Uranus

- Call when you say you're going to call. Because, otherwise, I will wait for you to call. And that's not nice.

- Don't call me if you haven't gotten over your last girlfriend/boyfriend/mother. I'm not an understudy for a psycho-romantic-drama.

- Don't lie. I am a professional—I can smell a lie a mile away. You see, I wrote the manual.

- Don't play footsie over dinner and then behave like nothing has transpired. Hello, have you not seen *Flashdance?*

- Don't tell my friends that you think I'm cool and special unless you mean it. Remember the rule of telephone: You tell my friends, they tell me. I end up thinking you're cool and special. Then, when you don't do anything I'll be forced to realize you're not.

- If you're bi, tell me up front. If you're confused about your sexuality, don't take it out on me or get me entangled in your web of confusion. Plus, if I dig it, think of all the fun junk we could do together.

- Don't monopolize the conversations with anecdotes about yourself (unless they're really funny). Remember to chat. Asking questions out of sincere interest is very attractive.

- Don't use the I'm-not-ready-for-a-relationship excuse. Cuz then I'll think you're trying to get rid of me by relying on stale, uninspired stock phrases.

- Don't screen my calls. It's weird, creepy, and lame.

- Do not pretend to like me in order to fuck me. If you want to fuck me, tell me. I can engage in sexual discourse without becoming emotionally attached. I can always use a boy toy.

*The **BUST** Guide to the New Girl Order*

- Do not tell me that you want to spend the weekend with me and then call me at 10:30 on a Thursday night to bail. Or not call at all. I won't be devastated/ emotionally crushed if you don't want to hang out. Of course, I will be disappointed, but being blown off/dissed is much less damaging than not knowing and wondering why, why, why. The latter is based on deception, which does not allow for resolution of feelings; the former is based on honesty, which demands closure.

- Don't kiss and tell. But, because I know you will, you slob, do me the favor of not degrading me. If you can remember to mention that I'm cool or funny or smart and that you're super lucky to even be telling your friend about my naked-action, you'll at least not be adding insult to the injury.

- If we live in different cities, and we know we are attracted to each other, don't get all huffy on me when I ask, "So, when will you be in town again?"

- Don't be afraid of falling in like with me just because I live in a different city. Long-distance romances have their advantages. Sure, it is hard to base your feelings on phone calls, but look at all the fun parts of a long-distance romance: we don't have to see each other all the time, it allows complete exploitation of one's own sexual freedom, and don't forget the keyword in romance—anticipation.

- Don't be afraid to fall in like with me, you big baby.

The Relationship

153

If we are involved in a healthy monogamous relationship, patterns of behavior will become established between the two of us. How we interact with each other as well as how we react to others around us will affect our relationship. Obviously, we will have some problems here and there and that's okay.

Men Are from Uranus

- Don't pester me with lame-ass questions like "Where is this relationship going?" A relationship is a dynamic and vital form of expression, not a bad plotline or two lost motorists.

- Stop whining about taking a blood test, especially if you have had needles in your arms for recreational use. I need to be safe about my sex and I ain't got time for your pre-me irresponsible behavior or your lame-ass questions.

- If we get into a long-distance romance, do not freak out when you ring me up at 3 A.M. my time and I am not there. I have a life too, but that does not mean I am out somewhere having sex with someone else.

- Don't get all bent out of shape if I earn more money than you. It's either old-school machismo or new-school oversensitivity. Just hang, bud, lunch is on me. Today.

- Don't try to one-up me. If my week was crazy, don't insist yours was crazier. If mine was fantastic, don't insist yours was fantastic-er. Be supportive. That always works wonders.

- Don't go on tour with your stupid band, on a boring business trip, or on the annual family vay-kay and only call me when you feel like it.

- Don't borrow my car to cheat on me. I don't want to make payments on the source of a painful memory.

- Don't tell me you were drunk and don't know how you ended up in some girl's bed naked with a couple of used condoms strewn around.

- Don't call ME a jealous freak and then act all jealous when you see me cracking up with other boyz.

- Don't tell me you are having lunch with her so you won't hurt her feelings. You're not that nice, she's not that weak, and I am not that stupid.

154

*The **BUST** Guide to the New Girl Order*

- Don't tell me in an exasperated tone that you have told her over and over again never to call. Here's a thought: If you hang up, she won't call back.

- Don't come home from vacation with: hickeys on your neck; strange underwear in your suitcase; receipts from Victoria's Secret; a box of condoms with a bunch missing; an unexpected rash; or scratches on your back.

- Do come home from vacation lovesick for me with a big cool present and a bouncy hard-on.

- Don't squeeze my juicy butt at parties to prove you own me. Squeeze it at home to prove you want me, right now.

- Don't forget to introduce me to your friends, unless you know I won't like him/her. In which case, hey, thanks.

- Don't try to get the waitress's phone number while I'm at the table, or wait until I go to the bathroom and then immediately break up with me upon my return.

- Don't show all the naked pictures you've taken of me to your loser friends.

- Don't pretend you were out with the boys last night when I know for a fact that you weren't.

- Don't put your friends before me. It's me, me, me, FIRST FIRST FIRST. Always.

- Don't put my choice of friends down. Remember, I never let them put you down, clown.

- Don't act like we never talked about going to the Virgin Isles together. I'm rarely given to complete delusion.

- No carnations or single red roses. Not that I want to be your personal Emily Post, but they're corny.

155

- Don't order me diet food while I am in the bathroom. Order me cake. Something with chocolate fudge would be great.

- Don't tell me: not to get hysterical; not to overreact; that I am imagining things; that I am on the rag.

- Don't forget my birthday, for God's sake.

- Do not raise your voice or it will only put me off and make me want to remain silent while you lose control of yourself, at which point you will no longer be in control—you'll just be wound up.

- PLEASE PLEASE PLEASE do not get possessive. Nothing scares a girl off faster than a possessive partner. If I am having lunch with a colleague and bump into my ex-lover at their office, it does not mean I stole a "quickie" in the bathroom while my colleague was getting her coat. Please. This cannot be stressed enough. If I am with you, there is a reason. Especially if I am no longer with him.

Sex

Here is a fact: We like doing it and chances are we like doing it with you! The way to keep our sex lives happy and healthy is to open the lines of communication. We want you to do certain things and we are not afraid to tell you, and we hope you will do the same thing with us. However, if you are going to be a jerk about our sex play, there will be problems. Here are some.

- Do not ever fuck me, come inside me, and then say "I gotta go," 'cause if you do, you'd better.

- Do not fuck me on Sunday and not call me till Wednesday. Call me on Monday. Remember this little rhyme: SunDay called MonDay in OneDay.

*The **BUST** Guide to the New Girl Order*

- Morning breath is not a disease. We both have it, so get over it and kiss me when we wake up together.

- Don't touch all the good parts while I'm sleeping unless it's with intent to wake me.

- Don't sniff my undies. It creeps me out.

- Don't keep telling me your parents won't hear us.

- Don't ask me to fuck your friends. How would you like it if I asked you to . . . wait.

- Your not ejaculating is a mystery to me and a source of extreme anxiety about my body. So, if it happens, bear with me, and help me realize it's not because I am unattractive or unsexy.

- Don't ask me how many guys I've slept with. I can barely keep count sometimes.

- Don't ever try to have sex with me with your socks on. It makes me think of Woody Allen and Richard Nixon. And look at them.

- "Don't touch" doesn't mean "Wait, touch."

- Don't forget that foreplay means the play before, and play is fun.

- It's embarrassing for both of us when the equipment doesn't work. But I still don't understand the mechanics of it all. I'll still like you if you 'splain stuff, so tell me.

- Don't forget that my nipples are not detachable, nor can they tune in Tokyo.

- Don't get uptight if I want to masturbate. Help or watch; it looks pretty cool.

- Don't ask me to count my orgasms after we do it.

Men Are from Uranus

- Don't tell me how any of your old girlfriends "did anything." Put that stupid shoe on the other foot and see how ugly it looks.

- Big boys, be gentle.

- Don't tell me I'm cute when I am trying to be sexy. Pay attention.

- Don't have sex while you're answering the phone. Get me?

- Don't say, "Thanks, it was fun!"

- Don't get lost in the mighty jungle. Remember what Dracula said? "Look into my eyes." Ditto here. When you're going down on me, look up, let me see your eyes. It'll turn me on more.

- The more the merrier. Just remember to invite me.

- Don't be intimidated by my vibrator.

- Kinky is good. Scary is not.

- Bring me to a hoo-ha and I will be yours forever.

- Finger condoms help keep, um, dirt from collecting under your fingernails. Invest.

- Don't use the following excuses to get out of spending the night with me: have to get up early; curfew; roommate may get lonely; must walk dog.

- Don't tell me to go down on you first if you are planning to absolutely not go down on me.

- Don't ask me to swallow anything you wouldn't swallow yourself.

*The **BUST** Guide to the New Girl Order*

- Don't tell me that: condoms don't fit; condoms don't feel good; you're allergic.

- Sex during my period? Ask me if I'm in the mood. See what happens.

- Don't watch TV during sex unless it's porn.

- Don't ask me if you're the best; it's not a contest.

- Don't tell me this won't hurt.

- Don't tell me you can pull out in time.

- Do not call me by any other woman's name.

- Don't tell me I'm not wet enough, like it's an insult.

- Don't ever ask me if my trip to the gynecologist is a turn-on.

- Do not insist on videotaping our sexcapades. If you want to make me your fucking costar, ask me if I'd like the part.

- If you can't come with a condom on, warn me. I may take it personally otherwise.

- Cuddling is an art form. Master it.

Talking Dick with Cynthia Plaster Caster

Interview by Betty Boob

Want your man to stay hard forever? Call Cynthia Plaster Caster, the legendary connoisseur of casting cock. *BUST* sat down and chatted with this High Priestess of Penis, who can be seen doing spoken word at a theater near you, regaling you with the colorful and interesting experiences of her life on her knees.

Were you a good girl or a bad girl?
I always thought I was a good girl. I obeyed my mother. She told me never go into a strange man's hotel room, so the first time I went to a hotel, I stayed down in the lobby while my girlfriend went up. Unfortunately it was the Rolling Stones' hotel room, so I should not have paid attention to my mother. I should have been a really bad girl, damnit.

Are girl groupies God's gift to boy rock stars?
According to this really cheap-ass dictionary that my father got for free when he opened a bank account, a groupie is a young girl who follows bands in order to have sex. I consider myself a groupie even though I haven't had sex in over a year, I'm not young, I have male friends who have sex with rock stars, and lately I haven't followed anybody any further than the Days Inn which is two blocks away from where I live.

What's the story of Cynthia Plaster Caster?
My girlfriend Pest and I were both virgins. We really liked British rock musicians; we liked their hair, we liked the way they wore tight pants and we could see these bulges that were, to me, a source of mystery because I had never seen a dick before—and we loved the music! We were getting hornier and I was getting more curious about sex because I had heard that it was for more than just reproductive purposes—that it actually felt good. That was news to me. We were reading about all these people losing their virginity before they were married and thought, well, maybe we should check that out, how do we go about it, we're too shy to seduce people. I had barely made out with anyone.

I was an art major and I got this homework assignment. My art teacher said, "Make a plaster cast. Pick an object that can retain its shape, that's kind of on the hard side," and I'm thinking, OMIGOD! I tried covering my face to try to hide my laughter, knowing exactly what I would cast. I'm thinking, in order to meet the bands, we have to slide our way past all the other groupie competition. We're gonna have to stand out in the crowd somehow. This is gonna be the perfect question to pop that's gonna draw their attention away from all the other girls! I ran into Pest and I said, "Guess what my homework assignment is?" We said, "Let's go for it! It's just so hilarious, let's make it more hilarious by making out like we're professional plaster casters." We went back to my school, stole some plaster, found a brown paper bag, and I drew this semiofficial-looking logo on it that said "Plaster." We tried to look like traveling plaster saleswomen.

We were to go hunt down bands that weekend. Dick Clark brought his Caravan of Stars to Chicago, where there were about ten or fifteen bands. Most of them were all staying at the same hotel. We knocked on this rocker's door and said, "Hey, we'd like to make a plaster cast of your rig" (rig was an English slang word for dick) and so he immediately whipped out his, this big old long semi-hard-on dick flagellating, kind of waving, in the wind! I had never seen a dick and I shrieked and ran away from the room. We thought, well, that was a good response, it was promising. So we worked our way down to another room. The singer was busy with a girl but he said why don't you come back tomorrow? We said we'll give it a shot. I wound up losing my virginity but I did not get a cast. The important thing was I got laid, I got pants down, I got the attention I was looking for.

Were you scared the first time . . .
. . . that I got laid? Oh yeah, I had no idea what to expect. It was painful and semi-romantic and it was really kind of rushed because the band had to be back on a tour bus in like an hour.

So you were still planning to cast?
No, so after all this was done, my girlfriend and I thought, Why don't we put together a kit? Let's figure out how to really make a plaster cast out of a cock and we'll just experiment on various rock stars and that will be our excuse to talk to them and

we'll ask them if they want to try melted wax or clay or aluminum foil around their dicks.

We showed up at a meet and greet for another band and one of the guys freaked out because we had already met him about two years prior. We still had the hots for him. He flipped out when we arrived with our suitcase with the logo "Plastercasters of Chicago" because he had heard of us and he didn't know that we were the ones that were THE plastercasters, so he freaked out so much that he started running around the stage in circles.

Then some promo man told Pest about dental molds and how that would be a good idea to use that as a mold so I went to some dental supply store and bought a can. I thought it was mixed already, the same as plaster and water, but oh no, you had to measure it really carefully. I discovered the hard way that if you try mixing it like plaster you'll just get water with floating chunks of alginate.

But the bands were into the idea even though you weren't getting successful casts?
Yeah, we would always always always get invited into the rooms because in those days it was really trendy to slip your dick into something new and different. It was an excuse to get into the room, meet them, and have a laugh with them. As long as we were laughing, we would feel more comfortable.

When did the casts really begin to work for you?
After a few of these always unsuccessful attempts, we realized we had to figure out how to do this right because Jimi Hendrix was coming to town. I practiced on two friends, I got my shit together, I figured it out. When Jimi was here I knew how to mix alginate. By this time we were sort of semilegends because dicks and rock 'n' roll draws instant media attention! That was really a source of major amusement to me and Pest because we were doing it just for a laugh and a joke. All of a sudden the media latched onto it, people were writing about us. I mean, that was never the intention—we wouldn't have minded being a household word among bands, but not the rest of the world.

What was your first successful time like?
Well, it was with Jimi Hendrix. I was nervous.

162

So you meet Jimi Hendrix and what does he say to you?

Well, it was after the first of two shows at the Chicago Civic Opera House. We pulled up at the hotel and said, "Hi, Jimi, we're the Plaster Casters," and he was like, "Oh yeah yeah yeah, I've heard about you from somebody in the Kosmos, come up to my room and let's do it!" And that was all there was to it.

Were you freaking out?

Yeah, I was using breathing control to try to hide the fact that I was very much freaking because they were my favorite band; I didn't think we would be successful. The whole band was up in this little room, I don't know if it was Jimi's or not. Then again it was the same hotel I had lost my virginity in! The Conroy Hilton was THE hotel in those days. I prepared this substance—by this time Pest had retired and my friend Diane took over—this was when there was a designated mold mixer and a stimulator called the plater. (Plater was slang for blow job, even though nobody under thirty has ever heard that term. In England it was a very popular word for blow job). Diane, she gave him a blow job and he deemed her the Queen of the Platers, because she had a really soft gentle touch. When my mold was ready he (Jimi) dipped but I forgot to lubricate his pubes. Somehow I forgot! I don't remember having pube problems with the first two people I'd done. Jimi's pubes were totally dry and as a result his pubes got stuck in the mold. That's the only part of the genitals that have to be oiled. By the time the mold hardens, the dick is usually soft enough to kind of slide out, but hair is really tricky, so I had to pull out one hair at a time to avoid him going through too much pain, but he didn't mind—he just fucked the mold while he was waiting. So I poured plaster into that mold and we went off to the second show. After the show was over we went to some party and we went back to the hotel, this was only six hours after. You really should let those casts sit for anywhere from twelve to twenty-four hours, but I was so anxious to see them that I cracked open the mold prematurely and it was not set yet, it was still soft and wet and in a hundred pieces. I didn't open it up all the way, I just very carefully closed it up like an envelope and let it sit for another twelve hours and when it finally dried it was broken into only three pieces, the head, the shaft, and the balls, so I just glued them together with Elmer's glue. It has this cool cracked kind of ancient effect. Journalists call it the "Penis de Milo."

163

I have to ask, is Jimi's the biggest?

Um—it's the thickest, but it's not the longest. It's fairly long. Sometimes they come out twisted or curled—I got about four of them that look like snakes or pigs' tails.

Can you ever tell the size of a guy's package just by looking at him?

Well you know what they say about noses and fingers and feet? Well, I find that guys with wide pelvises—they're kind of dorky and they walk like dinosaurs—almost always have big dicks.

How long does the dick have to be hard once it's inside the alginate?

They only have to be hard for anywhere from forty seconds to a minute and twenty seconds.

What makes a guy lose his boner in the middle of being casted?

Well, I think a combination of no direct stimulation, maybe a little stage fright, and the alginates are a little on the cold side, sometimes. They're not really cold—they're either room temperature or a little below that. I don't know. Maintaining a hard-on in a cold mold for a minute is a challenge. Judging from my collection, which is by average 25 to 75 percent capability, very difficult because they can't have direct stimulation down there, they can't have their dicks touched while they're immersed in the mold.

How many casts do you have?

I've made about fifty attempts but I've only succeeded in maybe 35%. I say fractions because sometimes I only capture their heads or half of their shafts or a third of their shafts with head.

164

Have you ever cast breasts?

Not yet, but I want to add tits to my collection!

Do you ever get a moistie when you're casting a dick?

I have no time to be turned on. I'm also not that turned on by the cast itself. It actually makes me depressed that I wasn't the plater.

The BUST Guide to the New Girl Order

Well, why aren't you always the plater?
First of all, nobody ever asked! In order for me to train somebody, alginates would have to be mixed and it was kind of expensive to train somebody. I was content to keep on mixing the mold. It is kind of fun and therapeutic for me to mix the mold, and it reduces tension. Strangely enough, lately there have been occasions where I just wound up being the plater. I asked the subject if he sees anyone that he would like to meet and somehow they just don't try to meet anyone and they come home with me instead. It's really only occurred in the last year or two.

Do you ever masturbate afterward?
I'm usually so pooped and wiped out by cleaning all the mess that I just pass out.

Biggest misconception about plaster-casting?
I think people think it's a lot sexier process than it is. My role is so mechanical and technical, I'm not very sensual and I think people expect it to be more erotic than it is. I mean, the plating is, but once we're in the kitchen it's pretty chaotic and kind of like a silent-film cops-and-robbers situation.

Why do you use the word "dick" as opposed to other penis words?
I used to use the words "rig" and "handsome wick." Handsome wick is Cockney rhyming slang for dick. I learned all these slangs words from the visiting British musicians in the mid-'60s. I learned about the existence of Cockney rhyming slang and I thought if I learned it, it would be an esoteric language with which I could communicate with rock stars. I wanted to get laid. I was a Catholic-trained virgin. I wanted to have sex with those bands but virgins did not lose their virginity unless you were married. Rig was the one Keith Moon used to describe his dick. But lately I really like to roll the words "dick" and "cock" in my mouth.

How about female parts?
I call it my twat or my pussy. Lately. I don't know, I gravitate. In '97 and '98 it's been twat and pussy. It was hole in the early '90s. *I* really love the word "cunt," it's another good word that feels good on the lips, on the tongue, I think. I also call people cunts. Certain guys feel better about themselves when they use that

165

word. It's really popular in Britain. That's why I don't find it offensive. It doesn't bug me.

Where does the feminist in you stand on casting?
I'm sort of more of an underdoggist rather than feminist. I'm on the side of anyone that's been fucked over, no matter what sex, inclination, or race. I don't cast for feminist reasons, to control guys necessarily. I do it for a laugh and I do it to just feel more comfortable. I mean, power to a lot of things about feminism. I'm one of those feminists that promote sex and being sexy. I can't articulate it very well—I just know how it feels. Man and woman are like one entity—it's a great sexual feeling!

Have you ever considered starting Cynthia's School of Casting . . . Dick?
Do you think I should?

I think you have a talent that you should share with the rest of us.
Like a workshop? We could all enlighten each other. I just love dicks attached to talented men.

What bands do you love?
The High Llamas. I'm quite smitten with them. Mekons, Dirty Three, Pulp, Supergrass, Françoise Hardy, Serge Gainsbourg, Tindersticks. I will crawl through a window backstage when Pulp are here if I have to.

Would you cast Jarvy?
Yeah, I tried a long time ago. They were about to leave town so there wasn't enough time. He may or may not have been really interested. I could never tell, he acted like he was. Maybe it was because he knew he was leaving town in two hours. I don't know if he would do it now, but that would be a hell of a dildo. That would be a cast I would like to do. He supposedly has a long skinny one. I read it in some British paper.

Did you ever cast any of the Stones?
No, no never. The first time they came to Chicago there were just five girls at the hotel—they were fairly unknown. I got Mick [Jagger] and Keith's [Richards] autographs

The BUST Guide to the New Girl Order

and I gave Brian Jones a box of cough drops. They were just recording their second album here. The next time they came back it was completely impossible to get anywhere near them unless you were really gorgeous or had lots of money or you had some connections. It was really difficult to meet popular bands in the very early days because you had to climb fire escapes. They would not allow so-called underaged girls into the hotels. Once the groupie revolution started, there would be hundreds of girls trying to get up to the floors the guys were staying on. It's easier now, there aren't hundreds, maybe tens and twenties.

Kurt Cobain . . .
I happened to be present at the Crash Palace in Chicago, this trendy bar where Nirvana went after their show, and Courtney Love turned up there. Courtney introduced us and I asked Kurt if he would be interested in posing for me. He said well you can cast my middle finger because it's representative of how I feel about the music industry. That was the night they consummated their love.

What do you mean when you say someone has a "great cock"?
Vaginal size. It's above average size, not too thin, not too long. I have tried casting this one rocker four different times. His dick is like a Bermuda Triangle—the mold has failed each time! I'm talking about different days when I don't mix fast enough or the water temperature is too warm. He's been so nice and sweet and patient. His ex-girlfriend thought I was doing this on purpose just so I could see his cock more!

Who else is on the future Cynthia P. Caster hit list?
All of them! They're all eligible. They're all on my hit list. Anytime I utter the name of somebody and I say I'm going to do, it never happens—it's like the curse of the caster. I'll hear that some band hopes I'll come watch them perform and see if they pass the audition.

What audition?
I call experiencing their music an audition and see if I think they're talented enough to add to my collection. I'm beyond musicians though. I'll do creative people, super-heroes. I'm obsessed with casting Michael Moore right now.

What does he think about that?

He doesn't know. He'd probably cringe if he found out. He appeared here recently with *The Big One* but I didn't have the nerve to approach him. He was standing right near Studs Terkel, another awesome creature that's probably too old to pose for me but still welcome in my collection.

So, what is dick?

What is dick? Oh, it's that magical, mysterious, cute, very unintimidating thing in the sky. It's much funnier-looking than I expected it to be. I thought that it would be some hot dog-looking shape. I didn't know there would be a head on it and balls. I think it's not a scary object at all; the shape of it is kind of clownlike and that's what I really like about it, it's almost like some little toy saying, "Please eat me, want me, love me!" walking around saying, "Notice me." Not a scary object at all.

My Brother, Myself

by Betty Boob

Have you ever had a best friend? I have. Quite a few, actually. Most have fallen by the wayside; the only one who has been a constant, on a best friend level, has been J. As it turns out, I am related to him. He's my brother.

My brother?

Yes, actually.

My father is somewhat responsible for this. When J. and I were quite young, my dad sat us down and said, "There are only two of you, so you better be nice to each other cuz you ain't getting any more brothers or sisters." (Whaddaya want from me? We're from Queens!) Of course, at the time, I figured he was just being a dad. Later on, I realized he had a point.

J. has left an indelible impression on me. Three, to be exact.

Me at age four: J, one. I was just a wee girl, he was newly born. Mom was spending all of her time paying attention to him him him. You know how it is. We were in the park this one special day, and there he was being swung in a swing—the kind with the sissy bar, so that the brat wouldn't fall out. I was jealous of course, having been an only child for so long, and I wanted all the attention to be sent my way for a change. So, there I stood, arms akimbo, right in front of the swing. As the laws of physics would have it, when the swing swung to, I was flung fro. The evidence is on the top right part of my forehead; eight stitches, in fact, of evidence.

What is it about my brother that makes him number one on the totem pole?

Lots of things.

He's been in my life since the beginning of time. My time, that is. I was four years old when J. was born. When someone has been in your life for that long, you have a lot of shared history. J. has lived it with me—being on the front lines of the family dramas, meeting the incoming friends, and watching the parade of outgoing boy toys. With J., the story of my life does not have to be rehashed time and again like it does with each new person I meet. I like this. I hate retelling the story of my life. *I was born and then I met you.*

With history comes trust, and my brother is a trustworthy man. Trusting a person is very important to me. I tell him things I dare not utter to anyone else. I feel like no matter what I tell him, no matter how far out it is, he will still be my friend, because he is my *brother,* not a Betty Boob flavor-of-the-month. Trusting him means I can count on him in times of need and *know* he will help me out—doing backbreaking favors (such as moving or cleaning my house up after a fire or two), baby-sitting my cat and dog when I am out of town, listening to me cry about a boy at four in the morning (he rolls his eyes whenever that happens).

Me at age eight: I had gotten used to having a little playmate, and this time, I was taking J. for a ride, on my back. It was fun until my glasses fell off my face. I panicked because I was rather near-sighted and as I bent down to pick them up (J. still clinging to my back) I went right cheek first into the corner of a brick wall and tore precious skin off my precious cheek. The missing skin scar still rests proudly.

He's a funny guy, my brother. He can make me laugh like no one else can—to the point where I'm wheezing. (Yes, it is true; we have the same laugh.) He understands me, knows me better than anyone else, although the fact that I attend movies alone is still a mystery to him. We have code words for things, and sometimes we will lapse into Hebrew when at a loss for English words, rather effortlessly. He likes dogs. In fact, he found my dog for me. I like the way he treats his girlfriends, although I must confess he has that annoying habit of dropping the world for his partner, which means I get left out of the picture when there's a new girl in town. But he is tremendously attentive to his girlies; I would want a boy to behave that way with me (considerate, loving, and a little ballsy). And I know why he is such a good boyfriend; he had a good role model—me!

My friends know him because I bring him along with me whenever I venture out into the real world. If I show up without him, there is always a little concern: "Where's J.? Is he okay?" I enjoy hanging out with him. He likes to do the same kinds of things I like to do: gazing at art, going to concerts, watching television late into the night, gobbling on pizza, cheering the Knicks on, and goofing around. It's almost like finding the perfect person to spend all your time with. Except, of course, I'm related to him.

Me at age twenty-six: Then-boyfriend Velvy (no I am not making this name up) and I planned a trip to New Orleans. Then he dumped me, and I had an extra ticket. This is where dear little bro came to the rescue—he took Velvy's already bought and paid-for plane ticket. On our first night there, the outer right part of my upper calf made friends with the corner of a pulled-out drawer. As J. delicately placed iodine on the gash, he warned that I would need to apply the burning ointment regularly. Of course I didn't. New skin developed, also known as a scar.

170

We are very close, J. and I. He has the keys to my apartment. I know what you are thinking—"What is she, nuts?" Yes and no. I like the fact that he can come and go; when he comes over, he is considerate, appreciative of having a home away from home (he lives with the folks). He always brings me little things, like my favorite flavor of Snapple, or a new item of clothing to snatch. When he is around, I feel comfortable, safe. I can talk to him, or not talk to him. I can be in the same room as he is and not feel like I am being crowded. When he leaves, there is an empty space.

Now don't get me wrong. J. is not a perfect specimen of boyness or humanness. He has his flaws. He can be a little temperamental: he has a stubborn streak that gets in the way of who's gonna walk the dog; he falls terribly, deeply in love with his girl-friends and gets attached at the hip to them (a big problem if it's a girlfriend I don't like, which has been the case lately. Unfortunately, he gets very macho about his girlfriends; when it becomes clear that I don't like them, he gets defensive, almost hurt that his pick doesn't meet my "approval." I just expect him to end up with smart, independent feminists, so it's always disappointing when he ends up with clingy, narrow-minded Schlafly-ites). He can be a little too protective of me, scowling at my boys he thinks are trouble—he's been known to charge at the few who have turned psycho; and he can be very critical of my lifestyle, something that can by annoying (like when I stumble into my apartment, all hot and bothered, ready to pounce said boy toy, and there he is, little boy J., looking like—*gasp*—a parent!)

We can argue about things—even fight—and make up without any grudges. It's this part of the relationship spectrum that makes friendships so special: forgiveness, empathy, love, respect. And this exists between us. Sometimes too much. But that's okay, too. Because if I didn't have him in my life, I would be so much more alone. I'd be without my best friend, my brother.

My Keanu: A Fantasy

by Lisa Palac

I am standing in front of Keanu's trailer. Not his Hollywood trailer, but the one in the trailer park where he lives. It's dark and I'm with my friend and we're standing in the gravel a few yards back from Keanu's living room window, spying. His place is filled with the kind of Early American furniture you'd see in a cheap steak-house, the walls are covered with paneling. My friend keeps elbowing me whenever

Steve A. Wacksman

I start to stare into the night or up at the moon, saying things like, "Keep watching because Keanu might take his pants off or something!" Now I am inside the trailer, lying on an uncomfortable green, prickly sofa. Keanu is kneeling on the floor beside me, stroking my hair. He tells me it is his birthday. I tell him how beautiful I think he is and how much I want to kiss him. So we kiss. Pretty soon Keanu starts taking off his clothes. Discreetly I give my friend, who's still standing outside the window spying, the eye, as if to say, "How's this for action?"

Keanu and I are taking a shower in a psychedelic locker room where the big white tiles go on and on forever. I'm on my back and he's fucking me hard. The water sprays down, dripping into our kisses. He pulls out because I want to give him a blow job. But before I can do anything, he comes all over my face. He is extremely embarrassed (about the prematurity of it all) and apologizes greatly (for the mess) and reaches for a towel to mop me up. Then, in that totally excellent way of his, he says, "It's not like we have to stop or anything because I've got another cock that's hard." And he flips his spent penis out of the way and right behind it is a slightly smaller cock-and-ball set that's all ready to go.

172

Did you know that Keanu means "cool breeze over the mountains" in Hawaiian? It also means "warm breeze between my legs" in the pornographic candyland of my subconscious. Not since Madonna have I melted-down so completely in the luminescence of a star. His mesmerizing beauty, of course, was the beginning. Looking at his face is like looking at a Botticelli or watching the snow fall. It's the sense of awe that comes simply from witnessing the beautiful. Sometimes all I have to do is look at him and I feel, wow.

The BUST *Guide to the New Girl Order*

I like his goofball deflections of life's complexity too, the way things can be totally excellent. And then, not so excellent. His understated alienation and his far-away brown eyes drift off the screen, I think. He doesn't have a place to live, except the Chateau Marmont. Apparently, he acts really weird during interviews. He retreats into manic laughs that cut off into sudden silence. He jumps out of his chair and recites obscure lines of dialogue. He answers the question "Why do you act?" with "You know, man, whatever." He crashed his Norton a few years ago in Topanga Canyon and it left him with a thick scar that snakes from his navel to his heart. But he's no James Dean. He isn't a bad boy, see. There's no tough shell, no unforgivables, no edges to soften. He's pretty on the outside. He's like a girl that way.

Keanu is my boyfriend. Occasionally I'll get a message on my answering machine sing-songing, "Your boyfriend is on TV tonight in *Dangerous Liaisons*" or "Your boyfriend is going to be on the next cover of *Wired*," or "I just heard your boyfriend is making a movie called *Feeling Minnesota* with your girlfriend Courtney Love." (Oh, to be sandwiched in the middle of that one.) Friends clip and save pictures of Keanu for me like so many coupons. Pictures of him as Prince Siddhartha in *Little Buddha*, where he has this bad Yul-Brynner-as-King-of-Siam makeup happening but he is mostly unclothed, which is very good. A few GIFS from *Speed*, old issues of *Details*, *Interview*, *Buzz*, *Entertainment Weekly*. There is a muddy, black and white taken by Gus Van Sant during the making of *My Own Private Idaho*, which I treasure, because Keanu tries so hard but his honesty gets in the way.

But my favorite is the one where he is wearing a black leather biker vest, unzipped all the way, and black jeans. His hair is parted in the middle and hangs in a sloppy bob just above his chin. He is not smiling. His hands are on his hips, and his hips I must say, have a bit of baby fat on them. He looks deliciously rough trade, showing off his rather hairless chest, his nipples and most importantly, his scar. For Christmas last year, I got a copies of *Speed*, *Point Break* and a dub of *Life Under Water*, a PBS drama starring Keanu and Sarah Jessica Parker. In one scene, he is completely naked—from the back—and if you watch it frame by frame, you can glimpse his scar when he turns, the scar up close, in real life? It might break the spell. The magic is made up of bits of ink stuck to glossy paper, projections on a screen, my dreams. Besides, why risk ruining the illusion when there are plenty of other people who are out to ruin it for me?

Men Are from Uranus

"He can't act his way out of a paper bag."

"Did you see *Dracula*? He was pathetic!"

"You know what the critics said about his performance as *Hamlet*? 'At least he remembered all of his lines!'"

Whenever I mention my thing for Keanu to outsiders, it's usually met with the slag, "He can't act." As if my enchantment is supposed to evaporate on the spot when I'm informed he might not be Oscar material. When the no-talent tactic doesn't work they bring out the big guns: he's stupid in person, his band Dogstar is shit, and maybe he's a fag on top of it all. The level of hostility is impressive. They're hell-bent on convincing me that he sucks. They attempt Keanu-intervention.

Keanu can act. Granted, some films are better than others and he is the first to admit it. "I didn't give a performance," he told *Newsweek,* referring to *Dracula.* Oh, so what. He was amazing in *River's Edge,* the story of a group of disaffected teenagers who discover one of them has killed his girlfriend. His character is stoned, streaked with compassion, and troubled that he can feel so much nothing for what is going on. Is it a great performance or is he just playing himself? Does it matter?

His performance in *Speed* was good. My only complaint is that there was no gratuitous male nudity. After all of those death-defying, sweat-soaked adventures, didn't Keanu need to take a nice, long shower? Or when he was under the bus dismantling the bomb, why didn't his shirt get ripped off so we could drool over his big scar and newly buffed torso?

I believe the "He Can't Act" vitriol is a symptom of something else. Do we really want to have a discussion about actors in Hollywood who can't act? Let me bring out my list. Kim Basinger. Matt Dillon. Tom Cruise. Demi Moore. Elvis Presley. But to be fair, they've all had a shining moment or two. Well, except for Kim Basinger. Perhaps we really want to talk about the envy and the unfairness of it all; that someone is making millions of dollars with their good looks and we're not. Ah, the aroma of jealousy fills the room. Not surprisingly, the rancor comes mainly from straight guys. They can dismiss his acting but they can't dismiss his beauty. In fact, they can't even allow themselves to recognize it long enough to reject it because they might wake up the next morning with the letters h-o-m-o branded on their forehead.

Now, there have been good-looking screen idols who have received the seal of approval: Brando, Newman, McQueen. Even dolls like Luke Perry or Johnny Depp get the green light. But they have the cool cachet of virility beyond their pretty faces. Keanu, on the other hand, is not the Marlboro man. Not simply because of his exotic comeliness but because of his innocence. Innocence, particularly sexual innocence, isn't what makes a man. Innocence is for children. Innocence is for girls. Or sissies.

Don't you know he's married to David Geffen? Everybody in Los Angeles claims to know someone who knows Keanu and says the rumor is true. Yeah, right. It doesn't matter to them that Keanu and Geffen repeatedly insisted they've never met.

Is he stupid in person? I've never met anyone who knows him in real life, so I wanted to see for myself. I flew to L.A. to see his band Dogstar play at the Hollywood American Legion on Highland Avenue. "I have restrained the rage of the dogstar," wrote Samuel Johnson, the famous eighteenth-century writer and lexicographer. What kind of rage does Keanu restrain, I wondered.

I invited my friend Cintra and her boyfriend Kevin to join me. I was buying. How could they refuse? As expected, Kevin pulled out all the stops about how lame Keanu was in the acting and brains department. But my loyalty wouldn't budge. I am so used to being publicly humiliated for my love interest, however, the occasional Keanu-bashing cannot dislodge my apostolic following.

The crowd was a mix of the Melrose Place chicklets with perfectly penciled and tweezed eyebrows, kneesocks, and brown lipstick from MAC; big-hair Valley babes in white heels flashing teeth at their pinky ring dude escorts, and club hipsters. White people with dreadlocks wearing flannel. Interestingly, I noted a fairly large contingent of Boho guys. Were they simply the boyfriends of the girlfriends who dragged them there? Maybe they were there to see the first band. Or perhaps to sleep their way to a major label deal?

The minute Keanu walked on stage and picked up his bass, the females started screaming. He wore a baggy black T-shirt and black jeans. A sea of short girls lapped at the front of the stage, giving me a continuously unobstructed view of Keanu but I still couldn't see his shoes, which would have given me much additional nonverbal information about his character. If only Keanu was into stage diving (like Courtney) and I could touch my Object of Desire. Touch. It's the mystical action that passes along the currency of soul, and hopefully leaves a trail of charm dust on your fingertips.

Keanu was gee-whiz gracious to his fans. Smiling, accepting their demo tapes, thanking them. Occasionally, some asshole would shout "Mrs. Geffen!" but mostly they screamed, "Keanu, I love you!" They threw flowers. I should have thrown my panties at him. Instead, I quietly enjoyed my buzz. This tingly sensation of, there he is. The boy in the pictures. It was like the time I saw the *Mona Lisa* at the Louvre. I'd seen reproductions of it for years and then finally, the real thing. Keanu is even more beautiful in real life. But the beauty trip only lasted about twenty minutes and then I came down. The band sucked.

They were beyond suck. The mix was so muddy, Dogbreath could have played the same chord all night and no one would have noticed. The lead guitarist, a rather unattractive blond with more talent for swinging his hair around than music, kept posing back to back with Keanu for a jam. Much to Keanu's credit, however, he did not head-bang or make rock-and-roll face. He only sang one tune, the barely decipherable "Isabelle." Cintra claimed the lyrics were Isabelle/Is a Spell. Man, like that is so deep.

After the show, we all walked back to the car. "So, did you get a moistie?" Kevin asked. It's the girl version of a boner.

"Yeah, I did. Did you?"

"Well, if I had to suck a dick, it would probably be Keanu's. He really is beautiful." The smart ones, they eventually come around.

Keanu's the lucky one who will always get the girl (or boy) in the end because he is so incredibly beautiful. Manly yes, but a bit of a dork. A bit of a femme, too. I like to imagine him taking a bath by candlelight, filling his place with roses, crying and finding beauty in melancholy, saying fuck you to failure, and then asking me to lick the blood off his face after a fight. He ain't always got something to prove, but I bet he could prove it all night if he wanted to. But what do I know? All I have are the pictures.

✕

Thurston Moore: BUSTiest Boy in America

Interview by Celina Hex

C: Are you a feminist?

T: Yeah, but it doesn't excuse me from being an asshole. The original idea for this interview was to have Kim ask the questions. We were midtour (Lollapalooza) and I kept procrastinating, fearful of some unknown intimacy. But I knew full well it would be fun, sexy, and challenging. By deadline I threw a fit (yelled and threw a handful of socks across the room)—humiliating myself and bumming Kim out. She's very aware of tour psychosis and mine was kicking in. And she brought me back with pure female consciousness. Beyond definition of philosophy or whatever. If Kim is a feminist than I'm a lover of it.

C: How do you define feminism?

T: Feminism, as an identity, exists in response to chauvinism's disrespect and ignorance toward female culture. Will the male culture ever overcome its envy and desire to dominate the mysterious, sophisticated female? And why are most men/boys insensitive to this situation as a complete social ill? Has male culture become so utterly sociopathic to where it must destroy the most important relationship it can have by confused emotional fallout?! I think anyone has the potential, through feminism, to be receptive to enlightenment toward the goodwill of Goddess culture. But feminism is societally denounced as an esoteric vision. And America does not historically encourage the intellectualism of esoteric thought (Japanese culture condones feminism as "failure"). So feminism, by its spiritual and physical claim, may well be defined as intellectual activism. At least that's how I ruminate it as a thirty-seven-year-old. I've read nary a word of feminist tract in my time and what I wrote above seems a bit hack-academic. But, for the most part, my conclusions are shaped by eyewitness account (as regards to the following question) . . .

C: Who are three women who have influenced you?

T: Kim, my mom, Coco—of course, those three, they're definitely the most personal—but, if you mean like writers, musicians, schoolteachers, landladies, etc., then my list

177

would have to include Patti Smith, the Slits, Penelope Houston, Lydia Lunch, Yoshimi Yokota, Sandra Bernhard, Bikini Kill, Julie Cafritz, the (original) Love Dolls, Hettie Jones, Dorothy Allison, the girl in Harry Pussy, Patty Waters, Yoko Ono, Rita Ackerman, Christina Billotte, Mary Timony, Banana Yoshimoto, the Wrecks, Edna St. Vincent Millay, Pearl S. Buck, Jocelyn Elders, Kira Roessler, Kate Moss, Jennifer Herrema, Chloe Sevigny, Daisy von Furth, Jane Alpert, Sally Banes, Yvonne Rainer, Suzanne Fasteau, Marilyn Crispell, Lorraine Geller, Michelle Orr, Pat Place, Connie Berg, and the Raincoats.

C: Who are three men who have influenced you?
T: Again, my dad, who died in '77—ummm . . . Richard Hell, Tom Verlaine, Johnny Rotten, Sid Vicious, Darby Crash, Mike Watt, Steve Turner, Joseph Jarman, Sun Ra, Byron Coley, Charlie Patton, Fred Sonic Smith, Steve Malkmus, Louis Barlow, Albert Ayler, Bill Dixon, Truly Justice, Derek Bailey, Cecil Taylor, John Coltrane, Evan Parker, Charles Gayle, Milford Graves, Karlheinz Stockhausen, Anthony Braxton, John Cage, Philip K. Dick, Jimmy Carter, and Morton Feldman.

C: What is your advice to guys who won't commit?
T: Commitment suggests monogamy and I think most men fantasize themselves as alleycats. It's a sex thing. A lot of guys don't trust themselves to be faithful. Most women seem to be into long-term love affairs (though I've known those who seem to have a depressing habit of cutting short whatever romance they fall into). My advice is to look at the bigger picture: by expressing devotion to one woman you are setting yourself up to be in very good graces to the queen bee. And her rewards are historically proven to be far more sensuous than a quick lay.

178

C: What do you think of porn?
T: You mean do I watch (and enjoy!) porn? Triple XXX porn? That's a secret. I think most guys totally (privately!) dig porn. It is so fucking LAME but it's super fantasy sex and it's there for any boy wanting to MASTURBATE. Imagine if hard-core porn was ever done with creativity and sophistication? With feminist creativity and sophistication? Lydia Lunch showed interest. The explicit *Fingered* was an intriguing attempt, but, like *Kids,* the sex was of an unfortunate perspective. There was no languished or

Cati Gonzalez

true-love/lust soul-beauty (though I'm sure the characters in *Fingered* would disagree). The basic no-plot porno-stars-fucking-like-crazy-on-a-couch film will always be more transfixing to any male's desire of arousal. But the porn stars are super-fuck-beings. They give a lousy sense of identity to both men and women. And that's where I find harmfulness in porn. It has the potential to terrorize anyone's sexual self-awareness. It's cheapo, degrading, and harsh. To see hard-core porn, with the specific effect toward viewer orgasm, portrayed in a more humanist, loving capacity would be radical. The fact that rental sales for "homemade/next door neighbor" porn have skyrocketed leads me to believe that market could leaven the insanity of porn. But who am I to tell what the general populace may want for fantasy? I for one don't get turned on by guys ejaculating on women's faces (a common occurrence in XXX films). But some people are into it. I vote yea to cruelty-free, consentive-adult porn as a safe-sex medium. But that's 'cuz I'm PC.

C: Why don't guys call when they say they will?
T: Well, I've had it the other way around too, y'know. I know it's more of a male stereotype that the boy doesn't call when he says he will. But . . . the simplest theory is that by not calling he's setting up a relationship where she's at the emotional mercy of he. And that's a traditional manipulation brought on by male fear of relationship equality, let alone dominance. You should just call him soon after he doesn't call and

Men Are from Uranus

say, "What the fuck's your problem?" and he'll either be delighted/relieved and ready to fall in love or be an asshole.

C: Do you have any tips for those of us *BUST* women who are looking for boyfriends?
T: I imagine *BUST* women are into music and/or books so I would just sojourn through record and book stores and keep an eye on who's looking good and what they're perusing and discreetly sidle up to him and say something about whatever he may be dealing with. Or ask a question about something you're looking at. Guys love it when strange women talk to them in stores. His initial response should give you some flash insight to his mental state. If you think he's totally available and worthy of pursuit, keep him chatting cuz he'll shy away easily and be gone forever. Cool guys are totally freaked out by girls so if he comes on all studly and self-assured he's probably a psycho. Be careful.

C: What do you think of men?
T: Most men are buffoons and I want nothing to do with them. The guys I like and respect I will certainly hang out with given half the chance, but my life revolves mostly around my marriage and baby. Kim has a few close girlfriends and I associate with them mostly, which I prefer. I've always preferred female friendships, though I love hanging out with a bunch of guys talking either dumb shit or intelligent shit and being totally fucking male-bonded. I was never the school heartthrob but girls always made friends with me and not with other guys. Which was weird cuz I'd invariably get crushes on them and subsist through months of torment. They'd fuck the jocks and cool guys or whatever but I would just be a friend. Kinda like that Krakow guy on *My So-Called Life* but more gawky and less math-whizzy. In retrospect, this was a thankful situation, but at the time it was teen anguish. I've always chosen to work with women before men as the intrigue of the feminine mystique lends constant inspiration to me as a musician. Actually I don't choose it—it just happens. I have no interest in impressing males.

C: If you were a girl, which celebrity boys would you have a crush on?
T: Good question . . . ummm—Eddie Vedder? He's got beautiful eyes but he's married. Steve Malkmus? He's pretty choice but he might be too easy to lose. Keanu Reeves?

180

*The **BUST** Guide to the New Girl Order*

He's kinda perfect but he'd probably never be around too much. Johnny Depp? He's probably a dick.

C: Who are the two girls in the picture with you on your album *Psychic Hearts*?
T: It's my sister Susie (on the right with her eyes closed) and our neighborhood friend at the time Ann Gardner (who I haven't seen since that time—1965, '66—I wonder if she'll ever find out she's on that CD jacket?).

C: With lyrics like "Kill the boys with their fucked-up noise, and all the bullshit they seem to enjoy," and "there was a time when God was dressed in pink," your album seems a lot like a riot grrl album. Are you sincere about these sentiments, or are you mocking them?
T: All the lyrics on that album are thematically involved with my personal life amidst female culture. They're directly inspired by emotions, both feminine and masculine, developed through female friend interaction. The original title for the record was "Feminist, Religious" (which Kim liked) but I thought it a little too scary and also that I'd probably get completely roasted for it.

C: Do you identify with the anger that women feel toward men? If so, how do you reconcile your feminism with your maleness?
T: I'm as aware as anybody of the shit male-dominated culture has served women. I choose not to reconcile whatever male guilt I may have but to learn and love those who have the oppressed voice. I can only sit quietly and hope to be identified as one who is ready to join hands. So . . . thanks for the honor of me being a *BUST* boy—I'm very into it. And I'll try not to fuck up too much.

Gillian Bell

Gillian Bell 5/98

5

Growing Up Girl

IN THE YEARS SINCE CINDY BRADY GREW UP TO BECOME
Courtney Love, the meaning of "girl" has been given a much-needed makeover.
The truth—that girlhood is more about insolence than innocence; that little girls
are made more of piss and vinegar than sugar and spice—is finally being told,
much to the relief of big girls and little women everywhere. Because, for the
longest time, our culture has been doing to little girls what little boys have always
done: ignoring them.

   I should know. When I was growing up, I was surrounded by boys. Although
I had only one brother, in the 1960s of my childhood, boys ruled the airwaves: there
was Timmy and his dog, Beaver and his brother, Eddie and his father. Sure, we had
the freckled and forgettable Buffy from *Family Affair*, but she seemed to do nothing

more exciting than squeeze Mrs. Beasley. In fact, the only girl who got to have any kind of fun in those days was a bitch: Lassie.

Not satisfied with having a dog as my role model, I tried to find my girl heroes wherever I could. I remember sitting on the floor of my dark bedroom every Sunday morning, watching old Shirley Temple movies. Hugging my knees to my chest, I'd be mesmerized by Shirley as she tap-danced her way through one tragedy after another. The fact that her movies made me cry was all the better: they fed my girlish desire to feel deep, sensitive, and a bit melodramatic. In books I could find a few girl characters I could relate to, but mostly, stories with girls at their center were few and far between. There was certainly no female equivalent to Huck Finn.

And then, in the '70s, when feminism was reborn, the word "girl" was suddenly stricken from my vocabulary. Up until then, ladies had no problem inviting "the girls" over for bridge, and the man in the gray flannel suit spoke with ease of "the girl" at the office, but now, a liberated woman would no sooner answer to the name "girl" than would a black man to the denigrating "boy." Feminists had argued, and convincingly so, that the girling of America had been a way of keeping women down, of belittling their wisdom and their abilities. Even I stopped referring to my ten-year-old classmates as "girls." I am *woman,* hear me roar.

In those years, girls seemed to be suffering from an image problem. Girl was cloying, girl was weak, girl was giggly. Tomboys were in; girlie-girls were out. Feminism, it seemed, was prepared to celebrate everything about womanhood—everything but the girl.

But, suddenly, "girl" is the word. From those T-shirts proclaiming that "Girls Rule" to pseudo-feminist bubblegum bands preaching about "Girl Power" to 1997's "Girl Issue" of *Spin* magazine, girl has gone from being a profanity among feminists to becoming practically a rallying cry. These days, enlightened women everywhere are embracing their inner brats, and TV shows like *Buffy the Vampire Slayer* and *Sabrina the Teenage Witch* are attracting teenage girls of all ages. Gwen Stefani, whose abs of steel could most likely kill a man, sings with mock helplessness about being "Just a Girl," while her pierced-and-combat-booted fans sit at home, painting their nails pink with Revlon's latest polish: "Girly." Women, step aside: the time of the girl is upon us.

The reevaluation of all things girl began in 1991. In that year, psychologist Carol Gilligan and her team of Harvard researchers reported that, contrary to popular belief, little girls were more confident, more assertive, and had greater self-esteem than their grown-up counterparts. In fact, they concluded, it was the process of becoming women that seemed to be stripping girls of their strength and courage. Their study, as reported in *The New York Times,* revealed that girls underwent a crisis of self-esteem during puberty from which they seemed never to recover. At age nine, a majority of girls answered "always" when asked how often they felt "happy the way I am," but by high school, fewer than a third of them felt that way. Boys were less happy in their teenage years, too (who isn't insecure in high school?), but the drop in their numbers was far less extreme. Clearly, something was happening to girls during their transition into womanhood that was bumming them out in a big way, and it was more than a bad case of acne could account for.

The New York Times article had women everywhere reflecting on their own girlhoods, and recalling the brazen beasts they had once been. Gilligan's study touched a nerve because it felt so right, making public something women had always known but had never quite been able to put their fingers on: that we had all been devilish little imps as children, who had clipped our own wings to fit into the portrait of a lady that was expected of us as adults. Maybe women were no longer required to bind themselves into tightly laced corsets; but even in the wake of the second wave of feminism, the self-denial and self-control that were demanded of us felt almost as restrictive. Our lives, as reflected in women's magazines and other media, seemed to be all about saying no: to calories, to inappropriate emotional outbursts, to men. We were expected to climb the corporate ladder and the Stairmaster; to get our hair, our bodies, and our emotions "under control"; and to take care of everything and anyone who came near us. Sure, we were strong—we were invincible, even. But suddenly we found ourselves looking back at the selfish days of our girlhoods with something that felt like longing. We were beginning to realize that, as girls, we had been more than just sissies—we had been *sassy.* And that was a quality that we, as adult women, needed to reclaim.

Speaking of sassy, right in the midst of the renewed hubbub about the crisis with American teen girls, a new magazine was born that was so full of attitude, you could practically hear the sound of gum-snapping emanating from its pages. *Sassy* was a magazine unlike any other: unapologetically feminist, smart, funny, and irreverent, *Sassy* spoke to its readers in the language of girl, a sort of "shebonics" shorthand

185

that conveyed both our girlie-giggles and our sarcastic streaks; our rock-and-roll poses along with our sentimental sides. It was written in the way that we spoke to each other, and any girl who read *Sassy* felt herself instantly transported to the world of girl, with a gang of wisecracking sisters who said, "Sure, being a teenage girl is harder than you expected. But just look at all the new freedoms you have, just look at all the music you can choose from, all the books you can read, all the opinions you can have, and, hey—just look at that cute boy over there!"

Sassy quickly became the cultural bible of a new generation of adolescents who took pride in their girlieness; who flaunted their Hello Kitty backpacks and Barbie barrettes like pink badges of honor. It was exactly the kind of thing that Mary Pipher, author of the best-selling *Reviving Ophelia,* an instruction booklet for concerned parents on how to keep their fearless little females from turning into anorexic, self-mutilating, pregnant teenagers, had prescribed. *Sassy* functioned like an antidote to what Pipher termed our "girl-poisoning culture": it turned the conventions of women's and girls' magazines on their heads by focusing on the pleasure, rather than the pain, of growing up girl. Older girls like Kim Gordon and Courtney Love said in the magazine's pages that they wished they'd had something like it when they were growing up, and they were right: it's incredibly important to see yourself reflected, accurately, in the media and in the world around you—because it makes you feel understood. And certainly, feeling understood goes a long way toward building self-esteem.

My generation of girls had that same overwhelming feeling of self-recognition when we read Judy Blume's *Are You There God? It's Me, Margaret.* How, we wondered, did this woman—this *grown-up*—know so much about our deepest fears and desires? How did she know how we girls talked, and what we talked about? It was a mystery to us (and it is still is to me, rereading the book twenty years later), but the thing was, she got it. We related to her characters in a way that we never did to Cindy, Jan, or Marcia. These were girls made of flesh, like us; they weren't all pretty, they were curious about sex, and they didn't come from perfect families. Her books talked about periods and breasts and smells and boys and we clung to her stories like life preservers as we navigated our way through our own ever-changing bodies. The fact that this book was banned from so many school libraries was a crime against girls everywhere.

The TV equivalent of Judy Blume's books came in the 1990s, in the form of the short-lived but highly successful show *My So-Called Life.* An instant hit, *My*

186

So-Called Life attempted to tell that great untold story: the story of girls. Through the characters of Angela, Rayanne, Rickie, and Jordan Catalano, we saw the friendships and crushes and rebellion and sexual confusion and parent trouble and terrible insecurity of girlhood presented in a raw and realistic way. It was a testament to the complexity of Everygirl.

Although a few things managed to get the girl thing right, for the most part, there's been a dearth of girl content in the media. Mary Pipher is right about the fact that girls get a raw deal: in children's programming, less than 20 percent of the characters are female. When girls do show up on television, they most often play a token role, in what Katha Pollitt has termed "the Smurfette Principle." According to her observations, the girl character is usually a combination of all the stereotypes of femininity rolled into one: she is both the love interest of the male characters and their mothering caretaker.

But, like stubborn weeds that grow up through cracks in the sidewalk, we girls survived a society that overlooked us by developing and nurturing our own collection of cultural references. Taken together they made up our very own "girl culture," one that we quilted together from the bits and pieces of the media that got it at least partway right. We read *Harriet the Spy,* the diary of Anne Frank, books about Madeline and Eloise; identified with Charlie Brown's nemesis, Lucy van Pelt; watched in awe as Nadia Comaneci won the gold medal in gymnastics; and fantasized about being Laurie Partridge: a cool keyboard player with a rock-and-roll mom who got to live with David Cassidy. We even read *Little Women* and developed a life-long fondness for the name Jo. We found our less-than-perfect, feisty girl heroines wherever we could, and held on to them, tight. And, just to make sure our own truths were recorded somewhere, we kept little locked diaries that filled in all the gaps where our stories weren't being told at all. If the world at large couldn't understand us, at least our diaries were always ready to listen.

And of course, there was Barbie. We all had at least one, unless our mothers, with their newly raised feminist consciousness, forbade them for the sexist playthings they were. They needn't have worried: Barbie didn't teach us so much about sexism as she did about sex. With her torpedo boobs and long legs, she lent herself to hours of sophisticated, perverse play, in which Barbie did stripteases for the other dolls, slept around with both Ken *and* Midge, stole other dolls' boyfriends, got into catfights, had her hair cut short or simply cut off, and had pins stuck into her head for "earrings." We were the furthest thing from the image of the innocent, sissified stereotype of "little girls playing with dolls"—playing with Barbie was serious business, and we created complex little soap operas with her plastic persona. Our Barbie, ourselves.

Today, as a generation of women are coming of age, our secret, hidden girl culture is busting out all over. Dorothy Allison's brilliant *Bastard Out of Carolina,* Mary Karr's *The Liars' Club,* and Sapphire's *Push* are all books that have thrown open the doors for other women to come out and tell the true stories of their girlhoods, no matter how harsh. In films, too, we're seeing more movies with complex girl characters at their centers, from *Manny and Lo* to *Heavenly Creatures* and *Slums of Beverly Hills.* And, even on TV, girls are getting a fairer shake. We've had fierce female characters in supporting roles for a while now—like the sharp-witted Lisa Simpson, and Roseanne's black-clad, rebellious daughter, Darlene Conner—but today's smart 'n' sassy girl characters are the stars of their own shows. Whether possessing a capacity for magic or the ability to do battle with the undead, there is no question that contemporary teenage heroines have power with a capital P. Even Barbie's been given a new lease on life, evolving from an evil sexist stereotype to a sort of feminist camp object. At last, the energy, adventurousness, and spunk of young girls is being celebrated, front and center, and no longer relegated to the darkened corners of sitcoms and storybooks.

Now that Girl and all her playthings have become a solid part of the mainstream, there's the danger that one inaccurate stereotype may simply be replaced by another. With everyone from magazine publishers to car dealers raring to jump on the girl-power gravy train, our pop culture is quickly becoming crowded with sneaker-wearin', gum-smackin', wisecrackin' chicas who take shit from no one, and buy their lipstick from Maybelline. It's important to remember that real Girl Power means that *real* girls have power, not just some commercial confection of what girls are supposed to be. We are, all of us, Sporty, Sexy, Posh, Baby, and Scary rolled into one—along with Crabby, Self-Conscious, and Stubborn, to name but a few. As long as we keep telling the truths of what it's like to grow up in a girl's skin, we can begin to show the world, and each other, what the world of girls is all about. Celebrating our girlhoods this way lets us take pride in our pasts, and can help build the self-esteem not only of girls, but also of women. You go, Girl.

—*Debbie Stoller*

The BUST *Guide to the New Girl Order*

Dear Diary

by Girl

It had a scuffed blue cardboard cover that locked with a tiny brass key which I kept hidden in a crevice down the spine, until I guess it got lost, or stolen. Then I had to rip the cardboard flap from its flimsy brass fastening, rendering permanently open, vulnerable, and public what had been my only refuge of at least symbolic privacy. Although I never had proof of prying, I always wrote, and hid, with the fevered and resentful conviction that someone (my sister Nancy) would be nosing around. There isn't much respect for boundaries in a family with eight kids, and though before I hit puberty even I, the youngest, had a room of my own, nowhere was really safe. (I had snooped plenty enough in the bedrooms of my parents, brothers, and sisters to know that.)

I never found anything really good in Nancy's room. I always assumed that since she was more experienced, more devious, and had far more to hide than I, she just had better hiding places. Most often I snooped in her territory for anything that belonged, or might belong, to me—a mutual, habitual strategy in our sister game. Reared in an anxious atmosphere of subtle hungers, inequities, and injustices, we could not resist the greed to possess each other's treasures, squashing them in drawers, in closets, and under pillows against their inevitable discovery. Earlier in childhood she and I were allies, but somewhere along the way we had become entrenched as adversaries in a perpetual war over psychic turf. Typically, one Saturday morning not along after we had each lovingly applied Archies rub-on decals (dug from our break-fast box of Honeycomb or Sugar Smacks) to the inside lips of our closet doorjambs (where Mom would never look), some casual infraction of personal space escalated through petty vindictiveness into a frenzy of retribution—until, at last, every one of those precious Jugheads and Veronicas had been cruelly clawed from the walls of our inner sanctums and we were left sobbing and broken. After that battle, and a few

189

similarly traumatic and bloody conflicts, we tended to invade only when the other combatant was not at home.

Anyway, my diary. A paltry thing with hardly a secret in it worth keeping, it still represented something desperate to me. It was the only private conversation I got to have with myself, the only outlet for my tiny little inner voice. Its existence told me, in a chintzy, dog-eared, pathetic cardboard way, that I was listened to. I didn't write to an imaginary confidante, like Anne Frank wrote to Kitty—and believe me, I was no Anne Frank. (I wasn't even a Go Ask Alice, the also tragically dead, anonymous confessor of lurid experiences—homelessness, homosexuality, hallucinogens—far racier than anything that went down in the Secret Annex, but closer to home somehow, and far more alluring than the Establishment propagandists who published her surely intended.) I encoded my diary for another self who would have to read between the lines.

After a few false starts at deflowering the virgin pages, in which I could never write "confidentially," I think I attempted to crib my most passionate innermost feelings without actually giving myself away. The risks of disclosure were too awful to engage. Rather than emulating the brave inspiring Anne, or even the ignobly admirable Harriet the Spy, I took no chances with honesty.

Anne embarrassed me, her frankness terrifying, her openness too raw, confused as it was in the clammy morbidity with which I obsessed over her photograph. How did she unbosom that stuff? She didn't seem to fear that it might be read. Here was I reading it without her knowledge and permission! How awful that her father was the one who survived to return and reclaim it, to invade her privacy in front of the entire universe. (For some reason it was this I found more upsetting than the unimaginable true horror of her fate.) And, sinisterly, his preface said that he edited out certain passages not for the eyes of the general public, which haunted me—what could it have been necessary to censor, to keep hidden, among all that he felt compelled to expose?

My mother, it seemed, had managed to find things—drugs in Nancy's macramé, pornography under my brother's mattress, things shoplifted, Ortho-Novum—without always choosing to acknowledge their discovery, so if she ever read my diary some quiet school day while cleaning the house, I never knew it. Not that she would have moved to confront me over anything that it contained, because my diary was pretty much a big cryptic bore.

Unlike Anne and Alice, I had no profound insights, no painful confessions, no adventures, no crimes, no revelations. In fact, apparently all I ever wrote about was what I watched on TV; I recorded the passage of several grades of elementary and junior high school merely by commenting on my nightly viewings. I wrote in script so tiny it was almost indecipherable, as if to make the dumbly precious words more hidden, more private. (I also wrote little stories in the same tiny hand, scraps of pulsating fiction on slips of notebook paper, but these were too dire a secret even to be kept with something so palpable and enduring as a diary. I hid those pieces wedged in between the pages of whatever book I was currently reading—the temporary possession of a book being one of the few sacred ownerships honored in our household—or inside my pillowcase, savoring them until it was time to destroy them.)

I think I labored about TV partly because it was shameful and partly because it was a mask for what was shameful—sex, mostly, was the subtext although I'm not sure how aware I was of that at the time. I found Starsky and Hutch somehow compelling (no matter how humiliated I would have been to admit it) in their eroticized buddyhood, in the hard-thighed tightness of their jeans. I was mesmerized, if also slightly repulsed, by the hammy bulge of Baretta's hog biceps, by the role-reversal foreplay between Stephanie Zimbalist and her boy toy Remington Steele, by Caine's sensuous asceticism. These were forbidden pleasures—shows too stupid to watch openly, much less discuss; not brilliantly stupid like Monty Python, but really stupid. I'm sure I was mortified to be writing about TV—why else was I using such microscopic script?—but it was better than writing about anything that was actually happening (or not happening) in my so-called life.

For me there was probably tremendous security in writing only of the trivial and banal. It reinforced the ultimate privacy of the inside of my head, one safe place in an unsafe world. Hiding was compulsive, if not compulsory, at home; deception and exposure were just part of daily life. Anne Frank had, in a way, nothing to lose; she could say everything. For some reason I felt I had everything to lose, and so I said nothing. It took me years to discover the liberation in brutal honesty.

What's interesting to me now is the sadness in remembering what I didn't write in my diary, what I couldn't afford to let be written, to let be read. All the things which held so much power over me through shame (because if there's a single word to sum up my entire adolescence, that would be it: shame), things I would not even allude to covertly, not on the page.

Like:

Getting my period but not telling my mom about it, ever.

Having to listen to my parents having sex on their indecently squeaking bed, and trying desperately to get away from the sound by going into the basement and turning the volume way up on the TV.

That I would sometimes steal Cokes from the Blomsteds' garage, and Sara Lee cupcakes from the Canteras' Deepfreeze.

That I took pleasure in the animal smell of my own vaginal secretions and explored the nameless thing which I later learned was my labia, feeling sort of dirty and abnormal and yet sort of satisfied.

That our neighbors' oldest son would sit too close on the couch and slowly, surreptitiously rub his crotch while we were all watching TV but no one else ever seemed to notice; that it became a torment I could not figure out how to escape, my eyes fixed on the TV screen, trying to ignore the stealth beside me, trying to squeeze myself to the edge of the seat, trying to think of an excuse to get up, hoping someone else would get up so I could take their chair without drawing too much attention to myself; wanting to call attention but knowing I never could; wondering why no one else ever noticed; feeling victimized by a horrible conspiracy of blindness.

That I was suddenly so curious about my best friend's body that I would try not to stare at her, self-consciously comparing my own body to hers, feeling awkward, staring helplessly anyway, wondering if this meant I was gay, and agonizing that I was abnormal.

That I would lock myself naked in the bathroom and decorate my new breast buds with soap lather, feeling vaguely dirty and evil.

That I would draw dirty pictures of naked women and men, but since I didn't know what men really looked like they came out unsatisfactorily, like anatomically incorrect Ken dolls.

All those things were hidden between the lines. A lot of it was shared, in guilty silence, with my sister; for some reason we could not have borne to acknowledge those things aloud, as I could not bear to acknowledge them in the pages of my diary.

I wish I still had it, but sometimes in my early twenties I must have destroyed it. Almost a decade later I was still capable of being ashamed of my own diary.

The **BUST** *Guide to the New Girl Order*

Electra Woman and Dyna Girl

by Tiffany Lee Brown

"Christina" finished cutting the peanut butter sandwiches into strips and arranged them in a circle on the plate. "I am going to have Sweet 10 in my iced tea," she announced. "It tastes great but only has ten calories per serving. Do you want Sweet 10 or sugar?" Puzzled, I asked why having ten calories was a good thing. "Because I'm on a diet," she explained. "Christina" was much bigger than me, she was tall and two years older and much stronger, too. But she didn't look like she needed a diet, and besides, as my mom would say, why should a healthy nine-year-old diet? "I don't want any sugar," I said. The tea tasted sweet to me already.

I followed "Christina" down the stairs, where she carefully put the peanut butter strips on the pool table and set the iced tea on the bar. I squeezed behind the bar and unlatched a little door in the pine-paneled wall. "Christina" was getting too big to climb inside, which made me glad because we used to play a lot in the little room inside. I didn't like small spaces, they made me feel weird and sometimes I would panic and start screaming and kicking like when my brother would stuff me in a sleeping bag and zip it up all the way, and I would squirm and cry and howl. I would try to pretend it was okay and be calm but I felt as though I was dying. But now I crawled into the little room long enough to find the big gold boxes and hand them out to "Christina."

When I crawled back into the rec room, the gold lid of one box was lying on the pool table, covering half the peanut butter sandwiches. Then "Christina" threw out the tissue paper and pulled out her dress. I started unwrapping mine slowly. I didn't really like mine; it was a pale salmon-y color that reminded me of my mom's kitchen tile. But I took off my clothes and "Christina" zipped me into the frothy strapless taffeta with the piles of tulle on the skirt part. I twirled around but had to keep holding it to keep it from falling down. The dresses were from "Christina"'s mom and her sister; they had worn them to the prom many years ago, so we had to be extra careful with them. The blue one, that looked like icing, stayed up on "Christina" now, and she swung her hips in front of the mirror for a while. She wore her dress shoes, which had little white heels on the bottom of them.

"I don't feel like playing dress-up," I told her after a while. I munched on a peanut butter strip. "Let's go outside and play Electra Woman and Dyna Girl. You got the walkie-talkies?" I always had to be Dyna Girl because "Christina" wanted to be the one who orders everyone around, but I thought Dyna Girl was prettier than Electra Woman anyway, and besides, even if she said less, she always figured out the really obscure parts of the mystery while Electra Woman was just running around in her red high heels.

"We're gonna play Wild West," "Christina" informed me. "What's your name?" I thought about going out to the woods to look at the miniature castles by myself or something, but decided Wild West would be okay. "Um, I'm . . . I'm Miranda," I said. "Christina" raised her eyebrows, and I could tell she was mad I had thought of such a dramatic name, a new one we'd never used in a game before. "I'm Beth," she pronounced proudly, pointing her chin at me. I didn't say anything. We both knew Beth was a boring name, from *Little Women.* She climbed up on the piano bench and pressed the eject button on the eight-track. I ran over to look at the tapes before she put the Carpenters on again. "I can't listen to the Carpenters anymore," I told her. "My mom's been playing them all the time." "But I want to hear the Carpenters," she whined. "No, let's listen to that other stuff. Look, your sister left her Beatles! Put on that!" "Christina" glared at me and I could tell she wanted to fight about it. "This is my house," she said sure enough, "and I can put on whatever I want." "I know," I answered. "Just put on the Beatles or anything but the Carpenters." I made sure my voice didn't sound like fighting. She hesitated a moment, then stuck in the Donna Summer cartridge. Towering down at me from atop the bench, she squirreled her eyebrows at me and let out a big huge sigh.

I didn't say anything and ate another peanut butter strip. The bottom of my dress dragged along the short carpeting, like always, but I started swaying to the disco song. "Christina" jumped down and rushed to the center of the room, flailing her arms in flowy motions and tapping her little white heels. "Ten cents a daaaance," she called out as usual. "Ten cents a daaance!" We made believe that cowboys had come in and we were dancing with them. I would keep dancing but not say anything, my

194

arm resting gently on my imaginary cowboy's chest, while I listened to her conversation with her imaginary cowboy. "Why, how dare you!" she exclaimed suddenly, slapping at the air. She marched off to the bar and took up her glass of iced tea. I kept dancing with my guy, asking him about where they had ridden in from. "I'm going to play your guy," "Christina" said in her normal voice, putting down the glass and bustling over to me. "My name's Nate."

She put her arms around my waist and I kept dancing. My voice was in a southern drawl, like my mom and I would always talk in for fun, like in *Gone with the Wind,* and it was really high up. "Christina" always tried to make a southern accent too, but she couldn't do it right and sounded funny. Now she talked real slow and made her voice low like a man's. "Tell me, little lady," she intoned, "how did you end up in a Wild West tavern like this?" I wasn't really into the game and couldn't come up with anything good off the top of my head, so I pulled away from her and shielded my eyes. "Ah'm feeling a bit weak," I fluttered in a breathy voice. "Could y'all get me a drink please, Nate?"

I leaned helplessly against the pool table. "Bartender!" Nate barked. "Bring me a beer for this little lady!" He brought it over to me, slightly concerned. "Here you are, sweetie," he said, leering at me somewhat. I drank gratefully, my cheeks flushing as I caught my breath again. "What did you say your name was?" "Ah'm Miranda, kind sir," I told him. Just then I felt faint with the weight of my poor plight, the crops dying, Mama falling ill, the long train trips out west, the long nights at the tavern. Water slipped down my hands as the glass fell toward the floor, but before it crashed to pieces Nate grabbed it. My head spun, and the orange dress was falling down. I was falling down. My eyelids were closed, the ground swam up to me and I fell into it.

The big-faced woman with the smelling salts scolded down at me. "You're supposed to dance with the gentleman, not faint on him!" She stood up, replaced in an instant by Nate, who leered over me like a big snake with beady eyes. "You're comin' with me, little lady!" he hissed gleefully, pushing the yellow beanbag chair across the carpet with me still on it. Straddling the chair so I couldn't move, he reached over and locked the door, then peered down at me again, smiling so his lips made a flat line. Nate hiked up her blue tulle skirt and lowered himself onto my stomach. "You want it, don't you, little Miranda?" he said.

I craned my neck toward the doorknob, wondering if I could reach it fast enough. Nate dropped the pile of frothing blue and his arms darted out like tongues, wrapping around my wrists and pressing them into the soft gelatin of the chair. "Don't even think of it," he drawled. "I am here to have some fun." I let out a squeal, or maybe a whimper, and Nate jerked my arms above my head, grabbing both wrists with one fat hand. The other closed over my mouth. I could feel "Christina"'s gold ring, the one with her birthstone in it, the real sapphire stone she said, digging into my cheek. "That's better," Nate said with an evil chuckle, and started grinding his pelvis into mine. This went on for a few minutes with nothing happening, so I started screaming underneath his hand. He pressed it tighter into my face and said, "Shut up, Miranda, you little whore."

Then she made a sound like "shlllorrp" and began pumping harder at me. This was the sound that meant the penis was supposed to be going into the vagina, which "Christina" said was how babies were made. "Shut up, Miranda, you little whore!" Nate said again, louder this time, so I pretend to struggle and yell. Nate kept going faster and faster, and my arms and hips started hurting. Then he sighed, a grunt kind of sigh, and let go of me. We lay still for a moment, listening to "Christina"'s mom walking up the steps from the front door.

"Whore," "Christina" said one more time, crossing the room to put on a Carpenters tape.

One Girl's Vise

by Marni Davis

My dad has never been a fix-it kind of guy. He's less so now than he was as I was growing up, when he at least pretended to be handy. Throughout my childhood, he maintained a manly workshop table, which occupied the entire left wall of the inside of our garage.

Dad had all kinds of cool shit: hammers and saws and power drills and a bazillion different screwdrivers. Boxes upon boxes of various sizes of nails and screws. A ten-piece ratchet kit in a red plastic box. He saved small pieces of scrap board and a pile of sandpaper for me, so I could hang out with him and sand wood and feel useful while he built ugly lopsided bookshelves.

Some of his tools fascinated me more than others. I was into the power drill, but it seemed dangerous and it made a scary noise, so I steered clear. I liked the level, too; I amused myself for hours by holding it on either end and trying to keep the little bubble steady between the lines. But I spent the majority of my tool-time with the vise.

It was clamped onto the workshop table by a huge screw, long and wide, pressed up tight against the table's underside. This screw—and thus the base of the mechanism—never budged. The only pieces that moved were a small, thin, dumbbell-shaped rod that turned with the touch of my little fingers, and the menacing-looking outer jaw of the vise itself. By spinning the dumbbell piece, I could change the pressure of the grip.

I'd first noticed the vise when I was around six, and my dad allowed me to twist the handgrip (under his supervision) and figure out how the thing worked. I experimented with the vise for a few months after that, and I soon discovered I far preferred playing with my dad's tools when he wasn't around. I spent this phase perfecting my one-fingered spinning technique, enjoying my ability to easily manipulate such an intimidating piece of equipment.

My curiosity blossomed around the same time I lost interest in my baby dolls. Coincidence? Maybe not—I'd been smashing my baby dolls' heads against walls for years (screaming "BAD baby! NAUGHTY girl!" and scaring the living crap out of my staunchly anti-corporal-punishment parents), so crushing their craniums in a vise seemed the next logical step.

I'd lay them down on the tool table, place their head in the device ("bad baby . . . shhhh . . . bad baby"), and slowly spin the rod. Some of my dolls had more pliable heads, so as the vise gripped tighter against their temples, their foreheads would bulge and their eyes would stare wildly to either side of the room, instead of straight ahead. The recurring stress eventually took its toll on the plastic, though, and they soon sported demented rips in their scalps and on their faces.

Of all my dolls, Chrissie was the baddest baby, and I took particular delight

Melissa Iwai

in bashing her around. The vise was her end; her head was less yielding, and I hadn't applied much pressure before CRRRAAAACCKK! Chrissie's skull caved in, and one of her eyes rolled off her face and back behind the table. She was a grisly sight, and I rushed her to the side of my neighbor's house and shoved her to the bottom of their garbage can.

A psychoanalyst would probably say that this experience—torturing and murdering Chrissie—had a profound effect on me, filled me with guilt and self-hatred. I might argue that I'd simply run out of baby dolls, and still valued my Barbies too much to destroy them. Regardless, my relationship with the vise changed drastically when I started tightening it on my hand.

It was initially a typical eight-year-old only child's solitary pretend game; I

198

was being held captive by evil forces, and, through cunning and magic, I would release my hand from their robot's jaws. I soon realized that making believe was more exciting when I was motivated by physical sensation. I tightened the vise, just so it hurt a little. I enjoyed losing myself in the drama, and the pain made it more real.

I don't remember when the game ended, but at some point it must have seemed superfluous, because soon it was just me and the vise. I'd place the palm and back of my hand against the grips, tighten it until it hurt like a motherfucker, stand there and wait until the pain was less excruciating, and then twist the little rod another millimeter to the right. I ended most rounds in tears and totally confused. Why was I doing this? Why couldn't I take more pain? What would my parents to do me if they found me standing in the garage, trying to crush my tiny hand?

I played this twisted game for only a few weeks. Fear of discovery, not fear of hurting myself, ended my obsession with my dad's vise. And it's a good thing that my superego stepped in, because I'm sure I would have broken some bones if I'd kept it up. I regarded the thing warily for a while, but by the time I was ten it was forgotten. I was by then obsessing on other activities, like playing "Let's Pretend Mommy and Daddy Are Dead" with my friend Maureen, and hanging out at the Burger King up the street with my neighborhood pals.

The vise didn't enter my consciousness again until very recently. Home for a long weekend and bored to the point of rage, I went out to the garage to see if my parents' old vinyl collection was worth pilfering. I can't say why I was drawn to dad's long-neglected workshop bench, but I suddenly found myself checking the base screw under the table and twisting the vise's handle. I looked around for something to crush in the grip, but decided against it and walked back to the house. I just didn't need the vise anymore; now my methods of tormenting others and causing myself pain are far more subtle and sophisticated.

Stealing Beauty

by Michelle Goldberg

The Mr. Cookie was right next to Unique Boutique in the mall in the town where I grew up, an arrangement that let me combine the greatest joys of my girlhood: sweets and shoplifting. Some of the girls and I would buy mini–chocolate chip cookies and then head next door to drop earrings, headbands, and rubber Madonna bracelets into our cookie bags. Other days, we'd go to Johnson's drugstore and steal pink mascara, violet eyeliner, Pizzazz hair color, and red lip gloss. At home, we'd examine our loot, give each other makeovers, paint each nail a different color, and then throw half the shit away.

Shoplifting is one of the most thrilling secrets of girlhood. Boys steal things like car radios and pornos, but for them it's more about getting the thing itself—if they had the money, they'd simply buy it. For girls, shoplifting is all about the taking. It's an empowering response to a society that can crush a girl under an avalanche of consumerism. It's a way of saying to the rapacious advertisers on TV and in *YM,* "Okay, if I need all this stuff so much, I'm just going to *take* it."

Shoplifting has always been associated with women. Fifties criminologists thought that it was related to women's inherent deceitfulness. I'm sure Freud had his own phallic explanation for why girls feel compelled to slip unpaid-for lipsticks into the purses he said stood for vaginas. Psychoanalyst Louise Kaplan devotes a whole chapter to shoplifting in her book *Female Perversions.* "Very rich women just shop and then shop some more and even steal a trophy or two, now and then, whenever they might otherwise get depressed or anxious. Not-so-rich women are kleptomaniacs who replace an experience of deprivation or anxiety with an impulse to steal what they feel deprived of. And poor women merely shoplift, steal what their families need in the way of food and clothing with an occasional extra—a trinket, a record, a bottle of perfume, some little trophy—to assuage the violence of deprivation," she writes.

Kaplan misses the exhilaration of filching, but she gets something right. Shoplifting was a way to beat back anxiety—the anxiety of being at the mercy of parents or boyfriends or baby-sitting jobs for all the adornments that we felt we needed in order to compete in the brutal world of junior high school. It made us

Marcellus Hall

generous, too. After I discovered stealing, I was able to get holiday gifts for every girl I knew. There was girl-to-girl gallantry in kleptomania. I'm not sure if I ever felt more heroic than when I was stealing a pregnancy test for a friend who waited shaking outside the CVS, or more grateful than when my friends did it for me.

Although it wasn't dick envy that made me take all those fake eyelashes, Freud's purse-as-vagina thing doesn't seem so far-fetched given the orgasmic rush

Growing Up Girl

that we thirteen-year-old girls felt snaking around the jewelry store, taking pretty things and shoving them down our pants or into our bras. My oldest friend, Tracy, says, "It was just like the excitement of when you like someone and you don't know what's going to happen. It's the anticipation. It was a group thing that said, 'Watch how good we are.'" While shoplifting, we felt slick and quick and smarter than anyone in the world.

When we called a girl a "kleptomaniac," it was a term of admiration. They were the ones, usually a couple of years older, who had graduated from stealing trinkets to the real thing—shoes, CDs, expensive clothes. At the time, they seemed exceptionally brave. Some of them got caught and had to go to court to be sentenced to community service. When I think about them now, though, I see that they were usually the ones with less money or cruel parents or some other circumstances that let them know early on that this world wasn't going to give them anything except when they could steal from it. I think their sense of entitlement was healthy. The worst thing that can happen to a girl is for her to start believing she doesn't deserve the very best.

Wayward Warden's Wicked War Against Womanhood

by Tricia Warden

I wanted to be tough and I didn't want tits. I thought that tits were the most repulsive things I had ever seen. To me they looked like the equivalent of rubbery alien tentacles, something that might reach out in the middle of the night and strangle you to death. They had no other purpose except to horrify and bewilder. My only live subject to judge from was my mother. She was overweight and her body seemed so foreign in comparison to my skinny flat child's body. I couldn't comprehend that we were the same thing or that someday I would eventually be that. This would not be the first time or reason this particular thought would flicker across my minefield mind. I felt oddly unprepared looking at her. It made me feel that I needed desperately to alter my genetic fate. Her tits explained this to me simply by looking gargantuan and hanging down almost to her waist. Super double-dare D's. I recall both a fascination and a repulsion; a gravitational pull toward them while squirming around on the toilet seat watching her undress in the bathroom.

I did not want to be a girl. I wanted to reject the whole thing. I just wasn't at all comfortable with the idea. This did not mean that I wanted to grow a dick. I did not necessarily want to be a boy either. I think I just wasn't into being a human but could not verbalize this feeling. The people and ideals that I had for examples seemed outrageously fucked. I did not want to belong to their group or change into one of them, so puberty horrified me. I thought for some cockeyed reason that I could bypass this required journey; it seemed apparent that I was some other strain of being altogether. This delusion proved to be very costly, for while my brain was forming this philosophy my body was already working against me. Puberty itself settled its jagged jaws in front of me and sucked me down into its black hole of indecision and humiliation.

One day my mother caught on to my mystified stare and said with a smile, "Don't worry, Tricia, every woman has them. Someday you will have them too." "No way" was my first response. I wanted to run away like a screaming maniac (an art I now have down to near perfection). I told her straightaway where my head was at. I said, "I don't ever want those." Much to my dismay she thought this reply was hilarious. In between laughs she nodded assuredly, "Someday you will be very glad you have them." I was outraged. I didn't want those huge mammaries hanging off me. My body was fine as it was. If they got that big I would have to cart them around in a wheelbarrow, and that would definitely cramp my style.

To combat this hormonal insurgence, I began my arduous pilgrimage toward its prevention. No boobs by any means necessary became my battle cry. I immediately made a vigil to God. Down on my hands and knees I prayed, "Our father who art in Heaven, don't ever make me grow breasts. I don't want them. They are the ugliest things I have ever seen. If you really love me you won't make me have them. I'll be

203

good. I'll do anything, I promise. I'll clean my room. Maybe I'll even wear a dress. Anything God, but no boobs. Thanks. Amen." Afterward I would genuflect, feeling as if I was taking some direct action against my seemingly miserable fate. My mother told her friends that I didn't want breasts. They all thought it was really funny too. They teased me, saying things like "Tough titty" or "Wait until ya have kids, then dey cutcha from ya crotch to ya ass. . . ." They scared me. But inwardly I could laugh at them, for they were unaware of my daily contact with the benevolent almighty. God will never make me like these people, I thought. Never.

As a result of what I could only attribute to the cruelest of the deity's tricks, my breasts began sprouting at age eight. By the time I was nine I had to skip the training bra altogether and go straight to the A. My mother took me to this women's store called Sylvettes. The woman with the teased bouffant behind the counter pushed her glasses down her nose and said, "Already?!" She came toward me with her trusty tape measure. I was mortified. I didn't want her touching me, especially there. My mother stood there beaming, seeming very proud for some reason. That day we left Sylvettes with two white bras with pink fucking bows sewn onto each of their centers. I ripped them off promptly as soon as the attention of my mother wandered. It was then I figured that God was definitely a man and that he hated my guts. There seemed to be no escape from my unavoidable destiny.

No other girls I knew had breasts. I felt like an ever-expanding abomination. Not only was my face ugly but the rest of my body seemed to be following the same route. I tried to ignore them. They just kept getting larger and larger as my shirts got baggier and baggier. The boys noticed as well. They began calling me "Toilet Paper Trish" because no one believed they were real. This made me feel worse because I didn't like the tits to begin with, and I definitely did not want to start defending them either. Eventually, I lost my shit.

I recall a kid named Dennis who came up to me during library period and called me T.P.T. I looked at him squarely and lifted my shirt to show him the real deal. I asked him while he stood there agog if they looked real enough for him. He just shook his head yes. This stopped this kind of remark for a short period of time.

Later on, a boy who must have been stupid or absent on the aforementioned day of my bust debut really reaped the benefits of my rage. The boy's name was Jimmy. I remember him well because he had this perpetual rash on both corners of his mouth and chin. The rash was a result of his compulsive gnawing of his dress-shirt collars. Poor kid. Anyway, one day he tosses out the old T.P.T. to me and I am in a foul mood to begin with. I have already decided I hate everyone. My parents are demons from hell and I am beginning to realize I have no choice but to live out the next excruciating six to seven years with them. As he said these old familiar words, something in my head just broke and my mind went black. When I came back I was pummeling Jimmy in the boy's bathroom. He was curled up in a fetal position, covering his face, lying next to a toilet bowl. I remember seeing the blue walls and freezing up instantly when I realized where I was.

Although the boys eventually stopped calling me T.P.T., the fun and stupid attention did not end there. The comments just graduated to another realm of unconsciousness that has yet to cease rearing its brainless head. This was an extreme bummer. Things seemed to be getting worse. I was changing and there was no way to hide it. I hated it. I was losing miserably. I was getting my ass kicked in what I thought of as the Vietnam of Hormones. I actually contemplated cutting them off with a kitchen knife.

Now I am no longer mammaphobic. I can enjoy breasts of all sizes in many ways. But oddly enough, I cannot see much purpose for my own contrary C's. They look nice; I'll give them that. It would be easier to run if they were smaller. It feels pretty good when someone touches, sucks, or bites on them. My memory of these simple pleasures often wanes because it has been so long since I have had sex with another individual. I know for a fact I will never use them for their ordained purpose, which is to nourish another human life. There is no way a child will ever sprout from between these legs and there are too many reasons for this statement. I have to admit, though, I have grown accustomed to my tits. I think I will keep them around. I don't use my spleen much but I would not want it removed.

Breasts were not my only problem. I started getting hairy as well. I remember the first time I realized I had pubic hair; it seemed to appear overnight. I was lying on the couch with a blanket spread out over me. I was stationed in the living room recovering from a recent tonsillectomy when I discovered this bodily rebellion. I had an itch, and when I decided to scratch myself, I felt a small tuft of hair there. I was paralyzed. I had tried so hard to be good. I could not understand why I was being punished so perfunctorily. It had been close to Easter and the rest of the family had been gathered around the

205

television watching *The Ten Commandments,* of all things. Oftentimes when I see or touch pubic hair I am flooded with the haunting visage of Charlton Heston.

Next was the period. I remember my mother informing me of this grim event outside my public school outlined by a clear, sunny day. My mother said it would be "our secret." She said there would be blood and that I should not be afraid. She said this could happen soon because the women on her side of the family were often early bloomers. She said there might be some pain called "cramps." I was terrified. I didn't understand why this would happen to me or why all women were "cursed." My mother said it was a "woman's curse" because Eve ate the apple. In Sunday school I was told it was "our sin" because some woman I had never met was dumb enough to share her forbidden fruit with some guy who obviously didn't appreciate it. The conclusive result of this historical event caused "us" to be jettisoned promptly from the safe confines of the boring painless paradise called Eden. Hence the rotten apple that spoiled the bunch. I couldn't see how this treatment was fair or why God hated all women because of a fucking piece of produce. It was just an apple. Why didn't he want them to eat it? What I especially could not comprehend was that he would still be pissed off about it and take it out on me. What a grudgefuck. How perplexing. At eight, standing in the sunlight, I knew I would be screwed. I would not be one of the chosen. I would not be ordained the new and improved Virgin Mary. I was marked like a casino deck and ready to be dealt.

My mother told me when I got my period that I was to tell no one except her. I was forbidden to bring up the subject if men or boys were present. The reason she gave for this was that the period was an extremely private thing. To give it that certain neurotic paranoid afraid-of-your-own-sexuality flair she gave it a code name. I felt like an agent of espionage. The code name was Rosy. In this way I could communicate with my mother if others, especially males, were present. She said I should say something like "Rosy came to visit me today and boy was she a pain!" Even at my tender age I knew she was out of her mind. This info just did not compute. Why was she so ashamed? If every woman had it, why was it such a secret? Were we trying to hide the fact that we were all damned by body-part association? Didn't every man and boychild know this already? All they had to do was watch television or read the best-selling book of all time, the Bible. Who was she trying to kid?

When the curse first arrived on the scene, I was alone in my room getting prepared for bed. When I removed my tan underwear with the patchwork letters that spelled out "groovy," something was not right. There was a dark spot the size of a quarter on the crotch. At first I was mystified; then it dawned on me. I figured I should go tell my mother. Since there were no men or guests in the house, I was thankful not to have to use the retarded code. I yelled upstairs for my mother. She answered in a kind, matronly tone, "What tha fuck do ya want now? Go ta bed already!" "I can't," I replied, surprised that anything came out at all. "Why tha fuck not?" was her warm response. "I have my period, Ma." "No ya don't! Go ta bed!" I felt an intense anger as I looked up at her from the bottom of the staircase. She was standing there in a gray-and-plum-colored bathrobe with the beige telephone cord wrapped around her body. She was talking to her friend Maureen. She glared back at me in an annoyed disbelief when I did not retreat from my stance. She lifted her hand up in the air. This simplistic body language said to me simply don't make me get off this phone and wack ya in tha head. I stomped back into my room to retrieve my bloodstained proof. I climbed each stair defiantly and produced my mark of the beast with righteous contempt. Her eyes widened when she saw the stain. She said quickly into the receiver, "Mo, I gotta go. Rosy just came to visit Tricia." Am I glad that now I see the humor and sadness in this statement, but at the time I wanted to yell so loud my liver would fly out. My mother was nicer afterward and explained that I probably would not menstruate regularly. She apologized and said, "I didn't realize." She also said if I bled more she would give me something to wear. The blood did not return again for almost a year, but the next time it would not be so painless.

When I was twelve I was in a gang of sorts with three other girls with views similar to my own (or so I thought at the time). My nickname was Fingers #14. They called me this since I was an expert shoplifter (a very short-lived career) among other things I did well with my fingers. We sought out trouble whenever and wherever possible. We acted like assholes a good amount of the time. I did everything first, both sex and drugs. I was trying hard to prove myself, but to whom I was trying to prove this I am not sure. The first time I had sex of my own volition was on a dare when I was thirteen. The guy I had it with tried to have his friends watch from the roof across the street.

Even though I had sex numerous times I never attained an orgasm. I had trouble figuring out this mystery. I had only acquired the knowledge of its so-called existence through its sketchy, nebulous mention in the porno mags I had found beneath the bathtub of our upstairs neighbors. I experimented a hell of a lot, but nothing seemed to cum from it. I did not feel so bad about this failure because no guy, not even the thirty-eight-year-old I was having an affair with in the eighth grade, ever gave me one either. I was relentless. I had to know. I got the guts up to ask other girls if they knew about this or if they had never experienced one themselves. They were all just as clueless as I or more so. (If they weren't, may they all get yeast infections this very moment.) I began wondering if the whole thing was a myth. I couldn't grasp why people thought sex was so great. It was all right. I liked the contact, but it was very apparent that the guys were having a much better time. My magic moment arrived when I was fifteen. I thought, Wow, if this is what being a woman is all about, then I'm all for it. I was straddled across the lap of my eighteen-year-old psychopathic Colombian boyfriend. I was grinding away while we were making out hot and heavy when I began to mount the edge of the most fantastic shivering spasm. I remember looking down at him and saying, "I don't know what is happening, but if you move I will kill you."

Now even though my cramps hurt more than having my arm torn open to the muscle I'm proud to be a woman and a feminist. I would never turn my tits and cunt in for anything or anybody. Even if some green genie popped out of my ass and offered to transform me into a man, I would plainly refuse. Only a fucking crazy loon would trade forty-five-minute orgasms for a higher-paying job.

The World Moves

by Dixie LaRue

You become an animal. Like a deer or a fox: listening, watching, waiting. Constantly alert, slow and easy on the surface, you're poised for action like a deer taking a tentative drink at the edge of a lake. Day by day, pieces of the human part of you drop away like molting feathers. At the start, you try to salvage comfortable bits of humanity as you cling to scraps of your former self. But what did that other self know about preserving itself, about the primordial need to *maintain*? Eventually you shed every layer of now-unwieldy cognition. There is no action, only reaction. You grab a toehold, and you hold on. Grown-ups are touching you *there*.

And so I've spent too much of my life listening to creaking boards. Too much time lying very still, deciphering footsteps. Too much time watching for venom in small acts, shrinking from too-loud laughter, waiting for violence. But as every forest creature knows, the promise of violence makes violence ever-present. In nature, peace is deceptive. Danger is both sudden and omnipresent. Violence is no longer an intrusion into order; violence becomes its own order. Violence roams the world like a wolf. I am a vanquished Red Riding Hood.

When we are children, the world is a big place ablaze with multicolors. In good and bad, there is black and there is white. Then someone you love, someone you trust, someone's tobacco breath is too close. And the world is no longer full of color. Good and bad are no longer black and white. There is only gray. Even though the rugged veil of child simplicity has slipped from the world, clarity becomes diminished, not sharpened. There is a luster to naïveté, and when it leaves, a vibrancy is lost that can never be recaptured. Nothing can be orange now, nothing can be certain now, only gray. You become wiser in a dimmer world. And as you walk through malls and grocery stores, you look at other little girls with sad eyes, and wonder. And always, always, look away to hide your own eyes.

Now I am a woman. I remember but do not grieve my wounds. I believe that if they ever existed, they have healed. I never changed. The world changed. It seemed to me then, as it seems to me now, that it was the world that shifted, not I. And so because the world changed, I sagely pushed down my innocence to a bottom where it could not be further burgled. I exchanged hope for cynicism, put away expectation and replaced it with wariness.

Betrayal can make the world's dogs less friendly, its seas less deep, its colors less bright, but it cannot, will not change me. I am the same, but the universe has moved a notch and can never return from where it slipped.

✕

Making It

by Anne Marie Yerks

It was straight from the movies: the colored pleats of her short skirt hung like a peacock fan around the wooden seat of the school desk; her legs—bare to the Michigan winter—were crossed at the ankles, and her feet were capped with purple-and-white saddle shoes. The back of her purple sweater was embroidered with her name, "Keli," in swirling fuzzy letters.

I was the new girl, having just arrived to the small-town Michigan school from North Carolina. In North Carolina, there were no cheerleaders in junior high. But in Michigan, things were different.

Before the day was over I had spotted each of the six girls who held the enviable status of Cheerleader. All six of these girls dressed in identical purple-and-yellow uniforms, and none of them seemed to mind exposing their bare legs to the icy November wind. In less than one hour at Onsted Junior High I decided that I too would tolerate chronic frostbite for the chance to serve as a cheerleader. But alas: my arrival in Michigan was several months too late. I would have to wait until the April tryouts to get my chance for the next year's squad.

Never disillusioned, I planned my strategy in algebra class while eyeing Keli's cheerleader garb. What I would have given to fasten a miniature megaphone pin to my collar! All at once junior high school held the promise of excitement, of more than homework, boring educational movies, and long bus rides. The problem was that none of the excitement could be mine until I was given the opportunity to don a cheerleader uniform.

A few days later, I gained the nerve to take the seat next to Keli and make an obvious attempt to befriend her. She was cordial enough to give me a brief biography: She had been going to Onsted schools since kindergarten. All four of her older sisters had also been cheerleaders, and as a matter of fact, her father was the mayor. Later, I pshawed Keli's family's elevated status in town politics. When cheerleader tryouts came, democracy would most certainly reign: The best girls would win!

My mother and I lived in a trailer three miles from the backside of the junior high school. I began to spend the afternoons that year by watching *The Guiding Light* and practicing cheers during the commercials: "Hey, Wildcats, get it right [stomp stomp stomp], hey, Wildcats, fight fight fight [dramatic pause] tooonight!" From a cheerleadering book secretly checked out from the school library, I learned the proper names of all the jumps: the Spread Eagle (extend arms and legs outright while in midair), the Russian Toe Jump (jump in air and touch tips of fingers to tips of feet), the Banana Jump (reach behind head and arch backward to form a banana shape with your body). I practiced shouting from my diaphragm: *Huh, huh, huh, huh.* And I learned the fundamentals: thumbs go *under* our fingers when making a fist, feet should be together when standing in place, and of course: always have a smile on your face.

During the course of the school year, I supplemented my secret after-school practice sessions with attendance at the football and basketball games, where the cheerleaders emerged in full feminine glory: It was on the field or in the gymnasium where those uniforms were snazzed up with something I wanted more than life itself, something for which I would have even traded a date with George Michael: Pom-poms! My feminist consciousness, still undeveloped, never led me to question why two wooden handles sprouting hundreds of swishing plastic strips should be the most esteemed token of midwestern girlhood. All I knew was that being the lucky mistress of those multicolored puffballs was to have achieved lifetime success at age thirteen, and I intended to do it.

During the games, I sat facing the cheerleaders on the closest bleacher seat possible and watched them. Eventually I learned enough to chant along under my breath. Whether the team won or lost, no game was a disappointment to me if I walked away with the words to a new cheer.

On the underside of my enthusiastic ambition, a wave of doubt was festering: Was I pretty enough to be a cheerleader? Was I too fat to jump high? And horror of horrors: What if I made it, and then none of the pleated skirts would fit me? It was true that Keli and her cohorts were stick-thin. And me? Well . . . I had hips to be sure, and thighs to be certain. But maybe with exercise I could slim down.

Onward ho! Nothing would stop me. There were more cheerleadering books at the public library—books that gave me helpful hints for tryouts: *Wear hair away from your face—cheerleaders do not look like sheepdogs. . . . Wear school colors at tryouts to show your school spirit. Make sure you are perfect from head to toe: socks folded, hair ribbons tied in perfect bows, shirt tucked inside shorts, face clean, and of course: a smile on your face. No matter what: always smile.* I locked myself in the bathroom and practiced smiling. A cheerleader's smile wasn't just an ordinary smile: it was a cultivated art. With enough practice, I could rouse a crowd of people to their feet by merely offering a spirited grin.

As the school year progressed, the advantages of being a cheerleader became more and more clear: not only did cheerleaders get to wear cute uniforms and megaphone pins, but they also had five other insta-friends and did not need to search beyond their sisterly elite for other pals. Girls like me—who wanted to be cheerleaders but weren't—formed our own posse, which was part cheerleader-admiration society ("Did you see Keli's new haircut? It's coo-el . . .") and part tryout support group ("Last year there were four judges on the selection committee . . .").

As if being a member of the most enviable sorority in the school weren't enough, the cheerleaders also had first grabs on the most desirable male members of the junior high school. Every Chad and Eric and Matthew would give his Hot-Rod car collection to date a cheerleader. Which of us didn't overhear the complimentary (and sexual) remarks the boys made when a cheerleader swished by?

By the time the local lake began to thaw, I had determined that becoming a cheerleader was the only way I could continue to live. I didn't just want to make it, I *had* to make it. Or else . . . or else what? Or else continue to walk in the shadow of six matching pairs of saddle shoes? No way.

Working diligently, I created and perfected my individual cheer, which was the tryout requirement. Every member of the cheerleader wannabe posse agreed that I certainly had the most creative and unique cheer. They were jealous. Graciously, I helped my forlorn friends compose their own cheers. I even revealed some of the secrets I had learned from the books. Together, we executed mock tryouts and took turns being judged. We tried hard to be frank yet courteous: "You should really *point* your toes when you jump . . . if you can."

Before too long, things became tense: the cheerleadering coach—a sinewy woman named Becky—had posted the tryout sign-up sheet in the girls' locker room. Within days, the troublesome word was out: four of the six current cheerleaders— Keli included—were trying out again. Even the most optimistic of us could not imagine

212

that any of the experienced cheerleaders would fail to make the new squad. That left two places for new girls.

My dedication did not falter: I extended my after-school practice sessions, feverishly rehearsing my cheer even while *The Guiding Light* was playing, even when I washed dishes, brushed my teeth, ate dinner. As the cheerleadering books said: "Your cheer should be a *part* of you."

One Saturday afternoon, my mother dropped me off at the local mall: it was time to spend my saved-up stash on the perfect tryout outfit. It didn't take long: purple athletic shorts from JCPenney, a yellow-and-white baseball shirt, white sneakers, anklets with yellow ribbons stitched on the sides, purple *Goody* ribbons for my hair. There was little joy in selecting these items; not only was I mentally chanting my cheer as if it were a prayer for the dead, but I was also fighting off the doubts that had plagued me since the beginning of the year: Maybe I *wasn't* a cheerleader at heart. All the books emphasized that a cheerleader was born, not made. My artificiality would show: the judges would see that I didn't have one shred of school spirit, that I really only cared about the pleated skirt and the pom-poms. I was a phony!

But wasn't everyone? I doubted that Keli's primary concern was the success of the basketball team. Surely she cared more about her own popularity. I went home from the mall somewhat assured and spent the evening planning out the week: tryouts were to be held on Wednesday. Four days left. And then? If all went as planned, a new life would open before me. A life of friendship and boyfriends and games and cheerleader tokens: a letter jacket, a pair of saddle shoes—and pom-poms.

> *Marie,*
> *you're so sweet & so nice! I'm glad we became friends. Remember when you first came here to Onsted? Now aren't you glad we're friends? I am!*
> *Love,*
> *Keli*

—From my copy of the 1983 *Onsted Yearbook*

Claude Lévi-Strauss could have written a book on the rituals I performed on the morning of tryouts: I spent at least 45 preparatory minutes in the bathroom, no square inch of my body left untended—hair washed and treated with deep conditioner. Legs shaved. Nails filed. Teeth brushed with Pearl Drops. Skin powdered with Jean Naté. As the morning light warmed the sky, I stood in my chilly bedroom and packed my bag: outfit (ironed meticulously the night previous) folded into a perfectly creased bundle, hair ribbons stashed in a velvet jewelry case, sneakers wrapped in tissue paper to preserve whiteness, the mandatory makeup (but not *too* much, warned the books), brush, comb, hair spray, and for extra good luck: my trial-sized bottle of Love's Baby Soft, which I would share with my new friends.

The day passed in a blur; everyone was whispering about what would happen come four o'clock. The gym was reserved for the occasion—the boys would have to find somewhere else to practice basketball that afternoon. Somewhere in the depths of my mental paralysis (I couldn't even chant my cheer anymore) I remembered all the rewarding afternoons I'd spent in the library looking for cheerleading books. The memory brought forth the smell of wood and ink and I longed to turn back time to the days when making cheerleading was a long-term goal—not an immediate challenge. I had learned enough to write books about cheerleading, but *becoming* one was a different story.

In my heart I knew that I belonged in the library, not the gymnasium.

School ended at three: we had one hour to get ready. In the locker room, everyone—cheerleaders and noncheerleaderers alike—congregated for the purposes of adornment and information exchange: The selection committee consisted of four teachers and the athletic director. After tryouts, the school principal would calculate the scores and then announce the names of the new squad.

I was too nervous to tie my sneakers. The words to every cheer and chant I had ever heard overlapped onto one another in a schizophrenic maze. I could not remember a thing. In a state of hyperdistress, I confessed to my friends: I was forgetting, yes, *forgetting* the words to my cheer! It seemed that the same thing was happening to them. The collective anxiety among us could have provided enough energy to topple the Empire State Building. Even the cheerleaders themselves were far from relaxed: Keli sat motionless on a wooden bench near the shower stalls, her eyes fixated on the tile floor, her lips moving silently.

Four o'clock arrived and I followed the parade of girls into the breezy gymnasium. Becky, the cheerleading coach, introduced herself and explained the process by which we would be judged: First, all of us would have to sit in the hallway and wait our turns. She would call us in one by one to appear before the selection committee.

Dutifully, we trudged into the dark hall and sat cross-legged on the floor against the wall. I counted bodies and with a deep heart noted that twenty-seven girls were competing for six places. When subtracting the four cheerleaders who would most certainly make the squad, the final tabulation was twenty-three girls competing for two spots. To make matters worse, a pair of twins was in our midst. What could be cuter than two identical girls in identical uniforms?

I was not the only one counting chances. Many of the girls plopped themselves resignedly on the floor and announced themselves sure losers. "I'm just here for the fun of it," said one of my friends, shrugging. If only I could have been so lighthearted! But somehow I had broken through to my second wind: the determination I had been accumulating over the past year electrified my every pore, and suddenly the words to my cheer came back to me. As Becky began to call the candidates into the gym, I closed my eyes and fell into a mental rehearsal of my cheer, relishing the security of those familiar words: maybe they were a part of me after all.

Finally Becky called my name. I walked toward the gymnasium entrance; my feet felt like rubber and my head like a balloon. As I passed by the string of girls, some reached out and lightly grasped my forearm or shoulder: "Good luck . . ." echoed the whispers.

The gym was cool and filled with yellow light. The five judges sat behind a long wooden table. I took my position behind the masking-tape line that Becky had planted on the floor. From where I stood, the judges looked like rag dolls, their faces emotionless, their pens poised stiffly toward the pads of paper resting in front of them; it was impossible to picture them in their underwear, as all the books suggested.

I began my cheer. The words and arm movements drained from me effortlessly. When I jumped, I was sure I almost reached the ceiling. Time must have moved faster during those moments, for I was finished in what seemed less than a second. Already the spotlight was over. The judges nodded and began to scratch their pens on the score pads. I was excused.

Back in the hallway, the waiting began. I had been one of the last girls to be judged. None of us knew how long it would take for the principal, Mr. Bennett, to calculate the scores. For a stretch of time we were in limbo: in those moments, there were no cheerleaders; for once, all of us were miraculously equal. Perhaps it was do-or-die, but the cloud of uncertainty brought all of us together as friends, no matter how temporarily. Last year's cheerleaders had no choice but to reveal their humanity and insecurities: their faces were pulled solemn, hands clenched, cheeks blotched.

A general discussion filtered among the group: Wasn't Christie Brinkley beautiful? Wasn't Prince a weirdo? Why were leather Converse All-Stars so expensive? My stomach was a burning pit. My breath was weak and sparse, making my voice come out as high-pitched as Michael Jackson's.

After what seemed like two or three hours, Becky came into the hallway and motioned us into the gym for the announcement of the new cheerleadering squad. The judges were gone when we entered. Mr. Bennett was standing in front of the table, which was covered with empty cups and stray papers. In Mr. Bennett's hand was a three-by-five index card—a card on which was most certainly written the names of the six most fortunate girls in Onsted, Michigan.

All twenty-seven of us sat on the floor in a tight cluster. As if by instinct, we each clutched the hands of the girls to our right and left. Mr. Bennett offered a blubbering preamble about how difficult and close the competition had been and about how all of us were certainly fit to be cheerleaders but unfortunately only six spots were available. My heart was thumping so hard that I could feel my pulse in my face and neck.

Mr. Bennett extended the index card in front of him and began to read the names. For the second time that day, time moved faster than normal, and in less than a moment, all the names were called.

My name was not one of them.

The gymnasium walls echoed the shrieks of the six girls who had made it. I was still waiting to hear my name. It wasn't until the chosen six, who turned out

216

to be all four old cheerleaders and the set of twins, formed a straight line in front of the table that I finally recognized that I was not among them.

The other twenty-one of us registered the shock in a collective cloud of doom. Our sentence had been cast: another year of anonymity. Another year of longing for striped sweaters, saddle shoes, and megaphone pins.

In the days that followed, I refused to admit—as some of my friends did—that I was not cut out to be a cheerleader. Instead, I allowed my resentment to transform into an aggregate of anger and determination. Being rejected only made me want to be a cheerleader all the more. After all, wasn't I smart enough to do whatever I wanted? I figured I had to at least be smarter than Keli.

But maybe I wasn't as smart as I thought. Sure, I could read books and think up clever cheers, but some of my friends knew enough to give up and not try out again. But me? No . . . I kept on going. Two more years of tryouts. Two more failures.

But then—in tenth grade—I moved to another town and started at a new high school. And when *that* school held cheerleading tryouts, I made it.

Falling from Grace

by Scarlett Fever

"If I had a daughter, I wouldn't let her hang out with you either," my mother once said. She said it after one of my little white-trash friends said that her mother didn't like us being friends. Her mother said I was a bad influence. My mother agreed. Years later, after graduation, after my friend married her high school sweetheart, after they had two beautiful children, she would abandon them all to run off with a Greek sailor she met one afternoon. I wonder if her mother blames me for that, too.

Fourth grade, fifth grade, sixth grade, seventh grade. Nine, ten, eleven, twelve. We shoplifted together, hid in my attic smoking cigarettes, looked at dirty pictures in my father's "art" magazines. We were the special ones all through grade school, the smart ones, the kids in the honor class. We banded together the ways kids do that are different. Banding together for safety and protection, for a sense of belonging somewhere.

We took field trips together, sitting scrunched together in the back of the bus. We ate over at each other's houses: Rice-A-Roni, tuna casserole topped with crushed potato chips, chocolate pudding, macaroni and cheese. Together we all marched off to junior high, graduating from grade school to something bigger. Graduating from whispered secret crushes on David Cassidy and Bobby Sherman to real crushes on the flesh-and-blood boy in the next row. From "Kissing Klubs" with guys from the neighborhood, to real boyfriends, to being part of a couple.

And it's all happening too fast and I don't know how to keep up anymore. Being smart is suddenly not enough. Becoming sexual is suddenly too much. Being bad turns from something exciting to something shameful.

I've become an embarrassment is what it is.

I say things at the wrong times. And I say them too loud.

I have too few secrets. I have too many secrets.

They pass me a note and it's over.

I have no more friends. I'm thirteen and no one will be my friend anymore. Because of puberty. Because I'm thirteen and I look eighteen and I don't know what to do with that. Because the only contact I've ever had with boys were things you kept secret. The sweaty groping hands of strangers in dark basements. Adult fingers and mouths in places they have no right to be. When people don't want you to tell things, they tell you, threaten you, warn you, scare you. I am the keeper of so many secrets that I believe everything else must be public knowledge.

I'm thirteen. I have no friends. I sit alone in my perfect room. Its freshly painted strawberry walls match the red and pink cherubs on the slipcovers my grandmother has made for my couch. The frilly crimson bedspread and dust ruffle

218

match the intricate cherry curlicues on the secondhand desk my mother has so painstakingly refurbished for me. Music and static sputter out of my little red plastic transistor radio onto the bed, cascading onto the floor.

It was all folded up and tucked into itself, the way you know how to do with notes only when you're thirteen, like the way you learn to make chains from gum wrappers. You learn that stuff from your girlfriends.

On the outside in big letters scrawled all around: U ASKED 4 IT. SORRY, BUT. FROM EVERY-ONE. SORRY.

I don't remember asking for it. I don't remember feeling like anyone was any more sorry than they felt they had to be. Not after we graduated high school. Not when I would run into them years later on the street, or in a bar, or in the supermarket. Not then, not ever.

Twenty-eight years later, I still have the note, written in ink, on a piece of lined paper, ripped out of a spiral notebook, folded seven times, and tucked twice.

I always know exactly where it is.

> *4/13/70*
> *The reason no one likes you is because:*
>
> *1. You're embarrassing to be by because you're so weird, and because your whole thing is embarrassing.*
>
> *2. You say things at the wrong time. Like when you said that to Judy about her smoking in front of her little sister and what you said that time at Martha's car on her camping trip. Those are what come to mind but there are many more.*
>
> *3. You think you can get attention from boys by doing retarded things. And it's sickening.*
>
> *4. You dish out stuff, but you get very mad and hurt and violent and stuff like that.*

219

5. They don't hate you but they're all getting sick of you. And don't think it's just from me because everyone else told me to write it and of course I am going to get the worst of it. But other kids are signing it too.

6. We're just ashamed to be seen with you. Why don't you calm down? (Not ashamed just embarrassed sometimes.)

I don't remember who Judy is or what I said during a camping trip I don't remember going on. But I remember those girls, my best girlfriends: Pam, the fearless one who would later abandon her husband and children; Lorrie, little and cuddly, the first of us to need and get a training bra which she showed us all in the dark of the Levittown movie theater one Saturday afternoon; Martha, her sensibilities so delicate that she was mortified when we got caught shoplifting together and our parents were called down to the store, but not so delicate that she wasn't having fun until we got caught; and Joanne, the one who replaced me, who wasn't one of the special ones because of her brains, but because she knew *how* to be in the world, a worthwhile skill faced with the onslaught of hormones and boys that is junior high—and a skill I didn't have with kids my own age.

I remember being friends for four years and four summers. Birthdays and slumber parties. Running home together after school to watch *Dark Shadows.* Séances and Ouija boards under a blanket. "Kissing Klubs" with neighborhood boys. Listening at the bathroom door while one of us was inside pretending we knew what to do during Seven Minutes in Heaven. Smoking cigarettes. Sneaking out of the house. Sneaking into the movies.

Like a salmon, I was headed in one direction, everyone else in the other. A note was slipped into my hand, as four backs walk away together; all shiny bouncy Prell-perfect hair, red, blond, and brown; white cotton kneesocks, pleated skirts and wool sweaters in fall colors, whispers and giggles, looking back at me over a shoulder here or there.

Standing in the hallway, the bell rings and kids charge in every direction around me, pushing, rushing, laughing. Looking down at the note in my hand I untuck, unfold, and unravel. The noise of thirteen is suddenly thunderous. The click

220

and squeak of Thom McAns and Keds, of kids laughing and shouting, the noise of rushing and growing and learning and flirting is deafening. A tidal wave of lonely rushes in, drowning everyone else in the hallway, in the world. The bubbles of their dying breath buoy me to the top as I float along the swift waters of rejection, out the door, out into the streets, alone.

I read the letter every year.

> *The reason no one likes you is because you're embarrassing to be by because you're so weird, and because your whole thing is embarrassing.*

I can't remember feeling a thing.

Kim Hiorthoy

6

Yo' Mama, Yo' Self

Mother's Day: established on May 9, 1914, by President Woodrow Wilson as a national holiday to honor thy mother. It would become a beloved Hallmark holiday celebrated on the second Sunday of many Mays to come.

I SHOULD BEGIN BY ADMITTING THAT THIS PIECE WOULD READ very differently if I were not in my mid-thirties, single, and child-free. I'm obsessed, you see, and it's not about the lack of a soulmate, but rather, the absence of a teeny little playmate. I'm virtually a cliché—*oooh, her biological time clock is in overdrive, buyer beware!*—afraid I'll miss the boat. The steady ticktock of my internal metronome instills this fear, rather than the Mystiquean sense of oppression it created for ye olde second-waver. Wanting a baby is no longer considered a violation of feminist doctrine, but a show of feminist pride. Plus, the wonders of science have turned pregnancy into a booming business, giving my generation of mama-bes choices galore. All of this has got me thinking—about how far the notion of motherhood has come in the last century, about my dear mom, and of course, my own situation: when I will (or will I?) be jumping on the baby bandwagon.

Is Every Child a Wanted Child?

Back in the day, many of our first-wave foremothers were married with children. For the most part, however, they did not consider motherhood to be detrimental to their activism. Elizabeth Cady Stanton, for example, argued "surely maternity is an added power and development of some of the most tender sentiments of the human heart and not a limitation." Stanton was no slouch; in fact, she managed to have it all: seven kids, and she was, along with her buddy, Susan B. Anthony, part of the dream team of the nineteenth-century women's rights movement. Say, you want a revolution?

Other suffragists, like Charlotte Perkins Gilman, recognized the burdens of being a working mom. Gilman advocated the establishment of communal baby-raising pools (you know, day-care centers) in order to lighten the load. One of Gilman's missions was to reform the institution of motherhood—to launch a "grand domestic revolution" because women were definitely not being "rewarded in proportion to their work." According to Gilman:

> We have so arranged life that a man may have a home, a family, love, companionship, domesticity, and fatherhood, yet remain an active citizen of age and country. We have so arranged life, on the other hand, that a woman must "choose"; must either live alone, unloved, uncompanied, uncared for, homeless, childless, with her work in the world for sole consolation or give up all world service for the joys of love, motherhood, and domestic service.

Little did Gilman know how important this idea of choice would become for the women's movement!

Until the early 1900s, choosing when and how to enter the maternity-wear elite was not an option. First came love, then came marriage, then came pookie in the baby carriage. Information on birth control was sparse. However, in 1912, Lois Weber directed a film called *Where Are My Children* that was practically an infomercial about the various forms of birth control. And then, of course, there was Margaret Sanger, who firmly believed that a woman's right to control her reproductive freedom was the key to economic and social equality. Sanger took her mission—to enlighten women everywhere about their choices—very seriously. (Sanger had watched her own mother endure eighteen pregnancies, only to die at the tender age of forty-nine.) She published her own 'zine, *What Every Girl Should Know,* and, in 1916, Sanger, with her sister Ethel Byrne, established the first birth-control clinic in the United States. In the first ten days alone, over five hundred women flocked to the small office in Brooklyn, New York, as Sanger sent out thousands of pamphlets informing women about their options. Surprise, surprise, Sanger's clinic was kiboshed within days by the moralizing U.S. postal inspector, Mr. Anthony Comstock. Sanger spent the next few years in and out of jails, fighting for her right to spread the word, until 1923, when she opened the Birth Control Clinical Research Bureau in Manhattan. (It would later get a makeover and be renamed the Planned Parenthood Association.) In 1936, *United States v. One Package* mandated that birth control "was not synonymous with obscenity and henceforth, mailing contraceptive information intended for use by physicians would no longer be illegal." Soon after, the American Medical Association voted to recognize "contraception as a legitimate medical service." Margaret Sanger had won, and it was a huge victory for women everywhere—they could have sex for, well, sex's sake. Now the idea of "planned parenthood" meant something, but not for everyone.

Black girls were still, well, not white girls. According to Dorothy Roberts in *Abortion Wars,* "The first publicly funded birth control clinics were established in the South in the 1930s as a way of lowering the black birthrate." To be a young single pregnant black girl was to be "not shamed but simply blamed," Rickie Solinger states in *Wake Up Little Susie: Single Pregnancy and Race Before Roe v. Wade,* blamed "for

225

the existence of unwanted babies and blamed for the tenacious grip of poverty on blacks in America." Later, in the 1960s, civil rights activities inspired fearful white men to issue "suitable home" laws, which were targeted at the black community and essentially declared that unmarried women were not capable of providing a healthy home for their children. So while unmarried pregnant white girls were shepherded into "rest homes," black girls went looking for a "cure."

Mama Mia, Here They Go Again!

You hear it all the time, but to be a mother in the 1960s was not considered all that. A lot of the female activists dropped diaper duty and took their place in the pro-test marches. Motherhood quickly became what Shari Thurer, in *Myths of Motherhood,* refers to as a "casualty" of the feminist war. Thurer argues that "while few feminists in the nineteenth century had felt that motherhood clashed with person-hood, activist women in the early stages of the recent women's movement con-sidered motherhood one of the major institutions that oppressed women and prevented them from taking more active control of their lives." As women were waking up from the doldrums of their suburban lives laced with Valium and mar-tinis, some women pointed their fingers at their mates, who had gotten them into this sticky situation. And it was verified by the crème de la crème, shouted from the feminist titty tops: *Sisterhood Is Powerful* declared that "pregnancy presents to the world visible proof of the husband's masculinity, his potency"; Shulamith Firestone said that "fatherhood is another term for the oppressive patriarchy"; and Ellen Peck urged women to "stop rocking the cradle and start rocking the boat." Rather than focusing on the strength and fulfillment a woman derived from being a mom, they focused on blaming the beast of burden. The second wavers' awakening drowned out any hint of a gurgle or a burp. The debate over "to be or not to be" was further complicated when along came a pregnant woman we would come to know as "Jane Roe."

In late 1969, a Texas lawyer named Sarah Weddington was determined to change the laws on abortion. She hit the jackpot when she met Roe (real name: Norma

226

McCorvey), who was in the early stages of an unwanted pregnancy. Weddington took Roe's case before the United States Supreme Court in 1971, arguing a woman's right to privacy and the unconstitutionality of anti-abortion laws. Finally, in 1973, the Court decided in their favor, and abortion was made legal. Weddington's victory in *Roe v. Wade* came too late for Jane Roe—she gave birth in 1970 and put the baby up for adoption—but not for countless other women.

By the mid-'70s, being antimotherhood was the accepted norm in feminist circles. Women were scorned for "just being a mom" or for staying at home while the activists went on marches—even though someone had to be in charge of the carpools while their fellow sisters were doing the women's work. However, the antis were barking up the wrong tree. Women were still having babies, babies they wanted to be having, because, as Anne Roiphe says in *Fruitful,* "this desire of women for children is not just some social construct, not some male misogynist plot, not some patriarchal desire to control the inheritance of the next generation. It is some unstoppable species urge, some delicate strand of our genes that makes so many of us smile back at a baby smiling at us. . . . The pull to reproduce was not a political decision but deeply primordial, a response to rhythms and tides not always accessible to reason."

So when Adrienne Rich announced in the late 1970s that "patriarchy was the oppressor and not motherhood," closeted as well as outed pro-mommy-ites breathed a sigh of relief. But once feminists accepted that being a mom did not mean giving in to HIM, they still had to deal with what Anne Roiphe refers to as "the fly in the feminist ointment: somebody has to bear children and somebody has to raise those children." Although women didn't (and obviously still don't) get paid to be "housewives"—a housework wage was bandied about in the early '70s but the idea disappeared into thin air—the money to raise these kids had to come from somewhere. Barbara Ehrenreich pointed out that "the economic stresses of the seventies split women into two camps: those who went out to fight for some measure of economic security (either out of necessity or choice, though the distinction is not always a meaningful one), and those who stayed at home to hold on to what they had." In the wake of a skyrocketing divorce rate, a battalion of single moms entered the workforce—independently, defiantly, and proudly.

Don't Call It a Comeback

The 1980s brought Ronald Reagan, family values, and the big catchphrase of "having it all"—could a woman really do it, could she bring home the bacon and fry it up in the pan? According to Sheila Rowbotham in *A Century of Women,* "women's representations in the work force increased from 51 to 57 percent and reached 70 percent in the twenty-five to forty-four age group" during the '80s and "the number of working mothers was still rising." As late as the mid-'80s only five states offered paid maternity leave to women (New York, New Jersey, Rhode Island, Hawaii, and California). Felice Schwartz suggested a superwoman's solution in *The Harvard Business Review:* a woman should work, but on a deferred schedule, one that allowed her to go home and sing lullabies. So, in order to make room for mommy in the office, employers eased up on their responsibilities and pressures. Talk about undermining a woman's potential—this little "favor" employers were implementing simply relegated women to positions with little or no hope of advancement, because they were now viewed as a "what if" factor. They even got a name: in 1989, *The New York Times* told us that these women were on the "mommy track"—oh, how flattering.

Adding insult to injury, women were not basking in the afterglow of the *Roe v. Wade* victory. All kinds of restrictions were being imposed every year. According to Marcy Wilder in *Abortion Wars,* "Between 1989 and 1992 more than seven hundred anti-choice bills were introduced in state legislatures across the country." Chips stacked against abortion? You be the judge: public funding was eradicated in 1976, which directly affected low-income women; contentious bills were passed, like 1977's Hyde Amendment, which limited federal funding for abortions needed to save a woman's life; waiting laws were implemented, meaning women had to hold off for twenty-four agonizing hours after being "counseled" before actually getting an abortion; parental-consent laws were required for underage women, which resulted in plenty of deaths (for example, seventeen-year-old Becky Bell died after an illegal abortion in Indiana because she couldn't, wouldn't tell her folks); even Medicaid does not cover abortion. And, of course, we are all way too familiar with the dangers of walking into a clinic these days: the threat of prolife vigilantes on Rambo-like rampages, murdering people as they enter and exit, is a reality. It's a war zone that forces nurses and doctors to wear bulletproof vests as they go to work in their bulletproof offices! To have an abortion is legal, yes, but safe? Depends on your definition of safe.

There are still stigmas to shatter in the 1990s, such as the "problem" of illegitimacy (the dictionary definition: a child born to a woman who is unmarried). It's a term that is still as harsh as the F-word. In Judaism, to be a "mamzer" is a curse: for ten generations, the lineage of illegitimate heirs cannot marry a member of the holy Cohain tribe. Harrumph. Numnuts like *Losing Ground*'s Charles Murray really stirred the pot in 1993 by suggesting that the I-word be this decade's McCarthyism, to ensure that "an illegitimate birth" remains "the socially horrific act it used to be." Here's a thought: If a man/husband were not necessary to legitimize a woman's existence, then maybe more women would not shy away from actually having children on their own terms, without the "threat" of being ostracized by their family and friends.

Mothers who do not spend "enough" time with their children are chastised unless, as Mary Pipher says in *Reviving Ophelia,* "their involvement is precisely the right amount," whatever that means. Mothers who hire nannies are especially easy targets. Witness the heartbreaking case of infant Matthew Eappin whose death in February of 1997 was allegedly caused by his nanny, Louise Woodward. Woodward was released after her conviction was reduced to manslaughter. Matthew's mother, a successful practicing doctor, was vilified by both the media and the public for having a nanny tend to Matthew while she was at work. She was asking for it, they practically said, even though that was certainly not true. The nanny had a job: to watch the baby. Matthew's mother had two jobs: as a mother and a doctor. Because of Deborah Eappin's status as a member of the so-called privileged class (i.e., being able to afford a live-in nanny), she was as much on trial as the nanny. Who is free. Mrs. Eappin is left to mourn for the child she once had.

229

It sucks that there is still a huge chasm between staying at home to breast-feed and working behind the checkout counter to pay the bills. "Western civilization has a history of unrealistic expectations about mothers . . . a double standard about parenting," Mary Pipher points out in *Reviving Ophelia.* A mother has to juggle, choose, struggle—compromising between what she wants to do as a mother and what she must do as a provider. The dual roles women have to play are a reality for us, the women of the '90s. And we are definitely up for the challenge.

Blinded Me with Science

Women in the '90s are finding more and more ways to have babies, with or without a partner. The sperm bank is probably not the right place to meet a man, but it is the right place to find, uh, the equipment you need to get pregnant. Artificial insemination does not conjure up images of romance, but for a woman whose partner's sperm can't do the backstroke, or for women who are going at it on their own or with female partners, this is an ideal place to collect. Plenty of ladies are going to the bank to make a withdrawal, and making a deposit where the sun doesn't shine.

Some women, however, do have more than most: a partner, some money, and a desire to be a mom. Surrogacy is a rich person's way to have a baby. You, the couple who cannot bear children, hire a vessel (read: a woman) to carry your young'n. She's inseminated with the man's sperm and violà, she's having your baby. Only sometimes it can get sticky. In 1987, the wanna-have-a-baby couple, William and Elizabeth Stern, hired Mary Beth Whitehead to carry their child. It was all very legal and done with an expectation that Ms. Whitehead be professional about being pregnant. There was nary a thought that perhaps an emotional bond between fetus and vessel might form through the course of gestation. (In this savvy, evolved media age, the stark negotiation of having a baby can be viewed as a technical transaction as opposed to a life-altering event that changes your body for nine months and, of course, you for a lifetime.) The Sterns armed themselves with lawyers when Whitehead reneged on the deal. Whitehead, in turn, fought to keep her child, Baby M, and got a partial victory. The courts awarded custody to the Sterns, but granted Whitehead visitation rights. The lesson: Surrogacy, while an option, can have very convoluted ramifications.

And then there's adoption, the route Rosie O'Donnell went when she wanted to be a mom. You don't have to be a straight married couple nowadays either—from gay couples to single women, adoption is available to anyone who can prove that she can provide for the child. Finding out how to do it is as easy as turning on your computer—you can go on the Web and look up www.adoption.com, where you'll find all kinds of forms and information. Imagine, you can adopt at the drop of a keystroke! Of course, adopting a kid has its own share of aches and pains: the waiting game, the are-you-good-enough-to-be-a-parent interview process, the not knowing if you will, in fact, pass the grade. But for the woman who wants to be a mom, it's yet another option available.

It's My Life and I'll Do What I Want

Accidents never happen in a perfect world, Elvis Costello has said. But sometimes the condom rips or the diaphragm slips at the wrong moment, and before you know it, there are a million smelly missiles looking for one good eggy. And with Viagra being covered by insurance nowadays (What is that? How long do we have to keep paying for birth-control pills? Next thing you know, Trojans will be covered too!), it's gonna be woodies galore! More opportunities, more mistakes, more unplanned pregnancies.

Single unmarried motherhood has become en vogue in a big commercial way. The one thing Madonna, Sandra Bernhard, and the girl next door (to me) have in common is that they went for it. Remember when a television character named Murphy Brown chose to have a baby without being married to anyone? Granted, I'm talking about a fictional character, a white upper-middle-class woman who could afford to have a baby on her own, a decision she was able to make without too many economic concerns. (How many of us are in that position?) But Murphy's choice had a resounding effect on her audience, composed of real live women. Depending on what statistic you are reading, somewhere between 34 million and 38 million Americans tuned in to watch this event, a ratings coup for the network and another step forward for feminists. Especially when Vice President Dan Quayle decided to ramble on and on about family values, proposing "dismantling a welfare system that encourages dependency and subsidizes broken families" and how "Murphy Brown mocks the importance of fathers by bearing a child alone and calling it just another 'lifestyle choice.'" How sensitive is Dan? Dan is very sensitive, very traditional, and very scary. I agree with a man named Frank Furstenberg, who says, "We walk a thin line when we attempt to promote matrimony as a public good." Waiting for the ring when you want a baby may not always get you the baby, so why wait?

I can't help think of a conversation I once had with Dr. T. Berry Brazelton, the renowned baby doctor, when I think of embryo transfer, fertility drugs (Oh my God! Your body gets forced into menopause for months before you can even begin the baby boot knocking!), in vitro, surrogacy, or any of the other wonders of science. I asked Dr. Brazelton what it would be like to raise a child without a partner, and he replied, "What will you tell the child about the father?" Dr. Brazelton raised this question to provoke thought, not ire. I spent ages wondering how a little version of me would react. But I think it's more like, What will you tell the child about its mommy? I'll tell you what I would say: Mommy wanted to be a mommy.

The idea of a *father figure* never occurs to me when flirting with the notion of being a single parent. Call it a sign of the times, or maybe it's just the good-boy short-age, I don't know, but the way my generation thinks about motherhood has certainly changed since the days of Lucy and Desi. We grew up watching fictional working women like Shirley Partridge, Alice, and that chick from *One Day at a Time,* Ann Romano, raise families on their own, and thinking, *We could do that?! Cool!* The thing is, they had babies the old-fashioned way: they got married. That's not necessarily the case for a lot of single mommy wannabes.

As Melissa Lutke says in *On Our Own: Unmarried Motherhood in America,* there was a time when "spinsterhood was the mark of a woman's disconnected life; now the absence of motherhood has displaced this earlier paradigm of women's deviance." Has my generation of women spent too much time "wasting" it on things like a career or finding oneself? I don't feel I have; I just haven't met "The One." For many single women, this is the case. Staying late in the office to finish a project isn't always a choice, it's a necessity. Not meeting people isn't deliberately self-sabotaging, it's a matter of circumstance. But because we have the technology, we don't really need much to have babies. What we do need, of course, is patience, and love, because the hardest job anyone will ever have is the lifelong career of being a mother. As we enter the next millennium, Making Mommyhood Mine is an opportunity waiting to be snatched. Ready, steady, go, girl!

My Mommy Dearest

It's only recently that I have been able to appreciate the pride my mother has in her lifework of being my mom. I'm fascinated by how she managed to do it, to stay married and raise us and work—she *has* been able to have it all! My mom was one of eight children who were raised in a just born Israel, a child of the '50s. She moved to New York when she married, and assimilated into the diaspora of American Jewish culture. She was alone, without many friends for a long time, which left her feeling lonely, sad, afraid. But she was a tough chick then (and still is now). Instead of lying in her bed, crying over split milk, she did things—went to school (to learn English), became an American citizen, learned to drive, got a high school diploma. And, of course, she took care of us. She made sure I got scholarships to private schools and plenty of food to eat, and that I always had the latest in platform shoes, Huk-a-Poo shirts, and Brownie scout uniforms. She encouraged my infatuation with all the *Teen/Tiger Beat* cover boys, to read but not in the dark, and to stand up for myself. My mother was not in a shiny, happy marriage: her "escape" was not Valium, but entertaining the attentions of many others, although she never ever ignored or overlooked her two children.

My mother did not have it easy, and yet, she made it feel effortless. We speak every day and it's always the same conversation: *Marce, when you gonna have a baby?* It's her thing, what can I do? She's my mom and she worries about me, always has, always will. I cringe when I think of the horrible teenager's phase of asserting myself, or the fights we've had, or the times I know she didn't sleep all night because of me; I regret any and every harsh word that's ever come out of my mouth in the heat of a moment with her. Of course, that's the kind of thing that comes with maturity, with looking forward, with wanting my own babies. I wonder what will be: Will I have children? Will she be alive to see it happen? Every moment I have with my mom is precious to me, it's not to be taken for granted, and while she drives me nuts sometimes, she's my mommie dearest, the woman I am the closest to in body, mind, and heart. She is the woman I owe my life to, and who I will spend the rest of my life keeping safe and protected, as she once kept me. She is my number-one gal.

And so, as you read what our *BUST*y sisters have thought about the reality of motherhood in their lives in the '90s, I leave you with something that Barbara Ehrenreich pointed out: even "President Theodore Roosevelt declared homemaking a career

233

more worthy of honor and more useful to the community than the career of any man no matter how successful." It's not easy being Mom, but it sure is worth it.

— Marcelle Karp

What to Expect When Your Best Friend Is Expecting

by Nancy E. Young

Although statistics show that many of us are waiting till later in life to have kids, eventually pregnancy and children impact all of us—directly or indirectly. Whether you're a *BUST* girl who is on the fast track to career success or one who's slacking through the scene, you'll find that a friend who's pregnant takes on another aura. She may no longer be into computer geek seminars or drumming for a downtown band, so here are some tips to help you understand your best friend.

1. *She wants you to be there for her baby.* Your friend will want you to confirm the fact that her child is the most beautiful, intelligent, well-behaved creature since Courtney gave birth. She'll want you to hold the baby, even if you're dressed in a uniform of black. It's best to get to know the baby first from its mother's arms. Don't reach out and grab. When the mother and baby are ready, s/he will be passed to you—and it could be for a long time!

2. *She wants you to be there for her.* Your best friend may need to vent about how no one ever notices her anymore. That when she got off the plane in Florida last week, her mom and dad ran to hold the baby and overlooked her. She'll also want to complain about how her man kisses the baby first, the dog second, and her third when he comes home from work. She needs to be reassured that she is still an adult,

that you value her opinions on Bosnia, breast implants, and boys. She needs to tell you how she is sick and tired of having no social life (and the baby is only six weeks old!). Your job is to be the yes-woman.

3. *She wants you to—hold that thought!* You no longer have your friend's undivided attention. When the three of you are in a room together, you are number three; when the two of you are in a room together, you are still number three. A Friday night rehash lasting hours is a luxury of the past. So, talk fast and get to the juice.

4. *She's worried about her looks.* It's hard to feel good right after you have a baby, especially when you see models like Nikki Taylor looking even more beautiful since the child danced out of her womb. Your friend will have dark circles, leaking breasts, stained T-shirts, and wet shoulders, and will be worried about the weight that didn't come out with the baby—get the picture? Try not to show up on your way to a black-tie, but dress down the first few times you go to see her. (After all, baby will want to drool and spit up on you too!)

5. *She might have a few mood swings.* On top of the hormonal changes of pregnancy, your friend will be suffering months, if not years, of sleep deprivation. She might tell you one minute that motherhood sucks, then the next hour she might say she could never imagine life without the baby. All of this is normal—just hold her hand and love her.

6. *You have to meet her more than halfway.* There's no two ways about it, right now the upkeep of the friendship lies with you. Obviously, she can't meet you downtown for drinks after work with the baby in tow. The social life the two of you share will change—for a while. Expect to go to her place more, and to spend time there with her *and* the baby. The good news is you can still have fun and enjoy each other—plus think of all the money you'll save by no covers, drinks, and tips!

7. *She'll count on you for entertainment.* At the beginning, especially for mothers who choose to nurse, she might feel imprisoned in her home. When you come, you need to tell her some social life tall tales. If you're in a dry spell, borrow some from other friends, because she wants to know what the scene is like, how unstable motherless life is, plus any dirt. Go ahead, give it all up.

One final important note to remember is that it's likely someday you and your friend will change places. She might be the mother of a placid six-year-old who plays well with others, while you are fainting the first time your baby spits up. So, be gentle and kind—your turn could be soon!

Two Girls and a Baby

by Thelma and Louise

Thelma's Story

When we're asked about our decision to have a baby, our favorite response is, "Oh, we'd already picked out a name for the kid on our first date." Picking out names, though, was a cinch. When it got down to picking out sperm—that's when the real challenge began.

With two grrrls, you have special fun in starting your family. Rather than spending time dating and looking for the right gene donor that way, we spent time poring over sperm bank catalogs: grade point averages, hobbies, statements about their reasons for donating, family medical history—how does one choose? I recall a coffee shop breakfast with a doctor friend during which I drilled her about the significance of a family medical history. We finally settled on a donor whose ethnic background and characteristics matched Louise's, the non-birthing mom. We also liked his occupation; he was a graduate student in philosophy.

Sperm choice out of the way, months of temperature and ovulation charts complete, the only thing left was alternative insemination. I love that phrase. Alternative insemination is the more PC version of artificial insemination. Basi-

Nicole Schooley

cally, both describe the delivery of sperm to the vagina without the help of a penis freight train (this could explain why some men are a bit threatened by the whole thing).

So, we're at the sperm bank, my legs are spread, the nurse has already sucked up the sperm into the syringe and Louise blurts out, "Wait—is he cute?" A moment's pause (during which we cringe) and she replies, "He's not a hunk, he's no JFK, Jr., but he's nice looking. More of a Tom Hanks type." Insemination proceeded. And we were convinced our child would be a Tom Hanks clone—as in Forrest Gump. (As it turned out, he's incredibly beautiful, turning heads wherever he goes.)

It took three months to get pregnant—a very short time in reality but an eternity in my mind. The second month we decided to do it ourselves. Let us just say that attempt number two, starting with lugging the large dry ice-filled tank home, via the Barnes and Noble cafe and Louise's therapy, and ending with much of that tiny bit of sperm on my leg, rather than inside, made me feel like we were Lucy and Ethel in a particularly stupid episode (and where's Desi?). The third try was done at the office, intrauterine (bypass that silly vagina), and it took.

The pregnancy meant a new level of "outness" as lesbians, as well as encountering an amazing new world of people's assumptions. From my mother's seventy-five-year-old friends to people of a much younger vintage, the query of the hour was, "How did you do it?" The questions sometimes bordered on the bizarre, such as whether I (the birth mom) would be genetically related to the child! The most common refrain was: "Isn't in vitro expensive? About ten thousand a try?" For the

237

record, AI costs about $500 a month for two tries. These conversations led me to believe that many folks out there just can't grid lesbian and mother as biologically compatible. People seem to think that lesbians don't have ovaries.

In fact, seeing people's almost totally positive responses after our beautiful son was born, (this past December, on the Feast of the Immaculate Conception, which pleased my mother no end!), I've concluded that the physical marking of pregnancy is a much more disturbing symbol of out-of-bounds lesbianism (an affront, so to speak), than a real live baby.

So now we're two lesbian grrrls with a baby boy. What's that been like? I've experienced truly unexpected levels of love, exhaustion, tenderness, and amazement. All, I expect, are fairly typical of what most first-time parents feel. Being part of a two-mom family has also had unexpected positive side effects. We often feel lucky to have two sets of nurturing hands and perspectives for our son's support. Sharing childcare (and breadwinning) as equally as possible was a given from the start. We both want to do it, and no one's barefoot in the kitchen except by choice.

Some feelings and issues, on the other hand, have presented unforeseen complexities in the two-mother family situation. For example, I've always felt that, as the bio-mom, I should make every effort to make Louise feel as secure in her position as I could, thus I often recede into the background when we're out in public so she can enjoy being seen as the mother of a young baby. When Brian was little, she was the one who most often carried him in the Snugly, for example. Sometimes I started to feel invisible, and even a bit upset by this, but I tried to keep in mind how important it was for her to feel as safe as possible about her position. Unfortunately, at this point Louise has no legal rights concerning Brian, and until we can change that it's important that she have every opportunity to both feel and represent to the world the strength of her bond and position *vis á vis* Brian as a full and equal mother to him.

I'd like to end with the story of a four-year-old. He inspired me to believe that it is possible to create a category called lesbian moms.

Louise and I were away at a workshop where she was teaching. Four-year-old Gregory lived next door and he and his sister had a full time nanny (his mom was the chef). He saw Brian with both of us, and one day as he and I were talking he asked if I was Brian's nanny. I told him Brian had two moms, and his response was, "If there's no Daddy, who plays rough with him?" I had to admit no one did, not even his

Grandpa. Later, his mother related how he told this story to her and her husband, and she'd asked him what he thought of two moms. He said, "Great!" What about two dads? "Great, too!" And what about a mom and a dad? "Well," he said, "that's no big deal." I hope Brian's whole generation will be like Gregory.

Louise's Story

When my partner Thelma and I started talking about how two girls could make a baby, I really wanted us to use a "known donor"—like a male friend or colleague. But Thelma was worried about our having a lifetime attachment to yet another adult (the two of us were hard enough!), so we went anonymous. The moment little Brian was handed to me in the hospital, a wave of deep relief swept over me that we'd gone that route. My first reaction was that Brian looked exactly like Thelma's brother—whom I wasn't speaking to at the time—and that made me feel suddenly insecure and left out of the family circle. When I remembered that we'd picked a Jewish donor, someone from my tribe (Thelma's Catholic), practically a relative, practically me, I felt back in the picture again. At that moment, I was really glad there was no known bio-dad out there to make me feel like a third gonad.

Thelma and I had really wanted a girl, but the moment we got our baby boy all of our prior prejudice dissolved. It was impossible to maintain the bad feelings I associated with boys (little Ninja Turtle–wielding frat thugs of the future) when faced with this seemingly gender-neutral, innocent, helpless creature, and we couldn't imagine wanting any baby but exactly him. Later, the feelings came back, though, and I found myself thinking it "boyish" when he flailed his little two-week-old fists around and made deep snorting noises. Then I noticed some girl babies doing the same thing, and realized something. By deciding to have a baby this way and taking the chance that it could be either a boy or a girl, I was committing myself to the belief that the unpleasant side of manliness was something men learned, not something they were born with. I knew I'd have to give up any lingering ideas that there was, say, a sex-linked arrogance gene. I had to really believe Brian could be the improved man of the future. (Of course, he'll probably rebel and become a football-playing Re-

239

publican.) Although I'd assumed that these boy misgivings had to do with our lack of intimate experience with guys, we were pretty surprised to find out that a lot of straight moms go through the same feelings about their boy babies.

Nevertheless, I didn't think our efforts to raise a well-rounded, feminist son were really being helped by the fact that as soon as he was born, Thelma started calling him Bucky, Buddy, Buster, and all sorts of other hulking names that started with B. At the same time, though, she had a hard-to-control desire to dress him in soft pastels, some of which were positively girlish. Although people have been really supportive of us in general, I've noticed a high level of freaked-outness in people over baby boy/girl stuff. For example, the head anesthesiologist stopped in the middle of applying Thelma's epidural to express her concern over the bit of pink clothing she saw peeking out our suitcase. My father, who never touched a sports object his whole childhood, being more of a chess-playing kind of kid, talks about Brian becoming a wrestler. Gifts from straight and gay people alike were blue, with tractors, trains, and tools on them. People seemed really anxious that he wouldn't be properly male-socialized by two women. And to tell the truth, they're probably right. Neither of us has a clue about hockey or golf.

Then there are our families, who've come a long, long way. My father, who hardly acknowledged Thelma's pregnancy, now calls every single day and asks if he can baby-sit. My mom custom tailors Hallmark cards to look like they apply to our family before she sends them. Thelma's mother is a little old religious lady, and she was the hardest of all—but we knew she had come around when she called my mother "Grandma Tilly" one day. In fact, our moms bonded and formed a solid wall of grandmotherhood at the hospital, sitting vigil twelve hours a day, armed with bottles and advice, and eating all the chocolate that people were sending us.

The hospital staff was a mixed bag. Our OB had to advocate for me every step of the way—something I hadn't thought about or expected. She was there to make sure I was really treated like the other expectant parent, that I was sitting by Thelma's side during the C-section, that the baby was handed to me, and that I got the bracelet that let me into the nursery. If it weren't for her, Brian's birth might have been a real battle for me. We'd thought it was great that she was also a lesbian mom when she chose her, but we had no idea how important her sympathy would turn out to be.

Being two moms means we have one particular problem straight parents

240

never have to face—the problem of being, well, two moms. When we planned it we had a very Utopian vision in mind of two earth mothers in love, both nurturing and nursing a lucky baby. Reality is different (but maybe more interesting).

For Thelma's part, she turned out to be less comfortable with the idea of two moms than she'd thought. She felt like we were competing for the same slot in his life. Competition for mothering roles was something I'd never thought of; as far as I'm concerned, the only difference between mothers and fathers is their genders, with everything else up for grabs. But deep down, parts of Thelma didn't feel that way. Before he was born, we'd decided we'd both breast-feed. I would use a gadget invented for adoptive mothers, a tube the baby drinks milk through while s/he nurses. (I've also heard of a non-bio mom who takes hormones to lactate.) Thelma thought breast-feeding was yucky, and was happy to let me do it. But when the time came, after Brian was born, she threw herself on the bed and cried her eyes out. She did not want that baby at my breast. She'd discovered she actually loved breastfeeding, and didn't want any competition.

I turned out to have wrenching insecurities about being the non-bio mom (which our breast-feeding conflict didn't help). Is he really my son? Am I really, really his mom? I wished sometimes we'd adopted—then I wouldn't be wondering this stuff. He would be equally the child of us both, period. But this way we were in wildly unequal positions. I wondered all the time if Thelma and I felt the same things about him—I loved him an impossible amount, I felt like he was an extension of my own body, but was she feeling something extra, something mysterious and secret that only a birth mother could know? I'd thought that since we'd decided that I'm going to carry our next child, it would all even out in the end, but now I feel like two or three years is a long, long time to wait for that to happen.

All these problems pale, though, next to the wonderfulness of our incredibly beautiful and sweet little boy; and we're going to do it this way again—we've already stocked up on more of the same donor's donations.

In the future, we hope he'll call us MamaLouise and MamaThelma. We really hope gay marriage becomes legal—we'd love to honeymoon in Hawaii and stop having to pay double health insurance. I plan to legally adopt him as soon as I can—something that's only become possible recently. But if we were legally married, we wouldn't have to go through the hassle of having a social worker come over and decide if I'm really the other mother, which is humiliating and really expensive. We worry about how having lesbian moms will be for him in school, and we hope he won't be tormented by the question of who his donor is. But we're convinced that if we give him lots of love and self-esteem, he'll be able to deal with whatever life brings him.

Abortion Story

by Simone de Boudoir

17

"Oh please God please—just this once let me not be pregnant." I'm chanting this over and over and punching myself in the stomach while I'm curled up on the bottom bunk-bed in my freshman dormitory room. The money is a big problem, I'm working two jobs part-time to pay my way through school; the two hundred bucks or whatever it would cost to get an abortion is simply not there. I'd have to tell my parents and get money from them. No, not my parents. They've hardly called me since I've been at this school, I can't talk to them about these things, they wouldn't give me money for anything. I can't tell them. Oh what am I gonna do, what am I gonna do? It's not like I can ask the guy to help, we've only had one date and I'm still trying to get him to like me. Oh why didn't I just stop to get my diaphragm in on time? Motherfucking stupid cunt, why do I get so drunk and so careless?

A few days later I get my period. I play out this same scene at least another twenty times in my years at college.

242

23

I'm in love. I feel loved. I've never felt loved before in my whole life. We fuck like bunnies for three straight years. He always asks to make sure I've put in my "frisbee." He won't fuck me if I don't. He once got a girl pregnant. He wants to make sure it'll never happen again. Nevertheless, we fuck, fall asleep, wake up and fuck again. I know the instructions on my frisbee say it's only good for two hours after insertion, not six. But I never get pregnant with him. Maybe I can't get pregnant. Maybe my uterus is pickled as a result of all the drinking I've done. Maybe all my eggs have rotted.

One morning after a huge fight I wake up in his bed. "It's over," he tells me. I feel it in my womb before I feel it in my heart. We used to talk about having children together; what we'd name them, what they'd look like, what we wanted for them. Now it's over between us, and he's taking all our children with him. The images of our potential children hover over my head like cherubs, then quickly evaporate. Maybe I can't have children, anyway.

26

Now that he's left me, I'm sleeping with everyone I can get my hands on. I'm out for revenge. On most of these nights I am so drunk I can't even remember whether I've had sex or not. Sometimes I see a used condom on the floor the morning after, and this is how I know that not only did I have sex, but it was protected sex. By some miracle, I don't get pregnant. I'm certain the alcohol has killed my womb; it must be floating in my body bathed in gin, like those fetal pigs from high school that were in jars full of formaldehyde.

27

I've stopped drinking. It's painful. I'm afraid of ever having sex again; afraid I won't know how without the prerequisite presex drinks. But I meet a sober man, and I kind of like him. We get close, slowly. It's not like all the drunken head-on collisions I'm used

to. We sleep together. We become a couple, but we keep each other constantly at arm's length. We have intense sex, when we have sex, which isn't often. He does not love me, I do not love him, but we need each other, we need something. We keep breaking up, then getting together again. On one of the nights we've broken up, he shows up at a café where I am. I want to make him jealous, show him how well I am doing without him. I'm all smiles, I laugh too loud, make sure I'm always talking to someone, anyone, not him. He comes over to me, grabs me by the arm. "We're going home," he says.

I follow him to his car. We drive to his apartment, not a word is spoken. Walk up to his room, go into the bedroom. He tears off my clothes, grabs me, holds me tight to the spot, impales me. For the moment, he doesn't want me to leave. For the moment, I'm happy to be wanted. There's no time to think of condoms. I lie in bed in the afterglow of something—a feeling. Desperation.

Weeks pass. I don't get my period. I do a home pregnancy test. It is positive. I know I don't want to have this man's baby; I don't even want to have a baby; I don't

The BUST Guide to the New Girl Order

even want to have this man. But surprisingly, I'm secretly happy, because at twenty-seven it's nice to know that I *can* get pregnant.

It's wintertime. In his bed I show him how large my breasts are getting; I show him the dark line that is already forming from my navel to my pubic hair. I am amazed at how fast the changes kick in. I tell him I want an abortion, he offers to pay half. Something about it is sweet. He holds me. I am carrying something of us inside me. I think we are both surprised that the two of us could result in anything at all, anything real.

Traveling on the subway in the mornings I feel like an alien spacecraft. I like it a lot. My little secret. My magical body. Still, I have no doubt that I am going to terminate this pregnancy next week—the week between Christmas and New Year's Eve. I have no affection for the "thing" in me; the thought of having a baby that is his does not appeal to me. The baby would be stupid. The baby would be ugly. The baby would definitely be an alcoholic.

"It's hard," he says, "with all of this happening right around Christmas. I keep seeing images of babies, and of angels. It makes me sad. But then I think, maybe it's God's Christmas present to you, to let you know that you *can* get pregnant." I like that. It does feel like a present.

The night before my "procedure" he brings me home, makes me dinner. Wakes me in the morning and we go to the clinic where I'd made the appointment. When we get there, there are at least one hundred women already waiting. They are there with their boyfriends, husbands, children. Crowded on benches and avoiding each other's eyes, they look like people on an uncomfortable subway car. It's depressing. "Forget it," I tell him. "Let's go to Planned Parenthood. There's one nearby."

When we arrive, there are only two people in the waiting room. I feel better. We wait awhile, then I go follow the nurse into another room. Fill out some forms. I'm going to have local anesthesia; the fact that the forms for general anesthesia warn that a side effect might be death creep me out too much.

I put on a paper gown. Wait in a hallway with at least twenty other women wearing paper gowns and paper slippers. I'm cold. I'm hungry. I wait for an hour, two hours. They put some of us in a different waiting room. We all wait. Another hour, then two. No one comes to our room. They forgot about us. We remind them. They move me to another hallway. Now I know I'm in the home stretch, sitting here on a bench across from a stupid mural of dancing women of many colors. They have us sitting off the same hallway where they wheel the women postprocedure to the recovery room. These women are coming out of general anesthesia; their eyes are rolled up in the backs of their heads, they are drooling and mumbling. I can't believe how much we are being treated like cattle. Is this some kind of punishment for being female? For having sex? I'm starting to get really angry; I had no idea it would be like this.

Finally, it is my turn. Somehow, I am the last one of the day. In a tiny little operating room, the doctor puts me on the table, my feet in stirrups, my naked body spread wide open. He begins to do something between my legs. I shut my eyes and try to relax. The door to the operating room opens. Another doctor walks in. "So, have a great New Year's!" he says to my doctor. "Thanks, you too. Glad to see you can finally leave," my doctor answers him. I'm lying on the table like a giant meat clump, no longer a human, just a body. The other doctor leaves. He leaves the door wide open. My doctor goes on inserting things inside my body. I can't take it anymore. "Can't you please shut the door?!" I yell, by now half crying. I'm exhausted. I'm frustrated. I feel victimized. Suddenly the doctor and nurse realize there is someone else in the room with them. It's me.

The nurse comes over. She holds my hand. The doctor turns on a big motor. The vacuum. I feel it sucking. It feels like the worst menstrual cramps I've ever had in my life. It hurts like hell. I clench the nurse's hand. She pats my forehead. "It's okay, it won't take long, it's almost over." Finally, some sweetness. I'm grateful.

After the abortion, I get to sit in an easy chair in the recovery room. They give me a few cookies and some water. I haven't eaten all day. I am bleeding profusely, I am wearing something like a diaper. Finally I can leave. The boy is there. He's exhausted, from waiting. He got lunch and did some shopping, but now he wants to go home. He drops me off at my apartment, and he leaves.

Two other friends come over to visit me. The three of us lie in my bed together and watch movies that I rented the night before; they bring me soup, they hold my hand. I'm relieved. I tell them how horrible it was.

The BUST *Guide to the New Girl Order*

Before I went for the abortion, I told my mother. I told her not to tell my father; he's never been very understanding, he lost my trust years before, he lost his right to my confidence. She was a bit sad, but mostly she was annoyed. "I don't understand how you, such a smart girl, could be so stupid." She was mad that I hadn't used a condom.

32

I am taking a walk with my mother. "Sometimes," she says, "I think about that child. I think of how old it would have been by now." Suddenly the dirt spaces beneath the trees growing out of the sidewalk look like small cemetery plots. I am single again, and still childless. "I never think about that," I tell her. It's true; I don't think of the child. What I do think about is the angel, the gift from God, who let me know my body was fine. Who warned me, who assured me that someday it would be possible. Ever since then, I've been preparing a space in my life for my future child. Now, when it comes, I'm planning to be ready.

Tie Me Up, Tie Me Off

by Scarlett Fever

Biologically speaking, I'm a breeder. That's what the gynecologist said. Except he phrased it a little differently. I believe his exact words were: "You're a lucky one. With those hips, you can drop one a year." I was fifteen years old and dropping one a year wasn't part of the five-year plan. In fact, it wasn't part of the any-year plan. I got myself on The Pill—and quick.

Unfortunately, Doctor Demento was right; I am a breeder. In the course of the next fifteen years, I became pregnant five times. In the days when I started taking it, there was no such thing as the minipill; they packed you so full of hormones that your breasts plumped up like ballpark franks just to make room for all that extra estrogen. While that made for a nice consolation prize, all those synthetic hormones were still no match for my own. I got pregnant twice. All The Pill did for me was save me the expense of a clinical abortion. I held on to each pregnancy for only a month or so, and then literally tossed the baby out with the bathwater. Still, the experience was too close for comfort for me. I needed to find something safer and more effective.

Doctors had a policy about IUDs at the time. They wouldn't give you one unless you'd already had a baby or an abortion. Sort of closing the barn door after the baby's already in the bassinet, isn't it? But I'm a good talker and I had those lovely wide hips and all, so I managed to bypass the IOU and got an IUD from the good doctor. I tried two different styles of that tiny piece of plastic, my favorite being the one shaped like the astrological symbol for Aries. Not my sign, but I was young and it felt sorta spiritual. It was, and the spirits declared me a breeder. I got pregnant two more times. Once for each style of IUD. Again, I held on to each for about a month and then spontaneously aborted, an innocuous, clinical term meant to sound simpler and less painful (emotionally, physically, and psychically) than the word miscarriage. It's not.

So I got back on The Pill, the New and Improved version, which seemed to work (or maybe I just wasn't getting it as often). I had those fabulous big plump boobs back and was a happy little bedhopper until they came out with all those damned studies. The ones that said The Pill caused cancer (which runs in my family). That it's worse if you're a smoker (which I was). That you had to get off it every coupla years or when you finally had a baby, it would be born with three heads. You remember those studies.

248

Once again I found myself looking for an answer and wishing I could just fall for guys who were sterile. Anyway, two weeks after getting off the hybrid hormone train, I wind up pregnant again. Did I forget to mention that The Pill acts as a fertility drug for the first few weeks after you go off of it? Where do you think all those quadruplets come from? So I'm pregnant and this one doesn't look like it's going to leave quietly like the other four, even though I gave it every reason to want to leave. Not wanting to get an abortion (and that was a strictly financial decision), I headed downtown and copped a blood-thinning brew, illegal in the States, but not in Chinatown, where nothing is impossible if you know the right pharmacist. Within a week the blood was flowing like, well, like blood. Unfortunately, it was coming from every orifice other than the right one. My nose, mouth, rectum, everything but my pootie. I'm a breeder, remember? My body didn't want to give this one up.

Well, biologically I may have been a breeder, but at the time I was an emotional and spiritual mess. There was no way I could take care of a baby—I couldn't even take care of myself. For Chrissakes, the next morning I couldn't even remember the name of the guy who got me pregnant, where he lived, or where we met. I debated the possibilities for about an hour and then it was back to see the Wizard. But I had so much Chinese Hot Sauce in me, the Wizard sent me home for two weeks to detoxify, afraid I'd bleed to death on his table. He was probably right, since at that point, every time I sneezed, I sneezed blood. So I had two more weeks to decide if I was doing the right thing.

I keep hearing women talk about the agonizing decision to abort. Not for me. I love kids. I really do—I used to be one. And I think they deserve the best the world has to offer: every chance, every opportunity, a house full of love, toys, curiosity, and patience. My house (and I mean this in the most esoteric sense) was full of shit. As well as hypodermic needles, coke spoons, faceless guys crashed out on the couch, violence, and empty bottles of whatever wine happened to be on sale. I didn't think kids deserved that. And I knew that it wasn't the kind of stuff you can change overnight just because you find out you're pregnant . . . again. Sure, you can clean up the stuff and toss the guy out into the street and swear you'll never get high again and maybe you won't, but probably you will, and if you can't even remember where you slept last night how are you gonna remember to feed and clothe and care for a tiny baby?

I opted for the abortion. As much for the baby's sake as for my own. I dragged my mother along with me. She cried a little, over the grandchild she wasn't going to get to love and spoil, but in the end she agreed with me. I wasn't fit to be a mother. I was barely fit to be a daughter!

249

After that experience I was determined to make sure the situation never came up again. What if next time the decision wasn't so clear? Time marched on and I found myself looking at mothers and babies in a different way than when I was younger, something more tender and maternal. I was afraid that maybe next time—and ya know with these hips there was definitely going to be a next time—I wouldn't be thinking so clearly and I'd keep it. What then? Then I'd have a beautiful baby of my own, right? Probably not.

Probably, if it was born alive at all, it would have fetal alcohol syndrome. Probably it would be way underweight, early, and sickly. Perhaps retarded. It was one thing to be pumping all that booze, drugs, and nicotine into an adult body, but babies and especially fetuses, they need gentler care to have a fighting chance. And I knew, deep in my heart, in the place where the truth resides and can't be denied, I knew that I was capable of losing my temper and hurting a baby. As horrifying as it was, I knew I could pick up a crying child, on a day when I was hungover or sleep-deprived or just generally miserable with myself, I knew I could pick that baby up and send it flying against the wall.

And that was the clincher. I wanted to make sure I was never given the opportunity to hurt a child. So, for my thirtieth birthday I got a tubal ligation. My doctor fought me—I was too young, he said. I fought back—my money, my body, my future, my decision, I said. This time, both my parents came and waited downstairs. This time my mom cried a lot for all the grandchildren she would never have. Upstairs, waiting to go in and have my fallopian tubes permanently sealed and cauterized, I ranted, raved, and cried. Screaming at my parents over the courtesy phone for having the audacity to call upstairs and see how I was, screaming at my doctor for even answering the phone and daring to give them any information at all. He must've thought I was insane, and I probably was at the moment. But after a few minutes in a small room with me and my temper, he stopped fighting and began to see the truth. I wasn't fit to be a mother.

My oldest friend at the time wouldn't come with me. She didn't talk to me for months afterward. I'd betrayed her. She wanted children. She loved kids and was horrified that I had closed off that avenue of possibility for myself forever. She didn't understand then, and I don't know if she even gets it now, that I did it because I love children, because I knew that I was capable of hurting a child. I couldn't control my temper, but I could control my ovaries, so I made the only possible decision. Not out of selfishness, but out of love. For all children. No one deserves to come into a violent household, and since I didn't know how to stop the violence, I did the next best thing. I stopped the babies.

It's been nine years since the operation. Ten or twelve since the abortion. And six since I've done any drinking or drugging. I know where I slept last night and with whom. I never think about how old my son or daughter would have been if I had had him or her. I never think about the others, the ones that slipped away quietly like thieves in the night. I don't think about adopting a child someday. I don't think about being a mother at all.

I get a little jealous when I see my friends with their new babies, or strangers on the street with happy little kids. I stop and lecture strangers who let their kids run around—wandering this way and that—so anybody could just come by and scoop the kid away. And I generally prefer the company of kids to that of grown-ups.

I get a little sad sometimes, too. For what I won't ever have, for the things I'll never know about loving a child. And I still know that I made the right decision. I'm sorry that my life led me to such a point of degradation and misery that I had to make it, but I'm never sorry I did.

Motherhood Lite: The Joys of Being an Aunt

by Tiffany Lee Brown

There's nothing like grocery shopping on a national holiday. Aisles teem with grumpy middle-aged men hauling cases of Miller Lite and buckets of salsa. Young lowlifes flex their tattoos and pocket soft packs of Marlboro reds. Above the hustle and bustle of Independence Day commerce can be heard a most distinctive and soothing sound: the lively chatter of children.

Yes, holidays mean Family Shopping Trips. What joy to hear the fresh young voices, as yet untainted by worldly cares and woes, screaming at their mothers: "Not the TreeTop Apple Juice! Get the Capri Sun, I want the coloring book!! I WANT THE COLORING BOOK!!" What a thrill to laboriously turn a blind corner and nearly snap a six-year-old's spine with my heavily laden shopping cart. Heavens, I almost interrupted his youthful activity—no doubt some whimsical game I've forgotten from my own sunny childhood, which apparently involves emptying the contents of each coffee bean dispenser from the bulk espresso bins onto the floor. And far away on Aisle 3 I can hear the sweet strains of the procreative lullaby: an infant, shrieking at the top of his or her little lungs.

Don't get the wrong impression: I'm not your classic single gal with the bitter beat of jealousy in her heart, masking her maternal desires with a cynical attitude. I didn't have a horrific childhood, and by some fortune I avoided the physical and sexual abuse that often makes people leery of having a family. Children themselves aren't a problem. In fact, I rather like children, as long as they belong to someone else and are kept muzzled in public spaces. Though I reserve the right to change my mind and squirt out brats later on, should the much-hyped biological clock suddenly take hold of my usually sensible uterus, for now I'm into letting other folks have the morning sickness, wild hormonal swings, stretch marks, and college-savings funds. After all, why be a mom when you can be an aunt?

Aunties, like grandmothers, get to play with children and watch them grow. Like grandmothers, we can spoil 'em rotten if we so please—the kids' parents will have to cope with the resultant tantrum of throwing things and foot stomping. Unlike grandmothers, we don't have to bring forth infants ourselves, and as Aunties we're often younger than the kids' parents. We can be a part of the beautiful cycle of life, the passing on of dubious genetic characteristics from one generation to the next, but without those pesky responsibilities.

While a mother has to spend most of her waking hours with an umbilical cord attached to her little ball and chain, an aunt can come and go as she wishes. The childless Auntie has a romantic and uneasy image in our society: the Auntie of books and movies might be a crazy old loner living in a haunted house with her dozen cats, a mysterious and witchy crone. She might be fussy and lovelorn on the surface, the sort of aunt who comes around the house entirely too much, like Charlotte in *A Room with a View*. Then again, she might be a dashing young career gal or entertainer, fluttering in only at Christmas to beguile the children with strange gifts from faraway lands. The intentionally childless woman is demonized, or at least considered suspicious, by straight America, but the loving Auntie is happy to satisfy her maternal instincts on a purely vicarious level.

In my family, the Wacky Auntie stereotype keeps things interesting. Without 'em, the whole family would devolve into a dull, whitebread, Christian remake of the 1950s. There were Clara and Louise, my great-great-aunts who lived as spinsters in some big ol' house back east, constantly sending me wonderful little boxes and jewels, handbags and trinkets, that dated from their swinging years in the '20s to their 1960s shopping extravaganzas. "The Aunties" were certifiably nutty and got me started early on a lifetime fixation with vintage shopping. My mother's sister D. had a kid, all right, but since she lived in a van and used to drop Owsley acid on the Haight in the '60s, Aunt D. supplied a much-needed awareness that there was more to life than our nice house in the country and the little white church where my brother and I went to Sunday school.

Aunt C.'s daughters might not have enjoyed her wild, arty lifestyle, but it saved my life. When I started acting, drawing, writing, and playing music as a wee tot, everyone could say, "Look, she takes after Aunt C!" I took it as a compliment, and Aunt C. became one of the very few people in my life I could actually look up to. In boring teenage years when I wanted to nuke the small town we lived in, I'd visit Aunt C. in Hollywood during the summer. She helped me fulfill my need for excitement, bright lights, big cities, weird people, trendy clothes, and trendier clubs—and to do it, I didn't even have to become a runaway and live on the streets. My mom, who sheltered us to the best of her abilities, probably considered Aunt C. a "bad influence" on me. On the contrary, Aunt C.'s willingness to introduce me to the Big Bad World kept me from discovering it all alone and in much more dangerous ways. Who'd you rather your daughter get drunk with for the first time: your bohemian sister, or a twenty-three-year-old crank dealer with a gold Trans Am?

Now I'm the Wacky Auntie. I'm very careful about my brother's family values: I don't smoke or swear around the kids, and when they talk about Jesus I just smile and nod. On the other hand, by the end of my Christmas visit a couple years ago, the kids were running around yelling, "I want a blue mohawk! I want a blue mohawk like Aunt TT's!" As my niece Sasha grows older, she may follow in her aunt's footsteps, and evolve from being bright and precocious to rebellious and angsty. If she does, I hope she knows there's someone cool around that she can run to: her wacky aunt.

What if you're an only child, or live far away from your estranged siblings, and would like to be an aunt? Fear not—all you need is a friend who intends to procreate. Family friends are routinely referred to as "aunt" or "uncle" in a society whose extended families tend to fragment or disappear altogether. It's pretty weird when close friends start getting hitched, settling down, and having kids, but playing Auntie is a way to enjoy the experience. It shows that you love your friend enough to be a part of his or her new lifestyle, instead of just pouting about it, and you get all the benefits of being around children, but on your own terms.

You can always find new friends to go on drinking binges with, or throw trespass parties, or to take backpacking in South America. If you don't want to stop doing those things just yet, hold off on motherhood and try the Auntie thing: Aunties don't have to drag the brats along to Safeway or miss a great show because they can't find a baby-sitter. Packed with flavor but only half the calories, being an aunt is like Motherhood Lite. Tastes great, less filling!

The BUST *Guide to the New Girl Order*

We Are Family (I've Got All My Goddesses with Me)

by Krista Franklin

I was one of the fortunate ones. Born the first female child of my generation in my family, I grew up surrounded by a bunch of female-loving women, and not just your regular kind—they were the ones who wanted to constrict your tiny baby body with girdles and corsets of crinoline and lace (though I did have that element to combat). I was born into a family of female-lovers who made it their job to determine for themselves what that loaded word "woman" actually meant, and who encouraged me all throughout my life to do the same.

I'm certain that my childhood has to be one of the most beautiful black girlhoods in existence. Sure, I had my hang-ups and brainwashings to overcome in adulthood like every American woman, but overall the experience was stellar. Blessed with educated, working parents determined to rear me in a neighborhood both safe and diverse (before that word became a national catchphrase, the cool, politically correct thing to be), I grew up surrounded by kids who didn't all look like me

Krista Hill

in a neighborhood where we held funky-ass disco parties in my family's garage and went rollerskating on Saturdays. The greatest part of my childhood, though, had to be my mother and her sisters.

Married to a man almost twice her age and deliberately childless, my aunt Sue was a teacher by nature and choice. A worldly woman and a voracious reader, she drove a smooth red Corvette, which she occasionally drove to pick me up from school. Sue flew me to New York City on my fifteenth birthday, where she exposed me to the art of fine shopping (an addiction I still can't seem to kick) and began to cultivate in me a love for live theater.

Bunni was the self-proclaimed "black sheep" of the family; the aunt with a history of spunk, rule breaking, and risk taking. She also happened to be the mother of my favorite hellraising first cousins: Kevin and Kerry, the 110 percent boys who preceded my birth, broke other boys' arms for me, brought back candy for me from their mysterious excursions, and made me laugh so hard my stomach hurt.

My aunt Bobbi was the woman with the great sense of humor and an uncanny knack for cooking and salting food just like I liked it. Bobbi was the one we left town to visit on holidays, the one who married the man who owned the best record collection in history, covering the gamut of musical experience from Santana to the Jacksons to Parliament Funkadelic; his collection even rivaled my father's.

But best of all had to be Mom. My mother—the quintessential, eternal tomboy. The woman who screamed at the top of her lungs about football plays gone wrong; the woman who could give more attitude than any man if playing baseball with a losing team; the woman who rode bikes and swam faster and harder than I and any other kid in the neighborhood did; went into any neighborhood she chose without ever being worried about what could possibly happen to her. She had an answer for my every question, a warm cup of hot chocolate waiting when I came in from marathon sledding sessions, and ice-cold Kool-Aid on the hottest summer days. My mom was the mom all the other kids wished they had. She was young, pretty, smart, and funny. She kept an open-door policy for all kids, including the ones on her social work caseloads, making sure our house was the beacon for any and every child, needy or not. My mother was, and still is at forty-eight years old, limitless and fearless.

The women in my family have watched me progress through my goth/progressive phase, my militant black power phase, and my Peter-Pan-never-wanna-grow-up phase (just to name a few). They have sat by patiently as I brought home boys with green hair, gay kids, straight kids, black kids, white kids, bi- and triracial kids, kids with long hair, kids with no hair, style or no style. They have maintained their grace as I've tried their patience, their pocketbooks, and their sensibilities—giving me enough room for self-definition, and attacking anyone who questioned my right to do so like a pride of lionesses.

Now a quirky, nontraditional twenty-six-year-old writer-poet, intellectual wannabe, and teacher in the making, I make up in fragments who these incredible women were and are. If there are goddesses in this world, they are the ones who created, reared, shaped, and mentored me. They compose me.

One's Not Enough

by Eve Shopsin

Large families certainly seem to be out of fashion these days, but as a mother of five, I can tell you that the benefits of mothering a large clan are well worth the gamble. In fact, it's easier to raise a large family than you might think.

For one, things you mom always did do not have to be done by you—a multi-kidded mom must creatively cut unnecessary corners. For instance, why do kids have to wear pajamas? Why can't they sleep in the nude? Why not sleep in their underwear or part of what they've worn during the day? Think of the money and hassle saved by the elimination of this ritual.

Lots of things normally thought to be necessary by smaller families are just impossible for a multi-child parent. You can't be active in fifteen parent associations,

Adrienne Yan

and you can't be active in the associations of only one or two kids. So you do what comes naturally—nothing.

An only child will use your total attention. Few are the moments such a child will let Mom out of sight. Not so with multiple kids. Having older brothers and sisters around provides the ultimate fascination for younger children. Baby's attraction to and need for his or her older siblings' attention creates a double plus for Mom. She can relax while baby is being entertained by older bro or sis, and the big kids get to feel a sense of worth and self-importance as a result of the baby's adulation. Mom also gets to appreciate her older kids and feel a glowy sense of family.

A large family frees one from the "Perfect Mom Syndrome." You cannot be the "Perfect Mom" to five kids. There are not enough hours in the day. Perfection is

*The **BUST** Guide to the New Girl Order*

replaced with a more relaxed attitude toward parenting. Doing your best becomes enough.

Having lots of kids frees you to say "No" or "Yes" easily in situations that a mom with fewer kids would need to ponder mightily or perhaps become racked with guilt over.

Being part of a large family encourages early independence on the part of the kids. You can't do it all for them for very long, so they learn to do for themselves. My kids became competent cooks before they reached double digits.

Having lots of kids frees you from many of the anxieties that moms typically suffer over. A mom always worries about her flock when they are away from home, but in large families this worry is balance by the relief of having fewer kids underfoot for a time. You are always too busy with the ones left at home to spend an inordinate amount of time worrying about the absent one.

It's harder to favor one child over another when there are many. A parent can't help but get more pleasure from one child at one time than another. In a large family a mom's favorite can change from week to week or day to day or even hour to hour. All get to be the favorite sometime.

People think I'm joking when I say I expect one of my children to be rich and take care of me if I'm needy. Having lots of offspring allows me to feel I will not be alone in the future.

Being a mom to many allows your children's quirks to be endearing rather than a failure on your part. All your hopes are not tied up in one basket. So what if one doesn't become a doctor, artist, or rock star? Maybe another one will.

Kids from a large family feel less lonely and more secure. They are always part of a group, so they are less likely to submit to peer pressure. I have never been asked to buy designer jeans by any of my children (although Nike sneakers are another matter). Amazingly, not one of my five children does drugs, alcohol, or tobacco. Although fights and "I hate you"s are not uncommon, a spirit of cooperation is more likely to be in evidence. My younger son has had much assistance ironing on camp labels from an older sister. He also gets plenty of homework help and encouragement from his older sisters. These everyday generosities have a twofold positive effect on Mom. The work gets done without her, and once again she gets that great feeling from seeing her family care for one another.

259

A difficult part of mothering is having the flock leave her nest, but having a large number of kids can soften this as well. My oldest son is now living in a different city. Something that has made his separation from me easier has been the joy and excitement evident in my other kids' faces as they speak with him on the phone.

My recent fiftieth birthday coincided with a visit from my oldest son. To see the ease with which he conversed with patrons in our restaurant and the happiness of all my kids to be with him and to be able to bathe in his success made a potentially traumatic day for me into a triumph.

I know this feeling will occur many times as my large family grows up. They are tangible proof of my success as a mom and as a citizen of Earth.

Mother-to-Wannabe

by Rose Tattoo

When I was eleven my mom made me this totally rad baby blue and mint green seersucker pantsuit with a pinafore top and huge bell-bottoms with bedspring fringe that hung down over my platforms and dragged on the ground. As I walked down the school hallway in that thing I felt like a million bucks—like sexy, cool-girl, boy-magnet womanhood was just around the corner. It was one of my favorite outfits of all time. I kept adding fabric in a desperate attempt to lengthen the legs, but I kept on growing and soon couldn't wear the damn thing anymore.

There aren't many things in life that become just plain impossible after a while. Everybody's always saying, "It's never too late to . . ." or "You're never too old to . . ." And if we're talking about becoming a concert pianist or a professional snow boarder or something, then, sure, I believe that. But twenty-plus years later, the end of my reproductive years hovers almost as close as puberty and all its dreams did then, and that pantsuit seems like a metaphor. It hinted at the majesty of femininity, but unraveled before the secrets did. Now it's almost time to wedge in the other bookend, and womanhood hasn't yet fulfilled its one promise that I have no control over. Well, biologically I guess I do. But by the time my seersucker was shredding, Helen Reddy was roaring in my ears that I could spread my wings wider than my elephant bells, and somewhere along the way life turned into a riddle. Yet even then I knew that I wanted kids—and all the accessories that go with them, like a husband and a home. And I'm scared shitless that I'll lose the race against time, just like I did back then.

I know plenty of women who don't want kids, and I respect that. But if there's anything I absolutely must accomplish before I leave this planet, it's to birth me a baby. I don't know exactly why, it just feels like an instinct that I can't intellectualize away. It's just there, like gravity or the tide. Every living thing on earth comes into existence, reproduces, dies. I am woman, I bleed. All I know is, life just won't feel complete until I'm a breeder.

And don't tell me that I can adopt. Or that there are already too many neglected children who need loving parents. Fuck that. I want unconditional love, and I *will* have it even if I have to make it myself! It's not about a kid, it's about *my* kid. It's about fusing a piece of me and someone I love into total oneness (even if the only one I end up loving is my disparate self!). It's about creating something greater than any artist ever could—a human that is an absolute extension and expression of my-self. It's living, breathing proof that there are things in me that are so good that they're worth repeating, and an excuse that I can't do a damn thing about my bad points, since they're biologically preprogrammed. It's the greatest challenge life has to offer: to mold a sane, functional, motivated being that doesn't turn out to be a total slacker or serial killer. It's about mortality, and my need to leave a little piece of me when I go.

So here I sit, basically ready. It's not like I need to have the kid tomorrow, but I'm ready in an abstract kind of way. I've gotten most of those other selfish needs out of the way: I've worked approximately 5,000 days now, and discovered that a career doesn't fill in the empty places that '70s- and '80s-style feminism said it would; I've traveled the world, so I don't long to sit on top of Montmartre with Pierre eating Brie and a baguette; I've looked for liquor and love in enough bars to know that one

261

doesn't lead to the other. Hell, I've even hobnobbed with famous people, and found them disappointing in just as great a ratio as regular folks.

Now, an alien bacteria has attacked my brain, and it makes me do things like turn down a night out to stay home and make those little candle holders I saw in *Martha Stewart Living*. That must be a sign. I think I've lived enough that I'm ready to give of myself without feeling like I'm giving up myself. I think. Maybe. Well, I'll never be 100 percent sure, but I feel more open to the possibility than ever before.

I have no desire to be a single mother. When I was young, I thought single moms were either slutty, stupid, or unfortunate. Now I'm ashamed of my youthful ignorance—I have incredible respect for single moms. I've had the chance to observe parenthood up close and personal, and it's hard work. Parenthood is physically, emotionally, financially, and socially draining. A kid needs parents who can survive that kind of stress with their love and grace intact. A single parent has to top this herculean task by providing a healthy balance of male and female perspectives, and somehow find enough hours in the day to be the sole proprietor of this little venture. Frankly, I don't think I have the courage.

Besides, I was raised in a mostly traditional family structure, and it left me with some mighty un-PC ideas of what a family is supposed to be. I'm not saying the male/female roles have to be so strictly defined—maybe I'm Ozzie and he's Harriet. But I find beauty and comfort in making a man my best friend, sharing the rearing of our very own kids, growing up and growing old with all of us there to love and look after each other. I also find potential boredom and total castration of my self, which is probably why I'm not there yet. But I think down deep I do want it.

Therein lies the rub: I may be ready, but my husband isn't. That's because he doesn't know he's my husband. In fact, he doesn't even know he's supposed to be my boyfriend. We haven't met yet—he's the winning number in my final round of *Beat the Clock*. It's only recently that I've started to take the game seriously, so I'm hoping my added concentration will sharpen my skills.

But just in case, I am chanting a regular mantra to myself that I do not need another half to be whole. I'm slowly trying to come to terms with the idea that I may not find my prince, or I may never be able to accept anything less than one (my mother calls this "being too picky"). I am a strong, powerful, *now* kind of woman who is emotionally and financially secure, with loads of friends and family to support me and my little bastard. I toy with the idea that I and all my other way-too-fabulous-for-men single-chick girlfriends with withering uteri will buy a big old Victorian mansion, find willing yet uncomplicated sperm donors, and live happily together in our little nursery/commune. Maybe I could handle single motherhood after all, or maybe time will teach me to embrace childlessness.

Yeah, right, and monkeys will fly out of my butt.

Sara Schwartz

Media Whores

WE LOVE THEM, WE HATE THEM, WE LOVE TO HATE THEM.
That's a pretty accurate description of women's relationship to the media over the past few decades. We eat up what they put out like it's chocolate cake, buying millions of women's magazines every year, traveling in packs to the movies to drool over Leo or Brad or Johnny, and making unbreakable dates with our TV sets to watch Xena slay her latest dragon. And then we trash them to pieces like they're in league with the devil himself, an unstoppable multibillion-dollar Beelzebub that's determined to keep us oppressed, depressed, and diet-obsessed. Over the years a number of diatribes—from *The Feminine Mystique* to *Backlash* to *The Beauty Myth* to *Reviving Ophelia*—have proclaimed that, if the medium is the message, then that message is misogyny.

Still, most of us '90s-type gals like to immerse ourselves in the current pop culture like it's a warm, scented bath. Sure, there's a lot of bad stuff out there, but when it comes to magazines, movies, and TV, most of us would rather fight than switch it off. Our favored weapon in this war against warped images of women is the smart chick's version of the kung fu kick: we study it, then slice and dice it, dissecting its context and content to reveal its underlying and often contradictory meanings. Like our '70s sisters who proclaimed that the personal is political, we know that so, too, is the popular, and we eagerly sign up for college courses with titles like "Feminist Film Theory" or "Madonna 101," honing our skills as feminist freedom fighters ready to enlist in some postmodern army. Besides, it's much more fun to be an activist when it involves sitting on your couch, munching popcorn, and watching the boob tube instead of marching for hours on the hot concrete side-walks of Washington, D.C.

But it's not just a cop-out that so many feminists of our generation have turned their attention to the media as ground zero in the fight for women's rights. It's clear to any of us who grew up in the '60s and '70s that the mass media have a massive influence on how we think about ourselves and the world around us. In this respect we have an entirely different perspective on the power of pop than do our second-wave foremothers, most of whom were born in the prehistoric age of radio. Douglas Coupland was the first to put his finger on this Generation X-related phenomenon, but even he seemed to overlook the fact that we're all looking at the world through gender-colored glasses; that the set of cultural references one finds most important might be quite different for Generation XX than it is for Generation XY.

In fact, as girls we've been targeted by the media in a way our brothers never were, bombarded by a relentless stream of messages encouraging us to buy buy buy, egging us on in an endless quest to locate that product that might rescue us from being a "before" and transform us once and for all into an "after." Although the TV producers of decades past seemed to have forgotten that they had a female audience at all, advertising executives never did. Through ads, they catered to our every desire and exploited our every insecurity, but at least they paid attention to us. This may be why we girls recall the advertising slogans of our girlhoods ("you tell two friends and she'll tell two friends and so on and so on . . . ") with a type of nostalgia usually reserved only for old boyfriends.

The **BUST** *Guide to the New Girl Order*

Our appreciation for the power of the media also explains why today's rebels are making 'zines, building Web sites, and recording rock songs rather than holding rallies: we know that we can effect change through pop culture; that it's worth our while to channel our efforts through TV channels. We've watched Madonna bring her material-girl feminism to the masses through MTV; observed Jane Pratt spread grrl power in the form of *Sassy* magazine; and witnessed Roseanne put the "broad" back into broadcasting with a hit show about an overweight, underpaid working mom. All in all, it's clear to us that the same media that can convince millions that a silicone-injected blond bimbo would make a believable lifeguard can also seduce us into accepting a fat lady with a big mouth as a genuine American hero. In other words, the effect of the media is far from straightforward. As feminist cultural critic Susan Douglas has said, "The mass media are both our best allies and our most lethal enemies."

The fact that women have been, until very recently, banned from social life—hidden away behind home and husband—has resulted in our having very few female role models in the public sphere. Perhaps this is why we have so greedily grabbed our heroines from movie and TV screens, lionizing the likes of Audrey Hepburn, Bette Davis, Lucille Ball, Pam Grier, Chrissie Hynde, Tina Turner, and Joan Jett. For us, these chicks have been as central in developing our idea of twentieth-century womanhood as Mom and Gloria Steinem. Men have not needed to be quite as passionate about their media heroes. With Lincoln and Kennedy, Plato and Nero, and Einstein and Schweitzer to look up to, how much excitement can one really muster up for the Fonz?

But even then, the version of masculinity we get from the media is more realistic—or at least more diverse—than that of femininity. Unfortunately, the media are still a big bad boys club, with most of the writers, producers, and directors of movies, magazines, and newspapers being male—hell, even the president of Lifetime, that cable channel devoted exclusively to women's programming, is a man. While there have been a few women at the helm of magazines (the Browns, Helen Gurley and Tina, come to mind), the pursestrings at both women's and general interest magazines are usually still held by men. So what does this mean for us girls? Is our worst fear true—that the media are powered by a room full of balding middle-aged men smoking cigars and plotting how they're going to put down women this week? Well, no, of course not. But we can certainly count on one thing: that the image of women we see in the media is most likely to be inaccurate. After all, man can create man in his own image, but he'll create women in whatever form his fantasies take.

Many critics have argued that this misrepresentation of women in the media does us a serious amount of harm. But the relationship between what people watch and what people do is hotly contested territory. Does pornography really make men go berserk and hurt women? Does fashion advertising really make women go berserk and hurt themselves? How much are the media responsible for negative attitudes toward women, and how much are they merely reflecting already held cultural stereotypes? These questions are not easily answered, and there's a large amount of contradictory evidence to support both sides. Nevertheless, it does appear to be hypocritical that the media will spend millions of dollars on advertising to get people to throw wads of money at their products, then turn around and claim that what people see in the movies and on TV has no effect on their behavior.

But, as the saying goes, just because you're paranoid doesn't mean they're not out to get you. In both Naomi Wolf's *The Beauty Myth* and Susan Faludi's *Backlash*—both best-selling books of the past decade—the claim is made that media images are consciously being used against women for the specific purpose of keeping men in power. Regarding the parade of images that have presented women as sex objects, stretching all the way from Venus to *Vogue,* Wolf says, "Women are mere 'beauties' in male culture so that culture can be kept male." In other words, men don't hold women in their place by keeping them barefoot and pregnant, but bare-breasted and pretty. Women's magazines, according to Wolf, are the greatest offenders on this front: "The beauty backlash is spread and reinforced by the cycles of self-hatred provoked in women by the advertisements, photo features, and beauty copy in the glossies."

Whether or not you're a woman who runs with Naomi Wolf, you'd have to agree with her that women's magazines seem to have fanned the flames of body dissatisfaction among women, making it an affliction that's more widespread than herpes. Yet, we girls can't seem to get enough of these rags. Why is that? Well, says Wolf, because we have no real choice. Women's magazines are the one place where women's concerns are taken seriously; in fact, they are perhaps the only mass-media product that is of the woman, by the woman, and for the woman. Feminists have long appreciated this fact, which is why a group of them held a sit-in in 1970 at the offices of the *Ladies Home Journal,* holding its writers and (male) editor hostage and demanding that they publish such articles as "How to Get an Abortion" and "Why Women Are Kept Apart."

And then there's Maude. Since its rebirth, feminism itself has been given air time on TV and in the pages of respected magazines, more often than not getting mangled beyond all recognition in the process. In the exact same way that advertisers can persuade us that using their brand of paper towels will make us more attractive to the opposite sex, the media can assure us that no one is more unattractive, hoarse-voiced, or humorless than a card-carrying feminist. According to Susan Faludi, the media have been on an out-and-out campaign to make feminism and the women who follow it look about as appealing as a dieter's cottage-cheese-and-tuna platter.

In *Backlash,* Faludi argued that television, film, magazines, and newspapers conspired in the 1980s to make feminism a big, bad "f-word," condemning it as the root of all contemporary evils, from single motherhood to men's wilting masculinity to the demise of lace panties. Their goal, Faludi contended, was to convince women that they were worse off now than they were before the women's movement. Finding antifeminist sentiment in every nook and cranny of the popular imagination, Faludi argued that such cultural events as the "man shortage" hysteria of the '80s was nothing more than a media concoction, intended to make women live in fear of becoming wrinkly old spinsters who were destined to be loved by no one but their eight cats, unless they renounced their evil, feminist ways. Enlightening and entertaining, *Backlash* found a large audience of feminists eager to join Faludi's media witch-hunt. But what both they, and Faludi, seemed to overlook was the fact that, even in the face of backlash, most women continued to live their lives in a modern, liberated manner, taking cover under the cloak of the infamous I'm-not-a-feminist-but routine that allows women who should know better to embrace feminist ideals, yet shrug off the label like it's some sort of cheap designer knockoff.

Happily, today it looks like feminism just might be fashionable again. The '90s has been the decade during which women finally gained some cultural ground, giving us media hounds the kind of characters that even a gal like Faludi could love,

269

from the over-the-top female bonding of *Thelma and Louise* and Patsy and Edina; to the strong older women of *Designing Women* and *Roseanne;* to the first lady of lesbianism, Ellen; to the Oscar-winning director Jane Campion and the resurgence of "the women's film" such as those based on the works of Jane Austen; the mighty single moms Murphy Brown, Rosie O'Donnell, and Madonna; to the powerful presence of girls in pop culture; to the raging rock stars Courtney Love, Liz Phair, and PJ Harvey and the female folkies of the highly successful Lilith Fair; to the rising stars of newscasters Jane Pauley and Farai Chideya; to cool and quirky female actresses like Janeane Garafolo, Jennifer Jason Leigh, and Parker Posey; to the chart-busting popularity of books about complicated women such as *She's Come Undone* and *Divine Secrets of the Ya-Ya Sisterhood;* all alongside best-selling feminist nonfiction, like Faludi's own book and those of Wolf and Paglia.

But, just as Faludi might have predicted, even in these times of profeminist sentiments, the backlash continues to rear its ugly head, leaving us to counter its effects again and again as if we were playing a perpetual game of whack-a-mole. It most recently popped up on the cover of *Time* magazine, in a story that tauntingly asked the question "Is Feminism Dead?" Pointing to everything from TV's *Ally McBeal* to music's the Spice Girls to literature's Bridget Jones, and even our own *BUST* magazine, journalist Ginia Bellafante waxed stupidly nostalgic for the ghosts of feminism past, claiming that "in the 70s, feminism produced a pop culture that was intellectually provocative. Today, it's a whole lot of stylish fluff." Just call me Debbie the feminism slayer.

Never mind the fact that *The Mary Tyler Moore Show,* which evidently earned Bellafante's feminist stamp of approval, isn't really any more intellectually provocative than *Ally McBeal*—in fact, except for the short skirts, the characters Ally and Mary have an awful lot in common: they're both single career gals with an ethnic best friend and a major propensity for pouting. The real hypocrisy is that *Time* magazine has never taken too kindly to feminism—not in its early days, and not now. In 1969, *Time* referred to feminists as "the angries" and remarked that "feminists . . . seem to be trying, in fact, to repel other women rather than attract them." And while Bellafonte complains that '90s feminism is "wed to the culture of celebrity and self-obsession," in 1968 *Time* criticized feminists for exactly the same thing: being too media-hungry. In a story on the Miss America pageant

270

protests, *Time* accusingly reported that "television and news photographers were allowed and even encouraged to photograph the pickets, and the women . . . escalated their activities when the cameramen arrived." Ten years ago *Time* was already declaring feminism to be dead: in 1989 they announced that "hairy legs haunt the feminist movement" and claimed that feminism was "hopelessly dated." Obviously, there's just no pleasing *Time:* as far as they're concerned, we girls are either too feminist, or not feminist enough.

In response to the article, many feminists shot back that it was unfair to draw conclusions about real women by analyzing fictional characters like Ally McBeal and Bridget Jones. Furthermore, they pointed out, there was plenty of political work being done by still-thriving bands of grassroots feminist activists. But these women were missing the point, because our pop culture is, indeed, an indicator of women's social status and an important influence on our cultural beliefs. It deserves all the attention it receives, and it's hard to believe that so many women, right along with Bellafante, still just don't get that. After all, it was feminists themselves who recognized the power of the popular, and developed a language for critiquing it, in the first place.

Both yesterday's postmodernism and today's cultural criticism have their roots in the work of feminist theorists and artists of the '70s and '80s, such as Cindy Sherman, Barbara Kruger, Anette Kuhn, and Laura Mulvey. And perhaps it should come as no surprise that the keys to cracking the coded meanings of popular images would come from women. We girls know all about how signifiers can signify, having learned right from the start that every element of our look would be thought to convey something about our sexuality, our morality, or our femininity. We have a lot to say about the meaning of blue eye shadow versus brown, flowery cotton dresses versus black velvet ones, or long red hair versus short blond pixie cuts. So maybe it's only natural that, when given the "texts" of popular culture, women would have a well-honed ability to read between the lines.

There's a saying that goes, "Keep your friends close to you, but keep your enemies even closer." Having accepted the idea of a politics of culture, contemporary feminists should be wary of ever turning their backs on the media. Instead, it is one of our most basic survival skills that we appreciate their importance and strength, and learn to carefully decode the myriad messages that they broadcast so innocently into our lives each day. If we don't, we run the risk that the media might one day

271

succeed at hammering the final nails into feminism's coffin, burying us alive. At the same time, we need to remember that we can use the power of the pop culture to our advantage as well. In fact, that's exactly why we thought we'd try to change the world with a little magazine called *BUST.*

—Debbie Stoller

That Cosmo Girl

by Carly Sommerstein

For the most part it pretty much rules, but it's not all some joyful Virginia Slims ad being an American woman. There are some consistently annoying things, and we all know it's the little things that bug you the most: women comics basing their acts around whatever tricks they may have with their vibrators and the Shower Massage; the Lifetime Channel—ultra-gal yet ultra-lame; the fact that on line at the Pathmark I always have to see the latest issue of *Cosmopolitan* staring back at me like so much come-hither girlie porn.

Although I might glance through the *Weekly World News,* intrigued by the headline "Female Alien Says: 'I Had Michael Jackson's Baby,'" I can't quite get myself to look at the 20 Things to Do with a Can of Tuna Fish–type magazines, and I usually pass over the fashion magazines. My objection to most of them is not that they're frivolous but that they're not frivolous enough. They kiss way too much rich and powerful corporate ass and are way too serious about being "with it." So I confess: in my supermarket boredom, I often reach for the latest issue of *Cosmopolitan,* which falls somewhere between the fashion mags and the trailer-trash tabloids in its appeal.

No women's magazine is quite as hilarious in its insincerity as *Cosmopolitan,* and no other magazine is as self-consciously yet unsuccessfully naughty. I read *Cosmo* for the same reason that wrestling fans are devoted to their favorite sport: for the big eyeball spectacle, the deliberate brainlessness of it all. *Cosmo*'s inseparable frappé of advertising and editorial, its boring vision of female beauty, and its feeble attempts at real journalism, all provide for twisted entertainment. Like the wrestling fans who "get it," I imagine that there are *Cosmo* readers who are also yukking it up on grocery store lines across our nation.

Still, *Cosmo* has a limited comic appeal. The laughs it inspires are goofy-stupid, not sexy-sly: more Jerry Lewis than Jerry Lee Lewis. Laughing at, not with, American women is a bittersweet pleasure at best. Mostly I wind up feeling pissed off. It sucks to finally realize that most of *Cosmo*'s readers are reading *Cosmopolitan* not as a hilarious parody of femininity, but for its ultra-lite fiction, prefabricated quizzes, bland-sexy attitude that passes for naughtiness, and most of all, for its normative bullshit about women and sex. In *Cosmo,* the dynamic world of women is reduced to some mutated Girls' Club, membership in which is contingent on one's ability to attract and (wo)manipulate men.

A lot of young women look to *Cosmo* as a psychosexual guidebook, and *Cosmopolitan* openly courts this demographic, as is evidenced by their recurring full-page ads in *The New York Times* featuring the waif of the week. They read like vapid mantras, with talk of beauty makeovers and pseudofeminist references to "the office," always ending with affirmations like "I really rely on that magazine . . ." or "I love that magazine. I guess you could say I'm That COSMOPOLITAN Girl." Who are these women, these reliant readers of *Cosmopolitan*? At work, at the gym, or at the tanning salon, she's That Cosmo Girl. After all, from Colorforms to Norforms, from Barbie dolls to phenobarbitals, the Cosmo Girl isn't born, she evolves—by way of all the *Cosmo*-advertised and editorialized crap and crud she eats, buys, and holds sacred. Here's how to spot her.

That Cosmo Girl puts food on her face, but rarely in her mouth. She might, on *Cosmopolitan*'s advice, concoct a honey-almond yogurt masque to firm her skin, but she'll only eat Jell-O made with Nutrasweet. Who uses those silly Aroma Disc Player machines? That Cosmo Girl buys up the scented records with names like Passion, Seduction, and Oriental Mystery. She thinks sex comes on discs, but only if it smells like it comes from a can. That Cosmo Girl makes a big effort to look wicked and considers being bitchy a compliment. Her makeup kit is as huge as it is lethal; on That Cosmo Girl, Prince Matchabelli turns Prince Machiavelli. But she never gets really wild. You'll never catch her downtown shaking it up in ripped fishnets and Jungle Gardenia perfume. More often she's seen supine at the beach, wearing a giraffe-print loincloth bikini and some stuff your grandma uses to fry chicken in. Sometimes you'll find That Cosmo Girl hanging around musicians, but the only thing she can play is the wanton. In other words, if That Cosmo Girl were a sandwich, she'd be a tuna melt on white bread. She is the enemy from within.

Recently, Bonnie Fuller, previously of *Marie Claire,* and before that *YM,* replaced Helen Gurley Brown as editrix in chief, but judging from the last issue it's in name only. Brown had been at the magazine for more than twenty-five years, and long ago laid down the law in the early '60s with her two books, *Sex and the Single Girl* and, later, *Outrageous Opinions.* The former is an especially great read, if only for Helen's goofy and twisted chapter "How to Be Sexy," wherein she evokes the name of sexologist/S&M scholar Havelock Ellis as one would a patron saint to help her explain female desire to her readers. Along with advocating that women go on a "helpless campaign" to enhance their desirability, the amusing madcap advice in this volume includes keeping married men as pets, pulling a Lysistrata with your date to get what you want, maintaining a lively interest in people and things that you really couldn't give a shit about, and my personal favorite, avoiding swarming in public with females so as not to broadcast to the world that you've given up all hope of romance. Such is the petulant and—hey!—sexist attitude that under the firm guidance of Brown informs *Cosmopolitan*'s editorial policy.

Excerpting its articles and fiction from various sources of floozydom, *Cosmo* runs borderline sleazy pieces like a profile of lady pimp Madame Claude, while its fiction is the serialized Danielle Steele–type dreck that floats in from romance mags like so much festering medical waste. Although Brown once advocated carrying around a controversial book like *Das Kapital* as date bait, she'd rather print tame crap like "I Slept with the Deliveryman." But the real problem with *Cosmo* isn't that its articles are cheesy, reprinted, or even dumb. It's that *Cosmo* addresses health and social issues in a matter so casual as to be potentially dangerous to its young readers. The most notorious example was *Cosmopolitan*'s late-'80s "Reassuring News About

AIDS: A Doctor Tells Why You May Not Be at Risk" by Dr. Robert E. Gould. It explained that a woman having so-called normal sex was not at serious risk of contracting the AIDS virus if she didn't think she had any open cuts or infections. This was some of the worst medical misadvice since the suggestion that one could catch VD from swimming pools. On the mental-health front, Irma Kurtz's "Agony Column" too often entertains such stupid and phallocentric anxieties as "Can the male still enjoy sex without an erection?" and "Can my boyfriend feel me while wearing a condom?" Who cares if he has an occasional limp chimp or if he doesn't delight in wearing latex? The *Cosmopolitan* Girl should be worrying about her own stuff, like why she isn't having multiple orgasms, or at least about the risks of skid marks from cheap rubbers.

With all this sex talk floating around the pages of her favorite magazine, you'd think That Cosmo Girl might eventually figure out that what she's being served up is more flash than trash. Even the cover of *Cosmopolitan* belies its boring, one-dimensional sex sell. Any real sexiness and individuality the *Cosmo* Cover Girl might have is well concealed behind her airbrushed fashion-plate disguise. She portrays The Sexy Image to her readers, eyeball to eyeball, a sort of girl-to-girl eye-fuck, but there is nothing erotic about her Sacvullo-ized gaze. The models—the usual crowd of leggy super-hos like Cindy "If I sell my own ass then it's feminism" Crawford—look taped-up, overstyled, self-conscious, and extremely uncomfortable. *Cosmo* seems to have solved the dilemma of the need for continuous creativity on its covers. The *Cosmo* Cover Girl is the same white woman each month, reappearing in a slightly different version, but always with the big nonhairdo, the long body accentuated by clinging clothing, the obligatory décolletage, the full-frontal vapid stare, and the omnipresent miniskirt.

I know, I know—it's all just harmless fun. Something to laugh at, rifle through when you're lying in bed with a bad period. Still, I really doubt that *Cosmo* is being laughed at by every one of the millions of women who read it; if so, then the joke's on me. Somehow I can't help but think that the joke's on us.

Ladies' Night: A Parody

by Wendy Shanker

Lately, my friends have been so busy. I feel like I never get to hang out anymore. Because of our jobs, or our relationships, it's just gotten to the point where I never get any real girl bonding time. Know what I mean?

I finally got sick of it. So last weekend, I call up all my closest girlfriends and I'm like, "This is what we're doing tonight. You're coming over to my place. We're gonna have makeovers, we're gonna eat s'mores, we're gonna watch the Spice Girls concert on pay-per-view, and do a sleep-over—the whole thing." Well, they loved the idea. As a matter of fact, my friend Gwyneth suggests we do it at her parents' place, because they are out of town.

That's so like Gwyneth—generous to a fault. If anyone is my best friend, it's her. I met Gwyn at a Learning Annex course, "Disempowering the Female Through the Scents of Calvin Klein," taught by Ivana Trump. It was an amazing class. If they offer it again, definitely take it.

Of course we invite Winona. Me and Winona are just . . . kindred spirits. Like in college, I joined the campus a cappella singing group, and Noni got really into plays.

And Uma. Uma is just fucking hilarious. You never know what's gonna happen when you hang out with her! Naturally, things aren't the same since that incident in South Beach. But just because I don't trust her doesn't mean I don't have fun hanging out with her. Like this time we were at Moomba (third floor, duh), and she tells this waiter, "No, you stick the steak frites up your ass!"

Guess you had to be there.

Gwyneth comes up with the great idea that each of us should be a different Spice Girl. I'm like, "I think that's a great idea, but there's only four of us. Who should be the fifth?" Gwyneth's like, "Let's invite Claire."

Claire's more Gwyneth and Winona's friend, but I'm like, "Yes, let's definitely invite her." Because every time I talk to Claire at a party or something I think, Wow, I know I could be really good friends with this girl. Yes, she's younger than us. But she's really mature.

The five of us go shopping to get supplies for the sleep-over. We stop off at the J Sisters Salon on 57th Street to get "The Playboy Wax." Uma wanted to drop by La Perla and pick up this thong thing that Sharon Stone had told her about. Then it's off to a facial from Marcia at Bliss Spa. Gwyneth just walked right in, can you believe it? The whole day is just really reminding me how wonderful it is to be around friends you really love.

We go to Ricky's to get some Manic Panic 'cause we're gonna dye each other's hair. While Gwyn and Claire are trying on Mattese makeup, which is pretty good stuff, I pull Winona into hair care. I tell her, "I know you wouldn't do it intentionally, but tonight is girls' night. I don't want that dumb ex-boyfriend of yours showing up drunk like last time." Winona's like, "What do you care? You're the one who ended up having sex with him." I'm like, "Hello, I did not have sex with him. I gave him a blow job. That's much different." Winona's like, "Fine, he's totally stopped bugging me. It should be okay." She's cool like that.

We get back to Gwyneth's, and we're all hanging out in the kitchen deciding who gets to be which Spice Girl. I get to be Sexy Spice, a.k.a. Ginger Spice, because it's my party. Gwyneth is Scary Spice, Winona's Posh, and Claire is Baby Spice, of course. Oh, and we make Uma be Sporty Spice, because she's the one that's pregnant and should get used to wearing warm-up suits. Uma bitches it for like nine years, then lights up a Dunhill. Claire's like, "Uma, you can't smoke, you're pregnant!" And Uma's like, "Courtney did and look how cute Francis Bean turned out." She has a point there.

Gwyneth checks her voice mail, and pulls me into the hall. I'm like, "What up, G?" Gwyneth's like, "Minnie wants to come to the Spice Girls party. She's in town, staying at the Soho Grand."

I'm like, "Gwyneth Andrea Paltrow, please tell me you did not tell Minnie Driver about my Spice Girls party." Gwyneth goes off on how she and Ben and some people were at the communal table at Asia de Cuba and Minnie was there with like Charlize Theron and they were all drinking and stuff, so she kind of let the Spice Girls party slip out.

Minnie's nice enough, I guess. But she's just . . . not like us. I don't know how to explain it. I guess it's like, in a room full of Prada, Minnie's resale Anna Sui.

So I'm like, "G, there are only five Spice girls. There's not enough room." And Gwyneth's like, "Well can't we make up another Spice Girl? Like Happy Spice, or

Funky Spice? That's what Minnie can be." And I'm like, "You can't just MAKE UP a Spice Girl. No." Gwyneth's like, "Listen, Minnie's a wreck. She's still so sad since Matt broke up with her."

It's kind of confusing, so let me back up. Claire had like this little fling with Matt Damon, then he starts dating Minnie Driver. Then Gwyneth starts dating Matt's best friend Ben. Then Matt broke up with Minnie, and Ben set him up with Winona.

So I'm like, "Whatever, Minnie can come. I just hope there's room for her huge angular face."

We're all in the kitchen eating full-fat ice cream when Minnie shows up. She immediately starts jawing on in her stupid English accent about Piccadilly Circus and the West End and Trafalgar Square, and how she lost all this weight after *Circle of Friends.* I can tell everybody is bored, but being nice. Claire asks Minnie how she lost all the weight.

Well, Minnie starts BAWLING. She explains that losing weight reminds her of Matt, because he lost all this weight for *Courage Under Fire,* and she lost weight for *Circle of Friends,* and they were both anemic and taking supplements and that's how they fell in love. I'm thinking, Oh please. But to my surprise, Gwyneth and Claire start sobbing all over Minnie. Even Uma is saying, "Oh, Minnie, I love your name. I'm gonna name my kid Minnie."

Rightfully so, Winona gets pissed off and leaves.

I'm thinking, Fuck, fuck, tension breaker. Who wants to do a shot of ginseng? So I'm like, "Hey guys, let's put away the ice cream and go upstairs. The concert is about to start, and they're opening with 'Spice Up Your Life.' I don't want to miss it."

But Gwyneth's still hugging Minnie. I overhear her saying, "Minnie, you should be Scary Spice." I'm like, "Excuse me, but why should Minnie be Scary Spice?" And Minnie's like, "Because I'm English, and the Queen Mum, and crumpets . . ." and on and on and on.

I grab my coat and go out to the garden, where I find Winona having a smoke. This whole ladies' night is really not going how I planned it. Winona's pissed, Gwynnie and Minnie are new best friends, Uma's yakking about Tibet or something, and Claire looks like she just wants to run and hide.

Luckily, I am one of those people who responds really well in stressful situations. So I take a deep breath. Aha, lightbulb. I pull Winona back inside and duck my head in the kitchen. I'm like, "Hey, I have a surprise. Come up to Gwyneth's mom's room." 'Cause that's where they have the VCR.

I pop in my copy of the Pamela and Tommy Lee tape (what happened in THAT relationship???), and suddenly, everything is normal. Gwynnie and Winnie are friends again; Uma's like, "Oh my God, his dick is so BIG!"; and Claire's eyes nearly pop out of her head. I'm like, "Does Claire need a permission slip to watch this? I think she does." I guess it's too much for Minnie's delicate composition, because she goes into the bathroom to throw up or something.

Not a moment too soon, it's Spice Girls time! I put on my red wig and my platforms, just like Sexy Spice. They end up opening with "Say You'll Be There." We're all dancing and singing. It's so perfect.

Then the phone rings.

Gwyn picks it up. She's like, "Hey. Yeah? Oh, how are you?" She frantically waves Winona over so she can listen in. "Yeah? Well, I don't know. We're doing Wendy's Spice Girls thing, so, it's like girls' night. I don't think so." Winona hits her, like, Are you crazy? But Gwyn hangs up.

I'm like, "Who was that?" Gwyneth's like, "That was Ben. Him and Matt and Skeet and these other guys are all going down to E&O. But I told him we were doing your Spice Girls thing, so never mind." I'm thinking, No diggity no doubt, it is ladies' night after all.

But now Gwyn and Win are paying no attention to the concert. They're just picking at their pixie hairdos and looking anxious. I'm like, "Do you guys want to go?" They're like, "No, definitely not, this is girls' night, we want to be here with just us . . ." Then Gwyneth launches into her "This is the first time in my whole life I'm not in a serious relationship" speech, about how much she treasures her independence. And just to prove how independent she truly is, she is gonna go straight to E&O right now and tell Ben that he is not her boyfriend; they are just dating.

I'm like, "Fine." Gwyneth's like, "Come on, Wendy, it'll be fun. I'm sure Ben can set you up with Cole or Casey or someone."

I turn to her, and I'm like,

"You know what none of you realize? These guys will come and go. But our friendships can last forever. Think about it. Who called me in tears when her fiancé broke off their engagement because she cut her hair?" I turn to Gwyneth, whose

279

mouth is hanging open. "You did." I whirl around to face Winona. "Who flew in from Petaluma, freaking out, when she heard Johnny Depp was lasering off his 'Winona Forever' tattoo, Noni? It was a long time ago, but you did." I stare at Uma. "And, Uma, you don't even like Ethan Hawke. No one likes Ethan Hawke!" She can't deny it. I continue. I can hear "When Two Become One" lilting from the TV set.

"When you're done with all these guys I know you'll come crawling back to me and want to spend time with me, and we'll say how much we mean to each other and talk about starting a production company together, and say that men suck, and what we should really do is become lesbians, and if we were going to be lesbians we'd be lesbians with each other, not that we'd ever really become lesbians even if we do get a little bi-curious when we smoke a lot of pot. But there's a lesson to be learned here, from the Spice Girls. I point to the song that put this super group on the map— 'Wannabe.' Did you ever listen to the words? Think about it.

'If you wannabe my lover
  You gotta get with my friends
  Make it last forever
  'Cause friendship never ends.'

"So if you want to run to E&O with Matt and Ben, and drink Cosmos and not eat your food, then great. Leave me here with the Bioré Pore De-Clogging Strips. But I say: Friends first, lovers later. That is what girl power is all about!"

Well, everyone left. Except for my new best friend, Minnie Driver, who I think is a very very talented and special individual.

280

"Women's Network," My Ass

by Wendy Bott

What the hell is with the Lifetime Network? Every week, the plot of their Movie of the Week goes something like this: Mare Winningham, unloved and under-educated, gets slapped around by her Wrangler-jeans-wearing two-timing husband, Tom Skerritt. And P.S., for reasons that may or may not be related to any of this, they're taking her kids away.

Now let's discus the movie *Why Me?* starring Glynnis O'Connor. Lifetime plays it all the time. If you'll remember (it's maybe twenty years old) it's about a woman who suffers through a hideously disfiguring automobile accident in which she smashes through a windshield and, as a result, loses her face. If memory serves (and often it doesn't), at one point Glynnis decides to spice up her now floundering marriage by seducing her husband in a teddy. Naturally, her husband demurs, citing a headache, because Glynnis is, after all, faceless. Shortly thereafter, her husband leaves her. Abandoned, but not yet defeated, Glynnis then undergoes painful facial reconstruction and, lovely by movie's end, hooks up with her plastic surgeon, played by—who else?—Armande Assante.

Let's get this straight. This is supposed to be the "Women's Network"? A place where women (the supposedly "sensitive" sex) can turn for comfort and under-standing in an, at times, demoralizing world? I've never felt worse in my life than I did after watching *Why Me?* or just the promo for the Mare Winningham movie. (What's with Mare Winningham, anyway? In real life, doesn't she have like eight kids? And wouldn't those eight kids be traumatized forever by turning on the Life-time Network and watching Mommy get slapped around or stuffed into a car trunk every other week? But I digress. . . .)

To put it bluntly, Lifetime's programming choices don't make much sense. Many of its movies are about women getting beaten up, stalked, and/or otherwise victimized beyond belief. What's the prevailing line of thought here? That women just can't get enough of that sort of thing? That they're dying to see movies of that ilk so that afterward they can get together and talk about how awful they feel over a delicious cup of Hazelnut Cream? What gives? Or maybe the thought is that women enjoy seeing movies about lives that are worse than their own. "Aw, sure I work in a diner sixty-five hours a week, but at least I don't have a two-timing husband, Tom Skerritt, stuffing me in a car trunk."

And the promos: Ewwwwwwwwww. There's the one about *L.A. Law.* This promo says, in thirty seconds, that the best reason to watch the show is because of the cute men. Oh, yeah, that's why the show won Emmys—cause of Jimmy Smits's ass. (On the other hand, maybe that is why, what the hell do I know?) Even their more general promos are insulting. Their "Lifetime Understands That Life Can Be Tough for Women" promos—they're patronizing. What if BET (Black Entertainment Television) ran similarly thought-out promos? They'd begin: " 'The Man' get you down today? . . . BET understands." Or "Having trouble getting a cab to stop and pick you up? . . . BET knows how you feel."

Add to this the horror that is the Lifetime Saturday Afternoon Movie. It's now promoted as part of "Mood Swing Saturday." Oh, that's great. Offer up movies for women under the auspices of a harmful, female stereotype. Way ta go!

All right, already. Enough haranguing. The thing is, Lifetime wouldn't be hard to fix.

Step One: They should get rid of their condescending promos. Whip up some promos that celebrate quality programming and call it a day.

Step Two: Get hold of some quality programming. Much of their stuff is good (*The Days and Nights of Molly Dodd, L.A. Law, thirtysomething,* etc.), but it should be cushioned by things other than *Battered Woman: My Man's Been Cheatin' on Me* movies. (Not that there's anything wrong with movies like that once in a while, but enough is enough—either the programmers over at Lifetime have no imagination whatsoever or someone's been working out some majorly personal stuff at the expense of the viewers. Really, now. It's time that Mare Winningham's black eye be allowed to heal—remember, she has children to consider.)

Need a reminder of the genuinely terrific movies of the last sixty years? How about cribbing from American Movie Classics' expansive library and running some Katharine Hepburn or Rosalind Russell or Bette Davis or Grace Kelly or Audrey Hepburn or Barbara Stanwyck movies? (Not to say that only older movies have value. The '70s and '80s both had their share of great movies starring Faye Dunaway, Jane Fonda, Barbara Streisand, Jessica Lange, or Meryl Streep to name a few.)

Step Three: Have fun. What's a "Women's Network" without a festival of cult classics such as *Cat Women of the Moon, Caged Heat, The Girl Most Likely To, Attack of the 50 Foot Woman, Barbarella, The Wasp Woman,* or *Switchblade Sisters,* to name a few, hmmm?

Okay, then. Enough already. The point's been made ad nauseam. Sorry. It's just that with television being what it is today (often, uh, crappy) it's natural to want this good idea (a "Women's Network") to live up to its potential. Now c'mon, is that too much to ask?

Bitch on Heels: Confessions of a Pop Culture Junkie

by Lisa Miya-Jervis

Everything sucks. Every fucking slick, glossy, gorgeous movie, TV show, magazine, and ad. They all suck. I hate them. I hate them so much I can't look away. Like that irritating, sexy, stupid, cool, infuriating, beautiful, immature, profound, unattainable fox we all had it bad for sometime during high school, the mass media are collectively compelling, repulsive, horrifying, and maybe the best fucking thing about being sentient. They hold an inescapable power over me that makes them all the more seductive. "Bite me," I want to snarl. "No, *harder.*"

When I come home from a hard day at work there's nothing I want more than to lie on the couch and mainline a *90210* rerun. Either that or the latest issue of *Mademoiselle.* I watch *Friends.* I saw *Showgirls.* I subscribe to *Glamour* and *Details.* I've been known to unmute the TV so I can hear an earnest eleven-year-old tell me that her overpriced running shoes constitute a protofeminist experience.

"Oh, I'm a cultural critic," I tell myself. "I need to do this, it's research." True enough—if I didn't watch, read, listen, how could I analyze the twisted pathologizing of teenage girls' sexual desire on *Geraldo,* the rank fear of female power in *The Craft,* the reduction of women to quivering masses of emotional need by countless magazines (aimed at both genders)? How could I discourse on the ways in which our desires are taken, re-formed, exquisitely packaged, and then sold back to us for huge profits, without opening the box?

Excuses, excuses. The other truth is that I love every minute of my immersion in the sick world of pop culture. There's a delicious tingle that I get from every overproduced, manipulative slice of the mainstream: think neoclassics of misogyny like *Basic Instinct;* the hip, sexy, and undoubtedly wealthy "Bacardi by night" club kids–cum–high-powered career babes; *Armaggedon;* lush photographs of Liv Tyler that illustrate those fawning so-young-yet-such-an-old-soul profiles. Yes, I know: queer women as ruthless murderesses; identities for sale cheap; men saving the world while women are left home to do nothing but serve as their motivation to return; hack writers projecting the same old fantasies onto a new screen (no matter how fascinating and talented that screen is). I know that the mass media are devoted to the manufacture of a self-serving desire that can only be satisfied through further consumption, whether it's of the movies and magazines themselves or the stuff they're shilling for.

I know all this and I can't stop looking. During summers, I pay my very own hard-earned cash to watch cars, trains, asteroids, and the White House explode. I can't help myself—I slavishly follow the crowds to the theaters, lured by shoot-outs, fires, and Demi Moore's pneumatic breasts. Who cares that the only woman in *The Rock* was nothing but a one-note baby-making heartstring tugger? Well, I do. More than anything I want action movies with real (and really important) woman characters, female secret agents who are more than high-priced whores, dialogue more intelligent and less badly offensive than "Winners go home and fuck the prom queen." But those fires . . . explosions . . . car chases . . . grand ridiculous plots . . . more, more, give me more. The sheen and lush gorgeousness of the big-budget aesthetic, the skill and savvy that renders manipulation discernible yet irrelevant—it's a great big turn-on.

Yeah, you heard me. And I'm not just talking about what a little hottie Nicolas Cage is, or Ben Affleck's chiseled cheekbones. Not the creamy-skinned appeal of Liv Tyler on those glossy pages, or the long thighs and sculpted pecs of a cK ad. No, it's the eroticization of the very act of viewing that gets me hot: holding the slick, scented pages that promise solutions to all your problems, easily purchased at your nearest department store; sitting in that darkened theater knowing that the images on-screen are nothing but a many-million-dollar whore meticulously constructed with no other purpose than to amuse you.

Let me be fair to myself, though. Sometimes it's my own capacity for feminist analysis and/or recuperative interpretation that gives the thrill. I loved watching Sharon Stone flashing those policemen—not for the sight of her lovely snatch, but for the spectacle of such a gleefully ballsy babe up there (literally) showing us all who's boss. I often go to the movies because I know something's gonna piss me off—and then I get to rant and rave and make a great big fun fuss about it.

But this leads to another problem: What's the difference between buying something to critique it and buying something to consume it? Well, nothing—for the person who's getting the cash. I'd love to make the excuse that all of this is just harmless brain/eye candy. But it's not—because if it were, I wouldn't bother to be writing this or anything else. The whore analogy works only if we ignore the obvious: that we're being sold something other than this single encounter. And if we buy it we're buying an entire world where women are often little more than canvases on which to project the hopes, fears, fantasies, and philosophical musing of men.

Does that mean I'm gonna shut my legs tight and refuse the pleasure of it all? No way—but I sure as hell am gonna remember to always wear my thinking cap at the movies. It's latex, you know.

Bring Me the Head of Melanie Banderas

by Dixie LaRue

"Why pick on Melanie Griffith?" you might ask (although you probably understand all too well). Is it because she is a subpar actress of limited ability, appeal, and intelligence? Is it because her personal life envinces a woman of coarse sensibilities and little sense? Or is it merely because she personifies all that women have been individually and collectively struggling against for the past three decades?

Certainly, there are any number of celebrities congesting the pages of *People* magazine and our corridors of justice that are practically crying out for my contempt. But there is something about Melanie Griffith's uniquely brazen vacuity that I find especially offensive. Both her on- and off-screen personas seem to say that it is acceptable, even attractive, to be an adult woman with a vacant look and an equally nugatory modus operandi that flashes "learned helplessness" in bright neon letters.

That Melanie Griffith is neither really talented nor attractive is only part of the problem. What I find most disturbing is that she is tarted up (pun intended) for public consumption as an actress and female icon, when, in fact, the emperor has no clothes. (Literally, in Melanie's case.) She exudes not one iota of intelligence, strength, or integrity, no matter what unlikely scenario scriptwriters and directors have dreamed up for her. When Melanie's being defiant, it has nothing to do with Good vs. Evil or Right vs. Wrong, but everything to do with tiny wrinkles around the eyes. When she exhorts us, in those Revlon ads, not to gracefully accept the aging process but to "Defy it!" she articulates what is likely the only stand she has ever taken.

In a republic where *The Bridges of Madison County* (or was it Madison Avenue?) is not only great literature but a cottage industry, should I be amazed that this breathy-voiced, habitually bimbo-esque mannequin is taken seriously as a glamorous actress? Her artistry consists of squeaking her lines as she lolls her head around as though her neck were a ball and socket. She often does this in her underwear. Nothing is authentic about Melanie Griffith. Even her breasts are fake. Yet we are meant to clasp her to our more genuine bosoms as America's sweetheart. We are meant to take her cyborg Betty Boop-on-Percodan impersonation as "sexy," or, even worse, "earthy." While it's not terribly surprising that men would buy into this caricature of feminine sensuality hook(er), line, and sinker, why are women colluding with this charade? Why is this skank being profiled in women's magazines (as if she were one) and help up as a modern beauty/career gal/mother when her entire being fairly screams "sloppy seconds"? Is it just Condé Nast, or has the entire world gone mad?

Speaking of poor judgment, I must say I question Ms. Griffith's. Consider the mounting evidence: (1) She has multiple tattoos, (2) she got breast implants *after* becoming a star, (3) she married Stephen Bauer, the poor woman's Lorenzo Lamas, (4) she married Don Johnson, and, perhaps most damning of all, (5) she married Don Johnson again.

Samuel Johnson once said, "He is not only dull, but he makes others around him the duller." For me, Melanie epitomizes our society's predilection for dressing up the skanky as sexy, the inane as art, and utter crap as noncrap. Even more insidious is her consistent undermining of the efforts made to tear down tired stereotypes and give women in media more varied, realistic representations of their lives and themselves. Take Griffith-Johnson-Bauer-Johnson-Banderas's film work (please). There's the ironic *Cherry 2000* (she masquerades as a robot), *Working Girl* (formulaic claptrap masquerading as Shavian satire), *Body Double* (misogynist insult to the opposable-thumbed masquerading as an erotic thriller), *Stranger Among Us* (gentile blow-up doll masquerading ever so believably as a tough cop and Orthodox Jew), *Milk Money* (offensive drivel masquerading as heartwarming family fare), and *Shining Through* (the less said the better).

So, women of America, join me in saying no to Melanie, Demi, and their whole mammary-augmented, stripper-impersonating ilk. Put down your Danielle Steele books, turn off *Baywatch,* and cast aside your Mariah Carey CDs. Embrace real women in the pop culture pantheon, three-dimensional women who act as much as they are acted upon. Worship women who, while they may dress "like hookers" (hey, nothing wrong with that), don't necessarily always play hookers. Explore your own authentic sexuality. Watch a Myrna Loy movie. And never, ever, plunk down another eight dollars to watch Melanie Griffith play another in that never-ending parade of ditzy yet lovable trollops.

Dancing to the **Tiger Beat**

by B. Young

I was lost from the moment I saw him: David Cassidy, my future husband. Even at the age of four, I was utterly convinced he would wait for me. (Thank goodness he didn't.) My parents gingerly tried to talk me out of my unrealistic fixation, but to no avail. Toddlers aren't too centered where reality is concerned. So Mom wasn't too startled when, at age six, I stopped her in the magazine aisle at Shopwell and asked her to buy me a copy of *TeenBeat.* She complied (those permissive Dr. Spock mothers of the '60s) and left me to tumble, headfirst, into the sticky abyss known as teenybopperdom.

I have no real memories of those early years—the David Cassidy/Davy Jones years. What pleasure would a six-year-old find in those saccharine poses, those tidbits of gossip, those mindless questionnaires that hundreds of has-been teenybopper stars must hear in their nightmares (What's your favorite food? What color are your socks? What do you look for in a girlfriend?). Could I have fantasized about them, even then? Did I really imagine myself on the arm of Keith Partridge, the sweetest, most baby-faced hunk in the world? Never underestimate the secret world of the little girl. I'm sure I didn't know what sex was back then, but clearly I knew all about romance.

My fixation with baby-faced (effeminate, even) teeny-hunks went on hiatus for several years, until Leif Garrett came into my life when I was a preteen. Leif was a bit of a teen magazine exclusive—by that I mean he seemed to appear exclusively in teen magazines and nowhere else. So my fantasies were allowed to flourish, undisturbed by his real voice or his real walk or his wooden acting. The magazines chattered on about Leif's many TV and movie projects, but they never seemed to materialize (aside from the cinematic marvel *Skateboard*.) Still, his friendships with *real* stars like Kristy McNichol emphasized his importance in the Hollywood world, and were fodder for my daydreams. Picture it: Leif arrives at the door, his dirty-blond, shoulder-length hair falling lightly in his face, a rose in his hand. He leads me to the door of his silver limo, which derives us to Shaun Cassidy's house. Kristy and her brother Jimmy McNichol are there too, and we all hang out and . . . what? It gets a bit hazy here.

Bitch about other celebrities? Do lines of coke? Fuck like dogs? All I know is there was never any sex or drugs in my Leif dreams. I didn't know about that stuff. Just a lot of niceness and caring and material wealth.

Leif became my roommate the day I noticed the posters. All the teen magazines had dozens of pull-out posters in each issue, and I destroyed my house's resale value in a single day by nailing twenty-six small Leif pinups to my bedroom walls. The posters were designed to follow you; wherever you stood in the room, Leif's gaze was on you. I checked it out from every angle, and even from under the bed Leif's eyes looked meaningfully back at me. He was my own personal big brother, my confidant, my familiar. I knew every inch of his face, I could recognize every shirt in his closet. None of my friends shared my fixation with Leif, of course; as I later discovered, that's part of the teenybopper dynamic. Every friend has to like someone different, so that nasty competition doesn't arise. Teenybopperdom is about girl-bonding, not backbiting. So Gail liked Les from the Bay City Rollers and Deb liked Donny Osmond and we could all share the latest gossip with impunity.

In retrospect, I see that Leif was a safe—and perhaps elitist—choice. Safe because there was no chance of ever having to face standing in line for a Leif Garrett stadium concert and experiencing the humiliation of realizing you are one in a million and you're nowhere near the top of the million. And elitist because I liked the fact that very few people knew who Leif Garrett was. I would happily and righteously correct people who (understandably) mispronounced his name "Leef" instead of "Lafe." I was probably one in a thousand and I liked those odds. It seemed all too possible that he would someday see me in a crowd and think, "She is my dream girl." And, since I'd memorized his likes and dislikes, I'd know just how to make him happy. By the time he got around to making bad records ("Finally," I can just see the PR woman's shouting, "a way to harness Leif's true star potential!"), I had dropped him like a hot potato.

At fifteen, I ran into trouble. I began to think of myself as a feminist. And I fell in love with the lead singer of Duran Duran. A queasy combination which became the bane of my existence. True to my elitist tendencies, I chose a figure whose band was totally unknown and whose personal attractiveness was frankly questionable. And they were English, so I wouldn't have to worry about them showing up in my neighborhood any time soon. I shared my discovery with my friends and soon everyone had picked her favorite band member by matching the photos with the pithy little bios in the magazines. I don't know why I picked Simon LeBon, other than that he seemed the most artistic and sensitive. He liked Iggy Pop and the Sex Pistols and wrote strange, pretentious lyrics. As I was an aspiring writer, that gave him serious bonus points.

Nick Rhodes was a wacky Warhol-wannabe and was just right for my flamboyant friend Kris. She later dyed her hair to match his. John Taylor was the cutest, and a fight ensued between several friends for possession. The loser was left with Roger Taylor, the ever-silent (but perfectly personable-looking) drummer whose nickname was Froggy and who many years later left the band.

I tried hard to divide my life into compartments. One part contained my smart life—my highbrow reading habit, my interest in women writers, my feminist leanings. The other contained my low life—my (by now surreptitious) collection of teen magazines, my correspondence with other teenyboppers, my LeBon daydreams. I found that a lot of my pen pals were similarly schizophrenic, though we never discussed it directly. We usually prefaced each letter by asking and answering Duran-related questions: Did you hear that they did a cover version of "I Wanna Be Your Dog"? Have you seen Simon's new girlfriend? Can you tape me that new import? After that, though, we pretty much talked about ourselves, school, books we were reading. We wanted so badly to connect, which is why it was so disappointing when a pen pal situation didn't work out (one girl couldn't spell, which freaked me out) or dissolved (one of my favorites switched to Menudo, a low blow).

Eventually I met some of my pen pals and we became real friends. Sandra, my pen pal from Oklahoma, called me long-distance a few times to discuss stuff. She had a thick southern accent and told me stories about stealing her uncle's pickup truck and hurricanes. This was Genuine Communion as far as I was concerned, and I explained to my mother that my love for Simon LeBon had made me part of a world-wide community. She looked a little concerned. But I was right: it was a community, a community of confused and hungry girls looking for other confused, hungry girls who weren't quite sure what they wanted in a boy or whether they wanted a boy at all. We wanted cuddly, asexual things who wouldn't impose themselves on us.

As the band's popularity skyrocketed, I began to panic. How to keep on top of the ever-increasing heap? I was now a teenager and beginning to feel like I should rise to the challenge of reality. I was smart and poetic and sensitive and reasonably pretty—didn't I have a chance with Simon LeBon? He would know instantly that I was more than a groupie—I could quote Sylvia Plath poems by heart. (I now know that Rod McKuen was more his speed, but love is blind as a bat.) He would introduce me to adult sexuality, and I would raise him to a higher plane where we would read philosophy and he would never be bothered by teenyboppers again.

My plan was a good one: I started a fanzine. While my male peers were out there creating their own indie-zine universe full of gritty hard-core bands and cooler-than-thou lingo, I was honing my sarcastic sensibilities on the foibles of a quickly rising Anglo-pop band. Readers' letters poured in. Never before had these girls (and they were all girls) been treated with decency, with the presumption of intelligence. Of course some of them were dumb as dirt, but even they appreciated the challenge. We dissected every move the band made, and when they came to town, we tracked them down and stood outside their hotel. When we got banned from the lobby, we checked into the hotel (eight of us in one room) and waited to pounce. They were nice and posed for photos. Our readers were ecstatic, and wrote worshipful letters to us—we had, after all, breathed the same air as [insert favorite band member].

The funny thing was that, when faced with the chance to talk to and touch my object of worship, I couldn't remember why it had ever been so important to me. I stood next to Simon LeBon, my heart beating 1000 bpm, and said nothing. I was a ghost, separated from my own body. He looked me in the eye, just like the posters, and his gaze rolled right off. It made me feel like there was something wrong with me—all the other girls were either screaming or hyperventilating or throwing themselves at his body. One girl tried to slip up to his room to, presumably, fuck him like a proper starfucker. (She didn't succeed, but only because his sweet not-a-model-but-soon-to-be-replaced-by-one girlfriend was in there with him.) I was beginning to see that I wasn't cut out to be a serious groupie.

And as the band grew more popular, the dream began to sour. I started hearing rumors that they were creepy, conceited people. Simon got bloated-looking, then plain podgy. They started dating supermodels, knocking us all out of the running. My fanzine became more cruel and cutting with each issue, and the circulation continued to rise as girls from all over America found a forum in which they could vent their "real" feelings. I got letters from young girls who'd sent the band presents, and were depressed that they didn't even get a form letter back; people who'd joined the slick new fan club and were bummed out to find themselves member #8653.

My father saw potential for serious profit and offered to fund my project, to turn it into a real magazine. The final straw came while watching the zombie-girl TV show *The Facts of Life:* Tootie mentioned my fanzine. I'll never know how they heard about it. But my career as a teenybopper had gone overground and I felt exposed, like a grown woman dressed in baby clothes. I did the only thing a smart woman could do: I gave it up.

Nowadays I rarely bump into my old Duranie friends. It seems most of us continued to exorcise our desire to participate in popular culture in one way or another. Some went on to a more hip, respectable form of fan worship by becoming serious indie-music fans. Some formed their own bands, others became rock writers, most just went to college and got boring jobs. A precious few tried their hand at star-fucking and found—as I sensed the day I met Simon LeBon—that being an imaginary groupie is a lot more satisfying for an intelligent girl than being a real one. But to this day, none of us like to talk about the dark, shameful past: our lips are sealed.

Desperately Seeking Farrah

by Jennifer Tillity

November 19, 1996

Farrah Fawcett
c/o Wolf Casteler

Dear Ms. Fawcett,
I am an editor at Ms. *magazine, but I write for this fantastic feminist zine called* BUST. *The next issue is the goddess issue, and I have*

been graced with the task of writing a piece about the Angels.
I'd love to interview you about what it was like to be a Charlie's
Angel, as opposed to wanting to be one (which was the option
and obsession for most girls I knew). What are your thoughts
about the cultural impact of the show? The women were portrayed
as strong, brave, and highly trained positive role models; yet,
typically, you were beautiful, thin, and sexy, too. You had
boyfriends or love interests on the show, but only for an episode
or two. That conveyed a girl-gang loyalty that I know inspired me
and my little friends. . . .

"Once upon a time, there were three little girls who went to the police academy . . ."

They excelled in all of the police-type skills (shooting, running, thinking), but the police academy, like the world it served, was sexist. So the three little girls (who were actually three skinny women) were assigned dull desk jobs and parking-cop duties.

"But I took them away from all that. Now they work for me. My name is Charlie."

The girls were promoted by Charlie-God all the way to Angels. No more drudgery. As Angels, they had to help humans and solve crimes, but they got to wear their own clothes, drive cars that matched their personality, and do good work that they could be proud of.

I wanted to be an Angel, and my friends and I would pretend that we were. I fought in order to be Jill Munroe. She was unquestionably the good one—all blond hair, erect nipples, and white teeth. The kind of all-American girl who drove a sports car and was effortlessly athletic. Kelly Garrett was the Lee jeans Angel to Farrah's Jordache: perfectly acceptable but less good. Sabrina Duncan was the flat-haired, smart, vaguely dyke-y Angel, a threatening idea. I never wanted to be her.

The Angels were totally loyal to one another. They always looked out for each other, protected each other, the way good partners and sisters do. If, say, Bri was in trouble and was forced to make a phone call saying that everything was okay, all she had to say in order to alert the team to the danger was say something like, "I noticed

293

your station wagon needed a wash, Jill." Everyone knew Jill drove a weird sports car called a Cobra. Jill and Kelly would pretend to take the bait and then go rescue Bri. One of their secret weapons was that no one took them seriously because they were gorgeous and perfect women.

> *"We were never typical actresses. We never competed for close-ups and costumes."*
> —Jaclyn Smith, *People,* 1994

My life was nothing like *Charlie's Angels.* Nothing. I was a kid. I had no power, no gun, no tight slacks, no bod, no cool clothes, no car, no big feathered hair . . . the list goes on and on.

Fargo '87

Aaron Spelling was conducting a nationwide talent search for his Angels reprise, to be called *Angels '88.* I missed the nationwide hunt for the new *Annie* in 1980, and I wasn't about to miss this one. I was seventeen, lived in North Dakota, did local theater, commercials, and modeling. I dreamed of the big time. I wanted out. I was graduating that year and hunting for a surefire path, a ready-made, immediate-gratification adulthood. I wanted to be an Angel.

I skipped out of *Sweet Charity* rehearsal on the day of the audition with two of the other Big Spender girls. At the cattle call we took our place in the swell of local actors, models, beauty pageant contestants, waitresses with big hair—all sharing dreams of escape from the flatlands and mundane concerns. After shuffling through the interview and monologue and depositing our 8 X 10's and résumés, we went back to rehearsal. The next day there was to be a list of ten regional finalists who would be given a screen test, which would be sent to LA.

I made the list.

I was ecstatic. It was so close, I could taste it. I knew I was going to be an Angel. I strode through the cruddy halls of South High with what felt like revenge at my fingertips. Preapproved. I have arrived. No more so-called life.

The night of the screen test I dressed carefully, put on a ton of makeup, poufed out my hair, gathered my photos (head shot and full-body) and drove through the frigid air to the television studio. I was proud that I was the youngest person there. It seemed to me like a good sign. The rest of the chosen (many were former Miss North Dakotas, Montanas, and Minnesotas) were in their mid- to late twenties. I was the only one who had done any acting. They had bigger hair and more makeup. I still had a retainer.

The plot: Charlie Townsend had decided to start another elite private investigating firm with beautiful women, but this time he wanted to hire three out-of-work actresses whose cop series had just been canceled along with their friend, a stuntwoman. These girls might have gone back to the casting couch or waitressing, but Charlie took them away from all that. The character I was reading for was dubious about Charlie's offer. She thought it would be too dangerous: "We have to think seriously about this. We're talking blood, not ketchup."

I stood in front of the camera and, cued by the casting director's assistant, gave the speech that could earn me my wings. I was stilted. We tried it again. My voice sounded flat and young. I could see my retainer glinting in the camera lens. I felt my future fading away. I wasn't going to be picked.

Farrah Fawcett
c/o Wolf Casteler

January 10, 1997

Dear Ms. Fawcett,
I wanted to try again, as valiantly as possible, to get an audience
with you, via telephone, and interview you for BUST. *I realize*
that you are very busy, but your input would make the difference
between this being another solipsistic yet funny pop culture remi-
niscence and something truly cool.

"There was nothing sexy in our shows."
    —Farrah Fawcett

Only one person was getting laid on *Charlie's Angels:* Charlie. He created the Angels, brought them to his detective agency realm, and assigned all of the cases. He never tried to date them or sexually harass them. In fact, the Angels never even got to see him. They could just hear the splash of the bikini-clad harem who accompanied him into the Jacuzzi, hear his groan of pleasure as his geisha masseuse walked on his back. He was Hugh Hefner and Big Brother, an always out-of-reach daddy.

> *"Cuddly David Doyle, as sidekick John Bosley, provided a safe male presence."*
> —*People*

Bos, on the other hand, was a eunuch, kind of a fag. But he had access to Charlie.

David Doyle died while I was writing this. Farrah eluded my faxes for months but, good God, her seventeen-year-relationship with Ryan O'Neal was breaking up. Kate Jackson, married three times, made one of the few queer movies in the '80s (her husband, played by Harry Hamlin, leaves her for another man), and a few years ago I read in *People* that she had breast cancer. Jaclyn Smith, also thrice-married but with two kids, fronts a line of clothing for Kmart.

> *"Some people criticized us for the bikinis and whatnot. But we understood that we were three powerful women who were the stars of the number one show on television."*
> —Kate Jackson

> *"But we never really used that power. Our characters were the same in every show, and we were never able to change that. Why couldn't I have been depressed on one show? Why couldn't I have cried? Once I went in to [executive producer] Aaron [Spelling]'s office and I said, 'Wouldn't it be great if in one show I took Kate and Jaclyn home with me, and they met my parents, and we explore the possibilities of these girls as friends?'"*
> —Farrah Fawcett

What do I have here? Writing about the Angels began with me thinking that I would argue about how campy, cool, and kick-ass they were. I loved them as a kid and wanted it to be because they clearly gave me a powerful role model. Of . . . policework. Being constantly jilted by Farrah as I sought an interview has somehow tangled up in my mind with my fierce, self-conscious loyalty to my friends, and how fucking *besmirched* I feel by moments of competition or envy. I try to avoid the goddess-propaganda, to resist my desire to be pinned down and approved. Like the model-mantra *I eat all the time—I'm just naturally skinny,* the Angels embody what women purport: *we never competed. If I win, it's not cuz I tried.* Being caught trying ruins the prize. *I'm not competitive, I'm not aware of being sexy, I'm not* doing *anything.* It's just *you,* retrograde girl, *you* that feels like a freak and has to try.

It's hard for me, a feminist, to reconcile those old ambitions to be a model or a stripper or a Charlie's Angel. I usually tell them as part of my kitschy Fargo, theater-fag past (always good for a laugh) and distance myself from that embarrassing girl. Underneath the joke of these experiences—such as when I competed in the excruciatingly cheesey World of Wheels pageant at the Fargo Civic Center or made the rounds of the modeling agencies in New York—underneath is a *deep* humiliation. I am ashamed of my serious desire to escape, to transcend normal human woman stuff—zits and small tits and lack of a look so singular that it's my career. But the shame is not so much from the desire to be, basically, Farrah; it's shame because I acted on that dream. . . . And failed. Or maybe it's that I was caught buying into it. Anyhow, the resulting itchy feeling makes me want to rip down those fucking Angels, to talk about brains and talent, and banish my openly competitive side into that eight year old. The one who fought the neighbor girls in order to be Jill Munroe.

And won.

A Vindication of the Rights of Cunt

by Jayne Air

Part of the experience of being a happening, smart, *BUST*y kind of gal involves the occasional realization that language hasn't caught up with you yet. When you're living like we do, you sometimes have to come up with your own vocabulary. Take the example of a particularly hip and innovative black girlfriend of mine who decided "def" wasn't speaking enough to her (too many overtones of gangsta rappers bitchslapping women and calling us ho's); she now has girls in the Bay Area using "deffa," a kind of feminine/feminist version of the same qualities of cool, minus the hateful crap. And while Gloria Steinem may have argued twenty years ago that "bitch" is the ultimate insult, we take it up when we feel like it, as a word that describes our femininity, our power, our PMS.

My newest favorite, like these other words, is more than mere nomenclature. It's about a mood, a lifestyle, an oppositional and in-your-face way of being at a party full of jerks, a restaurant where rude waitpeople are the rule of thumb, a concert where someone is raining on your parade, an office where your boss is too bossy, a roomful of your best girlfriends, at home alone because you feel like it. Whatever.

The word is CUNT. So many hate it. They say, "We've reappropriated 'bitch' and 'girl' but cunt is just going too far." They say, "Cunt is what really rude guys with beer bellies who hate us call us. Cunt is what nasty queens who find us disgusting call us. Cunt reduces us to—well—you know, a hole." Exactly. What I mean is, all those things are true. But they're precisely the reasons I love CUNT and find it so perfect. Cunt is taboo, and taboo things are scary and powerful. Somebody else isn't going to own that word. I figure it's so fucking dangerous, and it's so intimately about my anatomy, that it's going to be mine, too. Yes way.

But what, exactly, is cunt? What makes it lovable and good and bad? Cunt is different from bitch. Cunt is bitch's naughtier little sister. Bitch implies bitchy which implies all those "feminine" ways of getting even, like whispering behind people's backs and/or being arch instead of coming right out with it. Cunt is direct; it's unafraid to be what it is (lest we forget, cunt implies a whole messy, real thing, smells and juices and all—bitch is more sanitized). Cunt is a word that you just wouldn't say in front of your mother. Cunt is a word that can still make men suck in their breath uncomfortably and look down at the floor. It says, "There's nothing you frat boys can call me that I haven't thought of myself, before you. And I'm using it my own way, thanks so much."

Say you're in mixed company and you opine that, even though *The Specialist* was really dumb and Sylvester Stallone is an idiot, "Sharon Stone was a real cunt who almost saved that movie." Watch what happens. First of all, the women in the room are going to know you're onto something. You're obviously a feminist's feminist, cause you can admit it's fun to watch hot women in movies (maybe you don't think she's hot, but I do), and even more fun to watch them slug guys really hard in the mouth. Sure, some of your female compatriots might be taken aback. But they'll get your gist. I mean, you will have chosen your moment. You have some tact. You're one of them. The important thing here is that you're *not* a frat boy, or a guy who hates women, or whatever. In fact, you're stealing the only gynocentric term we have to say, "That women has balls." The guys will be freaking out, but who cares? This story isn't about them.

There have been lots of divine cunts in history. I think of Catherine the Great, who used her literal cunt to great effect. Mae West was considered a cunt because she was funny and sexy but also because she insisted on directing her own movies and slept with whomever she wanted, mostly male bodybuilders many years her junior. Often a cunt is a woman you hate, but you just have to hand it to her. For example, Auden read Marianne Moore, that accomplished poet who held her own in the boys club of poets, and said of one of her works, "It's very cunty, but I like it!" That is, it has woman written all over it. That's a fundamental aspect of cunt: being a woman who doesn't apologize. Other cunts include that opera soprano what's her name who was asked to leave the Met because she said her costume was smelly and she wanted more perks and some hot tea with lemon NOW. It goes without saying that Madonna has made a career out of being a bitch who is sort of a cunt but doesn't have the guts to go all the way, while Courtney Love is too much of a cunt to care if anybody calls her a bitch. By the way, Naomi Wolf is not a cunt, although she would love to be: nobody who would wash your mouth out for saying it is a cunt. Cunt is too insouciant for that. It implies a certain devil-may-carishness about rules and etiquette.

Cunt has all the power of a magic word. There are things that make it okay for us to say cunt while men can't, or maybe it's okay for gay men who are our best girlfriends, or straight men who have passed the litmus test. Anyway, this "magic word" aspect of cunt is best illustrated by concrete example. To wit, I was once a go-go dancer in Bridgeport, and I was working at a biker bar. And in order to remain sane, it was very important that I act like a cunt, because that's really the only thing the guys in the bar would respect (never mind admire—I was just looking to get my money and get out, because some woman was giving a guy a blow job in the bathroom and it was, I admit, too scary for me). Acting like a cunt meant not making eye contact—not because I was afraid, but because I was one tough cunt. It meant going into my dressing room and reading *The New York Times* instead of socializing with the customers between sets. (Some rapist wants to buy me a Coors and assumes that this obligates me to sleep with him? Charmed. I'll stay put.) It meant holding my own and not playing the nice girl.

So I'm on stage and one of these guys says, as a little conversational gambit, "You really have an attitude, don't you?" He doesn't say it very nicely. Then he says, "You know what you are? You're a little cunt!" And he lunges at me. At which point the other dancer on the stage very coolly grabs a beer bottle and hits him over the head with it, thus taming his impulse (don't try this one at home). Luckily, he came to his senses (losing consciousness can do that to guys) and things settled down.

When I asked my savior why she did what she did, she simply stated, "He called you a cunt," and went back to doing the splits for singles. The point here is that cunt is such a powerful word, with so many associations, that if it's used incorrectly it can set you off in all your feminine, avenging fury. Now, don't you want a word like that, carefully and correctly used, at your fingertips?

I have two final things to say about why I love cunt. First of all, the thing in itself. I can never find the right word for it. Pussy is so whimsical and euphemistic and pink ("Hi! I don't really fuck!"). Vagina is so darn clinical. Beaver, too '50s and ironic. Hole, already taken. Snatch, too '70s and dumb and boycentric (like, they want to snatch it away, or what? I don't get it). I'm not advocating we all start calling it "my cunt." But sometimes it sounds better than all the other options. More in control, more girl, more "Look, you can do whatever you want but I'm going to get backstage passes to this show." Cunt is in charge, take-no-prisoners, and brazen. Like women in my favorite porn movies, who say, "I'm going to devour you with my cunt! Put it in, now!"

Finally, cunt is about being an insider. Or making somebody one of you. My girlfriends and I use it with each other when we've done something particularly admirable ("You told your boss that? You brilliant little cunt!" "You bought a pair of Betsey Johnson gold satin jeans right after I did? You cunt! Let's both wear them to my cocktail party!"). And we use it when somebody needs to be brought back down to earth, when we need to remind ourselves that some scary, powerful woman who's treated us badly better get off her fucking high horse. As in "Margaret Thatcher—the cunt!" or "Look, Jeanie, we all know that your boss is bitter and threatened by you and she's going to make your life miserable and say you're doing lousy work even though you're not, whenever she can." "You know what? You guys are right. That cunt!"

For fun and for mean, for expression and for irony, cunt is it. For me.

Michael Lavine

8

Herstory: Girl on Girls

HERE YE, HEAR ME. IT'S TIME FOR YOUR BRIEF BUSTLINE OF
our feminist herstory. It's a dangerous thing to forget our roots, and I'm not just referring to our hair color, I'm talking about the feminist movement.

Once upon a time (actually, 1792), somewhere in England, Mary Wollstone-craft read *The Rights of Man*, written by her buddy Thomas Paine and went, "What the fuck?" In response, Mother Mary wrote her version of the chick manifesto called *A Vindication of the Rights of Woman*, where she stated:

> If woman be allowed to have an immortal soul, she must
> have, as the employment of life, an understanding to improve,
> and when she is incited by present gratification to forget her

grand destination, nature is counteracted, or she was born only to procreate and rot. Yet if love be the supreme good, let woman only be educated to inspire it, and let every charm be polished to intoxicate the senses; but if they be moral beings, let them have a chance to become intelligent; and let love to man be only a part of that glowing flame of universal love.

An instant best-seller it was not, but *A Vindication of the Rights of Woman* was one of the first bricks in the foundation of feminism. Ms. Mary blew the shofar for women's equality, for her right to work and to an education. "How many women thus waste life away, who might have practiced as physician, regulated a farm, managed a shop and stood erect supported by their own industry instead of hanging their heads?" she asked, tapping into ideas that were strangely missing from the American Constitution, which was written at the same time.

Over here in America, at the turn of the 19th century, women were getting involved politically—in the areas of temperance, abolition, and reform. Abolition was definitely *the* buzzword, and it was, according to the *History of Woman Suffrage in America,* "the single most important factor in creating the women's rights movement in America." As abolitionist women fought for the emancipation of the Negro slaves, it became obvious that they, too, were an oppressed people, and they were no longer content to take it lying down.

In those days, women were meant to be seen and not heard. As Connie Brown and Jane Seitz state in *Sisterhood Is Powerful,* a woman was considered "the guardian of the hearth, carrier of tradition, influencer of morality" as well as a "salve for men's consciences and a symbol of stability in a turbulent time." Whether a rich plantation lady, a frontier woman, or a she-slave, a woman was expected to embrace her role as the dutiful (house)wife and mother. Personhood was not a matter of discussion. Equality of the sexes? Feh! It was a version of *The Rules,* 1800s style: basically, if a woman curtsied and kept herself pretty in a big billowy skirt, she was behaving properly. A woman did not have property rights or a bank account of her own, she could not sue anyone, she could not run for public office, nor could a woman keep her own name once she was married (forget about hyphenation!). Voting? That was a white man's privilege. A woman was definitely not expected to pull a Lysistrata, to get all Mystiquean, or call herself a suffragist/first-wave feminist, and start a revolution—the kind where her agenda was to secure equal rights and the right to vote.

In 1828, Frances "Fanny" Wright, an abolitionist, started making noise, shocking the bejesus out of mostly male audiences by advocating equal property rights, fairer divorce laws, and more accessible birth control. Lucretia Mott and the Grimke sisters—Angelina and Sarah—were among the women who challenged the 1830s patriarchy. When Lucretia chaired her first Female Anti-Slavery Society in 1833, the Grimke sisters stood up and said, "Man has subjected Woman to his will and used her for his own selfishness and comfort. He has done everything he could to debase and enslave her mind."

Eighteen forty-eight was a benchmark year in the herstory of feminism, the first official year of the woman. It was then that the suffragists shifted into high gear, turning into righteous revolutionaries, ignoring the patronizing patriarchy as they began to win their battles. For instance, the Married Women's Property Act became law in New York State, ensuring that a married woman could retain ownership of her inheritance (although designed by *men* to protect their daughters' dowry, it was a step in the right direction). Amelia Bloomer started *Lily,* a women's fashion magazine which featured "rebellious" women wearing—*gasp*—pants. For Susan B. Anthony, one of the leaders of the first wave, dress reform was symbolic of the changes the suffragists were making in their lives. Eighteen forty-eight was also the year that the heroic "General" Harriet Tubman began schlepping slaves—19 times via her crafty "Underground Railroad" network—to freedom. And let us not forget that in 1848, five ladies—Lucretia Mott, Martha Wright, Jane Hunt, Mary Ann McClintock, and Elizabeth Cady Stanton—organized the first women's rights gathering in Seneca Falls, New York, where they announced, "We hold these truths to be self-evident, that all men and women are created equal." Their own girlie version of the Declaration of Independence, called the Seneca Falls Declaration, could be considered a precursor to the ERA, as their agenda included seeking full citizenship as people and gaining equal economic opportunities.

Naturally, all of this activity in Girlville made men nervous, and in many cases prompted them to ridicule, sneer, and jeer. The good gentlemen folk of a Philadelphia paper were so moved that they declared:

Herstory: Girl on Girls

A woman is nobody. A wife is everything. A pretty girl is equal to ten thousand men and a mother is next to God, all powerful. . . . the ladies of Philadelphia therefore, under the influence of the most serious sober second thoughts, are resolved to maintain their rights as Wives, Belles Virgins and mothers and not as Women.

Women were denied the right to exist separate and apart from men. They were to remain subservient, cute, and mute. For black women, it was worse, because they were not only oppressed as a gender, but also enslaved as a race. As slaves, they plowed the fields alongside the men, but as *female* slaves they were also degraded sexually by their white "masters," who regularly raped, beat, and bribed them to rear more children (in order to make baby slaves). Mistreating black women was a deviant act not exclusive to white males: white women were just as shamefully guilty of abusing their "subordinate" sistahs. Later, in the post-emancipation period, black women formed many girl-only organizations such as the Blackclubwomen's Movement, which were a preview of the women's consciousness-raising groups of the late 1960s. These collective lean-on-me associations provided emotional and practical support for freedwomen while financing orphanages, schools, and other community-oriented projects. As Stephanie J. Shaw says in *The History of Women,* these women "saw themselves neither as helpless nor as total victims."

The first-wave feminists had a political and personal agenda which begat many other uncompromising works of activism. In response to the Fugitive Slave Act of 1859, Harriet Beecher Stowe wrote *Uncle Tom's Cabin,* quite controversial for its time. The always outrageous Victoria Woodhull ran for president in 1872 on a platform that championed free love, shorter skirts, and legalized prostitution. Nellie Bly (née Jane Cochran) set the stage for Barbara Walters and Connie Chung in 1889 by being the first female investigative reporter, and stunned everyone by traveling around the world in less than 80 days. In 1890, journalist and crusader Ida B. Wells launched an antilynching campaign in articles written for the *Memphis Free Speech* and the *New York Age.* Wells further enraged southerners by suggesting that white women have sexual relations with black men as she attempted to debunk the myth of the pure white southern belle. In 1896, the National Association for Colored Women was formed in Washington, D.C., bringing together many black women's clubs under one umbrella. Finally in 1919, after years of campaigning, first-wave feminists celebrated the passage of the Nineteenth Amendment in 1919. Signed, sealed, delivered, the vote's yours, ladies.

Now fast-forward about forty years to the 1960s, as herstory repeats itself. Just as the first wave was born out of a civil rights movement, the second wave, too, began in a time of unrest. In the '60s, civil rights were on everyone's mind, as were race relations and the Vietnam War. All of this contributed to an era of unprecedented political action for men and women everywhere.

"What do you wish you had done differently?" Betty Friedan asked the alumni women of her high school class while doing research on an article she was writing for *McCall's.* These mostly middle-class white women told tales of settling into a somnambulant state of suburbia, their lives sugarcoated with Valium and weighed down by children. But wanting to be more than just another Donna Reed/June Cleaver prototype made the daydream nation of the average cocktail friendly house-wife feel guilty. Freidan called this feeling the "problem with no name," a domestic tyranny that left these women feeling quite isolated, and very, very angry. In 1963 Betty Friedan's book that started as an article, *The Feminine Mystique,* was published, changing the women's movement forever.

As female activists traveled south for marches and sit-ins, the reality of their oppression hit them. In 1963, the President's Commission on the Status of Women (a watchdog group that Eleanor Roosevelt urged JFK to create and which she chaired until her death) published its report, *American Women,* which "documented perva-sive sexual discrimination and the absence of support systems for women's changing lives." According to *The Reader's Companion to U.S. Women's History,* "The commis-sion's most enduring contribution was its role in helping to launch the contemporary feminist movement." Laws were passed: the Equal Pay for Equal Work Act in 1963, and in 1964, the Civil Rights Act, which was designed to prohibit discrimination in employing a person based on race, color, religion, national origin, or sex. But still, women weren't really getting an equal share of the pie. In 1967, Betty Friedan formed the National Organization for Women (NOW), and their version of the Bill of Rights was promptly published. It demanded, among other things, the passage of the ERA, the establishment of more child-care facilities, and that a woman have the right to

307

reproductive freedom. Nineteen sixty-seven also saw the birth of "consciousness-raising groups" (Kathie Sarachild affectionately called them "bitch sessions"). These meetings were informal bastions of bonding for women: individually, their tales of woe were personal, but en masse, their experiences formed a bigger, scarier picture—that women were still the second sex. Radical feminism made no bones about it: this was a battle of the sexes, as stated in 1968's *Redstocking Manifesto:*

> Women are an oppressed class. . . . We are exploited as sex objects, breeders, domestic servants and cheap labor. We are considered inferior beings, whose only purpose is to enhance men's lives. . . . We identify the agents of our oppression as men. . . . Men have controlled all political, economic and cultural institutions and backed up this control with physical force. . . . All men have oppressed women.

Women sought extreme measures to protest these inequalities—through demonstrations such as the one that took place during the 1968 Miss America Beauty Pagent. There, the New York Radical Women (Robin Morgan, Alix Kates Shulman, et al.) crowned a sheep in protest and threw their "instruments of torture" (bras, girdles, *Cosmos,* etc.) into the legendary freedom trash can; the press went wild and called the event a "bra burning," even though not a stitch got torched. Other gangbusters acts included WITCH's ("Women's International Terrorist Conspiracy from Hell" or "Women Inspired To Commit Herstory") raids of bridal showers—they condemned marriage, calling it "a dehumanizing institution—legal whoredom for women"; and the underground abortion clinic network, JANE, which provided more than 11,000 safe abortions in its four-year existence. Revolutionary works such as Valerie Solanis's *SCUM (Society for Cutting Up Men) Manifesto,* Shulamith Firestone's *The Dialectics of Sex,* and Kate Millet's *Sexual Politics* took on, among other things, the patriarchy's roles in women's lives. Meanwhile, declaring oneself a lesbian feminist became a political statement, but one not without humor, as they had fun reclaiming derogatory terms and turning them into positive slogans such as "Gay Is Good," "Take a Lesbian to Lunch," and "Super Dyke Loves You." In 1973, the National Conference of Puerto Rican Women, the Black Women Organized for Action, and the National Black Feminist

Organization were established. The NBFO took pains to establish itself as a movement addressing the needs of the black woman's presence and activism as women's libbers:

> The Movement has been characterized as the exclusive property of so-called white middle class women and any black women seen involved in this Movement have been seen as "selling out," "dividing the race," and an assortment of nonsensical epithets. Black feminists resent these charges and have therefore established the National Black Feminist Organization, in order to address ourselves to the particular and specific needs of the larger, but almost cast-aside half of the black race in Amerikkka, the black woman.

The consciousness-raising groups' "personal is political" mantra—that power relations between the sexes had to be examined and readdressed, in the workplace as well as in marriage—became the women's liberation battle cry. *Roe v. Wade* made abortion legal; Susan Brownmiller told us about the history of rape; Elaine Brown ran the Black Panthers; Gloria Steinem and Pat Carbine started *Ms.* Despite the movement's work, these second wavers were condescendingly brushed off as being nothing more than bored housewives going through a "phase." But the more resistance these women met with, the more they fought back. These sistahs were doing it for all of us, not just themselves. And we, the daughters of the revolution, have taken over, stomping in stiletto heels smack dab into the '90s.

The third wave is bubbling over with tremendous voices, visionary social, political and economic activism. Just look at the revolution, girl style, caused by Riot Girls. Writing "Bitch" and "Slut" across their arms and bellies in red lipstick, they reclaimed words that are meant to harm girls, and turned the tables, making the words sources of empowerment. Riot Grrls encouraged girls everywhere to start making music, making 'zines, making their voices heard. Today women are an active and vocal part of the labor force—from Gerry Laybourne, the founder of Nickelodeon, to my mom, a baby-sitter. We're consumers, players, activists. We know that Girl Power is more than just a marketing tool for the Spice Girls, it's a way of life. We can shout Shout Hip Clit Hooray! for prosex cheerleaders like Nadine Strossen, Betty

309

Dodson, Lisa Palac, Susie Bright, Annie Sprinkle—the women who keep reminding us about the power of pussy, that sex for one is fun, and that shtupping is good. Even Surgeon General Jocelyn Elders encouraged girls and boys to explore their "down theres" in our conservative society. Women can and do speak up and out, en masse and individually, changing history; whether it is the half million of us who attended the 1992 Pro-Choice Rally in Washington, D.C., or Shannon Faulkner taking on the military alone when she applied to The Citadel. Imagine, we can actually go to a theater and watch the playwright Eve "I'm worried about vaginas" Ensler take *The Vagina Monologues* to a new level of interactive performance by entertaining *and* raising awareness for the victims of domestic violence. Madonna encouraged us to "Express Yourself!" It has never been so easy.

We're at a point in time where we have the guts and the means to make choices, whether they are controversial or not. And while *BUST* has embraced the pleasure principle with a Magic Wand, sex isn't the only thing on our minds. We're worried about our futures, we think about the past, and we dwell on the good, the bad, the ugly. Some of us are here, are queer, and are used to it. We're not afraid to analyze, dissect, and debate the minutiae of our love lives, our economic situation, or the ERA—nothing is too trivial or too political. We have watched, listened, and learned, and now we do, do, do. We're bratty, we're angry, we're cool. There's room on our plates for all of our goals, whatever they may be. The nitpicking at our sister feminists, calling them da-duhists or bimbo feminists, is definitely something we don't need to do to each other—unless of course they are doing the antigirl thing—because we have enough opposition at our feet. Just take a ringside seat and witness the thrilla in Girlvilla: Faludi vs. Wolf; Denfield vs. Riophe; *BUST* vs. *Cosmo.* At the end of the day, we are all entitled to our opinion without another woman knocking it down. When we start sniping at ourselves, we end up with our own Judas: Bellafante (author of *Time*'s "Is Feminism Dead?") vs. The Rest of Us and crying *Et tu?*

A century of activism greets the millennium with a whole lot of something going on. We've entered an era of DIY feminism—sistah, do-it-yourself—and we have all kinds of names for ourselves: lipstick lesbians, do-me feminists, even postfeminism (which Simon Reynolds and Joy Press in *The Sex Revolts* describe as "playful where feminism is merely sober, flaunting an ironic sense of identity," cooler than the others, they argue, because "the earlier isms believed in authentic self"). No matter what the flava is, we're still feminists. Your feminism is what you want it to be and what you make of it. Define your agenda. Claim and reclaim your F-word. My definition of feminism is a simple one: that the sexes are of equal value. What's yours? The reality of feminism today is that men still have the upper hand: men's needs still come first (you just have to look how quickly health insurance companies were willing to include Viagra as a benefit, and yet women still must cover their doctor-prescribed birth control pills); men still earn more to the dollar than women; *Time* still has a Man of the Year issue. As Gloria Steinem once said, "If men could menstruate," oh, what a world this would be. We still struggle with being hassled in the street, with shattering the glass ceiling, without a woman in the White House. It's clear that we still have work to do. If it weren't for the blood, sweat, and tears of women like Margaret Sanger, Rosa Parks, and Bella Abzug, or Roseanne, Aretha, and Madonna, chances are I wouldn't even be able to challenge you to do that work. The torch, my dear, is in your hand now.

So what are you going to do with it?

— *Marcelle Karp*

Bad Like Me

by Courtney Love

I was born bad. My biological dad is a bad man, so Mama simply thought, "Ooh, she's got that bad blood seed in her." At heart, home, hearth, and boyfriend, I am a full-on good girl prude—but don't tell anyone.

When you're a bad girl, people are terrified of you. You don't get mugged or raped because you don't have any victim energy (I'm sure it's happened, just not as often). It's bad if you're a famous one, though, because the boys then all wanna fuck you, but when you get all girl-gooey and they go, "Oooh," because they thought you were gonna spank them. Duh, asshole.

When you're a bad girl, everyone does what you want. You have room to grow. Bad girls are kinder than good girls and they are better to other girls, mostly, unless said other girls are boy-pleasin' users who want a little bad girl spice rubbed off on 'em like so much perfume. Bad girls are also more spiritual and less prone to drug addiction, or, if they have it, when they quit they *quit*.

Bad girls know genius before the other dumb good girls do. They get the hot guys first 'cause they aren't looking for that big stamp of popularity approval. In *Amadeus,* Salieri says Mozart is ugly; the Soprano (a naughty bad girl) replies, "A woman of taste only thinks of genius." Bad girls love boy flesh that has an astronomical IQ.

Most bad girls are *not* as libidinous as good girls. Sex is intrigue, not looks; it's buildup and mind warping.

Bad girls love like lions and kill those who fuck with their kin.

Good girls steal bad girls' boys. Bad girls fuck your boy-friends, yeah . . . but we feel shitty about it, sort of. You're there to take care of the dog, to have the BBQs. We're there to fly into New York or LA or Paris and lock up in a four-star for three days while your boyfriend and we do things you'll never know about and he'd never dare to do to you. And it makes us feel a little guilty.

312

Bad girls are "femmenistes"; we like our dark Nars lipstick and LaPerla panties, but we hate sexism, even if we do fuck your husbands/boyfriends. We understand men, we love them, us hetero/bi bad girls.

We are not psycho bad girls; those are evil and in a class of their own. They are usually considered good girls by the community. (E.g., the Oly girl, in her high, quaky voice and "widdle gurl" act. How could she be capable of severing the head of a kitty and putting it on your front porch with a syringe in its cornea? No, not that widdle good gurl!)

Bad girls will get obsessed if you dump us nasty, but instead of resorting to evil good girl tactics we will do things like: make your band open for us someday; send all your mail to a Der Wienerschnitzel in Watts; get a guitar for revenge; do genius comics; and be a genius such as my favorite NYC bad girl, Dame Darcy, goddess supreme. We met on the one day I'd uttered her name in a foreign country. She is a bad girl; she's friends with Lisa Suckdog, who has that great zine *Rollerderby.* Lisa tries to be a bad girl, crawlin' around nekkid and stuff, but I think she wasn't born with it—but hey, I could be totally wrong.

Like Me

Dame Darcy

Darby from *Ben Is Dead* is a bad girl. She makes fun of me but bad girls do that to each other, unfortunately. Shouldn't we all be piling up on Juliana or something?

Cristina Martinez of Boss Hog is a Hot Babe bad girl—some day she'll lose that Spencer guy and come into her own fabulousness. She's got a swinging bad girl Spanish booty. Man, you don't wanna get on the wrong end of her rattail comb. See, bad girls get fucked up like me or Cristina or Inger Lorre—she's a natural star

313

and the baddest girl of us all. We just cannot cross the line from bad girl to evil girl, leave that for the . . . oh, no point in naming names.

Alanis Morissette won a bunch of Grammys and she went to the Grammys. No bad girl would go to the Grammys.

Don't dump a bad girl 'cause one day you'll have to come back and grovel for something; watch it, man—hell hath no fury like a bad girl dumped ill.

Bad girls can deal with a little infidelity; good girls will leave you on "principle." Bad girls can be as classy as Jackie O., who was a bad girl, she just didn't think it was our business to know that.

My sister Ms. Barrymore is a way bad girl. We are going to wear acid-wash to the Academy Awards. Of course, bad girls go to Academy Award parties. Only if you get nominated are you *busy*.

Good girls live in a state of sulking or gloating, 'cause they are getting their butts kissed or having to kiss butt. But my friend—who's a good boy on the outside, but a very bad boy on the inside—told me that there's a middle state wherein, like, if you go to the Academy Awards, you are going out of your way to get your butt kissed, and that's lame.

We can be *total* media whores; we can also be completely mysterious.

All bad girls in the NYC and LA areas have slept with other girls just because.

Bad girls love like no one else.

Bad girls swallow—it is sooo rude to spit, but don't do it the first time. I don't know why I think that, I just think the good girl part of the bad girl says they know you give good head, so make the worms wait.

If you're a single girl on the make, I suggest power. You have to work hard to acquire it, and no one will help you. You will gain many girl enemies. That's 'cause you eventually wind up playing the wife of a huge publisher—who is alive and happens to like you—in some big movie and all the lame-o's that work at his magazines you could have chopped but you won't 'cause BAD GIRLS DO NOT EVER ABUSE POWER once they have acquired it, except occasionally for sexual purposes only.

Bad girls do not fake orgasms, or they betray only themselves.

Bad girls have bad boy boyfriends but mostly good boy boyfriends 'cause the sweet-faced angelboy is really horrid and Mr. Gnarly is a big wimp who wants to know what sweater to wear onstage tonight; blechhh!

Bad girls sometimes wimp out and call; that's separating the wheat from the chaff, the men from the wimps. If you can't be friends with him, forget it. If he doesn't know how to actually get you to shut the fuck up, it's not worth *that* much. Fuck the phone game; other games are way funner. I'm a loser at the phone game. If you want to be a femme fatale, go for it and never call back, tally up, etc. The good ones do not even *get* the phone game. It's hard to believe but true. Cat and mouse is for Elizabethans and Victorians.

Bad girls will always give you the shirt off their back.

Bad girls are vulgar, but we have the potential for *total* class.

The rest is *my* business, not the *New York Post*'s.

Gloria Stein-mom

by Amelia Richards

I was about to begin my last year of college when a friend called to say that Gloria Steinem needed someone to help her with research and fact-checking. I had anticipated continuing an internship from the previous semester at Christie's Auction House, where I constantly felt underdressed, underprivileged, and overly caring, so this was a welcomed opportunity.

When I came into Gloria Steinem's life, I wasn't really sure of who "she" was. Although I was raised by a single mother in a home that always had stacks of *Ms.* magazines lying around, the name "Gloria Steinem" only conjured up the distant image of someone who was famous, but how or why I wasn't certain. Now, five years

315

after I began working for her, I am still in her life and can't imagine where my life would be had she not been in mine. Our relationship includes everything from friends to employee/employer, roommates (thanks to her generosity), coactivists, sisters, mentor/mentee, and mother/daughter. It encompasses basically everything but lovers, despite what some people have thought. On occasion I have felt like the mystery woman. "A twenty-four-year-old assistant sleeps in the loft above the dining nook," *The New York Times* reported two years back. Yes, I'm the guest that never left. I came to look after the cat, the mail, and other things while Gloria was on a book tour. She encouraged me to stay on for a while after she came home, and somehow, it just worked. Neither of us would have thought that living together would have worked for us—but it did.

Gloria is the perfect girlfriend. She helps me get ready to go out—"I have the perfect belt for that outfit"—and when one boyfriend calls while I am out with another, she simply says, "I expect her home later." When I regret plans I committed myself to, she always offers to call in sick for me. She is also the best mentor. When a reporter wants to interview her about young women and feminism, she says, "There's a young woman here right now, you should really talk to her." When I am all excited about my latest "theory," she always encourages me to write about it, and when I am nervous about something or having anxiety attacks, she shares her experiences to calm me down. As a roommate, she is always there helping me set the table for some dinner party I'm having or asking me what I think of the latest household decoration. And as an employer, she knows that a flexible, supportive, and trusting work environment creates the best employees.

The primary reason Gloria and I are able to have the mother/daughter relationship we do is because I have an overly nurturing, encouraging, and loving biological mother. This makes the boundaries of my relationship with Gloria a little less blurred. I can have my cake and eat it, too: a mother/daughter thing that still allows me a certain amount of privacy and separation. I think it's easier on her knowing that I am not trying to make her my mother. After all, she spent her childhood mothering her *own* mother, her reproductive years either thinking "later" or mothering other things, like organizations, magazines, and movements, and is constantly having to rerespond to the media's barrage of questions with "No, I do not regret not having biological children."

Timing is also a crucial factor in my relationship with Gloria. She came into my life just as I was becoming more comfortable with who I was, and excited to explore all the possibilities that lay ahead of me. I came into hers at a similar point in her life. She was transitioning out of being a daily presence at *Ms.* and beginning to commit more time and energy to books she had always wanted to write; she was "freeing up the part of her brain" that had otherwise been occupied by sex; and she was able and willing to share her life and home now that she had "one of her own." This timing has also allowed me to share things with Gloria that I never shared with my mother. With Gloria I am totally comfortable talking about the drugs I experimented with, how I lost my virginity when I was still too young to know what virginity even was, and all those other things I did to constantly challenge my mortality. Growing up, these were things I couldn't share with my mother, nor would she have wanted me to.

Then there are also all those years I spent rejecting my mother. In most instances, these things are so hurtful, embarrassing, and stupid that I hate to be reminded of them—like making up a mythical nuclear family for my friends because I somehow thought that my one-parent family wasn't good enough; threatening to get married and start a family and forget the education and opportunity for a career that my mother worked so hard to provide for me; and constantly being embarrassed by her feminist values. It took time, experience, and Gloria to make me rethink all of the above.

I remember the first time my mother met Gloria. It was at a rally where Gloria was speaking. Afterward, in the midst of a crowd, I introduced them. Gloria was a bit distracted by the rally itself, yet she was clearly excited about meeting my mother.

Beegee Tolpa

My mother was overwhelmed by the introduction—she was thankful, excited, and appreciative—and her eyes were filled with tears. I know that my mother is at times jealous and envious and that she thinks I will forget that she is my *real* mother. You know those fathers—usually divorced or separated ones—who only show up for the good stuff and leave for the bad? Although she never said so, I think this was how my mother initially viewed Gloria's role in my life.

317

Still, I know her good feelings far surpass the awkward ones. It must be a little weird—and somewhat exciting—to know that your daughter has daily contact with one of your heroes. My mother bought the first issue of *Ms.* magazine and became a lifetime subscriber, and she is an active feminist (as opposed to those inactive ones). For the past fifteen years she has been in a women's group where she and her friends exchange life-changing information and learn that they are not alone. This consciousness-raising group is an example of one of those things I couldn't appreciate as a little kid. Now, I know that these gatherings were the backbone of the feminist movement.

Although coincidence is partly responsible for my relationship with Gloria, I believe that fate also had something to do with it. We both escaped from midwestern cities, spent a portion of our lives with single mothers, were active throughout our lives, and have always had an unhealthy balance of (too much) work and (too little) play.

Through all of the time we spend together and all of the things we share, I sometimes forget that Gloria is *Gloria Steinem.* Fans we run into on the street, otherwise loquacious friends of mine who become speechless in her presence, and dropped jaws when I tell people where I work help keep me in check. In a sense she is the "mother of us all"—or at least most of us self-respecting young women who grew up with a feminist consciousness. While personally she has helped me to make sense of my life, the intimacy I have with her and her work helps me to make sense of the world, particularly the world of women. Because of her I know the possibilities, and also the realities, of what we can accomplish. And I know that the least I can do in exchange is to share the benefits of this relationship and all that I have learned.

This is only the beginning of that sharing.

❈

Pirate of a Lady

by Scarlett Fever

My father was a swashbuckler at heart, and that's the legacy he's passed on to me. I was raised on beautifully illustrated books full of adventure, like *Robin Hood* and *Sinbad.* In a small book of my father's, its pages already yellowed with age when I found it and read it for the first time, were stories of lost treasure: Dillinger's buried loot; Captain Kidd's hidden doubloons—boy stuff. But hidden inside all that rough-and-tumble sword- and gunplay was the story of Mary Anne Blythe: the G-string Buccaneer.

She quickly became my muse. Like me, she was tall with a fiery temper, and I liked to imagine myself being as beautiful and as vibrant as she was. According to the story, she was only fifteen when the terrible pirate Blackbeard boarded the ship she was traveling on. Wearing lit matches and red silk ribbons entwined in his long thick beard, he relieved her ship of all its treasure and killed most of the crew. When he returned to her and tried to rip off her dress, she laughed and slapped his face. Captivated by her courage, he was transformed into a perfect gentleman, and escorted her with a curtsy to his ship. There, dressing in men's clothing, she became his protégée, learning all manner of things sexual or seafaring, and mastering the art of piracy. By the age of twenty she'd earned a ship and crew of her own.

While she could handle a cutlass and pistol with the best of the buccaneers, she had her own secret weapon: women. Lots of them, each as immodest and headstrong as she herself. She knew the power of sexual desire, and used it to her benefit. Her girls would stand at the railing of her ship, sliding their loose tops from their shoulders and waving at the crews of passing merchant ships, while Mary Anne herself wore little more than a G-string and a pair of boots, her dark red hair catching in the wind. As the sea-weary crews of the merchant ships pulled beside them, ready to board and relieve themselves after months of only the ocean and the company of other men, her crew of bloodthirsty bandits would jump from their hiding places and capture the vessel.

Mary Anne did not only use her sexuality as a tool to manipulate men; she indulged her appetite for masculine booty as much as she did her desire for material booty. After taking over a ship, she would have her male captives line up on deck. From these, she would pick a young and handsome man as her lover, keeping him only until he bored her, which could last anywhere from a few hours to a few months (a woman used to so much adventure bored easily). When she was through with him, she would cut his throat and toss his lifeless body overboard.

She wreaked havoc on the high seas for years, entertaining Blackbeard while her young lovers entertained her, until a young Spanish sailor captured her heart. She kept him for three years, but when Blackbeard's jealousy threatened them both, the two lovers stole away on a ship bound for Peru, never to be heard from again.

Mary Ann Blythe was my goddess, my role model, my heroine. In my own way I sought out the Blackbeards of today: gangsters and bikers, murderers and thieves, charming them all with my bravado and *cojónes*. I dyed my hair red and when I danced topless on stage I wore nothing but a G-string and boots. I carried a knife in my boot or on my belt. I took lovers with abandon, and left them when they bored me.

I've always wanted to know more about this six-foot-tall, titian-haired woman who served as my secret alter ego for thirty years. But when I began researching her life, what I found instead were histories of *other* lady pirates. Alwilda, a Swedish princess who captained a pirate crew somewhere in the Baltic Sea until the prince of Denmark captured her ship. The young and pretty Mrs. Hon-Cho Lo, who, after the death of her buccaneer husband, became an admiral of sixty oceangoing junks, with which she earned a terrifying reputation, sacking villages and pirating the seas. And then I found the story of Anne Bonny and Mary Read, the Thelma and Louise of the high seas.

Anne fell in love with a penniless sailor and ran off and married him, only to be first disowned by her father for her act of insolence, then abandoned by her gigolo husband for her poverty. Not the type to lie down in the face of hardship, Anne had once beaten a man who'd tried to force himself on her—beaten him so badly that he was confined to bed for weeks. She met and took up with another handsome rake, the pirate Calico Jack Rackham. She soon found herself pregnant, and he let her ashore on Cuba with friends, but she returned to pirating immediately after the baby was born (and this is the last that's heard of the child!).

Upon returning to the ship, Anne spied a handsome young sailor and set her sights on him. Cornering him with seduction on her mind, she revealed the luscious

320

body she had kept hidden under men's clothes. To her shock, her intended paramour did the same, opening "his" shirt to expose a pair of breasts! Mary Read and Anne Bonny had been keeping the same secret from the crew and each other, and that discovered, the two became fast friends.

Mary had spent years in male drag in the army, until the day she fell in love with a fellow infantryman. She revealed herself then too, and the two were happily married until his untimely death. Now a widow, Mary had returned to male drag and taken to the seas. She'd joined Rackham's crew when he overtook the merchant ship she'd been working on. While pirating under Rackham's flag, she fell in love again, this time with a young craftsman, and again secretly revealed her gender. When her gentle lover was challenged to a duel by another pirate, knowing he couldn't use a weapon, she picked a fight with the bully and fought him herself, shooting him first and running him through with her sword for good measure.

The two ladies kept their secrets from all but their lovers and each other. They cursed, drank, and fought like men, and better than many. When Rackham's ship was finally taken by the authorities, he fled to shore and the crew hid below-decks. Only Mary, Anne, and a lone seaman stayed up top to fight for their ship. Mary yelled for them to come up and fight like men, and when they didn't, she fired into the hold, killing one crew member and wounding another.

Finally, they could hold the ship no longer and were arrested and taken to prison. Only after the crew was sentenced to execution did the two women reveal their sex. They pleaded "their bellies"—both of the friends were pregnant—and the judge stayed their executions. Mary died of prison fever before the birth of her child. Anne gave birth in prison, then received a reprieve.

On the day of his hanging, Calico Jack came to Anne's cell to visit his love one last time. She was disgusted at the way he had abandoned his ship and his crew. She blamed him for Mary's capture and death, but agreed to see him anyway—it seems she wanted to speak her mind before it was too late. She turned and told him that "if he had fought like a Man, he need not have been hang'd like a Dog."

As hard as I tried, I was unable to find records of anyone named Mary Anne Blythe. It seems she is not much more than a fictionalized delicacy created from equal parts each of Mary Read and Anne Bonny, then topped with the whipped cream of male fantasy. But she served me well for thirty years, and what she led me to find was even better than the fantasy. Instead of one woman making her way alone in a man's world, I found several women—real-life adventurers in a time when women didn't venture out at all.

They married, took lovers, snatched up armloads of pleasure, drank big gulps of life, regretting nothing and never looking back. They were women who, when told what ladies can't do, simply spat, grabbed the wheel, and became fierce ruthless men to the world, and fiery lusty women to their men. They fought for what they loved and fought because they loved it; they stood together and refused to go gently into that good night.

Tura, Tura, Tura: An Interview with Tura Satana

by Mae Jest

Wonder Woman. Jaime Sommers. Princess Leia. Name a female action icon, and I betcha 50 bucks Tura Satana could kick her ass. With her star turn as Varla, the villainous ringleader of a trio of thrill-seeking go-go girls in the epic bad-girl flick, *Faster Pussycat! Kill! Kill!,* the exotic beauty tough-talked and karate-chopped her way to midnight movie immortality.

But there's more to the baDDest of the bad girls than one campy role and a brick shithouse build. Tura Satana's life is as dramatic and complex as a B-movie plot. Details of her life and long career unfurl like a Vegas Oliver Twist—full of sex, violence, and triumphs of spirit. Through multiple incarnations—singer, stripper, actress, wife, mother, and now, retired cult heroine, martial artist, and grandma—Tura Satana remains every inch the sexy, good-humored, take-no-shit *BUST*-style goddess.

Mae: So you're finally writing your autobiography?

Tura: Yeah, well, this fellow in Germany had apparently been delving into my past. He was going to do an unauthorized biography, so I figured, why not collaborate on it?

M: Sure, if he's gonna do it, he might as well get it right. Let's start with your girlhood. It was pretty wild, huh? Gangs, reform school, stripping, and of course karate. All by the age of what, fifteen?

T: Um, you know, I think I'd done all that by thirteen. Except the stripping—I was fourteen and a half.

M: How did you get your start?

T: I started out as a singer in Calumet City, Illinois. I was fourteen and a half at the time. If they had known how old I was, I would never have gotten the job. Thank God I looked older than I was.

M: What was the routine?

T: There was a show called "Galatea," the statue who came to life. And the gal who was doing it left. So the guy who ran the show asked me if I would do it. I said, "But will I have to take off my clothes?" And he said, "Yeah." And I said, "Well, then I want more money." See, at the time, a "legitimate" dancer only made seventy-five bucks a week. He said, "Okay, I'll raise you up to $125." So that's what I got.

M: You had a pretty big female fan club. Was that unusual?

T: Yeah, that was definitely unusual for most strippers. Often females feel intimidated, or have a lot of animosity toward women who strip. These ladies were mostly housewives, and they just enjoyed watching me twirl my tassels.

M: Speaking of which—what's the trick?

T: (laughing) Muscle control. It's all muscle control.

M: Nothing you can teach me?

T: No, not over the phone.

Herstory: Girl on Girls

M: You had some pretty dangerous curves back in the day? What were your stats?

T: Back in those days? 36DDD, with about a 21-inch waist, 36- to 37-inch hips. Very long legs, they used to say.

M: When did you first make the transition from stripping to acting?

T: That was in the '60s. The first thing I did was a show called *Hawaiian Eye.* It was a series and I played a secretary.

M: When you first got the script for *Faster Pussycat,* did you have any idea that it would be such a huge cult hit?

T: No. I had no idea. To me, it was just a lark. It was something that was different from the things I was doing, that looked like fun.

M: When people meet you, do they expect you to be Varla?

T: Oh yes. Everyone expects me to be Varla.

M: Well, there are some similarities, aren't there?

T: Varla is very much a part of me. Not necessarily her sexual tastes, but definitely her temper. And her violent nature.

M: Now, we all know Varla survived. Where is she?

T: Well, Varla is just basically biding her time. Haji and I are thinking about bringing back a re-creation of Varla and Rosie. We'd have to find somebody who's really into that type of thing. Haji used to date a lot of stuntmen, so she can do a lot of stunts. And I can do some of the same things that I used to do with my karate. She and I talked about taking an act on the road.

M: So you keep in touch?

T: Oh sure, Russ and Haji are still very good friends of mine. We talk about once every couple months. I was in New Jersey not long ago for the Chiller Expo [horror/cult film convention]—we had a ball doing that. If Haji had made it there, we coulda whipped that whole thing into line. You never can tell with her.

*The **BUST** Guide to the New Girl Order*

M: Did you save any souvenirs from the movie?

T: Actually, no. The boots got worn out very shortly after. My gloves—one of my gloves is on Russ's wall, on a plaque—and the other I donated to a library in Mississippi. They wanted some memorabilia for an auction, and I heard it sold for about $100 or so. For one dirty old glove.

M: Are you still practicing karate? I heard you were a security guard.

T: Well, I still do some of it, but not a whole lot. I was in an auto accident and broke my back. So, I can't do *all* the things I used to do, but definitely some.

M: Let me switch gears a little. As one of four sisters, and the mother of two daughters, how do you think things have changed for women from one generation to the next?

T: Well, I would say that a lot of things have changed. The way I raised my girls was basically the way I was raised—you respect other people. You don't take any crap off them, but you don't force your opinions on anybody, either. I feel that women need to be recognized as a force all their own, and that if we do the same kind of work, we deserve the same kind of pay. Right now that's still not true. I raised my girls to be independent, to be able to function on their own.

M: Are you a feminist?

T: I don't know if I'm a feminist or not. I mean, I like men opening doors for me and if I smoked anymore, I imagine I'd like having my cigarettes lit for me and stuff like that. I believe that females should be treated like they're females, but if she wants to be independent, let her be independent. I have never known a female who couldn't handle her own life. The only thing that screwed it up was guys.

325

M: Speaking of which: let's talk about a few of the ones in your past.

T: Oh, I've known quite a few interesting ones.

M: Who comes to mind first?

T: Well, I would say the best memories I have are of my second husband. He treated me like an absolute goddess. Nothing I did could ever upset him. The other is Rod Taylor, who I was very much in love with. I still have really fond memories of him.

M: How did you meet Elvis?
T: Elvis I met working in Chicago and down South. He came to catch my show in the theater, and wanted to meet me 'cause he liked my moves. He said they were really good, so I taught him some.

M: True or false: you were almost the first lady of Graceland?
T: That was a long time ago.

M: Colonel Tom must have had a stroke.
T: I don't know about a stroke, but he sure wasn't too thrilled. For starters, I was of a different race and he didn't care for that, and then I got Elvis all into the martial arts 'cause I told him that that's where I got most of the moves for my routine.

M: About the race issue—how did you deal with it? I know you were pigeonholed quite a bit.
T: Shit, I had a lot of trouble when I first started because I was Oriental. People always wanted to bill me as "the Oriental Tempestt Storm" or somebody else with big boobs, and I was like, "Hey, I'm my own person." I told 'em, I said, "My title is Miss Japan Beautiful," which I won legitimately on my own and that's the way I wanted to be billed, not as the Oriental anybody else.

M: There weren't many minority headliners back then, huh?
T: There were a lot of Chinese women. But they all—I guess in some ways I paved the way for them, because I stood up for me and everybody else, and didn't take no for an answer. But mostly they were all Caucasian—usually blond or maybe redhead.

M: So how did people react to you?
T: The reaction I got, when I first started, was very strange. In Little Rock, Arkansas— I'll never forget that place—they didn't care for my routine until I started twirling my tassels. After that, I could do no wrong. In Atlanta, Georgia, when I first came out

there was a Japanese scientists' convention, so I had my own fan club. The governor invited me out to his house for a barbecue. I was the only stripper I know of who was there.

M: What is the most common reaction you get from fans today?
T: Mostly they say, "You haven't changed a bit." I just tell 'em it's been thirty years. Everybody changes in thirty years.

M: How have you changed?
T: I think mostly I've just kind of mellowed out. Settled down. I'm a grandmother, you know.

M: How old are your grandkids? Have they seen your movies yet?
T: Oh yeah, every one I've ever been in. Let's see—one is twenty-one years old, that's my oldest grandson, then I have one that's sixteen, one that's eleven, one that's five, and one that's two.

M: And your daughters? Any actresses?
T: No. One's in information systems—y'know, computers—and the other is a dental assistant.

M: Who were the women who have inspired or influenced you most along the way?
T: I would say Joan Crawford is one. People used to say that I reminded them of her. And Rosalind Russell. I figure that Joan Crawford and I were alike as far as maybe being a little hard or pushy when we wanted to get our own way, but I don't know about Rosalind Russell.

327

M: What about them did you admire?
T: Ah, I admired Rosalind Russell's talent. Jane Russell, too. She's a wonderful person. Just a down-to-earth gal. I met her once, she's a very classy lady. And Stunning Smith—she gave me some very, very good advice when I was just starting out as a dancer. I had never worked in a theater with a big stage before, and she took me aside and said, "You have the talent. All you have to do is learn how to use that stage, every

inch of it. Just imagine that it's all your family out there, and you'll never go wrong." That's one of the things that I learned to live by, and she was very right. Backstage, you know, was like a family. Most people think that burlesque people have very low morals, but they have higher morals than most churchgoing people.

M: What do you think about the state of stripping today?
T: There are just no artists left to do it. These girls today think that acting like you're screwing a pole is going to make you a star. You've got to have more talent than that. You've got to enjoy it and make others enjoy it, too. Anybody can walk around with their clothes off. You have to do it with style. And class. You have to be able to entertain.

M: Let's talk entertainers, then. What do you think of Madonna?
T: I don't care for Madonna. Sexploitation is about the top word I can think of for her.

M: How about Roseanne?
T: Roseanne is too crude for me. I believe in women's lib and all that, but there are some things I draw the line at.

M: Who do you like?
T: I dunno. I like Kathie Lee, she's good. Demi Moore's okay. I don't necessarily care for too many of the ones that are coming up. Ursula Andress is a great gal. Janet Leigh was good. Y'know who I really respect? Debbie Reynolds.

M: Really? How come?
T: 'Cause she had the balls to do it on her own. She got married to an idiot, to two idiots, actually. Eddie Fisher was stupid enough to let her go, and her next husband was a showboater who left her with a lot of debts. She really had to almost work herself to death to pay them off. I have the greatest respect in the world for her. And she raised a great daughter, I like her daughter. She [Carrie Fisher] is a good kid. She had a drug problem, y'know, but she kicked it. I never had to rely on drugs. That's one of the things they teach you with martial arts, not to screw with that shit. If I had done drugs, I wouldn't look like I do today.

*The **BUST** Guide to the New Girl Order*

M: Is that it? That's your secret?

T: That, and believing in yourself. I don't know anyone who is as happy as I am right now. I've accomplished all of the things I most wanted to accomplish.

M: Any regrets?

T: No. Never regret living your life.

M: One last question: what's a girl's best friend?

T: Her own self-respect. And a lot of cash.

She's Gotta Have It: An Interview with Nina Hartley

by Betty Boob

When you think of a porn star, smart, edgy feminist is not a description that pops into your mind at first. It's more like blond, silicone, druggie—stereotypes that imply things that are slightly more derogatory. Well, the legendary Nina Hartley is blond and she does have implants, but she's not a druggie and she's not a victim. She is a fiercely feminist porn star, having been in over 350 porn flicks (you can also see Nina as the philandering wife in *Boogie Nights*). In addition to being a magna cum laude graduate, a registered nurse, a producer-director, and having her own Web site (www.nina.com— you can find out where she is performing and read up on her feminist manifesto!), Nina is funny, she's passionate, and she's got a thing or two to say about a girl's pleasure.

So you are this legendary porn star . . .

I am evolving into the teacher, the yenta, the mentor, and the big sister as well as the sexy older woman. I'm here to share my sexual experience with people in hopes it will help them and to say it's worth every effort you make to get at peace with your body, it's worth every piece of shit you go through, every fear, every terror, every whatever you personally have to go through. You need, you must, you're obligated to make love with yourself and love yourself in a sexual manner. If you can't do that, you are never gonna be any good to a partner. I really encourage the readers to do what it takes to understand your sexual nature and to be okay with whatever it is as long as it doesn't involve underage people. The best thing I ever did for my sex life was put a mirror next to my bed big enough to see all of me and all of him when we were having sex and realized I looked pretty darn good thank you very much.

Does society have an obsession with tits?
Well, in a perfect world we'd be valued for our hearts alone, but, yes, our culture has an adolescent breast fetish. We should have an ass and hips fetish cuz that's where sex happens, not in the tits, but that's another century or two. If a person is getting cosmetic surgery because it's gonna change their lives and make them feel better, they need to really think about this and probably not do it. I didn't get breast implants till I was twenty-nine and I'd been working in the sex business for years. I was no longer comfortable being naked because my tits didn't match the rest of me so I went up a cup size. If I had gone to a double DD, then we're talking *Nina you need a fucking hole in the head.* I have to admit they seem extremely obvious. They don't hurt; they're saline. I didn't put my health in danger except for the operation. I'm not carrying silicone time bombs. I know in certain angles they look weird. I know how guys get about women like that, about women who need to put makeup on in order to feel good about themselves, who really spend all their time vying for the attention of men, who feel unwhole without that attention. I used to feel very sorry for those women and I saw them as unliberated and poor unenlightened souls. On the other hand, if a woman is heterosexual, you gotta do certain things to get the attention of men. That's the way it is. For women who still like and enjoy and appreciate the attention of men, it's perfectly appropriate for them to wear cosmetics, and to shave their legs, and to wear dresses that are a little revealing. This is a perfectly acceptable thing. Sometimes all I want is to be someone's sex object. Sometimes I don't want to be known for my mind, I want to be known for my body, like when I'm horny. There's a time to be known for your body

and not to be worried about Bosnia. We can talk about Bosnia tomorrow morning over French toast.

What was your first job in the sex industry?

I actually go way, way back. I got my first job in the sex industry when I was fourteen years old, at a Renaissance Fair here in California in the drench-a-wench booth, which is a fancy name for kissing game. It was great. I was kissing all these guys with no worries, and there was no attachment. It was out in front of everybody. I got really good at kissing that summer. It wasn't until later on that I realized that was sex work, even though the clothes stayed on and there was no genital contact of any kind. It was still sensual and erotic in intent, and very sexual in nature, and I liked it. I really really liked it. But after that I didn't work in the sex industry till I was twenty-one, and got a job doing live lesbian shows in a peep booth in SF. That job was my first paying job in the sex industry; I was going to school five days a week, working one day a week. That was in 1983; by '84 I graduated to doing movies and dancing, and I've been there ever since.

So you were in school and working at the same time?

Yes, and I wanted to finish school because I wanted to be a midwife. I'm a radical child-birth advocate. That's actually how I got into my feminism—when I was eleven years old, I read about the natural birth movement and how it politicized women. So I went to nursing school to be a midwife. I am still a health care professional. And I also happen to be a sexual professional—instead of midwifing babies being born, I get a great deal of pleasure out of midwifing people's sexual birth experiences.

What was dancing like?

It was great because I got to eat pussy, suck titty, dance around naked, look at myself in the mirror, and I got to masturbate! If I looked real closely, I could sometimes see the guys masturbating. I got to see all these dicks, no hassles, no dating, no wondering if I was gonna get killed, raped, murdered, none of that. It was like Yea, this is fabulous. It's normal and natural to wanna look at naked girls; what's not moral or natural is the desire to hurt them. That's culturally induced. I knew it was possible to objectify and not disrespect, to objectify and not wish harm upon a person. I wanted to share a

331

pleasure. For me that's feminism. I grew up with "It's my body, I can do whatever I want to." It's my choice and not only could I say no, I knew also how to say yes. And for me, I wanted to get comfortable in my skin. I wanted to explore my exhibitionism because I didn't like being uncomfortable in my skin. It wasn't that I felt ugly. I just didn't feel at ease in my body yet.

How did you get comfortable with your body?
I was never particularly athletic, but I was very much into dancing as a creative thing. It also helps you get in touch with your body, helps you feel comfortable with your skin. You know yourself, you like it, you can move easily. I learned how to release the energy in my hips. I learned how to dance African and jazz style, then I learned how to dance sexually. The hard part was learning how to dance in front of one person and not crack up laughing with embarrassment and giggles. Then the next step was the stage. It took years from the time I started working on that part of myself until the time I did it, from thirteen to twenty-one to get to that point. I'd always wanted to be comfortable in my skin. I didn't know what I would have to do, but I wanted those feelings about myself—sexual confidence and sexual competence—and I set about getting that for myself. So for me it was a very wonderful journey, and I put myself through a lot of pain and a lot of growth, but I wanted it. I didn't care if it hurt to learn how to breathe. I knew I had to do it. It had to get done.

Did sex freak you out?
When I was twenty, I really feared, and was uncomfortable around, the sexuality of twenty-one-year-old men. I grew up in a time that said, on one hand, sex is very natural, like *The Joy of Sex*. But also, books by Susan Brownmiller saying, "Every man will rape you if he can," which was based on a fear and mistrust of lust. A feeling that sex was icky; that men and their cum were distasteful; that need and desire and urgency were something to be condemned. And that's just Victorian prudishness to its highest degree.

The more I am comfortable with my skin, the more I am comfortable with flesh, the more I am comfortable with my sexuality, the less threatening men are; because I understand it now. I look at twenty-one-year-old men and go, "Is that all it was? That's so sweet," cuz no one ever told me, "Put your hand on it. They'll calm down in five minutes. It's no big deal." Men stopped being so scary to me when I stopped being scared of sex.

Because I *had* sex. It was nothing they gave me. Nothing they did to me. It's something I did. And that was a powerful moment when I finally figured that out.

Why did you make the transition from dancer to porn star?
I was so ready for it. It's not like I went from being a topless dancer to porn movies. I was doing live sex—showing my pussy to men, talking about my clit and what I got off on, and how you can touch your girlfriend's pussy and make her feel better—and fucking myself onstage with a large black dildo.

So it was really not a problem for me. It was more a question of, "Am I ready for a permanent record? Am I ready to be written up in the history book? With stripping, you can just walk away, and no one ever has to know about that part of your life. I was more worried about the acting than the sex. I did it so I could start talking about sex from a point of view of experience. My first boy/girl scene was with Billy Dee. My first girl/girl scene was with Karen Summer, known as a very vocal girl in the early '80s, who had a nice furry treasure trail. It went from her navel to her tits. Sometimes they made her shave it off, sometimes she tried to keep it.

What's a day on the set like?
It's so personal. You come to work, you pick up your script, you say hello to people you know or you don't know, find out what the call time is, have some coffee, get made beautiful, pick out your costume, say hello to your coworkers, go to scenes, do your dialogue. Master shot, his POV, her POV, and eventually you kiss and take it from there. The basic rules: kiss kiss suck suck lip lip fuck fuck in that order. It's very cut-and-dried. If you have ambivalence about what you're doing, work is going to be difficult and draining—working with someone you don't know very well, that kind of thing. For me, I like sex with people I don't know, as long as I know my physical safety is taken care of. As long as I know I'm not gonna end up dead or in a ditch or in a closet by some wacko. I really love juggling all the things you need to juggle in the scene to make it look as effortless and passionate and real as a possible. His level

of horniness, time of day, hot or cold, hungry, tired, mom sick, car in the shop, cat died, rent overdue—all the things you have to figure out.

And he can't ever know it. You have to make it as easy on him as possible. I know a lot of people are gonna go, "Omigod, servicing men servicing men, eek!" but I'm servicing myself. If I make the scene more difficult when I don't have to, we all take longer to get to lunch. I'm there getting a crick in my jaw and a cramp in my knee. Who needs it? I like what I do and I'm gonna go out there and have fun with it. I have to admit I get a thrill, and I love the fact that I'm good at what I do. I love putting the guy at ease and putting a woman at ease, and bringing out and drawing out of them a good performance, because they are relaxed.

Is it more fun with women?
I especially like working with women. I can always get a good performance out of women, especially now that I'm a veteran. It's calming for a woman's first time because I can do it with love and affection and no emotional entanglements, and just give her the experience to let her know that her body works just fine. And she could go off and do it on her own. It's just wonderful having someone like a Stradivarius under your fingers going, "Do me, baby." It's like, "Okay, I will." There are a lot of genuinely affectionate, well-adjusted, touchy-feely bisexual women who love having sex for an audience. *It's great for people to work with.* There are still women in the business who are into it for the money, and it hurts their spirits, but there are probably two for every one of those women who have found their home, and are like people in an oasis, having the time of their lives.

Is it ever romantic?
It's relatively mechanical, it's not super duper erotic. There's not a lot of pre-ejaculate, actually, the way it would be in a session at home. The movies have very very little of that because the guys don't ever have a chance to be that turned on, truly aroused, because we're not making love; we are having sex, and we have five sex scenes to shoot today. So at that level there's a distinctly unromantic undertone to most professional productions. You want romance? You want real heat? It's easier to get real heat out of amateur movies, because people are doing it for the love of it.

It seems to me that the porn industry has come a long way since the days of the Mitchell brothers.

Commercial pornography is extremely corporate. There is a twenty-four-hour counseling available, life insurance, medical insurance, dental, that kind of thing. The business is just now twenty-five years legal from being criminal activity. There's a lot of old guard still in charge and there are people who will work you till you die. There's more and more guys getting into the business who are nice and good-looking so the ladies at home will have more fun watching. If you are in here to save yourself, there's plenty of people who will help you do that too. It isn't as monolithic as the antis will have you believe. It's a much more wide-open entrepreneurial field, almost like the Wild West. Anything goes.

How do you make sure your fellow actors aren't stinky?

Word of mouth and gossip in this business is very quick and rapid. Quite frankly if you get the reputation of being smelly you stop getting work cuz no one wants to work with you. People are hyper about showering, mouthwashing, and brushing teeth. The hygiene issue is a question of constantly raising consciousness with people, so they start demanding more and more protection for themselves. Condoms are permitted. Hey, it may cut into your work, but you are allowed to use them. As a producer/director/actress, I don't permit noncondom anal scenes in any of my movies, unless the people in question are an off-camera couple. Otherwise I don't think it's a good message to send.

What's up with HIV?

We all get tested once a month. You show me your test, I'll show you mine. A lot of people say the threat of HIV is so great, how could I possibly do this? Humans take risks for things we want to do. We drive without seat belts. We eat too much red meat. We drink too much. We smoke cigarettes. We parachute. We hang-glide. We do all kinds of things that are dangerous because we like what they do for us. However, I wouldn't take a stranger home and permit him to fuck me without a condom because I don't know his ejaculatory control; I know the ejaculatory control of the people I work with—they're a proven commodity, they cannot fail, they may not fail; they must, with plenty of time to spare, withdraw their penis and ejaculate somewhere else than inside my pussy.

So if I were a porn star, and I was feeling uncomfortable about my costar wanting to go freestyle, what would I do?

If it doesn't feel right, you have to bring it up to the director. You don't have to yell and scream, but pull the director aside and say, "Look, I know you say this is a shaving cup, but I don't buy it. I'm not gonna fuck the guy without a condom." These days, unlike three years ago, the director has no legs to stand on. Set your boundary, make your safety area your concern, and don't leave it in somebody else's hands to decide. You, as a mature woman who's not a victim, but an independent agent, are responsible for taking care of your safety boundaries, and that's an important lesson every girl in the business must learn (though some do take longer to learn that than others to learn it).

I can't do an interview and not ask for some tips!

I have a tape, 800-765-ADAM. It's "Nina Hartley's Guide to Better Oral Sex."

Come on!

The most important thing is two or more willing people. With fellatio, it's not about putting your mouth on it and going into pound-pound-pound. It's a question of putting your hands on it, playing with it, pulling it, stretching it, and talking to the person and looking up into his eyes and giggling and stroking it or maybe having them stroke it for you. It's about pleasing your mouth as much as it is about pleasing them. Your mouth has a tremendous erogenous zone. If you're having fun, they're gonna be hard; it's not a problem. Just as a woman can get dry and go wet, men will go up and down several times during a blow job. Don't trip on it! Two biggest problems women have with fellatio: if they touch it too gently it tickles and irritates, or if they grab on it really hard trying to make it hard. I get a lot of oral gratification from giving head. It feels so good in my mouth. I try this and I try that. So I'm having as much fun as they are.

What about cunnilingus?

With women you have to coax the pussy to come out and play. You realize that indirect stimulation of the clit is always much better than direct stimulation. Just because she has one, do not, repeat, do not pull the lips back and lean in. It doesn't work, it's not comfortable, it's painful, she will slap you. And any woman who sits there and lies there and doesn't moan or move or show him with her hand what she likes and then has the gall to say he's a bad lover, I just want to spank her. That is being childish. Men cannot read minds. They're totally thrilled to be helping out, their egos stay totally involved, its a win-win situation. I firmly believe it's up to the woman to get the sex she needs out of the guy. Most people desperately want to be present, and hopefully helping a woman, when she has an orgasm. It's the next best thing to having a baby. It's just tremendous. The more you know about your response cycle, the more you can help the other person help you get there. Most important, don't trip on it. You cannot force an orgasm out of a woman. You cannot finger fuck her frantically enough to make her come. You must realize that oral sex, like all sex, is about the journey; not the getting there. You can't *make* her come. You can make it safe for her to come. You can only make the space so she'll feel safe enough to go for it.

What about masturbating?
Men, normally speaking, barring alcohol and other impairments, have a much easier orgasmic reflex. They practice it more. They masturbate more than women. The single best thing you can do to give better cunnilingus, the single best thing you can do to be a better receptor of cunnilingus, is to masturbate, masturbate, masturbate. Know your own sexual response cycle, know what you like, and be able to communicate that to the other person with ooohs and aaaahs. You are a grown-up girl now. You are having sex. You need to know what your body likes. Get in front of the mirror, masturbate, look at yourself in all stages of arousal. Prance around in your silk lingerie or whatever turns you on. You need to look at yourself in the mirror as a sexual thing.

Is watching porn a good stimulus?
Put a tape in the video, and when it gets to the part you like, pause and rewind, and go, "That move right there. I like that same thing." With guys, be able to articulate to her what you like: "I like it when you suck the head off." Porno really helped me a lot to get over the embarrassment of saying I want you to ____ my ____. Once I realized I needed to say, "Oh yes, suck my clit a little more, oh yes," they would do it.

What's a turnoff?

I used to bark orders. People could not wait to leave me. It took me years to realize I must have sounded like a fucking witch. But then I learned how to talk in bed. "Omigod," I'd say, "to the left, no to the left, more to the left, to the left, gentle, oh yeah, like that." I'd get exactly what I needed.

Do you have a fetish?

I do admit to one fetish—Barbie doll high heels. I grew up with Barbie, and while I did leave her naked and tortured and tied up half the time, she had the coolest shoes—these little Marilyn Monroe things. I really admire the twenty-somethings to this day. You can wear the riot grrl gear, and the cool shoes, and the big army boots, the flat shoes, and I have to admit I don't have the nerve to wear those kinds of things, because I still love the stiletto heel thing. But there you go.

As a veteran of the porn industry, what can you bring as a producer-director that has not been done before?

Feeling. Everything's been done before, every combination, every possible grouping, every possible act, every possible setting, every possible plot, it's all been done before. It's kissing, licking, sucking, fucking, solo masturbation, girl/girl, boy/girl, girl/girl/boy, boy/boy/girl. That's all there is. I'd bring the woman's point of view. There are things I want to say sexually. More women are directing and producing porn than ever before, a lot of them for themselves, in amateur films, and the longer it goes on, the more it will happen. Candida Royalle was the first person to identify the women's and couples market. She created it, identified it, went out and did it. Many people have tried to copy her, but she still is the one and only original. My new movie with her is called *The Bridal Shower* (from Adam and Eve). I like producing and directing sex education films. I like the idea of gonzo—which is all sex, no plot, more cinema verité. And I like getting a good performance out of people.

You are very outspoken about gender issues.

The two big things I've come to realize, where I believe strongly the early feminist movement got lost, were creating this monster of objectification, and also not realizing the evils of patriarchy. In the first flush of anger, they weren't able to see that in a class society, most men are victims of patriarchy, as well as all women. Actually, because of our pussies, women are given tremendous tools for at least getting their own out of the patriarchy, if they're willing to use it. I'm not saying it should be that way, but I'm saying it is. We have to get past this. Somebody has to be the nurturer in our culture. Somebody has to be able to take care of the hurt feelings. And I've started feeling tired of being resentful of men in my life. It's wearing me down without giving up anything of myself. Most guys our age are as clueless as women are. They're walking around wondering what the hell is going on, and how they're gonna fit into the gender roles, and most of them don't benefit from the patriarchy any more than we do.

What's your biggest gripe about the way some feminists view sex work?
For me, my big rant with the feminist movement these days is that if they cannot legitimatize the existence of sex work as a pay field, we will not get anywhere. We have to stop making sex a battlefield. So many of the old-wave feminists are shown to be very humorless, very joyless, and there's truth to it. I really think the feminists of today would do very well to embrace a little more of the sex radicalism, the ultimate sex positiveness in their own lives. It helps you reach joy and understanding, letting go of the anger. If you can cultivate pleasure and joy in your life, and if it happens to be from sex, so much the better.

Okay, how do you feel about Kitty MacKinnon?
Don't even get me started on Kitty MacKinnon. A year ago, I would want to scream at her. Now I'd just look at her and shake my head and go "tsk tsk tsk," and say, "You know what, I'm really sorry you are that bitter and angry, cuz that's what it is. It's her fuel. It's what drives her. It's not that she is not smart, but I do believe she is deluded, and I do believe anger and fear and jealousy and resentment and frustration and out-and-out prudery are what drive her, are her motivating forces. Carol Queen writes in *Real Live Nude Girl* an absolutely fascinating essay where she talks about people like Catharine MacKinnon, and why they are the way they are. MacKinnon really does feel like she is helping women, while at the same time, she and Dworkin and their ilk silence women. They won't listen to our stories, our truths. Somehow a woman's ability to tell her own story, to talk about her own life, the teller of her own truth, is a no-go.

339

Let's talk about the power of pussy.

Women are given tremendous tools, if they're willing to use it. We have to stop making pleasure, having fun, procreation, getting nasty and horny the enemy here. Even if I wasn't in the sex biz I'd still be a sex radical, I'd still be a swinger, I'd still be a bisexual, I'd still be a femme top. I'd still be exhibitionist. I got the first edition of *Our Bodies, Ourselves* for my thirteenth birthday when I had my first period and it was the most powerful book I'd ever read next to *Sex for One,* which I got when I was fourteen and it saved my life. Sex is enlightening. The reality is that once a woman knows that the pleasure goddess is at the end of her arm then she can swing her hand in front of her crotch anytime and whoops! there it is, anytime she wants. It's really easy—let's see: teddy bears, folded blankets, Jell-O's, washing machines, Jacuzzi jets, vibrators, cunnilingus, fucking, ooh, lots of things can do it. Women are denied pleasure because pleasure is very, very powerful, very very potent. You're no longer at the mercy of men when you understand that. It lets you see clearly and it makes you powerful, makes you confident in your sexuality.

Oh, Yoko

by Larry Marotta

It's just after midnight and my wife and I are watching TV. We switch to VH-1 just in time to see a rerun of an old episode of that quintessential '70s gem, *The Mike Douglas Show,* featuring none other than cohosts John Lennon and Yoko Ono. We are fascinated, shocked, repulsed, and utterly amazed all at the same time.

Yoko did most of the talking. First she led the audience in a primal scream therapy session. Mike displayed Yoko's current work in progress: a canvas sat in the studio all week upon which guests and audience added drawings and doodles. Mr.

ex-Beatle did little more than take orders from Yoko, mainly laboring to assemble a broken teacup for the camera in the name of conceptual art.

"No wonder why they hated her," my wife comments matter-of-factly.

She's right. Yoko Ono is hated. And it is exactly this woman who I am going to nominate for goddesshood. After all, being hated is kinda sexy in a way. In fact, one of the things that attracted me to my wife in the first place is that my fellow bandmates at the time were afraid of her.

But calling Yoko Ono a goddess is setting yourself up for ridicule. And for a skinny white-boy rock guitarist like myself, it can appear like the chickens erecting a monument to the Colonel.

This is because Yoko Ono is one of the most reviled figures in our popular lexicon. She is the supreme temptress: after all, she broke up the ultimate boys club, the Beatles. She is the supreme dominatrix: she turned the angry rock-and-roll voice of his generation into an Alan Alda–like, card-carrying feminist Mr. Mom. She is the supreme charlatan: a bizarre, no-talent poseur who wreaked her goofy pointless "art" in the wake of a supremely gifted spouse.

In any event, I'm going to be called onto the carpet by many for this act of heresy. Yoko? A goddess? It's certainly something I couldn't safely announce to a room of strangers. So, how does one clear Ms. Ono-Lennon's rep?

First of all, let us recall what an incredibly cool artist Yoko (who's name means "ocean child") was, and is. A lot of what we are led to believe about her is the result of pop culture versus the avant-garde, Mop-Tops versus Fluxus, Mike Douglas versus John Cage. We are dealing with the sorts of people who prefer van art to Jackson Pollock.

Far from riding on John's coattails, Yoko was a successful artist in her own right, a pioneer in a field that did not include many women (let alone Asian Americans). Starting in the late '50s, she gave performances which combined radical music and theater in her Greenwich Village loft, events that were given clout by the attendance of artists like John Cage, Andy Warhol, and Jasper Johns.

And the ideas she was dealing with were not going to reach the average audience, either. While her future husband was wanting to hold your hand, Yoko was writing about imaginary cities that contained devices like word vending machines, traffic lights which ordered "Dream" and "Fly" instead of "Stop" and "Go," and a parking problem solved by putting signs on cars that said "This is not here." These are ideas that stood in a stark Eastern contrast to the dense pop complexity of *Revolver* or *Sgt. Pepper.*

Let's face it, her vision was just too cool for most folks. For example, the Zen koan–like art suggestions compiled in her book, *Grapefruit,* are simple and powerful because they offer so many possibilities and so many ideas. "Lighting Piece" suggested, "Light a match and watch it until it goes out." Or "Painting to Hammer and Nail," which asked the reader to "Hammer a nail into a mirror, a piece of glass, a canvas, wood, or metal every morning. Also, pick up a hair that came off when you combed in the morning and tie it around the hammered nail. The painting ends when the surface is covered with nails."

Then there was the infamous painting featured at the gallery where she met John. Mounted on the ceiling, it was blank except for the word "yes" printed on it, which only became visible using a magnifying lens, and then after the viewer had ascended a ladder. They all laughed, but it is beautiful, a sublime affirmation. It's so simple, it's so heavy. Put into the hands of a shallow, blockheaded press, such works could easily be made to look trivial.

And, as far as this breaking-up-the-Beatles thing goes, that's sexism talking. Has your boyfriend ever taken you to band practice? Then you know what I mean. Somehow, like Yoko, you are violating some deep, intense male bonding ritual. Now, I'll admit the scenes from *Let It Be* where John and Yoko are glued together in the studio while the Beatles are recording are kind of annoying. But there are greater things that broke the Beatles up: poor management, lousy business decisions, and just plain growing up. John married young. He actualized himself when he met Yoko. For better or worse, John realized the limitations of the pop medium and found a universe of other topics to explore. Likewise, once Paul met Linda, he stopped being the gentleman dandy, the teddy bear he was, now letting his hair and beard grow. John became what he always was down deep: an everyman rock-and-roll singer who spoke for his generation, while Paul became the consummate popmeister à la Wings.

Ultimately, what people couldn't stand about John and Yoko was their relationship. They couldn't understand how their god was pussy-whipped by a small, strange, daringly nonsubordinate Asian woman. John went from spouting lines like "I'd rather see you dead little girl than to be with another man" to "Woman is the nigger of the world." When Yoko felt that John needed some emotional growing up to do, she kicked his ass out of their house and set him up with another woman just so he could sow his wild oats. And when he returned, presumably drained of excess testosterone, John played house husband to son Sean, letting his recording career go by the wayside for five years while Yoko wore the proverbial pants of the family.

Now there's a woman of power, a goddess. No wonder why they hated her.

If you're with me so far, but the artworks are still not your cup of tea, then her music is a good way to appreciate her. It is as a musician that she has had the biggest impact on me. Laurie Anderson, Diamanda Galas, Lydia Lunch: these are women who have entered the art world through the door Yoko Ono helped open.

For me it's the voice, that visceral wail, that shriek, that just speaks of such pain, anger, and passion. It's a sound that slices into your head, your soul, and wakes you up. It was punk before punk, only much more intense than most people want to deal with.

"She delivers with such emotion," said the British mag *Melody Maker* in 1972, "that you think she's going to end it all right there on stage."

Definitely check out her 1995 album *Rising*. You can listen to the goddess moving into a new realm as the older survivor, supreme mother artist. Losing a husband/soul mate and being the target of journalistic derision have transformed her voice into a supreme caterwauling cry, a weapon. On the opening track, "War Zone," you'd have a hard time believing that this woman is now more than sixty years old. Hell, she's older than my mom.

Rising gives me strength like nothing else. Through it, I realize that I need never fear growing old, that age is only a mental thing. I have friends who were dead by the time they were twenty-five, and here Yoko is, rocking as heavy as bands like the Jesus Lizard or Sonic Youth, screaming at you to wake the fuck up.

Yoko is everything I think a goddess should be: strong, maternal, creative, successful, and a bit bizarre. And, like many strong women, she will be hated for it.

Would You Want This Man to Be Your Dog?

Interview by Areola

If you had to ask me or any of my *BUST* friends to name the sexiest rock star ever, we would surely all say Mr. Iggy Pop. Forget those bubblegum pop stars, Iggy is what our cool older cousins and brothers listened to while we were growing up. He's wiry, tight, sexy, dangerous—not to mention the original punk rocker! I was ultra-nervous about spending the afternoon with my idol, but soon found out that Iggy is warm, incredibly humble, and an all-around nice guy.

A: So, you got a chance to look at *BUST* . . .
I: Yeah!

A: So it's like, a lot of women, right . . .
I: Yeah, I know, I read it.

A: So, my first question is, since this issue that we're doing now is the "Men" issue, is there a particular man that influenced you?
I: A particular man? Oh, wow! Rock stars, probably. Seeing Jim Morrison was a big influence, and, other than that, the thugs I went to high school with, very much.

A: Were you a thug, too?
I: No, I wasn't a thug! I was bordering on nerd, and I always admired the thugs.

A: How old were you when you saw the Doors?
I: Nineteen. They played the homecoming dance for the University of Michigan. The guy was stoned out of his mind, and was singing in a falsetto voice. He refused to play the songs properly, which the band couldn't play anyway, and his eyes were just giant pupils. He was out of his mind on some psychedelic, I'm sure; he was insulined to the point where they had to leave the stage after like fifteen minutes or they would have gotten their asses kicked. They had just had their first hit single, and I loved the fact that he basically gave the finger to five thousand guys who used to kick my ass,

The BUST Guide to the New Girl Order

and I thought, "This was great." At the gig I ran into this little French American chick that I used to fancy, and I just remember that during the gig I was humping her.

A: Had you started the Stooges by then?

I: I had the Stooges. And we did not have the balls to get out and do it. There were two things that made us do it; one was seeing that show, we saw that show and I just thought, well, this is so brazen, there is no excuse for us not to do it anymore. And the other thing was we went to New York. We had gone to New York a couple of months before that just to check out the scene, and we had never been to a place like New York. I was loaded out of my mind, and we went down around Eighth Street there, where all the young tourists hang out, and we met these girls from New Jersey, from Princeton, they had a band called the Untouchables, and we're like, "Oh, you've got a band, sure, ha ha ha," and they said, "Well, come to our house and see us play." And we didn't have anywhere to crash, and they let us crash, and they played for us, and they completely rocked, and we were really ashamed. We were like, "Ah, fuck!"

Other than that, I had a teacher, who was most probably gay—I didn't think about that at the time—and he encouraged me. He was like, "You can do this," you know, and he really made me feel like what I wrote was of interest, like I had a talent.

A: What about women? Are there women who influenced you?

I: The Ronettes. Ronnie Ronette, and also the girl in the Shangri-Las. When I was a teenager I used to get pickup gigs, to drum once in a while, and I actually drummed behind them once. Man, she was so cute, I was just like, "Ah, man." She was like really, really cute. She had a certain kind of complexion where the color of her hair and the color of her skin and the color of her eyes were all about the same, this indeterminate sandy look, and it really looked cool, it really looked great. Girls like that. And basically what really used to influence me were girls that were in high school when I was in junior high, which means, their look was like beehive hair, big pointy bras, wasp waists, and then you'd have a skirt, I don't know what the line is called, but it made their asses look really wide. This was very fantastic, you know, it was just like, "Wow." It kind of went with the cars, y'know, the Cadillacs and everything at the time. The big fins, big chests . . .

A: Have you ever had any women in your bands?

I: I don't think I've ever done that, no. The closest I came was there was a gorgeous chick, who was a good simple player too, and I met her one night jammin' with Bad Brains at A7, back when this neighborhood was really bad—that was in 1981 or '82. I can't even remember her name. She was super hot, and I was hanging with her, sleeping with her, for like a couple of weeks. But she had a bad habit—she liked heroin. She got my Telecaster. But no, I don't think I ever have. I've worked with them before, but I don't think I've ever had them in the band. I think I could now, at this point. In fact, I may use a keyboard the next time I go out because there's a lot of my stuff I can't cover without it. And if I did, there's some girls that know how to play that, 'cause I hate guys that play licks, you know? A lot of the best bands now are girls, anyway.

A: Why do you think that is?

I: It's shifted right now because what's happened is that the men have gone bankrupt. It's a down period for guys and they don't know what the fuck to do. Whereas the girls are somewhat fresh to it, and also people aren't used to looking at girls in that role, and, you know, they look better. So you can see them and go, "Oh wow, that's interesting." You know, I paid $2.50 last night to see the Elastica video on "The Box." That's the first time I've ever paid, but I wanted to see it, you know, I wanted to see that video. I know those girls, I went to their gig, and I want to see what it looks like. I think it's just a time-link thing, I don't think that's necessarily gonna last. I think it just means that, in the end, it can equal, it will balance out. Or else maybe everyone will just stop doing it, and do something else. They'll all get bored! [Laughs.]

A: You have a son? Do you have two kids, or just one?

346

I: No, I just have one kid—apparently—and he's going to community college in Prescott, Arizona.

A: Do you hang out with him a lot?

I: Not too much right now, but we did for quite a while. He was on one tour with me. The whole thing, and that was an interesting experience. He went pretty wild. He's a pretty nice-looking kid, he's a hunk, or whatever.

*The **BUST** Guide to the New Girl Order*

A: Do you think he's into doing music?
I: Nah, I don't think so. Uh-uh.

A: Now, I know you're married . . .
I: Yeah.

A: Well, a lot of the women who write for *BUST* have like, serious issues with men. You know, they're kind of pissed. What do you think about relationships?
I: Oh, you mean they have serious issues like, *against* men?

A: Well, not really, but you know . . .
I: Well, I think that's great, I mean, come on, let's compete, bitch! (Laughter)

A: Well, I mean, you know, sometimes guys can be kind of like, dogs.
I: Right, sure.

A: What do you think about relationships between men and women now in the '90s? Do you think it's the same as it's always been?
I: Well, I think that there's a wide range of ways that a human being will act toward another one given the chance. A very wide range. And then I think people are influenced by what they are taught is acceptable behavior, or "I can get away with it" behavior. On the other hand, you have this whole other issue, which is that there are some people who are just by nature more nice, or more interesting, or happen not to be, more brutal. I'm fascinated by the whole range of the whole thing. You know, like, my son's mother is gay. And she's a really cool chick, right, and I respect her. And I was with him the other day and we were in a cab, and we were out in like bumfuck land in Arizona, and this cabdriver says—what was it—oh, Melissa Etheridge was singin' and so I sort of went, "Wow, she can really belt out a tune." I wasn't sure it was her, and I said, "That chick's got a lot of voice," and the cabdriver went, "Yeah, her girlfriend thinks so too." And I went, "Whoa," and of course, it really offended my kid too, 'cause you know, he's sensitive to that. And we didn't say anything. I mean, I guess we were supposed to buddy in and say, "Hey, yeah," but we didn't. And this guy—he looked just like a normal human being, I guess; he looked clean [laughter]—

347

he actually said, "Yeah, when I read that it made me sick. It made me sick." And I was like, "Whoa," y'know? So that would be, I guess, an extreme case of, like, certain guys I went to school with who were like, "All you can do is fuck 'em and that's it." And that was never my orientation.

When I was young I learned a lot from women. I had more girl friends when I went to high school than guy friends, really, and mostly what we'd do is play records after school, 'cause that's what I was into. It was fine until once I got a job to chauffeur the Rolling Stones. I only got the entourage, I didn't get the band, but I was driving the courtesy car. This was in '65, I was a senior, and I took two of my girl friends to the concert, and as soon as we got there they were like, "Oh my God," screaming and crying, and they're just crying real tears, pouring down their face, there's like five or six thousand girls crying at once, and I was really impressed. And I remember thinking really clearly, they don't see this the same way I do. Although, maybe they did, but here's probably the difference: because of my sexual role, I was empowered to think I could do something about it. I could be that guy up there. To them, that was far enough removed that all they could do was scream about it.

Now there's a good side and a bad side to that, because it's a shame that no one screams now—that that's gone.

A: I think the teenyboppers still scream.
I: Yeah? Is that still going on? I've never seen it the same way as it was. I think people are getting more blasé toward that thing. I think it's great when people think they can access things. What I don't think is great is when people think that the things that they have to access are so completely dumb-ass and horrible, which is usually what happens. For me, you know, I've gone all different ways. I've had like those friends that I had in high school, and then I've had periods when I've just strictly gone through rock-doggism. And also periods when I had, like, a lot of unrelationships. I just wanted somebody for the sex, or I didn't even know why I wanted them around, and then as soon as I got any hint of what the person was like, or even if they were like *anything*, I was like, "Get out of here!" You know, at this point, I check everyone out and everything, but I don't feel entirely correct, you know.

348

A: I know you spent some time with Nico. Tell me about her.

I: She was wonderful. She was the first girl who told me, she said, "You know, there's something very nice you can do for me." I was like, "Oh yeah, what's that?" [Laughter.] "Oh, let me show you," she said. I thought that was pretty funny, pretty hilarious. She was like, hanging out with her was like fucking your older brother. She was about ten years older than me; she was thirty-one, and I was twenty-one. And so, it was like somebody older and a lot hipper and very strong in her opinions and also incredibly fucking talented. The album she had just made at that time was just a phenomenal piece of work. So she had that, and then she was highly eccentric and also dangerous, and at the same time, where the dangers came in too, was that she was very vulnerable.

She was wild, she was a boheme, she was serious about her art, and I just welcomed the chance. I hung out with her day and night for about a month; a couple of weeks here, and a couple weeks there, and then, inevitably, the strain. There's a certain strain when you're trying to create with your mind, especially when you're very young, it comes with a lot of serendipity. It's difficult to have somebody around, and so there was turbulence there, and the band of course really wanted her out, they were jealous, and they would walk around the house imitating her accent and stuff. She would come to our rehearsals and she'd tell me what she thought of the shows, my haircut, and every other damn thing. It was highly provocative, and I did probably my most destructive stream of shows; one of my most destructive periods was right around that time. A lot of people, other people besides me, were getting hurt. I was learning how, she taught me how, to drink. She was like, "Don't drink that Ripple!" I mean, I thought Ripple was like a good wine, you know? I got, like, "Wow! Beaujolais! This is great!" Prefiguring Marla Hanson's situation, she had cut someone with a broken glass about that time. Someone who she thought provoked her, someone very socially correct. She gave 'em a little slice, you know. It was not as litigious a country at that time, so, I didn't know, maybe there wasn't serious scarring, but there was this other side to her, you know, a you-better-not-fuck-with-me side, although I never . . . I mean, she was bigger than me.

She didn't do any drugs then. Neither of us did. I would smoke my grass, she would drink her wine. That's probably why she was with me, because I didn't do that stuff, and I didn't realize it. And so, she was probably running away from something.

That's pretty possible. But she knew how to dress, and she was one cool chick. After that I came back to New York to do some gigs—we had progressed and we were starting to play more like we played on *Funhouse,* a harder sound—and a little time had gone by, and I came to stay at the Chelsea. She was staying there, and she—she always had a cute man around—she had some new man, a French guy, and I was kind of like, "Who is this French guy, anyway? What are you doing with some French guy? Who's he? Let's have a look at him," and I went to visit her in her room. I was really excited to see her, and she was sitting there, she had a harmonium. I'd never seen her play her harmonium, it was just a little thing, about three feet long and about three and a half feet high, and she's playing on it, and she played this song, "Janitor of Lunacy," which is on one of her records, and she sang the words: "Janitor of lunacy, paralyze my infancy." Just like, you know, very good poetry, just kind of like hearing her doing that right there, complete, in the Chelsea, and that was the way it was gonna go on the record. I was very very impressed with that. And I also knew that she was going farther and farther from the New York counterpart of the swinging London scene, she was going off the let's-be-happy-pastel-videos mainstream. But she was great.

A: Yeah, it's too bad she's not around.
I: Yeah, well, I saw her later, and we had our differences. I got stoned with her many years later on some heroin and it was not pleasant, she did not look well, and I did not react well, and I wasn't such a gent about that and so there's some regrets there.

A: Did you ever have any male groupies?
I: Yeah, I had a very intense and interesting bunch of male groupies. And I'm really perversely proud of it in a way, 'cause in the '70s when I was my baddest, when I was absolutely . . . it was just after *Raw Power* had been out, and it was down in the 30-cent bins, and I was dropped by the record company, suspended by the management, and I had nowhere to live, and I was also the most hardcore performer in America. And these guys, these fags from San Francisco decided, "He's the one." I mean, basically, they just wanted someone to party around with. They started this Iggy Pop fan club and they sent me this package with all these good drugs, which was really bad 'cause I would take them all.

They were basically these San Francisco gay junkies who were living on ATD, which is Aid to the Totally Disabled, which means they'd get a really big check from the government, and they were hustling. That was the first time I ever saw the word "hardcore" applied to music, basically it was "Iggy Pop Fanclub Harare." They publicized in things like *Creem* magazine: "Send in your money and you get a silver membership card," but these guys basically just liked to party and have a good time and they'd indulge me in whatever adventures I wanted to get into. Sometimes that would turn out really good. They'd do stuff like get me a photographer's roll, you know, like a big roll of that paper, and rent me the stand, and I'd paint for a week while they'd make me stuff, and it would be really cool stuff, and sometimes it would be really sordid, and once in a while, once in a while, if I was like really asleep and they didn't think I was watching or anything they'd come and they'd try to pull my nuts. And I'd go, "No! Get off me! God, you boys." But I liked them, because I'd never been a big fan of Butch America, it's just too fucking stupid, and they were culturally really aware and I dug that.

A: Do you have any favorite female bands?

I: There's something really nice about Slant 6, there's something really attractive about that bunch, but on the other hand, I've seen them play live, and it was pretty shaky, but they've got something that's just attractive, and I dig that. There's something spooky about them. Die Cheerleader was good, I took them on my tour, that's who opened for me on my tour of Europe. I liked the first Liz Phair album a lot. I gotta say it was totally obvious that she saw she had to make the big dollar-onies and rushed out the second one, which absolutely is not up to the quality. Because it takes time to come up with stuff, generally speaking. And you could really tell the difference, and the quality went down, down, down. I can't picture being that age and what I was doing at that point and be in that kind of position where some major guy is saying, "C'mon, give us product right now, you'll make money." I don't think it was wise that she did that. Hole's a really, really good band.

A: What do you think about Courtney?

I: She was fine to me. I met her at somebody's gig—the Lemonheads gig—she was hanging around. It was the first time I'd seen her play; she came out and did two

351

songs alone. And it was very, very high quality. It's very hard to do, to deliver a song alone. Particularly to a large room, particularly one that's just been through a rock concert, but she did it. That is a genuine talent, to be able to deliver the serious goods. I'd heard, you know, "Oh, she's a terror," and you know, I'm really experienced with divas, I know lots of them, so I thought, "Oh God, it's gonna be diva-time," but she wasn't diva-esque, which I really enjoyed. She was just sort of, regular, and, you know, la-di-da, and that was okay, on that level. And since then, like anyone else, if you see anyone ad nauseam in the media you start to get sick of 'em, I'm sure she knows that too, but she has something to sell out there right now, so she's gonna be as visible as she possibly can be to sell more units.

A: A lot of people think she's a lot like Madonna.
I: I think there's certainly a case to be said that there is a role for a blonde that was invented a long time ago and has been recycled into an American archetype. Marilyn would be one that everybody knows. There is a blonde role and somebody has to fill that role, and Courtney's doing it right now, and Madonna did it a little before her, and of course, the requirements—what you have to be able to fill that role—shift and change constantly, and she's done a good job of seeing what that is, and doing it.

I mean, to me, that sort of thing is ultimately not gonna be as interesting as what the music is gonna sound like five years from now. That'll be more interesting, to see how it sounds after a while, y'know. What's happening right now, the way I see it, with the rock-and-roll bit, is that the means of disseminating it and selling it has become so efficient and so large that everybody goes overboard on whatever's happening at the time. Everything inevitably is overrated the way Guns N' Roses was, and I think Nirvana was, frankly, and people don't realize it yet. And that's really good, solid music, too, but people tend to get on this hypnotized tangent and then later things will look different. So I'm more interested in how it looks up the line, because I'm older, and my orientation is different, and it will be really interesting to see the ups and downs. 'Cause I've seen so many come and go now. I can remember idols from twenty-five years ago that absolutely, like, if they shit, people wanted to eat it and wear it, and now, nobody cares. So, it's interesting.

A: When you're performing, are you out there, are you in another place?

I: You mean, what do I think about? [Laugh.] Well, the worst is when you think about something like, "Oh God, I left my pants in the other suitcase," or, "Oh God, that guy owes me $15 and he hasn't paid me in four years!" Once in a while that'll creep in but not usually. No, I'm not out there at all.

A: You don't sort of get into another plane? I mean, sometimes it seems really intense.

I: I would say, only in the sense that I concentrate. When it's good, I have the ability to concentrate entirely on what I'm doing. I don't think many people experience that. I mean, even to listen to music, to actually really listen to music is really hard. People think they do, but many people don't; the music's on, but they're really thinking about who can they pull tonight, or, "I'm hungry, I want some food," you know, whatever, "Am I cool?" And I'm just thinking about what I'm doing and really reacting to it. I really get into, like, "Oh my God, that guitar, what a rush!" Or, "Shit, I don't hear the guitar. Let me move over three steps . . . ah, that's better," or how the thing feels, I'm sort of into that, y'know. What's happening at that moment, basically. It's like flying kind of, I guess.

A: A lot of people see your performances as being very sexual, almost kind of like the way a woman would be onstage.

I: Hmmm . . .

A: Do you think about that?

I: No, but that's interesting. It feels like a place where a lot of stuff can come out, basically. You know, all sorts of stuff can just come out there which is really, really nice.

A: Do you ever get backlash for that type of thing?

I: Oh God, yeah, totally. Nobody really went along with what I was doing for the first fifteen or twenty years. Nobody was going for it. And it was like, some people would wanna kick my ass, which happened a few times, but not really when I was playing, it was when I'd be out and around just being myself. And the closest I ever came when I was performing was once I did a gig where the Allman Brothers' roadies opened for me, in Nashville, and [the crowd] chased me and the guitar player into the toilet, and they were pounding on the door. "You guys got pussies or what? You got pussies, c'mon, we want your nice pussies!" And I was like, ah, mmm, 'cause we had a lot of makeup and stuff.

Basically what would happen is I would just think, yeah, this looks cool, and sure, part of it would be sexual, and this feels cool, and there would be a lot of different things mixed in. A lot of it was from watching cats and dogs, and how they act and move too, and just all kinds of things: watching other performers, what mood you're in that day. Sometimes it switches and I get real angry, like if I'm in a bad mood, I start breaking shit, y'know. And it just comes in a lot from the music and how it makes you feel. If you get attention it gets your adrenaline up. When I first started playing I would look in the room, and it was like it was a cutout, nothing really moved until we were done, or sometimes someone would just say, "I'm determined, I'm gonna do something," and that would always be a negative, that would generally be some guy that wanted to give us the finger or hiss.

That sort of stayed for a long time, and I just got used to the fact that that's how it was, and so a lot of people would come and like us, but there was no joining in. And then all of a sudden, I sort of dropped out of things for a few years, and then capital-P punk happened, and then I went out and did a gig and all of a sudden they were all doing what I do, they were all spitting and pogoing and doing all this stuff and it was a whole different ball game.

A: **What did you think of that?**

I: I was shocked. I didn't like the spit all over me. I was like, ewww. I played a gig in London and Rat Scabies was in the front row—I didn't know he was Rat Scabies then—and he could pogo really high enough so that he could get up and get a good aim and then he'd spit on me; I mean, I was just covered in gob. And it pissed me off, but after a while I'd just roll with it and go, "Hey, I used to spit on people," and I could be really assholey too if I got stoned enough. Anybody can. Especially when I got older and got in my thirties, cause thirties I think is a horrible age for guys who do what I do. It's when you start losing your baby looks, and so you go through this whole fucking number, and you have to shift, and it's a hard shift.

354

A: You've still got your baby looks, though.

I: Well, you know what I mean. You're not all cute and pretty, and all of a sudden your going, "Aaah . . . ," you know.

A: Do you have any music plans now?

I: I'm going away in a week to make my record. I'm all excited; I think it's really good. I did rehearsals for it and taped them up in Context, and it sounded really good and I've got the tape to prove it. I had to go through all this shit, like I had to hand in demos, because basically I was naughty and my last record was a hard sell. They were like, "No more of those. We don't want any more of those *American Caesar* records." But I'm really excited. And it's my same band, I managed to keep together a band, that's really important. It's starting to sound better and better; it's like anything else, you work on it enough, it'll get better. That's what I feel strongest about. While I was writing this stuff for this record—you know, you can't write songs all the time—I kind of did the start for another book. It's a sex book, it's all my sex life, and I wrote down fifty-two girls that I remember—because I thought there's fifty-two in a deck of cards, I thought, that's a nice number, right?—and whenever I'd remember one, I'd write it down, including totally explicit detail, exactly what I did with her, but also including the emotional side of it, and also weird shit that happened. I did ten of them and then I kind of put it away 'cause I have to get this done. But, it's kind of not bad, I mean I pick it up and go, "Oh my God"—it's a little, it borders on, like Geraldoism, and I don't want to get into that. It's kind of interesting to do that. I've got that going, you know. Those are the main things right now.

A: What about acting?

I: I did a little thing in *Dead Man;* I had a tiny part in *Tank Girl*. The best thing I've done is this Spanish movie called *Atoyadero*. It may come out here sometime, it's not out yet, and I play the bad guy. A gunslinger of the future, kind of like a gay Yul Brynner type of thing, that's the best way I can describe it. I wear all black. They gave me a real Uzi, and they always kept my hair done up. It's a real sick, nouveau-Spanish film. It's really good; that's coming out.

355

A: What happened to the other Stooges?

I: Well, the two brothers, they get some checks from publishing and some small royalties and they have bands in Detroit, and one of the guys has a side line in B monster movies, but locally, I mean, infinitesimally low budget monster movies. They're eccentric people, you know.

One of the guys died, Dave Alexander, the original bass player. I'd kicked him out of the band 'cause he couldn't fucking play, well, at one point he just wouldn't do the work basically, and then he made a lot of money on the stock market, and drank himself to death. He died of pneumonia, complicated by alcoholism. He died in his twenties.

And Williamson, the last guitar player, he's done well; he's doing something in Silicon Valley, with computers. He's like sort of a tennis-playing BMW-driving, cappuccino-sniffing dude.

A: Okay, well, I ran out of questions. Thank you.

I: Thanks!

Are You There Judy? It's Me, Tori

Interview by Tori Galore

[At the time this interview was being conducted, Judy was writing *Summer Sisters*.]

Nervous? You bet. But different from meeting a dishy actor or famous rock stah nervous. More personal, slightly vulnerable. Like the nervous I get when I'm meeting Some-Guy-I-Really-Like's mother for the first time. Except in this case, the mother in question has known me longer and more intimately than any man. She saw me safely through puberty. My first bra. First period. First kiss. Omnipresent, silently winking. She was loyal and kept secrets. A true friend. So when she opened the door and welcomed me into her home, it was all I could do not to give her a big hug and thank her. Not that she would have minded. She is relaxed and chatty and . . . is it me, or do we immediately lapse into an age-old-gal-pals vibe, figuratively lying on the lime shag rug in my old bedroom, on our stomachs, gabbing. She slips off her shoes and, tucking under her feet, cozies into a big, wumpfy couch. I sit across from her, reveling in the glory of the setting sun which literally consumes her luscious Santa Fe–esque home on Manhattan's Upper West Side. She is fifty-eight years old, dressed comfortably, in great shape, sexy, cute, and smiles often as she talks. She looks fucking amazing, friends. Everything I imagined and yet not what I expected from someone of my mother's generation. Which I strain to remind myself of, because she was one of my best friends growing up. She was all our best friend.

Did you consciously set out to fill a void in young girls' literature?
I set out to do nothing, I didn't know what I was doing. I was desperately in need of something but I didn't know what. I was married when I was a junior in college. I had two children (a son and a daughter) before I was twenty-five. But that was what we did, and many, many young women growing up in the '50s did that, but then everybody didn't go cuckoo. And I think I would have, if I hadn't found this thing. I loved having babies, but I had to have something else. The women's movement was very late coming to suburban New Jersey. I didn't know anyone who worked, but I still had a deep personal need to be involved in creative work. That's what was missing from my life.

Why do you think you gravitated toward pubescent girls and not women your age?
Because that is what I knew best. That is what was real to me. That is what came back easily. You don't decide what you're going to write about, it just comes. I had, then, almost total recall of my childhood.

That's clear in your style, the nuances and details are so lovely.
I think when I was young, it seemed to me that there was every possibility. That I could do or be anything. And then somewhere after fifteen, it wasn't that anyone told me I couldn't, it was the shift in my life from identifying with my father, who made everything seem possible, who adored me and never told me I couldn't do anything.

He was the parent who was fun and he was the nurturer, he took more care of me when I was sick than my mother. I didn't want to be in the kitchen. I wanted to be the hero, the cowgirl, the detective.

And what switched at fifteen?
I think I began to identify more with my mother when I got into the whole dreamy adolescent boy thing with fantasies of growing up and getting married and having babies.

Which seemed less enticing than being a cowgirl?
No, I replaced my save-the-world fantasies with romantic fantasy. So maybe the romantic fantasy is the downfall of the young woman . . . hmmm . . . I don't know.

Was the idea of writing about being a woman in her late twenties, married with two children, just too terrifying . . . too close to home?
It never occurred to me. I wasn't ready for that until I wrote *Wifey*. That took a long time. Because I was living that life. I wasn't ironic about that life. It was "Oh shit, this is what I wanted and now I'm stuck with it." What do you do with that? I made these choices. I listened to my mother. I should have listened to my father. I had adult responsibilities, but I didn't feel grown up.

So, you're a wife and mother trapped in suburbia, spending all your free mind time writing about being twelve . . .
Yes, but that was more adult than anything else I was doing. That gave me a sense of my self. Writing saved me. It gave me a life.

Was *Wifey* [her first adult novel] a rebellion?
In the context of what was happening in the '70s, everybody was free to do all these things. I had never done anything and I wanted desperately . . . (pause). If my husband had said to me (and I don't think he should have), "Go out there, have sex with everybody, and anybody, get it out of your system, experiment, you have my blessings. . . . " I wonder what would have happened. I never had an adolescent rebellion, my brother was so rebellious that my role in the family was to make everybody happy. I'm still fighting that.

*The **BUST** Guide to the New Girl Order*

Photo courtesy of Judy Blume

Did *Wifey* rock the world of those around you?

I got zillions of letters from women. It made a lot of men very upset. But I was gone. Taking my two kids, then twelve and fourteen, I left my husband and moved far away, first to England, then to Santa Fe, and then I wrote *Wifey*.

If you hadn't left, do you think you could have written it?

I never could have written it when I was still in that marriage. But he and I are quite good friends now. And I think he handled it brilliantly. We never talked about it. I remember giving it to him, and asking, "If there's anything in here that really bothers you, I'll change it."

Before it was published!?

I think so. And he didn't say anything. He stayed out of it. I think that was really very smart. I admire him for that. *Wifey* was my coming of age. I thought, "I'm not just this twelve-year-old." It was time for me to deal with this other me. This woman . . .

—who had never been explored?

Right. And this life that my mother led me to believe I wanted left me unhappy. So it was a very freeing experience for me. A very necessary experience in my evolution.

Were you aware at the time that junior high students all over America were dog-earring the pages of *Forever* that contained the sex scenes and passing them around study hall?

Yes. Good. Well, what did you think when you read *Forever*?

359

I was overwhelmed, I was stunned. It was a little scary. I was maybe thirteen and sexually, a late bloomer. What you were describing was so out of my context.
Did you feel betrayed?

Yeah, I probably did.
Wow.

I remember telling my father that I thought I was the missing link of female genetics when I still hadn't gotten my period at fourteen . . . "When will it happen to me?" Reading *Are You There God? It's Me, Margaret* placated my fears, suggesting that I be patient. Now, I'm in a somewhat similar scenario as my friends pair off and have kids. . . . Do you feel any responsibility to have your characters grow up, for instance Margaret or Deenie, and negotiate adult relationships?
No, I don't want Margaret or Deenie to grow up. But I am writing a book about two women who become best friends at twelve, in 1977, and I take them through their thirtieth birthdays.

I think it's unfair for us to want you to come through for us—
—I'd love to come through for you. I love your generation. You're my first readers. You're my most loyal readers. I meet you at book signings and it's so unbelievably sweet. These young women come up to me and they look at me and I look at them and then we start to cry.

I've found the mention of your name elicits a visceral reaction from my generation—
I can't wait until you're all running the world.

There are going to be statues of you all over the place. Who were your female heroes growing up?
I don't know that I had them. Because who did I know who was out there doing things? . . . I didn't know any women who wrote. I didn't think of writers as being living creatures. I knew movie about stars and stage actresses. I wanted to be Margaret O'Brien dancing "The Unfinished Dance," I wanted to be Esther Williams. I wanted to swim underwater and smile at the same time, the way she did.

What about the women around you?

My aunt was a teacher and then a principal of a school. That was something back then! She was married but never had children. Miss Fae, who I thought was very glamorous, worked for my father, who was a dentist, for thirty years. She never married. She took me to the ballet. She had a roadster with a rumble seat. She smoked and could tell dirty stories with the guys. She seemed to me exciting. Although the reality was that she lived in a little house with her father and widowed sister.

She must have been a pretty powerful alternative to your mother.

My mother did not like it when Fae came and taught me how to put on mascara for the prom, because my mother never used mascara. Fae drank scotch on the rocks and my mother never drank. My mother thought that my father enjoyed being with Miss Fae a lot . . . maybe too much.

So as a girl on the cusp of womanhood, your immediate choices were between becoming your mother and becoming Miss Fae . . .

But my mother had the husband and the house and the children. I don't know . . .

Sounds like we're becoming a generation of Miss Faes. We're independent and confident. We have our own careers, and sexuality. We can smoke a cigar, tell a dirty joke, and throw our heads back when we laugh, but we're living alone.

So was Miss Fae. Maybe that's what I should write a book about. There's an idea. And also my aunt seemed to me quite independent and had all the books in the world.

So, does a woman have to choose between the Mother, Miss Fae, and the Principal or can she be all three women at the same time?

You can be all three women in your lifetime. I'm not sure you can be all three women at the same time. Can you have it all? Yes. Can you have it all at the same time? I don't think so. You can have successive lives

One of the issues that the women of our generation have with the men of our generation is with their mothers. In your book *Smart Women*, the character Margo says,

361

Herstory: Girl on Girls

"No woman would have been good enough for their son, which is why their son treated women like shit." Do you think that mothers of sons have a responsibility to train their sons to be the kind of men they would want in a partner?
I do. And I think it's very tempting to spoil your son. I think the mother-son relationship is very tight. But yeah, I think we should have that responsibility.

We discuss the differences in the generation of men she was supposed to marry versus the generation I'm supposed to marry, responsibility versus commitment, the evolution of male/female friendships, the insistence that mothers don't do their sons' laundry past the age of eighteen. I remark that it sounds like she's done a good job of raising her son.

So why isn't he married? Why isn't he having children?
He's waiting to meet the Mother, Miss Fae, and the Principal all rolled into one. Yes, well . . . waiting for that kind of perfection . . .

I also have this theory, that when people are really ready, the next one who comes along—
—yes, the next gal who walks by . . .

At this point, I pause to savor the moment. Hmmm. Moving on, we discuss her marital history. Married sixteen years to a nice, sensible Jewish lawyer as her mother had prescribed, Judy divorced and married the next man she met. She sums up those years as "incredibly stupid," having put not just herself through "four years of hell," but her kids, which she "can never forgive herself for." At the conclusion of her second marriage, she resigned herself to the notion that, at forty-one, she would never have that intimate relationship that she had "always chased." A couple of months after her second divorce, she was fixed up on a blind date. On their third date he moved in. They have been together seventeen years.

I was never single.

Do you regret that?
I think it would have been wonderful to have been single while I was young, like you, and have the chance to figure it all out, but then maybe I never would have figured

362

out anything. Instead I just rushed in. I gave much more thought to my first marriage partner than I did to my second or third. And my second was a disaster, and my third is heaven, it's everything that one could wish for. I get by in life a lot on instinct. I can't say that I recommend it.

Do you consider yourself a feminist?

Yes, I am a feminist. That doesn't mean I don't like men, I've always liked men. We are different, I accept that. Sooo different. But it's interesting to figure out those differences. I began to think for myself somewhere in my late twenties and thirties, I began to question my way of life, that authoritarian male society. I accepted it throughout my first marriage, I never tried to get my husband to change. *Fear of Flying* was a very, very important book to me at that time.

How?

I was becoming aware of the possibilities. My husband blamed *Fear of Flying* for my unhappiness, which is simplistic to say the least, the way many men blamed *Wifey*.

Do you have any regrets?

How can you live fifty-eight years and not have regrets? If you haven't made mistakes, there's something wrong. What's the point of mistakes if you don't learn from them? I don't have the regrets about things I haven't done, because I've done a lot of things. My regrets have nothing to do with unfulfilled fantasies because I've pretty much lived out those fantasies. Rather they have to do with any pain my choices caused those closest to me, which would be my kids. I wish they hadn't had to suffer through my mistakes. But that's a mother's guilt for being less than perfect. And it was all so long ago.

363

When are you happiest?

It's hard for me to say when I'm happiest. Most days I feel happy. The question is, when am I least happy? I'm unhappy when my kids are unhappy. I have a friend who has said to me, "A mother is only as happy as her least happy child." And I think that is absolutely true.

We wrap things up. She walks me to the door. At this point, thanking her seems insignificant, so I don't. Her husband arrives home and she beams. She reminds me of my best friends. A pleasant prophecy of afternoons to come. And a kind reminder of a puberty long gone, thank Goddess; I look forward to rereading her books with my teenager someday. Hell, I may not wait that long. I leave, wishing I'd thanked her.

Bibliography

BOOKS

Banner, Lois W. *American Beauty*. New York: Alfred Knopf, 1983.

Bly, Robert, *Iron John: A Book About Men*. New York, Vintage, 1992.

Bordo, Susan. *Twilight Zones: The Hidden Life of Cultural Images from Plato to O.J.* Berkeley: University of California Press, 1997.

———. *Unbearable Weight: Feminism, Western Culture and the Body*. California: University of California Press, 1993.

Bright, Susie. *Sexwise*. San Francisco: Cleis Press, 1995.

———. *Susie Bright's Sexual State of the Union*. New York: Simon & Schuster, 1997.

Brownmiller, Susan. *Femininity*. New York: Linden Press/Simon & Schuster, 1984.

Brumberg, Joan Jacobs. *The Body Project: An Intimate History of American Girls*. New York: Random House, 1997.

de Beauvoir, Simone. *The Second Sex*. Translated and edited by H.M. Parshley with an introduction by Dierdre Bair. New York: Alfred A. Knopf, 1953; reprint, New York: Vintage Books, 1989.

Douglas, Susan. *Where the Girls Are: Growing up Female with the Mass Media*. New York: Times Books, 1994.

Douglass, Marcia, and Lisa Douglass. *Are We Having Fun Yet? The Intelligent Woman's Guide to Sex.* New York: Hyperion, 1997.

Dworkin, Andrea. *Intercourse.* New York: Free Press, 1987.

Ehrenreich, Barbara. *The Hearts of Men: American Dreams and the Flight from Commitment.* New York: Anchor Books, 1983.

Ehrenreich, Barbara, and Deirdre English. *For Her Own Good: One Hundred Fifty Years of the Experts' Advice to Women.* New York: Anchor Books, 1978.

Ehrenreich, Barbara, Elizabeth Hess, and Gloria Jacobs. *Re-making Love: The Feminization of Sex.* New York: Anchor Press, 1986.

Faludi, Susan. *Backlash: The Undeclared War against American Women.* New York: Crown, 1991.

Firestone, Shulamith. *The Dialectics of Sex.* New York: Bantam Books, 1970.

Fisher, Helen. *The Anatomy of Love: A Natural History of Mating, Marriage and Why We Stray.* New York: Fawcett Columbine/Ballantine Books, 1992.

Friday, Nancy. *The Power of Beauty.* New York: HarperCollins, 1996.

Freidan, Betty. *The Feminine Mystique.* New York: Laurel/Dell Publishing, 1963.

Furstenberg, Frank, Jr., and K. M. Harris. "When Fathers Matter/Why Fathers Matter: The Impact of Paternal Involvement on the Offspring of Adolescent Mothers." In *Young, Unwed Fathers,* edited by R. Lerman and T. Ooms. Philadelphia: Temple University Press, 1993.

Giddings, Paula, *When and Where I Enter: The Impact of Black Women on Race and Sex in America.* New York: Quill, 1984.

Greer, Germaine. *The Female Eunuch.* New York: Bantam Books, 1971.

Heywood, Leslie, and Jennifer Drake. *Third Wave Agenda: Being Feminist, Doing Feminism.* Minnesota: University of Minnesota Press, 1997.

Hill, Anita. *Speaking Truth to Power.* New York: Doubleday, 1997.

Jong, Erica. *Fear of Flying.* New York: Signet, 1974.

Juno, Andrea, editor. *Re/Search #13, Angry Women.* California: Re/Search Publications, 1991.

Kaplan, Laura. *The Story of Jane: The Legendary Underground Feminist Abortion Service.* New York: Pantheon Books, 1995.

Lefkowitz, Bernard. *Our Guys: The Glen Ridge Rape and the Secret Life of the Perfect Suburb.* Berkeley, California: University of California Press, 1997.

Lemoncheck, Linda. *Loose Women, Lecherous Men: A Feminist Philosophy of Sex.* New York: Oxford University Press, 1997.

Lieberman, Carole, M.D., and Lisa Collier Cool. *Bad Boys: Why We Love Them, How to Live with Them, and When to Leave Them.* New York: Dutton, 1997.

Lord, M. G. *Forever Barbie: The Unauthorized Biography of a Real Doll.* New York: William Morrow & Co., 1994.

Ludtke, Melissa. *On Our Own: Unmarried Motherhood in America.* New York: Random House, 1997.

Lumby, Catherine. *Bad Girls: The Media, Sex and Feminism in the '90s.* St. Leonards, Australia: Allen & Unwin, 1997.

Lundarini, Christine, Ph.D. *What Every American Should Know About Women's History.* Massachusetts: Adams Media Corporation, 1997.

Mankiller, Wilma, et al. *The Reader's Companion to U.S. Women's History.* New York: Houghton Mifflin Company, 1998.

Mann, Judy. *The Difference: Growing Up Female in America.* New York: Warner Books, 1994.

Martin, Wendy. *The American Sisterhood: Writings of the Feminist Movement from Colonial Times to the Present.* New York: Harper & Row, 1972.

Mitchell, Sally. *The New Girl: Girl's Culture in England, 1880–1915.* New York: Columbia University Press, 1995.

Morgan, Robin, editor. *Sisterhood Is Powerful.* New York: Vintage, 1970.

Orenstein, Peggy. *Schoolgirls: Young Women, Self-Esteem and the Confidence Gap.* New York: Anchor Books, 1994.

Papachristou, Judith. *Women Together: A History in Documents of the Women's Movement in the United States—a Ms. Book.* New York: Knopf, 1976.

Peck, Ellen, *The Baby Trap*. New York: B. Geis Associates, 1971.

Peiss, Kathy. *Hope in a Jar: The Making of America's Beauty Culture*. New York: Metropolitan Books, 1998.

Pipher, Mary. *Reviving Ophelia: Saving the Selves of Adolescent Girls*. New York: Ballantine Books, 1994.

Politt, Katha. *Reasonable Creatures*. New York: Alfred Knopf, 1994.

Queen, Carol. *Real Live Nude Girl: Chronicles of Sex-Positive Culture*. San Francisco: Cleis Press, 1997.

Rapheal, Amy. *Grrrls: Viva Rock Divas*. New York: St. Martin's Griffin, 1994.

Reynolds, Simon, and Joy Press. *The Sex Revolts: Gender, Rebellion and Rock 'n' Roll*. England: Serpent's Tail, 1994.

Riophe, Anne. *Fruitful: A Real Mother in the Modern World*. New York: Penguin Books, 1996.

Rossi, Alice S., editor. *The Feminist Papers: From Adams to de Beauvoir*. New York: Bantam Books, 1973.

Rowbotham, Sheila. *A Century of Women: The History of Women in Britain and the United States*. New York: Viking, 1997.

Sexton, Adam, editor. *Desperately Seeking Madonna*. New York: Delta, 1993.

Sher, Lynn, and Jurate Kazickas. *Susan B. Anthony Slept Here: A Guide to American Women's Landmarks*. New York: Times Books, 1994.

Sidel, Ruth. *Keeping Women and Children Last: America's War on the Poor*. New York: Penguin Books, 1996.

———. *On Her Own: Growing Up in the Shadow of the American Dream*. New York: Penguin Books, 1990.

———. *Women and Children Last: The Plight of Poor Women in Affluent America*. New York: Penguin Books, 1986.

Smith, Joan. *Misogynies*. England: Faber and Faber Limited, 1989.

Solinger, Rickie. *Abortion Wars: A Half Century of Struggle, 1950–2000*. California: University of California Press, 1998.

———. *Wake Up Little Susie: Single Pregnancy and Race Before Roe v. Wade*. New York: Routledge, 1992.

Stan, Adele M., editor. *Debating Sexual Correctness: Pornography, Sexual Harassment, Date Rape and the Politics of Sexual Equality*. New York: Delta, 1995.

Steele, Valerie. *Fashion and Eroticism: Ideals of Beauty from the Victorian Era to the Jazz Age*. New York: Oxford University Press, 1985.

Steinem, Gloria. *Outrageous Acts and Everyday Rebellions*. New York: Plume, 1983.

Thurer, Shari. *The Myths of Motherhood: How Culture Reinvents the Good Mother*. New York: Penguin Books, 1995.

Tisdale, Sallie. *Talk Dirty to Me: An Intimate Philosophy of Sex*. New York: Anchor Books, 1994.

Tobias, Shelia. *Faces of Feminism*. New York: Westview Press, 1997.

Vance, Carol S., editor. *Pleasure and Danger: Exploring Female Sexuality*. Boston: Routledge & Kegan Paul, 1984.

Weatherford, Doris. *American Women's History: An A to Z of People, Organizations, Issues, and Events*. New York: Prentice Hall, 1994.

Weddington, Sarah. *A Question of Choice*. New York: Penguin Books, 1992.

Wilson, Elizabeth. *Adorned in Dreams: Fashion and Modernity*. Berkeley: University of California Press, 1987.

Wollstonecraft, Mary. *A Vindication of the Rights of Woman,* in *The Feminist Papers: From Adams to de Beauvoir,* edited by Alice S. Rossi. New York: Bantam Books, 1973.

Wolf, Naomi. *The Beauty Myth*. New York: Anchor Books, 1991.

Yalom, Marilyn, *A History of the Breast*. New York: Alfred Knopf, 1997.

ARTICLES

Breslauer, Jan. "Stacked Like Me." *Playboy,* July 1997, 64–68.

Arndt, Bettina. "Men Under Seige." *The Weekend Australia,* May 22–23, 1993. Based on a paper given by Bettina Arndt at the Sydney Institute.

Bellafonte, Ginia. "Feminism: It's All About Me!" *Time,* June 29, 1998, 48–54.

Daley, Suzanne. "Girl's Self-Esteem Is Lost on Way to Adolescence, New Study Finds." *The New York Times,* January 9, 1991, sec. B1.

Friend, Tad. "Yes." *Esquire,* February 1994, 48–56.

Gillespie, Marcia Ann. "Mirror, Mirror." *Essence,* January 1993, 73.

Johnson, Allan G. "Can Men Take Responsibility for the Patriarchy?" *Ms.,* November/December 1997, 60–63.

Murray, Charles. "The Coming White Underclass." *The Wall Street Journal,* October 23, 1993.

Powers, Ann. "The Male Rock Anthem: Going All to Pieces." *The New York Times,* Sunday, February 1, 1998, 46.

Schwartz, Felice, "Management Women and the New Facts of Life." *Harvard Business Review,* 67, Number 1 (January–February 1989), 65–77.

"Do Men Get It?" *Ms.,* November/December 1997.

"The Girl Issue" *Spin,* November 1997, 74–139.

Meet Some
of Our Contributors

Jayne Air lives in New York City. She has taught literature, film, and cultural studies classes at Yale and Parsons. She's written so many bitchy things about people and magazines she might need to work for some day that she can't use her real name here.

Areola (Laurie Henzel) is the Creative Director/co-publisher of *BUST* magazine and resides in the bohemian enclave of Greenwich Village in New York City with her husband, photographer Michael Lavine, and their two daughters, Olive and Penny. In addition to working on other graphic design projects, she has been known to haunt church thrift stores in search of the perfect Pucci bikini, and other scathingly brilliant artifacts to be had for under a dollar.

Isadora Bimba (Syma Sambar) is a Lebanese-Palestinian chick living in sin in New York City. After breaking all Arab social rules, she convinced her family that "ladies can do that, too." Coincidentally, her boyfriend is Jewish-American and, yes, tampons are a part of her regular menstrual routine.

Wendy Bott is a freelance writer living in Los Angeles, California.

Training Bra (Iness Moskowitz) has been a frequent contributor to *BUST*. When she's not trying to make her big hair smaller, she manages the creative department of an entertainment-branding company in New York. She loves going to the movies, long walks on the beach, and strawberry daiquiris. Unfortunately, much to her dismay, she's begun letting her friends touch her boobs again—all in the name of drama.

371

Lu Cashmere (Lucine Kasbarian) is a former New York City restaurant reviewer and United Nations correspondent. She writes for Manhattan-based magazines and is the author of *Armenia: A Rugged Land, An Enduring People*, published by Dillon Press (a division of Macmillan Publishing).

Jimmy C. A-Go-Go (Jimmy Cohrssen) is a New York-based photographer whose work appears in *Metropolis* and other magazines. He is very in touch with his feminine side.

Marni Davis is an aspiring American historian and, when her studies permit, a freelance writer and editor. She lives in New York City.

Scarlett Fever is a New York-based freelance writer. Her work has appeared in *BUST, Penthouse, Playgirl, Cosmopolitan, STIM,* and *Best American Erotica '95.* Under her natural born pseudonym, Jodi Sh. Doff, she is also a contributor to the upcoming *Without Child* anthology. She is currently not working on her memoirs.

Tori Galore Chickering is a writer and filmmaker whose essays and interviews have appeared in *BUST, Cosmo,* and the anthology *A Girl's Guide to Taking Over the World.* She has written and directed for MTV, Comedy Central, Lifetime, and PBS, as well as a short film starring Isaac de Bankole and a documentary on New York's alternative comedy scene. She is presently having a ball writing feature screenplays.

Girl (Fran Willing) is a painter who is only able to write for *BUST* under the pretense that she is sending off postcards to her bestest friends—which isn't so far from the truth. She lives on the Bowery, works at the best museum in the world, and she comes in colors.

Girlbomb (Janice Erlbaum) is a writer/producer in Brooklyn, New York, and has been a *BUST* contributor since 1994. A former founding member of two "spicy" third-wave phenoms, Pussy Poets and Minxmag.com, she has recently quit gender politics, and is currently building a holodeck in her apartment where everybody agrees with everything she says at all times.

Lisa Glatt's poetry and fiction has appeared in magazines and anthologies, including the *Indiana Review, Columbia,* and *Spelunker Flophouse.* Her book, *Monsters and Other Lovers,* was published in 1996 by Pearl Editions. She teaches in the Writers' Program at UCLA Extension. And no, she has never participated in "water sports," though her narrator in "Waste" did so that one damn time.

Michelle Goldberg lives in San Francisco with her boyfriend Matt and their pet fish. She's the arts editor of the *San Francisco Metropolitan* and a contributor to *Salon, Speak, The National Post* and *Avant-Guide San Francisco.*

Ester Gyn (Elizabeth Schroeder) is a health-care activist turned registered nurse. She's currently working as a home care nurse to elderly and pediatric patients, and is studying toward a Masters degree in nursing.

Mae Jest (Laura Herbert), when not actively pursuing her childhood dream of becoming the first Dallas Cowboys Cheerleader in Space, is a twenty-seven-year old web producer/digital prankster with a dangerous obsession for risque collectibles, pop culture phenomena, and self-deprecation. She discovered the beauty of *BUST* in 1994 and resides in a tiny, crap-filled apartment in New York City with her multi-colored beau, Elio, and Lucy, their four-legged lovechild.

Dixie LaRue is a gorgeous redhead who left her stint fan-dancing in the Congo after she tired of trading gunfire and snappy patter with the locals. Retiring to New York City as the deceptively mousy Sarah Feldman, she spends most of her time watching old movies—and eating a staggering variety of children's cereals. Currently sought for "questioning" by the authorities, neighbors describe Dixie as "quiet," "polite," and incorrigibly scantily clad.

Tiffany Lee Brown has always wanted to use that cliched bio: "Tiffany Lee Brown is a freelance writer living in New York." Well, now it's true. But she's the editor of *SIGNUM* (www.slm-net.com/signum.htm) and the assistant editrix of the *Fringe Ware Review* (www.fringeware.com) as well. Also known as Magdalen, her online pseudonym of seven years, Miss Brown sings and reads teen magazines in her copious amount of spare time.

Lust is an editor at a national consumer magazine. She writes about travel, cooking, and sex (and all combinations thereof). Her freelance projects have included writing for *Playboy*, Cosmomag.com, *Travel Holiday*, The Disney Channel, and *BUST*, of course. She's currently developing a book and dreams of working at *Dog Fancy*. She lives in New York City with two cats, a husband, and one cherished copy of Russian Master Dog.

Ann Magnuson is an actress, writer, singer, and part-time performance artist. She has appeared in such films as *Making Mr. Right* and *Clear and Present Danger* and co-starred on the ABC-TV sitcom *Anything But Love*. She continues to write and perform in one-woman shows and with her band in her terminally unique cabaret extravaganzas in both New York City and Los Angeles. For more info check out AnnWatch at http://www.burningboy.com/annland.

Lisa Miya-Jervis is the editor and publisher of *Bitch: Feminist Response to Pop Culture*. She has also written for *BUST, Hues,* and *Salon,* and the anthologies *Adios, Barbie* (Seal Press, 1998) and *I'm Too Sexy* (North Atlantic Books, forthcoming). She lives with her husband in Oakland, California, where it is her nightly habit to read *Glamour* and *Entertainment Weekly* while watching syndicated reruns of *Friends*.

Cassandra O'Keefe is an actress, artist, and writer. Prior to this publication, this piece appeared on refrigerators of single women worldwide. She is profoundly grateful to her beautiful daughter Shelan and her partner, Drew: her two true loves who led her from there to here.

Lisa Palac is the author of *The Edge of the Bed: How Dirty Picutres Changed My Life* (Little, Brown), the producer of the erotic Virtual Audio CD series *Cyborgasm,* and the host of www. lisapalac.com. She lives in Los Angeles with her husband, Andrew Rice.

Tabitha Rasa is known as Barclay A. Dunn in "real" life, where she works as producer for Entertainment Weekly Online. She has written for Enterzone (http://ezone.org/enterzone.html) as well as *BUST*—in the same confessional tone, but she still does not feel forgiven. She has been compared to kewpie dolls and Betty Boop. She never operates heavy machinery after taking soporific medicine.

James "Squeaky" Reling is a harmless cute-boy from the shiny Bay Area. He likes kittens and the Spice Girls. He once did a zine called *Static* and is now co-owner of Unamerican Activities, an organization dedicated to providing Quality Rebellion at Affordable Prices. Please E-mail him kisses at Squeakystatic@hotmail.com.

Amelia (Amy) Richards is a young feminist activist and organizer. She is a co-founder of the Third Wave Foundation, a contributing editor to *Ms.* magazine, and a research, editorial, and political advisor to Gloria Steinem. She is the voice behind "Ask Amy"—an online activist advice column located at www.feminist.com. Her writings can also be found in *Listen Up! Voices from the Next Feminist Generation, The Nation, Ms.* magazine, *The New Internationalist,* and *BUST.* In 1995, *Who Cares* magazine chose her as one of twenty-five Young Visionaries and in 1997 *Ms.* magazine profiled her as "21 for the 21st: Leaders for the Next Century."

Chessie Sequel's (Lianna Hawes) Puritan ancestry dates back to 1654 when her family first arrived on New England shores. She was born and raised in central Maine and has always had a love of storytelling. An alum of Boston's Emerson College, Sequel did graduate work at New York University's School of Education and traveled to the Central African Republic where she did her independent study in narrative patterns. She is currently a publicist living in Manhattan.

Talin Shahinian, since writing "Both Sides Now," has completed extensive research on men which has rendered her less curious and more jaded. Nowadays, she's Post-Bisexual, and says "Bah!" to dating any gender. She enjoys collecting Hello Kitty/Sanrio products, xnet.goth list mates, reading voraciously, indie film, zines, thrift stores, music, and all her best friends who know who they are.

Wendy Shanker wrote and performed *Look! A One-Woman show About Beauty, Brains, and the Pursuit of Perfection*—in which "Ladies Night" first appeared—to packed houses and rave reviews. She has written for ABC, Lifetime, MTV, VH1, and Comedy Central. Wendy contributes to magazines like *Mode, Hues,* and of course, *BUST*. Plus she knows an awful lot about Madonna.

Eve Shopsin is a native New Yorker and a Hunter College graduate. Eve is a natural mother of five, and mother of the moment to the hundreds of customers who eat at the Greenwich Village restaurant that she runs with her husband.

Carly Sommerstein's writing has appeared in *Mademoiselle, NY Press, Jane,* and the *Utne Reader.* While not obsessing on depictions of women in pop culture, she is hard at work on a novel.

Ayanna Sullivan is a freelance writer who resides in Brooklyn, New York.

Rose Tattoo (Marcia Zellers) is a multimedia producer and freelance writer. She recently bolted after twelve years in New York City for the sunny skies of Los Angeles, where she hopes to discover a new community of equally *BUST*-y chicks.

Thelma and **Louise** are a musician and a university professor. They are the proud parents of a three-year-old boy who loves vehicles and tool kits, and who also likes to wear lipstick, nail polish, and clothes with pink hearts (which his moms almost never wear). They hope one day to reverse their bio/non-bio mom roles with a second child.

Jennifer Tillity (Jennifer Baumgardner) was born May 15, 1970. She grew up in Fargo, North Dakota where her teen years were spent doing the prairie version of *Waiting for Guffman.* She emigrated to New York's East Village in 1992 and toiled as an editor at *Ms.* magazine until 1997. Her work has appeared in *BUST, The Nation, Jane, Out, HUES, Glamour,* and *Ms.,* among other magazines. She has also written for the book Alt.culture, and contributed a chapter with Judy Blume to the forthcoming *Letters of Intent.* She is at work on a book about the state of feminism, co-authored with Amelia Richards, called *Girl, You'll Be a Woman Soon.*

Hapa Wahine (Doreen Hinton) did not attend any illustrious university, has not been published in any major nationally distributed magazines, and is not releasing a book coming out next year. She is a freelance writer based in her only true home: her mind.

Tricia Warden is a person with a lot of hammers. She is also the author of two books, *Brainlift* and *Attack God Inside,* both published by 2.13.61 publications. She is currently editing a book of short stories entitled *Death is Hereditary* and writing a novel with the working title *3315 Pleasant Avenue.* She performs in the New York City area both by herself and with a band called Vagina Dentata. One of her favorite sayings is "There's so much shit hitting the fan that I just can't feel the breeze."

Nancy E. Young shies away from pseudonyms but answers to a dozen or so nicknames. She prefers to write in a pink bathtub by candlelight with lots of bonbons. Her published work includes letters to the editor, poetry, and a chapter in a crisis-management book. She is a reformed vegetarian who occasionally eats meat but never eats flowers.

Meet Some of Our Contributors